Lights, Camera, Feminism?

Lights, Camera, Feminism?

CELEBRITIES AND ANTI-TRAFFICKING POLITICS

Samantha Majic

UNIVERSITY OF CALIFORNIA PRESS

University of California Press
Oakland, California

© 2023 by Samantha Majic

Library of Congress Cataloging-in-Publication Data

Names: Majic, Samantha, author.
Title: Lights, camera, feminism? : celebrities and anti-trafficking
    politics / Samantha Majic.
Description: Oakland, California : University of California Press, [2023] |
    Includes bibliographical references and index.
Identifiers: LCCN 2022056853 (print) | LCCN 2022056854 (ebook) | ISBN
    9780520384880 (cloth) | ISBN 9780520384903 (paperback) | ISBN
    9780520384910 (ebook)
Subjects: LCSH: Feminism—Political aspects—United States. |
    Celebrities—Political activity—United States. | Human trafficking—
    United States—Prevention. | Equality—United States.
Classification: LCC HQ1150 .M345 2023 (print) | LCC HQ1150 (ebook) |
    DDC 305.420973—dc23/eng/20221222
LC record available at https://lccn.loc.gov/2022056853
LC ebook record available at https://lccn.loc.gov/2022056854

Manufactured in the United States of America

32   31   30   29   28   27   26   25   24   23
10   9   8   7   6   5   4   3   2   1

To Mary Fainsod Katzenstein, for being a brilliant scholar, mentor, and friend.

CONTENTS

In graduate school at Cornell University in the early 2000s, my friends and I created our own version of an "academic journal exchange," where we circulated the likes of *Star, Hello!,* and *Us Weekly* through our mailboxes in the Government Department. These magazines, which were full of celebrity gossip, provided relief from the massive quantities of scholarly reading that we had to complete for our courses and field exams. Fast forward over a decade and I am a tenured professor in New York City. On my way home from a long day of writing, teaching, and meetings, I stop at the newsstand near the Columbus Circle subway station and purchase a copy of *InTouch Weekly*. I make my way down to the platform, and by the time the train pulls out of the station, I am engrossed in stories of celebrities' marital problems, real estate sales, and wardrobe choices as the day behind me fades away.

I am not the only person for whom celebrities—persons well known for their athletic, artistic, and other endeavors—offer a much needed respite from the grind of daily life. Their performances on stages, screens, and stadiums entertain us, and their lives, replete with designer fashion, luxurious vacations, and beautiful homes, offer a window into a glitzy and glamorous alternative universe that now, thanks to social media, we may peer into at any moment of the day. Yet celebrities do more than simply entertain and distract us: they have brought their fame to bear on issues ranging from the Vietnam War (Jane Fonda), to police violence against racial minorities (LeBron James), to feminist politics through #MeToo. Furthermore, they routinely serve as ambassadors for major NGOs, address high-profile audiences ranging from the United Nations to the US Congress, and use their fame to run for elected office. Who can forget that Donald Trump—a real estate heir who attained celebrity status through decades of tabloid coverage and multiple seasons of *The Apprentice*—ran successfully for President of the United States in 2016?

As a citizen who loves celebrity gossip, and as a feminist scholar who has spent her career researching and writing about political engagement among marginalized communities, celebrities' prominence in politics—and feminist politics in particular—both entertains and worries me. On the one hand, it's easy to dismiss their activism. Surely, celebrities only make political statements (or even run for office) for the attention, and what harm can they really do, especially if they use their high profiles and legions of fans to rapidly draw attention to important issues such as gender inequality? But on the other hand, celebrities' growing presence in political life should also make us deeply uneasy. Despite their lack of issue expertise or experience, they routinely access high-profile organizations and audiences, and outside of electoral politics, it remains difficult to discern the impacts of and even hold them accountable for much of their political work.

How, then, do we think about and assess celebrities as political actors, and as feminist activists in particular? What broader lessons can we learn from their political engagement? I wrote this book to help us answer these questions and make sense of celebrities' roles and power in contemporary democratic politics. To do this, I decided to focus on celebrities' efforts to raise awareness about and shape laws against human trafficking, an issue I have long been familiar with through my research on policy and activism related to the sex industry. Human trafficking is a high profile issue that has garnered much public and political attention, particularly since 2000, when the contemporary anti-trafficking movement came to prominence and Congress passed the Trafficking Victims Protection Act. However, even as human trafficking occurs in a range of industries, dramatic narratives in public discourse have long conflated it with *sex* trafficking, a feminist issue par excellence. In these stories, circulated through the news and entertainment media, (foreign and/or non-white) men or criminal gangs capture innocent (white) girls and women and force them into sexual slavery until law enforcement rescues them and prosecutes their captors.

Celebrities have featured prominently in the anti-trafficking movement, and their activism here illuminates their role in feminist and democratic politics more broadly. Coming into this research, I assumed that the majority of celebrities would promote the dominant, made-for-TV sex trafficking narrative and its attendant carceral politics. But as I explain in this book, I found something more varied: the celebrities featured here illuminate not only the diversity of anti-trafficking politics, but the dynamics of celebrity feminism and the promises and perils of political representation within an increasingly elite-dominated polity. Consequently, I am now more convinced than ever that we as citizens, scholars, and activists cannot dismiss celebrities who engage in politics—in any way, about any issue—as quirky and harmless distractions from our lives. Instead, we must understand them as multi-level actors who are increasingly inserting themselves in political life, much like other powerful, unelected elites, ranging from philanthropists to corporate titans. I hope this book urges readers to hold celebrities (and other unelected elites) accountable for their actions *and* to continue working to address the social, political, and economic conditions that have facilitated their political ascendance while marginalizing those for whom they claim to speak.

ACKNOWLEDGMENTS

Writing a book is always a long journey, and I am grateful that I did not have to make this one alone. Since I began working on this book around 2015, a village of people and institutions have supported me.

This book would not have been possible without Maura Roessner, my editor at the University of California Press, who championed this project from the start. Maura also connected me with three incredibly smart and thoughtful reviewers. Renée Cramer, Anthea Taylor, and Tiffany Willoughby-Herard, thank you for reading this manuscript in its entirety and for pushing my thinking and writing in so many ways. At the Press, a special thanks also goes to Madison Wetzell, Emily Park, and Sam Warren for their editorial support (especially for answering all of my questions about image permissions!), Catherine Osborne for her copy editing, and Cynthia Savage, at Savage Indexing Services, for creating this book's index.

I am also grateful to the many institutions that provided resources I needed to complete this project. The Professional Staff Congress-CUNY (PSC-CUNY) grant program (award numbers TRADB-46–135, TRADB-49–124, TRADB-51–64, and TRADB-52–221) provided me with essential time away from teaching and funding for research assistance. A special thanks also goes to the PSC-CUNY for their collective bargaining efforts, which ensure that we have paid sabbaticals to work on projects like this. The Office for the Advancement of Research (OAR) at John Jay College also provided funding for various images and indexing costs through its Book Publication Funding Program, and its Midcareer and Senior Scholar Award Programs provided me with course releases.

Dhanya Babu, Lauren Moton, Katheryne Pugliese, MG Robinson, and Be Stone were my invaluable research assistants. Thank you for your insights, organizational skills, and patience with my endless requests that sent you down many celebrity gossip rabbit holes over the years. Andrés Sebastian Besserer Rayas also provided additional research for chapter 4. I could not have completed this book without any of you. Thank you.

I have been incredibly lucky to discuss and develop the ideas in this book with so many formidable people. I completed my research during my sabbatical year (2017–2018), which I spent as a visiting scholar in the Department of Gender Studies at UCLA. Here I am forever grateful to Juliet Williams and Kate Norberg for their hospitality and unwavering intellectual support, and to Jenna Miller-Von Ah and Richard Medrano for being so helpful about all things UCLA.

Over the years, I was also very fortunate to present my research and receive feedback in a number of other forums, including at the Lilly Family School of Philanthropy at Indiana University-Purdue, the Department of Gender Studies at UCLA, the Maryland Discussion Group on Constitutionalism at the University of Maryland School of Law, C4: Conference on Contemporary Celebrity Culture at Drake University, the Program in Gender & Sexuality Studies at Princeton University, the American Studies Workshop at Princeton University, and the Comparative Politics Workshop at the CUNY Graduate Center. I also benefitted from the feedback I received at the annual meetings of the American Political Science Association and the Western Political Science Association, and from the support of my colleagues in the Interpretive Methodologies and Methods Group, the Feminist Institutionalism International Network, and the Women and Society Seminar at Columbia University.

As I wrote and revised this book, I am eternally grateful to all of the incredibly intelligent people who generously read various chapters. Aisha Beliso-De Jésus, Natasha Behl, Abhishek Chatterjee, Dan Brockington, Melissa Ditmore, Nancy Hirschmann, Marisa Lerer, Stephanie Limoncelli, Jillian Locke, Felix Pedilla Carbonnell, Zein Murib, and Michael Saward: your critical, insightful feedback has only, I hope, improved the final product, and I owe each and every one of you as many reviews as your hearts desire!

I've also had the opportunity to develop many of the ideas in this book through a range of publications. Here a very special thanks goes to Michael Bernhard and Dan O'Neill at *Perspectives on Politics* for supporting me in the development, guest-editorship, and publication of a special issue on Celebrity and Politics (vol. 18, no. 1 [2020]). Portions of this book are also derived and/

or developed further from Majic (2017); Majic, Bernhard, and O'Neill (2020); and Majic (2021).

I've also benefitted from all manner of intellectual and other support from many phenomenal scholars. Ujju Aggarwal, Nikol Alexander-Floyd, Chris Anderson, Karen Baird, Lehn Benjamin, Elizabeth Bernstein, Lorna Bracewell, Alexandra Budabin, Susan Burgess, Allison Carruth, Michael Jones Correa, Susan Fischer, Farah Godrej, Jeffrey Isaac, Julia Jordan-Zachery, Mary Fainsod Katzenstein, Regina Kunzel, Alexandra Lutnick, Timothy Pachirat, Shannon Mariotti, Gregory Mitchell, Jennifer Musto, Kimala Price, Amy Cabrera Rasmussen, Andy Sabl, Svati Shah, Carisa Showden, Peregrine Schwartz-Shea, Jacqueline Stevens, Dara Strolovitch, Stephanie Wahab, Laurel Weldon, Elizabeth Wood, and Dvora Yanow, thank you for all of the conversations, collaborations, invitations, letters of recommendation, and everything else you've done to help me get from there to here.

The further along I get in my career, the more I realize how lucky I am to have truly amazing colleagues at John Jay College-CUNY. In the political science department, Andrew Sidman and Jim Cauthen have been the most incredible chairs, and Monica Varsanyi is a brilliant reader who generously offered incisive feedback on many iterations of this project. I am also lucky to know and work with Amy Adamczyk, Alexa Capeloto, Preeti Chauhan, Kathleen Collins, Kashka Celinska, Katie Gentile, Richard Haw, Susan Kang, Olivera Jokic, Lila Kazemian, Debi Koetzle, Kyoo Lee, Sara McDougall, Allison Pease, Gohar Petrossian, Dan Pinello, Caroline Reitz, Jennifer Rutledge, Deryn Strange, Lucia Trimbur, and Liza Yukins—thank you for being great colleagues and friends, and for listening to me complain about this project over drinks and food at many of the mediocre bars and restaurants near the college.

I would also like to thank Lee Ann Fujii, in memoriam, for her friendship and pathbreaking work in the field of interpretive research. When I thought that this project was going nowhere, Lee Ann assured me that I was wrong, and she helped me find my way out of a deep hole of self-doubt. I did not know that this would be our last conversation, so thank you, Lee Ann, for being you.

A number of people in my life have always offered great conversations and made sure that I went out, laughed, ate good food, and watched a lot of reality television. Thank you Firouzeh Afsharnia, Brooke Beardslee, Miranda

Bryant, Hillary Caviness, Lauren Esposito, Jennifer Forster, Cynthia Gozberk, Alison Lang, Sheron O'Brien, Dana Pellicano, Melissa Renwick, Mary Sum, Jeremy Trickett, Elspeth Tory, Andy Wald, Hilary Walker, Melissa Weber, and Brooke Wells. I also want to thank my family for their support over the years; Joel Ramsey, for keeping me in shape; Katie Quinn, for making sure that I don't look like a mess; Lisa Borneman, for helping me keep it together; and Beyoncé, whose album *Renaissance* dropped just when I needed the energy to get this book into production.

Finally, my deepest gratitude goes to John Rasmussen, the person who always supports me, put things in perspective, and makes me laugh every day. Thank you for being here for this book, and for everything else.

LIST OF ACRONYMS

AFESIP	Agir pour les Femmes en Situation Precaire (Acting for Women in Distressing Situations)
ASSET	Alliance to Stop Slavery and End Trafficking
BBC	British Broadcasting Corporation
California ACTS	California Alliance to Combat Trafficking and Slavery
CAST-LA	Coalition to Abolish Slavery and Trafficking in Los Angeles
CATW	Coalition Against Trafficking in Women
CIA	Central Intelligence Agency
CNN	Cable News Network
CSR	Corporate social responsibility
CTSCA	California Trafficking in Supply Chains Act
DHS	Department of Homeland Security
DHHS	Department of Health and Human Services
DNA	The Demi & Ashton Foundation
DOL	Department of Labor
DSB	Don't Sell Bodies
ECPAT	End Child Prostitution and Trafficking

FEC	Federal Elections Commission
FMA	Feminist methods of analysis
GEMS	Girls Educational and Mentoring Services
HRC	Human Rights Campaign
ICE	Immigration and Customs Enforcement
ILO	International Labour Organization
IMA	Interpretive methods of analysis
IMDB	Internet Movie Database
IRS	Internal Revenue Service
MCF	Male celebrity feminism
MTV	Music Television
NBA	National Basketball Association
NCSL	National Conference of State Legislatures
NGO	Non-governmental organization
NIJ	National Institutes of Justice
NOW	National Organization for Women
NYPD	New York Police Department
PAC	Public awareness campaign
PBS	Public Broadcasting Service
PPF	Political performance framework
PSA	Public service announcement
PSI	Population Services International
RMF	Ricky Martin Foundation
SAP-FL	Special Action Programme to combat Forced Labour
SESTA/FOSTA	Stop Enabling Sex Trafficking Act/ Allow States and Victims to Fight Online Sex Trafficking Act
STEM	Science, technology, engineering, math
SSU	Sonoma State University
SVAW Campaign	Stop Violence Against Women Campaign

TIP	Trafficking In Persons Report
TVPA	Trafficking Victims Protection Act
UN	United Nations
UNICEF	United Nations Children's Fund
UNODC	United Nations Office of Drugs and Crime
USAID	US Agency for International Development
USC	University of Southern California
WNU	Women's Network for Unity
WJSFF	Will and Jada Pinkett Smith Family Foundation

Introduction

CELEBRITIES, FEMINISM, AND
HUMAN TRAFFICKING

IN THE 2008 ACTION THRILLER *Taken,* the actor Liam Neeson plays Bryan Mills, a former CIA operative who is trying to develop a closer relationship with his seventeen-year-old daughter Kim, an aspiring singer played by Maggie Grace.[1] While overseeing security for mega-pop star Sheerah (played by Holly Valance), Bryan saves her from an attacker, and to thank him, Sheerah offers to listen to Kim sing. But before Bryan has a chance to tell Kim, she asks for permission to travel to Paris with her best friend, Amanda, where they would stay in an apartment with Amanda's cousins. Leery about her safety but wanting to make her happy, Byran grants Kim permission for the trip. But when Kim and Amanda land in Paris and arrive at the apartment, the cousins are nowhere to be found. As Kim calls her father from her cell phone, she realizes that a group of men have entered their apartment. "There's someone here," she says. "The cousins are back?" asks Bryan. "No," Kim says, before exclaiming, "Oh my god, they got Amanda." Bryan snaps into agent mode. "Stay focused, Kimmy," he tells her. "You have to hold it together."

In the scene that follows, Bryan tersely instructs Kim to go into the next room and hide under the bed. "They're going to take you," he says. Kim's face contorts into a panic as Bryan instructs her to leave her phone on the floor and call out everything she sees. The men—Albanian human traffickers—enter the room; from Kim's vantage point, we only see their feet. The room goes silent. "They're leaving. . . . I think they're gone," Kim whispers to her father. But within seconds, she is pulled screaming from under the bed, yelling a description of the abductor. The camera is now back on Bryan, who hears breathing and realizes one of the abductors has Kim's phone. Stoically, he tells the abductors that if they return his daughter now, there will be no

I

harm, but if they don't, he has "skills I've acquired over a very long career. Skills that make me a nightmare for people like you . . . and I will kill you." After a pause, the voice on the other end of the phone says, smugly and ominously, "Good luck."

Grossing $226 million at the box office and followed by sequels in 2012 and 2014, *Taken* catapulted Neeson to action star fame *and* activist status. Although Neeson served as a UNICEF National Ambassador for Northern Ireland since the late 1990s, in a case of art mimicking life, on March 29, 2011, UNICEF announced that it was elevating him to serve as a Goodwill Ambassador, in which position he would engage in humanitarian work to help the world's most vulnerable children. As an article in the *Sunday Mirror* declared (before Neeson assumed this new position), here he would face "his toughest real-life role yet—war against ruthless sex traffickers" (Jones 2009, 16). Noting his role in *Taken,* the actor said the movie offered "a fresh reminder of the urgency in addressing the problem of trafficking and exploitation and standing up for the rights of children—on a global level" (*Look to the Stars* 2011). But Neeson was not the first celebrity to raise awareness about human trafficking. Celebrities, who are people well known for artistic, athletic, or other endeavors, and particularly those based in the United States, have long been involved in the anti-trafficking movement, speaking publicly, influencing legislators, and devoting significant resources to this cause (Haynes 2014).

As Elizabeth Bernstein (2018) documents, the term human trafficking first appeared in a 1976 *New York Times* article about the trafficking of persons from East Germany, and it was not until 2000, when the United Nations adopted the Protocol to Prevent, Suppress, and Punish Trafficking in Human Beings, Especially Women and Children (hereafter referred to as the 2000 UN Protocol), that the term entered global discourse (see also Molland 2013). The 2000 UN Protocol defined human trafficking as

> the recruitment, transportation, transfer, harbouring or receipt of persons, by means of the threat or use of force or other forms of coercion, of abduction, of fraud, of deception, of the abuse of power or of a position of vulnerability or of the giving or receiving of payments or benefits to achieve the consent of a person having control over another person, for the purpose of exploitation. Exploitation shall include, at a minimum, the exploitation of the prostitution of others or other forms of sexual exploitation, forced labour or services, slavery or practices similar to slavery, servitude or the removal of organs (United Nations 2014).

A purportedly massive and gendered problem in the United States and internationally, human trafficking occurs in a range of industries. The Global Slavery Index estimates that there are 40.3 million people trafficked worldwide, and they, along with international governing bodies such as the UNODC, estimate that the majority of victims are women and girls (UNODC 2016; Walk Free Foundation 2021b). Human trafficking has thus become a feminist issue par excellence (Lee 2011; O'Brien 2011), not only because it is a threat to women's rights and equality globally, but, as I show later in this introduction, because it has been conflated with sex trafficking and sex work—two highly contentious topics of feminist interest. As a result, feminists across the spectrum have debated human trafficking and worked to shape related laws and policies. However, I also show later the *anti*-feminist consequences of their many endeavors and achievements here, especially in the United States. By centering sex trafficking and promoting criminal justice solutions over those advancing social and economic justice, contemporary human trafficking discourse, laws, and policies often undermine feminist goals such as gender and racial equality.

Among the many feminist issues that celebrities have engaged, human trafficking both confirms and challenges our ideas about what constitutes a "celebrity-friendly" topic. On the one hand, it is the perfect issue for celebrities. Since their status depends on sustained attention, they tend towards high-profile issues that are relatively uncontroversial and supported by broad audiences (Keller and Ringrose 2015; Van den Bulck 2018). Human trafficking fits the bill here: no one in her right mind defends it, and it is a "made for TV" issue that quickly grabs attention. Replete with sex, violence, victims, villains, and organized crime networks, mainstream media representations of the issue in films like *Taken* resonate strongly with the contemporary cultural milieu across the Global North (Szörényi and Eate 2014). All of this makes it easy, in a sense, for celebrities like Neeson to take on human trafficking.

But on the other hand, celebrities' anti-trafficking work challenges the notion that they tend towards simple issues with specific, short-term solutions (Van den Bulck 2018). Human trafficking is in fact a complex and contested issue that requires significant expertise to understand and time to address because it is actually very difficult to define. Even as the 2000 UN Protocol guides how many nations legally define human trafficking, it remains imprecise, never specifying what, exactly, is meant by force, fraud, coercion, vulnerability, and exploitation (Bernstein 2018). While it is true that these actions may occur as they do in *Taken,* there are many cases where workers in legal businesses are subject to force, fraud, and coercion, such as in New York City nail salons, where the *New York Times* reported that workers (many of whom are immigrant women) are routinely subject to fraudulent, exploitative working conditions that include wage theft, forced silence, and no breaks to eat (Maslin Nir 2015). In another example, news reports showed that at Packers Sanitation Services, many workers felt forced and/or coerced to accept its poor workplace safety record because the company hired them despite their felony convictions and paid above minimum wage (Martyn 2021). Given the range of situations that may fit the definition of human trafficking, it is easily confused with a wide variety of practices such as migration, human smuggling, kidnapping, and debt bondage (among other activities that involve labor, coercion, and movement). Moreover, many government officials, the media, and various advocates further complicate things by referring to human trafficking as "modern day slavery" and, in more gendered and sexualized incidences, "female sexual slavery" (UNODC 2016; Salazar Parreñas, Hwang, and Lee 2012).

Definitional confusion, combined with its status as an illicit practice that often goes unreported, makes human trafficking a difficult issue to study and quantify. Since victims may be unwilling to come forward and speak about their experiences due to stigma, their uncertain legal status in many countries, and fears of deportation (among many other reasons), estimates of human trafficking's prevalence remain tenuous and imprecise at best (Gozdziak 2015; Reinelt 2016; Merry 2016; Bernstein 2018). For example, estimates of people trafficked into the United States each year have ranged from a low of 14,500 to a high of nearly 50,000 (McGough 2013). By extension, there is no typical victim profile or known cause. While women may be the majority of victims, according to current estimates, a growing number of men, boys, and transgender persons are vulnerable as well (UNODC 2016; Gozdziak 2015; Showden and Majic 2018). Furthermore, research indicates that while individual men and organized crime networks may cause some human trafficking (à la *Taken*), structural factors including but not limited to the demand for cheap, exploitable labor, economic deregulation, dislocation as a result of wars and/or economic development projects, and racial and gender discrimination often increase vulnerabilities to sexual and other labor trafficking (Doezema 2010; Hoyle, Bosworth, and Dempsey 2011; Sharma 2003; Copley 2014; Malloch and Rigby 2016; Showden and Majic 2018; Peksen, Blanton, and Blanton 2017).

Despite this complexity, US-based celebrities have joined the anti-trafficking movement, often citing "the data" as their motivation. As Neeson declared, he was "haunted" by sex slave statistics he saw when making the violent thriller *Taken,* adding, "I had access to facts, figures and numbers of children who disappear from Eastern Europe and Asia. They would make the hair on the back of your neck stand up" (Jones 2009, 16). Yet even as he and his celebrity peers may access research and other information proffered by high-profile and authoritative bodies like the United Nations, they are not issue experts who understand human trafficking's complexity and the related challenges of collecting data to represent it. Instead, celebrities' strength rests in their capacity to reach and present uncomplicated, often dramatic narratives to the broader public (Kogen 2014), as illustrated by celebrities like Neeson, who tell the story of human trafficking as sex trafficking. But since they are not elected officials, they are rarely held accountable for their issue representations, which shape public discourse (Haynes 2014).

To date, scholars have provided an overview of celebrity anti-trafficking activism, considered its online connections and networks, and examined individual case studies of various celebrity anti-trafficking films and awareness campaigns (see, e.g., Heynen and van der Meulen 2021; Baker 2014; Haynes 2014; O'Brien 2013). However, there remains no comprehensive accounting for and analysis of celebrities' anti-trafficking activism over time as a form of celebrity feminism. As I detail more in the following chapter, celebrity feminism is a hotly debated form of activism through which celebrities mobilize their fame to publicly articulate and promote various feminist interests and ideologies, which I understand broadly as sets of beliefs about and solutions for achieving gender equality and justice—related concepts that, following Mala Htun and Laurel Weldon (2018), encompass "equality and autonomy for people of all sex groups and gender identities" (7), as well as efforts to understand *and challenge* the social and political structures that shape their identities and their opportunities to participate and flourish in social, political, and economic life.

Analyzing celebrities' anti-trafficking activism as celebrity feminism is thus instructive because celebrities are increasingly visible in political life, and in feminist debates specifically, where "[s]ex trafficking remains one of the most widely and vehemently contested issues" (Szorenyi 2014, 21). Therefore, by inserting themselves as leaders who weigh in on sex and other forms of trafficking—sometimes in ways that lack nuance and obscure structural analyses, sometimes in a range of other ways—celebrities are engaging in feminist politics. In so doing, they potentially illuminate and promote a wide range of feminist interests and ideologies including, but not limited to, carceral feminism, which describes gender justice in terms of criminal justice, where criminalization, prosecution, and incarceration are integral to women's liberation and gender equality; liberal feminism, which roots gender inequality in unequal individual legal, social, and political rights and promotes legislative, marketized, and individualized solutions; and a more structurally intersectional feminism that emphasizes how capitalism, patriarchy, and racism (among other macro-structural factors) interact to further gender inequality (Bracewell 2021; Epure 2014).

Studying celebrities' anti-trafficking efforts, then, draws our attention to how celebrity feminism may advance *and* constrain efforts to promote gender equality and justice, while also raising and engaging broader questions about the role and influence of unelected elites in the polity. To this end, I raise and respond to four interrelated empirical and interpretive questions. First, I consider how and to what extent US-based celebrities raise awareness about human trafficking. Second, given celebrities' capacity to inform and influence large segments of the population about issues of concern, I ask how they represent and propose solutions to human trafficking, reading the feminist interests and ideologies they advance from here. Third, given celebrities' need to distinguish themselves from their peers and members of the general public, while also maintaining their fans' attention, how may we account for variation among their anti-trafficking activities and representations? And finally, I consider what this all means for how we understand celebrities'—and other unelected elites'—political power and responsibility, particularly in broader movements to end oppression, exploitation, and marginalization. Are they merely engaged in high profile "virtue signaling," or are they contributing to meaningful change?

To answer these questions, this book draws from an original dataset that captures US-based celebrities' anti-trafficking activities from 2000, when the contemporary anti-trafficking movement came to prominence in the United States and globally, to 2016, the end of the Obama administration. I focus on the United States because of the reach of the nation's media and cultural/ celebrity industries, and because it has declared itself a global leader for addressing human trafficking. In addition to being a key destination for victims, the United States is home to many of the most prominent anti-trafficking NGOs, and anti-trafficking efforts now influence the nation's foreign policy interventions in areas ranging from aid distribution to international security (Heynen and van der Meulen 2021; O'Brien 2011).

The analysis of celebrities' anti-trafficking activism in the following chapters complicates how we understand celebrities' political engagement over time. Challenging assumptions that celebrities are merely uninformed elites who mainly engage in political activism for branding and marketing purposes, I argue broadly that we should understand them as multi-level political actors whose varied interests, actions, and issue representations are shaped and mediated by a range of personal and contextual factors. To illustrate this argument more specifically, I show in response to my first question that celebrities from a range of fields—and white women actors in particular—raise awareness about human trafficking through predominantly high-profile, media-friendly activities, the most popular of which include supporting organizations, appearing in documentaries and awareness campaigns, and engaging with Amnesty International. In response to my second question, then, I find and show that these activities, which I understand as political performances, offer more varied representations of and solutions to human trafficking—and hence feminist interests and ideologies—than we may expect. Indeed, many celebrities do promote the dominant *Taken* narrative and its attendant carceral and liberally oriented feminist ideologies; however, over time, celebrities also complicate and challenge the dominant narrative to highlight other forms of labor trafficking and signal the importance of non-criminalizing solutions, thereby endorsing a more structurally intersectional feminist ideology.

What, then, per my third question, accounts for this variation? Why do some celebrities reinforce the dominant narrative and its attendant power arrangements while others foment dissensus? Since nothing automatically associates celebrities with human trafficking (or feminism, for that matter), I argue that the answer to these questions emerges when we examine their personal motivations for engaging with the issue and the temporal and organizational settings for their activism. This means that two factors—their positionality and how they became interested in human trafficking ("the personal"), and the time period during which they initiated their activity and the organizations they work with ("the contextual")—play a key role in shaping their interest in the issue, how they represent it, and the feminist interests and ideologies they communicate as a result. Considering how these personal and contextual factors shape celebrities' representations of human trafficking thus furthers efforts to map "the shifting terrain of celebrity feminism" (Taylor 2016, 12), namely by complicating assumptions that celebrities are a seemingly coherent group of powerful individuals with similar motivations and goals.

As a result, the answer to my fourth question is not clear-cut: we cannot understand celebrities' anti-trafficking (or other) activism as either high-profile virtue signaling *or* the key to ending oppression and marginalization. Instead, as I theorize more extensively in this and the following chapter, their activism draws our attention to how power operates in our increasingly unequal and elite-dominated polity, where individuals with abundant resources often engage in what I term representation-at-a-distance. By this I mean that their fame, which commonly affords them immense resources and privileges, places them at a great remove from those they claim to represent. Indeed, elected officials may operate at a similar remove, but celebrities are further above the messy fray of electoral, grassroots, and other political efforts to illuminate issues, change public opinion, and shape laws and policies. In this representative position, celebrities thus indicate the recursive and contested nature of their power in political life. On the one hand, they draw attention to issues *and* to themselves, thereby furthering their status and power. But on the other hand, celebrities' visibility and constant exposure to public scrutiny also influences and, even, checks their actions (Driessens 2013). Given all of this, the very things that fuel their celebrity, such as near-constant media and public attention, also, in turn, allow us to scrutinize their activities, critique them, and work to check their power.

CELEBRITIES AND POLITICS

Understanding celebrities' political engagement and power requires us to interrogate the meaning of "celebrity" and how it came to confer various privileges to those who attain this status. While the term may bring supremely beautiful and talented people to mind (think: Beyoncé), it remains diverse and vague, synonymous at times with "hero," "star," "personality," and "idol" (Driessens 2013). Therefore, despite extensive scholarship on the topic, celebrity remains a slippery concept that has eluded any real sense of definition (Cashmore and Parker 2003), especially since almost anyone may fill this role in the age of social media (think: the Kardashians). Therefore, in this book, I draw on the extensive literature in celebrity studies to understand contemporary celebrities as both constituted by and displaying the following features and processes.[2]

With roots in the Latin "celebritas" (fame) and "celeber" (frequented) (Boorstin 2012 [1961]), the central characteristic of a celebrity is that she is *widely known*, and scholars have traced some of the earliest celebrities to the twelfth-century saints, who attracted attention and large crowds (Brockington

2014a). In the contemporary context, this "known-ness" (Boorstin 2012 [1961]) is a *production*: it is not an inherent quality or condition but a process that is linked to technological and commercial developments in film, cinema, and commodity circulation since the 1900s (Drake and Higgins 2012; Brockington 2014a; Farrell 2019). Since then, as Graeme Turner (2014) summarizes in his review of the history of celebrity, developments in modern media technologies, aided by the growth in public relations industries, facilitated the invention of the celebrity. Today, persons with celebrity status become known and celebrated through a combination of texts (e.g. television shows), producers (e.g. publicists), and audiences (those who encounter and use their images) (Gamson 1994; Rojek 2001). Given this, ongoing *media exposure* "is the oxygen that sustains the contemporary celebrity" (Drake and Miah 2010, 55). The mainstream media (television, newspapers), social media (Instagram, Facebook, etc.), and other online media (e.g. the blogosphere) publicize the celebrity's particular sporting activity or movie performance, while also covering elements of the celebrity's life that are not related to his or her specific talent or activity (Turner 2014). These ongoing, accumulated media representations make the celebrity recognizable and constantly evaluated in terms of the scale and effectiveness of her visibility. As a result, celebrity status is inherently unstable and can change overnight (Driessens 2013; Boorstin 2012 [1961]; van Elteren 2013).

Linked as they are to the rise of capitalism, celebrities are also a *commercial* phenomenon, in that their presence and/or the activity for which they are known is commodified and marketized in some way (Brockington 2014a; Marshall 2014; Wheaton and Nandy 2019). Here celebrities operate as a brand that draws attention to and fuels the consumption of a particular product, be it a television show, album, tickets to a sporting match, or any other consumer good that is associated with their activities, talents, and/or image. In short, this commercial element is what distinguishes celebrities from the merely famous (Turner 2014; Marshall 2019). Their ability to capitalize on their fame thus epitomizes the dominant ideologies of contemporary Western culture—individualism and market capitalism—while serving as signs through which these ideological discourses get passed on to the population-as-audience (Marshall 2014).

This general definition of a celebrity—a person who is known, produced, mediatized, and commercialized—likely brings to mind individuals in entertainment and sports, and this book focuses predominantly on these celebrity types, as they are the most visibly engaged in anti-trafficking work. However, celebrity is also relative: if one mainly follows professional sports, her notion of who counts as a celebrity may differ significantly from someone who only follows country music. Moreover, celebrity is ever-shifting. As social media has expanded, many individuals have attained this status (for example, as "Instagram influencers"), albeit often with a more specific, self-contained audience (Taylor 2016). While these "micro-celebrities" (Marwick and boyd 2011, 140) may not be the focus of this book, in the concluding chapter I discuss the importance of studying them in future research.

Even as celebrity is a constantly evolving concept, it grants individuals significant "celebrity capital"—a stock of wealth that includes their recogniz-ability, popularity with a large fan base, communication skills, financial resources, and social networks—all of which may be converted into other resources to advance various causes (Driessens 2013; Gunter 2014; Chidgey 2020). The political realm, broadly defined, is among the many places where celebrities may spend this capital, and scholars have documented and debated how they engage here in activism, defined basically as efforts to fur-ther social, political, economic, and other changes (Van den Bulck 2018), most often by running for elected office and/or engaging in advocacy (Street 2012). For the purposes of this book, I focus on celebrity advocacy, a com-municative form of activism whereby famous people work in service of some cause other than themselves by speaking out on issues and fundraising, among myriad other activities (Brockington 2014a; Van den Bulck 2018). As Dan Brockington (2014a) shows in his historical overview of celebrities' political advocacy, this is a relatively recent phenomenon linked to the emer-gence of modern democracy and the concomitant belief that anyone may achieve anything, despite their social and economic position at birth, and to media and technological developments like the printing press, which dis-seminated large volumes of information about individuals and their activities to audiences.

In the following pages, I draw on existing scholarship to sketch the broad contours of celebrities' political advocacy in the United States, the focus of this book. The bulk of research in celebrity studies indicates that celebrity entertainers actually played a relatively *minor* role in US politics until the mid-twentieth century, due in large part to the constraints of the Hollywood studio system that dominated the US entertainment industry from the 1920s to the 1950s. At this time, huge film studios contractually "owned" the stars for a period of time (usually seven years), and they exerted this ownership by constraining their roles on screen and in public, especially as the studios were on the defensive against government accusations of communism (Demaine 2009; Spohrer 2007; Gamson 1994). These Cold War politics meant that the government often worked *with* celebrities and the broader entertainment industry to disseminate anti-communist messages. In one cruelly ironic example, the US government deployed African American jazz musicians in a cultural battle with the Soviet Union to promote the virtues and freedoms of capitalist democracies, despite the prevalence of government-sanctioned racial segregation in the United States (Brockington 2014a).

However, scholars of Black politics and culture have shown that Black actors, artists, musicians, and athletes have long used their celebrity platforms to challenge injustices, including well before the decline of the studio system. The singer and actor Paul Robeson offers one of the most notable examples here. The son of an escaped slave, Robeson—a four sport athlete at Rutgers University who earned a law degree from Columbia University in 1923—was "the first African American to obtain crossover celebrity status and arguably the first modern celebrity of any race in the United States" (Sarah Jackson 2014, 20). But even though he was a brilliant polymath, Robeson faced the dual constraints of racism and the studio system, which initially limited his political advocacy. While he supported popular civil rights initiatives like anti-lynching laws early in his career, in the 1920s he was "largely silent on more controversial issues, believing his inclusion in white public arenas represented some progress" (20). However, as his celebrity grew and he became internationally known, his "fame in the entertainment realm gave him access to the political realm" (Spohrer 2007, 163). By the 1930s, Robeson was publicly challenging the limited roles for and portrayals of Black people in Hollywood films, and by the 1940s he was staunchly opposing racism and colonialism, while also expressing pro-labor and pro-Soviet sympathies in the United States and abroad. His advocacy came with considerable costs: the US government characterized his statements as anti-American, seized his passport, and subjected him to investigation by and testimony before the House Un-American Activities Committee in 1956. Although Robeson did return to speaking and performing internationally, by the 1960s, health issues pushed him into retirement (Thompson 2019). Yet even as his entertainment career declined, the power of his artistic and political endeavors endured. As Shana L. Redmond writes in *Everything Man* (2020), which examines Robeson's continued resonance in culture and politics, his songs "were fundamental to the transnational Black and working-class political cultures that by midcentury galvanized the rebellion of entire nations" (xiv).

Robeson's pathbreaking work, combined with the political and commercial changes occurring in the 1960s, provided a critical juncture in celebrity advocacy, setting the stage for more celebrity entertainers to become politically active and oppose injustices. As the Hollywood studio system declined and the music industry changed as more independent labels emerged, stars had more freedom to make political statements, especially as there was mounting social turmoil in the United States (Brockington 2014a). As Lisa Ann Richey and Stefano Ponte (2008) document, Dr. Martin Luther King and the US civil rights movement inspired a wave of celebrity activism that coalesced around the anti-Vietnam war movement in the United States. Freed from their studio contracts and eager to speak out, many celebrities embraced this moment enthusiastically, taking at times radical stances on controversial issues. To name just some instances in the entertainment realm, singers Woody Guthrie and Pete Seeger wrote popular folk protest songs, Jane Fonda visited Vietnam, Charlton Heston and Paul Newman debated nuclear disarmament on national television, and Eartha Kitt criticized and linked the Vietnam War to racial and social unrest among young people in America's urban centers (Demaine 2009; Brockington 2014a; Sarah Jackson 2014). Examples also abound in the realm of sports: boxer Muhammad Ali famously refused to participate in the Vietnam War, and three-time Olympic gold medalist Wilma Rudolph declined to attend a celebration in her honor because the event would be racially segregated (Sarah Jackson 2014; Towler, Crawford, and Bennett 2019).

By the later 1970s, and into the 1980s, this more radical celebrity advocacy shifted in response to developments in media technologies and the ascendance of neoliberalism. The invention of the television (followed by computers and the introduction of the internet, cell phone technologies, multi-channel cable networks, iPads, and other personal electronic devices) facilitated what Jesper Stromback and Frank Esser (2014) term the "mediatization" of politics and society—a social change process in which the media became increasingly influential in and deeply integrated into different spheres of society, constituting the public's most important source of political and social information, independent from other institutions. Alongside mediatization, neoliberal thinking also became a significant feature of late modern societies since at least the 1980s, emphasizing, among other things, the role of markets, individuals, and civil society to solve social problems (Harvey 2005; Brown 2015; Yrjölä 2011a). And so, as mediatization allowed the public to draw closer links between celebrities and topical issues (Biccum 2011), and as civil society increasingly overlapped with the state and business sectors, celebrities' political power and influence expanded: not only could celebrities cross these blurred boundaries, they were savvy at drawing media attention to themselves (Brockington 2014a).

This relationship between mediatization, neoliberalism, and celebrity is especially apparent when we examine US celebrity activism in the 1970s and 1980s in the international humanitarian realm, which, broadly speaking, attempts to alleviate human suffering and bring about a more humane, peaceful, and cooperative world, often by casting a unified "humanity" against individual victims who must be cared for (Yrjölä 2011b; Ticktin 2016; Fassin 2012). At this time, many US-based celebrities expanded their advocacy from domestic issues to include more global humanitarian concerns such as HIV/ AIDS, famine, disease, rape and genocide, child soldiers, refugee crises, and human trafficking (Hozic, Majic, and Yahaya 2018). Of course, it bears noting that celebrity engagement in this realm was not new, especially for performers and other celebrities of color. Paul Robeson had an extensive record of international humanitarianism; many celebrities, beginning with actor Danny Kaye in 1953, engaged in global humanitarian advocacy as UN Ambassadors (see chapter 5 for more detail); and singer Harry Belafonte, who followed in Robeson's footsteps, opposed apartheid in South Africa.

However, the late 1970s and 1980s offered a very different setting for celebrities' international humanitarian advocacy. The public now had more access to television and other media technologies, and a neoliberal political ideology expounding less government and more individual, NGO, and for-profit sector responses to global (and domestic) humanitarian issues was also ascending, all of which increased the appeal of this advocacy for celebrities (Jeffreys 2015). Here perhaps the most illustrative example was Bob Geldof's recording of "Do They Know It's Christmas" (billed as "Band Aid") in 1984 and the related "Live Aid" concerts of 1985 (Richey and Ponte 2008). Engaging dozens of celebrity musicians from the United States and United Kingdom, ranging from Sting to Robert Bell of Kool and the Gang, an estimated two billion people watched the concerts on television. Furthermore, in accordance with the neoliberal ethos valorizing privatized (Global-North-led) responses to social problems (especially those in the Global South), the telethon raised almost $150 million for famine relief in Ethiopia.

Since the 1990s, US celebrities' advocacy efforts expanded and altered in character as the Cold War ended, media and other related technologies advanced, and neoliberal politics continued their ascendance. Certainly, in this context, celebrities continued to use their platforms to raise awareness about a growing range of issues. For example, as Yvonne Bynoe (2004) documents, after the police violently beat Rodney King in Los Angeles in 1991, many rap artists became political spokespeople against racist police brutality through their music and other performances. Celebrities also shifted their advocacy to increasingly formalized and institutionalized philanthropic structures, favoring those that eschew the more traditional practice of "check-writing" for ventures that are more business-like and transactional in form (Jeffreys and Allatson 2015). Furthermore, celebrities have used their position in what Johan Lindquist (2010, 227) terms the "humanitarian media complex"—an ever-evolving assemblage of films, investigative reporting, and documentaries, among other media formats—to shape public perceptions of issues ranging from AIDS, to lowering poor countries' debt payments, to the genocide in Darfur, to human trafficking, the focus of this book.

But even as they seem to hold and mobilize significant influence, the more concrete results of their efforts here are somewhat underwhelming. Although some recent studies conclude that "the prestige-generating power of success makes celebrities special and gives them the power to exert normative influence" (Lindenberg, Joly, and Stapel 2011, 103; see also Budabin 2015), the public and political leaders alike do not always see them as credible and reliable sources (Archer et al. 2019). As a result, their impact on public opinion, policy development, and other political decisions is largely limited to date. As Asteris Huliaras and Nikolaos Tzifakis (2010, 263) summarize in their review of celebrity activism worldwide, "the results of celebrity activism are not very impressive." While they have done well at drawing attention to various issues and supporting the NGO sector's work, celebrities rarely follow up on and deliver legislative or other programs to substantively address issues such as poverty, police violence, international development, and so many others (Bynoe 2004, Brockington 2015).

WHAT IS POWER?

The expansion and uncertain outcomes of celebrity's political activism raises questions about power, which we may understand broadly as *the (in)capacity of actors to mobilize means to achieve ends*—a force that may be possessed and exercised, and that is both enabling and constraining (Avelino 2021, 440, emphasis in original). As this section shows, celebrities have positioned themselves as "big citizens" (Rojek 2013) who independently mobilize their resources to represent issues and populations to the public and political leaders alike. They do this in a broader political context that rewards and invites their efforts—namely, the mediatized, neoliberal, post-political, or, post-democratic moment, defined by significant inequality, where powerful elites' efforts to make the political and economic system work for them surpass those of the masses (Alexander-Floyd 2021; Crouch 2004). But while celebrities may have the power to illuminate issues and impacted populations, and to shape public discourse and policy in this context, I posit that they more reliably draw attention to *themselves,* in ways that enhance their own power and the neoliberal ethos of individualism more broadly.

Powerful individuals (and the groups representing their interests), from the "Robber Barons" of the early twentieth century to the hedge fund titans of today, have always engaged in and influenced political life, sparking long-standing debates about the extent to which politics and political ideologies are elite-led (Majic, Bernhard, and O'Neill 2020; Harris-Perry 2004). However, as Mike Savage and Georgia Nichols (2018, 299) note, "in the last 20 years of the 20th century, we have seen the most dramatic shift of income, assets and resources in favour of the very rich that has ever taken place in human history." As these wealthy individuals and the highly organized groups representing their interests contribute record amounts to political campaigns, and as leaders in governing bodies increasingly rely on them to address various issues in a complex world, political authority is increasingly delegated to private, elite actors in global governance (Partzsch 2017; Goss 2016). Here Lena Partzsch (2017) identifies three types of these non-state agents, with different sources of power, who are among the most visible and significant individuals in this emerging constellation of elite private actors. There are social entrepreneurs who deliver new ideas and shape how people think about the options for dealing with the issues at stake, such as economist Mohammad Yunus, who founded Grameen Bank. There are philanthropists, such as technology billionaires Bill and Melinda Gates. And finally there are celebrities, who are increasingly mobilizing their resources to raise awareness about and ameliorate public problems.

In a more crowded, corporatized, and consolidated media environment, celebrities are uniquely positioned to capitalize on and mobilize their key resource—fame—to achieve their ends because they are often charismatic performers and highly skilled communicators (Demaine 2009). Consequently other elites, including philanthropists, corporations, and NGO and government leaders, deploy celebrities to promote their agendas. Oftentimes, these agendas involve efforts to ameliorate the plight of far more marginalized groups, whose members may not need or want help from the elites who often benefit from and sustain the very power arrangements that have contributed to their oppression. Indeed, as decades of scholarship indicates about the political activism of sex workers, racial minorities, welfare recipients, and many other groups, marginalized groups have long relied on and benefitted from *their own* collective efforts and action to gather resources and mobilize their community. Their work to this end often begins (and continues) as grassroots, collaborative endeavors to draw attention to their community's plight and challenge the dominant power arrangements that sustain their vulnerability. These political struggles and their outcomes are often messy, conflictual, and incomplete, involving negotiations and interactions within groups, and with broader institutions and social structures, about their goals and how to best achieve them.

In contrast, powerful non-state agents' (including celebrities') efforts to raise awareness about and address the issues facing marginalized groups indicates how power operates when it is divorced from collective struggle. Like the other elite private actors noted above, celebrities' power derives not from an authorizing constituency, or from shared grievances that unite and move a group towards collective action, but from their individual achievements and resources. Specifically, they mobilize their fame as a form of "soft power" to bring issues to the broader public and policy-making agenda (Van den Bulck 2018, 60). Indeed, celebrities' exercise of this power may raise awareness about issues and even challenge the various conditions that sustain inequality and marginalization; however, these actions most reliably draw attention to the celebrity herself, augmenting further her fame and power.

This enhancement of individual power is the real cause for concern because it ultimately furthers a neoliberal ethos of individualism. With its emphasis on individuals (and markets) as drivers of social change, this ethos minimizes and distracts from the broader structures that create vulnerabilities for any number of groups (poverty, racism, etc.), while maintaining dominant power arrangements—namely elite control and the expansion of global capitalism—that sustain them (Alexander-Floyd 2021; Strolovitch and Crowder 2018). Furthermore, this ethos of individualism detracts from more collective mobilizations to reform and rebuild these structural arrangements and promote democratic engagement more broadly. Put differently, while celebrities may draw people to a cause, this is not a shortcut to constituency-building, because oftentimes the crowd is gathered first and foremost to see the celebrity (Bynoe 2004). However, these power relations and dynamics are not a *fait accompli,* and to critically interrogate celebrities' political engagement and power—as well as the personal and contextual factors that may shape and mitigate this—the remainder of this book considers their engagement in anti-human trafficking politics.

HUMAN TRAFFICKING: A FEMINIST ISSUE

Concern about human trafficking has a long history, and in the pages below I illustrate how racialized, gendered, and anti-immigrant/post-9/11 anxieties variously fueled the creation and circulation of a dominant narrative that conflates human trafficking with *sex* trafficking. Promoted largely by feminists and conservative advocates in the West and their allies, this narrative has rendered human trafficking a feminist issue par excellence and shaped related public discourse and policy, albeit with decidedly *anti-*feminist consequences. Namely, as I show further in this chapter, in the United States, the dominant narrative's influence on the nation's anti-trafficking efforts has done relatively little to identify and assist victims while variously reifying racial, gender, and immigration status hierarchies.

In the United States, human trafficking has long been framed in terms of innocent victims and guilty predators, but in the nation's colonial imagination, notions of innocence have always been synonymous with whiteness and purity, as indicated by scholars who trace the dominant human trafficking narrative to the "white slavery" panics of the Progressive Era, when stories circulated that foreign men allegedly lured white girls into prostitution (Kaye 2017). Emerging in response to a range of social changes and developments— including challenges to white male dominance, changing sexual and gender norms, and anxieties about citizenship, (im)migration, and empire, among others—these stories tapped into "white supremacist narratives of Black male sexual predation that fueled lynching in the late nineteenth and early twentieth centuries ... [and deployed] gendered assumptions about the importance of (white) girls' sexual innocence and racialized threats to their sexual purity" (Baker 2019, 774).

As a result, these stories largely erased from anti-trafficking discourse the many Black women and girls in the United States who have long been coerced into sexual and other labor. As Siobhan Brooks (2021) writes so succinctly in her article about the binary framings of sex work and trafficking debates, terms such as "white slavery" and "sexual slavery" overlook

> the historical reality of chattel slavery and its continuing effects on Black women and girls in the Americas, effects that have lain the groundwork for their uniquely exploited position in the sex industry. Black women were not seen as human but as chattel, and as a consequence they were largely viewed as breeders of slaves for the economy: a slave woman's function was to reproduce slaves for a capitalist market, and her own life was not valued. Not only were Black women not viewed as needing protection, they were also seen as sexually deviant compared to white women and thus deserving of their exploitation (516–17).

These gendered and racialized assumptions about who is "innocent" and therefore "worthy" to be designated a victim of trafficking have continued to inform and infuse public understandings of the issue, especially since the Cold War ended and violence against women became a key issue for feminists globally. At this time, the pace of economic globalization increased, and growing numbers of people, notably women, moved in search of economic opportunities (Larner 2000). Racialized anxieties about migration, opening borders, organized crime, state sovereignty, and what "loomed" behind the Iron Curtain fueled international efforts to tighten borders and expand punishment and policing (Kempadoo 2005; Andreas and Greenhill 2010; Lee 2011; Limoncelli 2010; Baker 2013; Milivojevic and Pickering 2013; Fukushima 2019). To navigate these conditions, in many cases women (and others) moving for work engaged the services of traffickers and smugglers, who frequently lied about the terms and conditions of their future employment (Sharma 2003). Their stories came to the attention and illustrated the concerns of the growing transnational movement to end gender violence and promote women's human rights and gender equality, which argued that violence against women—including that which occurred in exploitative labor situations—impeded women's social, political, and economic well-being and mobility (Krook and True 2012; Weldon 2011, 2006; Htun and Weldon 2018).

However, as Wendy Hesford (2011) documents, even as transnational feminist advocates successfully highlighted the link between violence and gender inequality, the media remained inordinately drawn to spectacular representations of *sexual* violence against women and girls that mobilized gendered and racialized tropes. Internationally, these representations were apparent in media stories of Latin American, Eastern European, and Asian women who moved and were coerced (that is, trafficked) to work in brothels and other sex businesses in Western Europe and the United States (Gozdziak and Collett 2005; Soderlund 2005). In the United States, these representations reflected contemporary racialized panics about sexual predation in the nation. As Roger Lancaster (2011) documents, the growth of the victims' rights movement through the 1980s and increased media reporting on crime and racial antagonisms had already shifted societal anxieties to "special monsters" like "sexual psychopaths" and predators, and sexual "stranger danger" emerged in public and political discourse as an especially horrific problem meriting state attention, more so than poverty or other social ills (see also Fischel 2016). In this context, the media—and, by extension, activists and politicians—began circulating stories of predatory men capturing and forcing women and girls into the sex industry that drew upon longstanding gendered and racialized notions of victimization (Baker 2019). Although, as Mireille Miller-Young (2010, 222) writes, "African American feminist scholars have written a great deal about the issue of sexual representation, focusing on the exploitation of black women's bodies within patriarchal, racial capitalism in the USA," these media stories remained stubbornly ignorant of Black and other women of color's experiences of sexual (and other labor) exploitation. Instead, in media stories about sexual predation and exploitation, girls' and women's involvement in the sex trade was commonly presented "as an 'urban' problem invading suburban and rural communities, [with] portrayals of the issue often focused on rescuing white girls victimized by Black men" (Baker 2019, 744).

It is not surprising, then, that by the 1990s human trafficking soon became associated with *sex* trafficking in public discourse, and feminists were the leading advocates in the broad-based and powerful anti-trafficking movement that coalesced at this time. Even though not all human trafficking is for the purposes of sex work, and not all trafficked workers were and are women, feminist attention to sex trafficking reinvigorated long-standing debates about whether sex *work*—the voluntary exchange of sexual services for cash or other trade—perpetuated women's subordination and enslavement in society (Chateauvert 2013; Szörényi 2014; Bracewell 2016). However, many scholars and activists of color had long indicated that binary framings of debates about sex work and sex trafficking emphasizing innocence-versus-guilt and choice-versus-force did not "address the actual needs or political desires of sex workers, especially Black women" (Brooks 2021, 513), to say nothing of Black and other women of color working in a range of other potentially exploitative industries. Unsurprisingly, public and political discussions of human trafficking quickly fell into old patterns, framed "largely by moral distinctions between those who are considered to be the victims of trafficking and those who choose sex work as a form of survival" (Hesford 2011, 126).

In one camp were what one may broadly term anti-sex work carceral feminists, who opposed any legal recognition of sex work and employment protections for sex workers and framed human trafficking as *sex* trafficking and as a problem of male violence against women (Szörényi 2014; Reinelt 2016). Drawing from media and NGO accounts of women and girls who were coerced into the sex industry in the United States and abroad, these anti-sex work carceral feminists and their supporters conflated human trafficking, a *humanitarian* concern, with sex trafficking, a highly gendered *crime* that, by most estimates at the time, affected mainly women and girls across the globe (Zimmerman 2005; Bernstein 2018). Among them, the most vocal and powerful were predominantly white and economically privileged US-based feminists who formed the Coalition Against Trafficking in Women (CATW). Emphasizing deviant individuals over institutions, carceral approaches over redistributive welfare state solutions, and beneficence over empowerment, they argued that male clients, traffickers, and other facilitators trick and lure women and girls into prostitution and must be punished to end their "demand" for commercial sexual services. These women and girls, in turn, should be rescued and diverted from the criminal justice system and offered social services that help them exit the sex industry (Bernstein 2018).

These activists clashed with a range of sex workers, feminists, labor activists, and other so-called "critical trafficking" scholars who problematized the anti-sex work carceral feminists' conflation of human trafficking with sex trafficking. In addition to challenging its inherently gendered, heterosexualized, and racialized framing of the issue, they argued that this conflation "transforms sex workers from workers who can claim their rights into either criminal 'sex traffickers,' subject to punishment, or else passive 'victims'" (Chapman-Schmidt 2019, 182–83). Furthermore, they argue, this understanding "effectively neutralizes domains of political struggle around questions of labor, migration, and sexual freedom" to reductionist tropes of "prostitution as gender violence" and "sexual slavery" that only the criminal justice system and global capitalists, working in tandem, can help combat (Bernstein 2018, 10–19). This approach minimizes how law enforcement disproportionately targets racial-minority and other marginalized sex workers over those holding more privileged identities. And it does little to address the conditions that create vulnerabilities to human trafficking, which include, but are not limited to, poverty, global wealth inequality, racial discrimination, destructions from wars and environmental disasters, and insufficient labor protections (Baker 2018, 2019). Therefore, in contrast to anti-sex work carceral feminists, critical trafficking advocates argue for framing human trafficking in ways that account for "broader dynamics of globalization, gendered labor, and migration" (Bernstein 2018, 19). They propose more structurally oriented solutions that address the conditions that create vulnerabilities to human trafficking, and they also support granting all workers, including sex workers, autonomy and labor rights (Zheng 2010).

These divisions between anti-sex work carceral feminists and critical anti-trafficking advocates manifested in the late 1990s in international and US policy deliberations about whether to single out prostitution as a specific form of sex trafficking, or to acknowledge individuals' capacity to consent to prostitution, even under constrained circumstances (Doezema 2005). The 2000 UN Protocol, which over eighty countries signed in December 2000, reflects these divisions in a somewhat confusing and circuitous way. While its definition of human trafficking (presented above) labels the use of coercion, abuse, and deceit as key elements of trafficking, it also distinguishes between trafficking and prostitution, stating that prostitution must occur as a result of one of the deceptive or coercive "means" listed in the definition to be classified as trafficking (Wijers 2015). Yet even with these divisions and confusions, Prabha Kotiswaran (2019) shows that the 2000 UN Protocol sparked the development of an extensive, highly influential, and poorly institutionalized transnational legal order. The United States quickly claimed a leadership role here, and its resulting laws came to reflect the interests of anti-sex work carceral feminists and other advocates who framed human trafficking through the now dominant *sex* trafficking narrative.

However, as Alicia Peters (2015) documents, anti-sex work carceral feminists' influence was not immediate. When the Clinton administration began to consider human trafficking in the 1990s, it understood the problem as one that occurred in all sectors of the economy and also involved men and boys as victims. But this more expansive understanding of human trafficking and its victims was short-lived, as anti-sex work carceral feminists soon formed a "coalition of strange bedfellows" (Bernstein 2010, 65) with right-wing religious groups and a number of powerful conservative political leaders. Their combined neo-conservative commitments to abolishing sex work, enforcing a particular view of sexual morality, and being tough on crime helped them advance an anti-trafficking agenda that largely emphasized sex trafficking (Bernstein 2010; Peters 2015). To both anti-sex work carceral feminists and conservative elected officials, the (non-white/foreign) sex trafficker was the worst predatory offender, and catching him aligned with the neoconservative moral imperative to "rescue" women and root out organized crime networks, particularly from the Global South, where "dark, menacing criminals" would threaten homes, families, and ways of life (Milivojevic and Pickering 2013, 588).

This agenda was publicly and politically appealing because it tapped into longstanding gendered and racialized tropes of victimization *and* it exploited anxieties about declining white male dominance that escalated with post 9/11 fears about terrorism, (im)migration, and national security (Szörényi and Eate 2014; Baker 2019). American assertions of masculine dominance and empire, including gendered and racialized law and order approaches to human trafficking, also aligned with the "War on Terror" that followed the events of September 11, 2001. At this time, as Lila Abu-Lughod (2013) writes, Western publics were increasingly exposed to stories of the alleged horrors of life for women in Muslim countries, and soon a moral crusade to rescue them from their cultures and religions swept the public sphere and justified all manner of humanitarian and military interventions. In line with this, federal interest in prostitution and trafficking reached a fever pitch when the Bush administration adopted anti-trafficking as a key humanitarian initiative in the post 9/11 period (Soderlund 2005), declaring human trafficking a "special evil" in 2003 (Chang 2013, 56).

The Trafficking Victims Protection Act (TVPA), which the US Congress first passed in 2000, responded to and reflected these anti-sex work carceral feminist and conservative concerns about human trafficking (O'Brien 2011; Peters 2013). Originally designed to stem the flow of trafficked victims into the United States (Chuang 2010), the TVPA, which has been subsequently reauthorized as part of the Violence Against Women Act, promoted a "3 Ps" approach to human trafficking, focusing on "protection, prosecution, and prevention, but ... prosecution above all" (Merry 2016, 117). (The Obama administration added a fourth P, "partnerships," to emphasize the role of NGOs and other organizations). The law also establishes the US government as an international human trafficking monitor by conditioning other countries' receipt of US foreign aid on their rankings in the annual Trafficking in Persons (TIP) reports (Kelley and Simmons 2015a; Wilson and O'Brien 2016). Assuming and promoting the superiority of American values, the TIP reports judge other countries' anti-trafficking efforts according to US standards, which effectively pressures countries to fight trafficking through the "4 Ps" approach and criminalize trafficking in their domestic laws (Merry 2016; Kelley and Simmons 2015).

As a result of these advocacy and legislative efforts, the US government now devotes significant resources to fight human trafficking. At the federal level alone, Katheryne Pugliese, who assisted with my research for this book, found in her review of TIP reports from 2000 to 2020 that the Department of Health and Human Services (DHHS), Department of Justice (DOJ), State Department, Department of Labor (DOL), and US Agency for International Development (USAID) have received the bulk of funding—totaling at least $1,953,289,228—for anti-trafficking efforts to date. While funding data was not available in these reports for all years, it is worth noting the anti-sex work carceral feminist and conservative influence on these funding allocations. Pugliese found that the State Department, which largely focuses on criminal justice responses to human trafficking (and sex trafficking in particular), received the largest share ($637,541,119, total, since 2000), while the DOL, which focuses on addressing trafficking in *non-sex* industries, received the smallest share ($209,178,000, total, since 2000).[3]

But even with these laws, policies, and resources, many believe that human trafficking still occurs on an enormous scale in the United States (and worldwide), even as it is difficult to quantify. While multiple US government agencies collect data about human trafficking victims, the nation's privacy laws and agency rules prohibit them from sharing personal information; as a result, there is not one, central set of victim statistics (Walk Free Foundation 2021a). NGOs and other interest groups have stepped in to estimate the number of victims in the United States and the Global Slavery Index, one of the more prominent sources here, estimates most recently that "on any given day in 2016 there were 403,000 people living in conditions of modern slavery in the United States, a prevalence of 1.3 victims of modern slavery for every thousand in the country" (Walk Free Foundation 2021a)—numbers that presumably exclude those who are engaged in forced labor in the nation's prisons.[4] However, from these estimates, the National Institutes of Justice (NIJ) finds that "only a small fraction of trafficking victims are currently identified" (Simich et al. 2014, 2), and the same goes for the number of traffickers. Numerous NGOs, alongside local, state, and federal government agencies, variously interact with persons who may fit the definition of a trafficking victim or perpetrator, but if we look at just a small selection of the organizations that do identify victims and perpetrators in some way, their numbers are far smaller than the aforementioned estimates. For example, in 2020, the Polaris Project, which runs the National Human Trafficking Hotline, had 10,583 situations of human trafficking reported, involving 16,658 individual victims (Polaris 2021b), a number far smaller than the Global Slavery Index's estimate. And on the trafficker side, very few perpetrators have been formally identified (at least by arrests), relative to the estimated number of victims. The Bureau of Justice Statistics reports here that the number of arrests reported for human trafficking involving involuntary servitude increased from 66 in 2015 to 146 in 2019 (before declining to 92 in 2020), while those involving commercial sex acts increased from 684 in 2015 to 880 in 2016, before declining to 301 in 2020 (Lauger and Durose 2021).

In addition to shaping an arguably ineffective response to human trafficking, the dominant narrative has had other decidedly anti-feminist consequences, as indicated by the ways in which contemporary anti-trafficking laws and policies variously further race, gender, and immigration status hierarchies. Because lawmakers in the United States have largely conceived of human trafficking as sex trafficking through the dominant narrative, police departments—and vice departments in particular—tend to spearhead the bulk of human trafficking investigations. Consequently, these investigations focus more on illegal sex work (such as prostitution) instead of labor in licit industries such as agriculture or the domestic sector, where trafficking is likely far more common (UNODC 2016; Peters 2015). Moreover, these investigative efforts replicate longstanding tendencies to target men and women of color for related offenses. Here, cases involving children and young people in the sex trades—a major focus of law enforcement and other human trafficking investigative efforts since 2000—are especially instructive. Law enforcement has disproportionately targeted Black men as perpetrators of prostitution and, by extension, sex trafficking. As *Reuters* reported, "Between 2005 and 2015, 57% of defendants in U.S. federal minor sex trafficking trials, a focus for prosecutors, were African-American, even as only 13% of the U.S. population was African-American" (Murray 2020). On the victim side, although the TVPA automatically identifies any person under the age of eighteen who trades sex as a trafficking victim, Alexandra Lutnick (2016) illustrates that police arrests of young people initially *increased* for the first ten years after the TVPA was enacted. And these arrests were (and are) not race-neutral. As Carisa R. Showden and I find in our review of research in this field (2018), due in large part to the effects of structural racism and poverty, Black girls are more vulnerable to engagement and exploitation in the sex trades. But given longstanding stereotypes about their sexual maturity and promiscuity, they are also more likely than white girls to be arrested instead for prostitution (see also NBWJI 2022).

Furthermore, the trafficking victims among the many young people and adults who continue to be arrested for prostitution (and other offenses) are not often identified as such, even after multiple arrests. Because trafficking investigations in the United States have disproportionately focused on the sex industry, victims in many *other* industries, ranging from agriculture, to domestic service, to the garment industry (among others) remain underidentified. As a result, many victims of trafficking, who are often vulnerable by virtue of their race, income, gender, and immigration status, may never secure access to critical services and support. These risks are especially apparent when we consider the DHS's "T-Visa" program, which offers temporary immigration relief to up to five thousand foreign nationals who are victims of trafficking in order to "strengthen law enforcement's ability to investigate and prosecute human trafficking" (DHS 2021). Since these victims must cooperate with law enforcement in order to obtain this visa, it is not surprising, as the 2021 US TIP report showed, that the DHS only granted T-Visas to 1,040 victims in 2020 (up from 500 victims in 2019), leaving one to wonder what became of the many victims who could not qualify for this visa.

PLAN OF THE BOOK

Despite decades of anti-trafficking advocacy and law and policy development, individuals continue to be coerced into dangerous and exploitative work situations globally. In response, the diverse and diffuse anti-human trafficking movement has continued to grow, and it now includes celebrities like Liam Neeson, who use their high profiles and media savvy to both draw attention to existing efforts to address human trafficking *and* promote their own understandings of the issue's forms, victims, causes, and solutions to the public. Therefore, by comprehensively accounting for and analyzing celebrities' anti-trafficking activism over time, we also expand our understanding of celebrity feminism *and* celebrities' political roles and power more broadly.

To this end, the following chapters introduce my theoretical framework, provide a broad overview of celebrities' anti-trafficking activism, and offer illustrative case studies. In chapter 1, I draw from theories of celebrity feminism, political performance, and representation to argue that understanding celebrities' anti-human trafficking activities as political performances draws our attention to the dynamics and nature of political representation—in this case, how highly visible and unelected political actors highlight an issue and its impacted population to the general public through representation-at-a-distance. Following this, I outline my qualitative-interpretive and feminist methods of data collection and analysis, which I use to capture the extent of celebrities' anti-trafficking activities and analyze how they represent human trafficking's forms, victims, causes, and solutions to promote various feminist interests and ideologies.

In chapter 2, I use Shirin Rai's (2014) framework for analyzing political performances to present an overview of US-based celebrities' anti-trafficking performances along two axes, the first of which are the markers of performance—the performers, sites, and audiences. Drawing from my dataset documenting celebrities' anti-trafficking work from 2000–2016, I show that predominantly white women actors engage in a range of high-profile, media-friendly activities to diverse and diffuse audiences. Turning then to the second axis—the performances' effects—I elaborate the representational and discursive effects of celebrities' anti-human trafficking work, demonstrating here that celebrities offer a wider range of representations and, hence, feminist ideologies than we may expect, and various personal and contextual factors help us interpret and understand this variation.

To then illustrate in more depth how and why celebrities' anti-trafficking activity varies over time, the following three case study chapters compare the most active celebrities' anti-trafficking advocacy. My goal in these chapters is to illustrate broader themes and trends discussed in chapter 2—namely, how celebrities' personal stories and the context of their engagement variously shape their representations of human trafficking to promote different feminist ideologies.

Chapter 3 compares Ashley Judd's and Jada Pinkett Smith's anti-trafficking work to understand how celebrities appoint themselves to represent human trafficking and its impacted populations by demonstrating their connection to the issue. Specifically, I consider in this chapter how the actors' personal, familial motivations and the time period in which they became active around human trafficking shaped their engagement with and varied representations of the issue, which offer a range of feminist ideologies that challenge and reinforce race and gender hierarchies. I conclude the chapter by discussing the mixed effects of their activism: while they draw attention to human trafficking and challenge various Hollywood norms, they also illustrate celebrities' oft-limited accountability for their political advocacy.

Chapter 4 then turns to singer Ricky Martin and actor Ashton Kutcher in order to explore the possibilities and limits of so-called "male celebrity feminism." I show how personal and contextual factors shape their interests in and representations of human trafficking, and the sex trafficking of children in particular. Namely, Martin's longstanding interest in helping vulnerable children in his home of Puerto Rico and his partnerships with international NGOs have informed his somewhat complex narrative of the issue, whereas Kutcher's introduction to and engagement with the issue through celebrity philanthropic consultants and technology investments has contributed to his reification of the dominant narrative. Like their woman-identified celebrity feminist peers, Martin and Kutcher both emphasize solutions to human trafficking and circulate carceral, liberal, and structurally intersectional feminist ideologies. Kutcher also promotes a cyber-feminist ideology that celebrates the liberatory aspects of technology. As prominent men in a women-dominated activist space, their activism also draws attention to and complicates traditional gender ideologies, most notably hegemonic masculinity.

Finally, chapter 5 compares actors Mira Sorvino and Julia Ormond, who became anti-trafficking advocates at the invitation of the United Nations. While we may reasonably assume that they would give global purchase to the dominant, American-centric narrative in this setting, their anti-trafficking performances challenge this logic. As a result of personal and contextual factors, they *destabilize* the dominant narrative on at least two levels: first, by rejecting the notion that sex trafficking merits the most attention, and second, by drawing attention to a range of structural factors that create vulnerabilities to human trafficking. Yet a closer interpretive analysis of their efforts reveals the limits of even this most structurally-intersectional celebrity feminism. By reinforcing American imperialism and failing to call for deeper market reforms, Ormond and Sorvino also uphold and reproduce numerous Western gendered and racialized power structures.

The concluding chapter discusses the broader implications of this book's findings for how we think about celebrities as self-appointed political representatives, particularly regarding their political authority and responsibility in movements to end marginalization and oppression. Here I discuss the lessons that their anti-trafficking activism offers about the varied actors and settings in our contemporary, elite-dominated polity, and about anti-human trafficking and feminist politics going forward. I conclude by proposing a number of individual, institutional, and systemic ways to better hold celebrities accountable for their political work, and I indicate directions for future research.

ONE

Theory and Methods

CELEBRITY FEMINISM, PERFORMANCE, AND
POLITICAL REPRESENTATION

> Your Excellencies and Distinguished Guests, I am Ashley Judd and amongst
> other things, I am an actor. I have appeared in scores of films and on
> Broadway. I would understand if you might be wondering right now, how
> dare she imagine she has something to contribute to the urgent, charged
> debate about the scourge of modern slavery, of human trafficking? Actually, I
> believe wholeheartedly the real question is, 'How dare I not? How dare I not
> stand before you with all of the earnestness at my command and witness to
> you what I have seen?'
>
> ASHLEY JUDD,
> *speech to the UN General Assembly (Judd 2008)*

IN 2008, STANDING BEFORE UNITED NATIONS DELEGATES and
human rights activists, among others, Ashley Judd shared stories about a
young girl in Cambodia who was "sold for sex," and a mother in Thailand who
"had paid sex" to feed herself and her son. These were just some of the individuals she identified as sex trafficking victims through her work as a Global
Ambassador with Population Services International (PSI), a US-based NGO.
In so doing, Judd engaged in a long-standing feminist tradition of "visibility
politics," presenting an image of an issue and its impacted population in an
effort to raise awareness about their plight and spark social and political transformations (Whittier 2017; Ayoub 2016; Pachirat 2011). Yet unlike many
feminists and other stakeholders concerned with sex and other forms of
human trafficking, Judd had no direct experience with or scholarly knowledge about the issue. Instead, her opportunity to speak to and potentially
influence the UN audience was largely a function of her celebrity capital.

Of course, Judd is not unique here, and the remaining chapters in this
book illustrate how she and her celebrity peers access similar resources to
raise awareness about human trafficking. This chapter offers a theoretical

framework for thinking about and analyzing these activities by first situating them as a case of celebrity feminism. Given that celebrities are rarely connected to or officially authorized to speak for trafficking victims, we must look critically at how they represent them and the issues they face. To this end, I propose in this chapter that we understand celebrity feminists as unelected representatives whose political performances offer what I term representation-at-a-distance. That is, they speak for issues and impacted communities with little direct connection to their struggles on the ground. To develop this proposal, the following pages outline key concepts, including celebrity feminism, representation, and political performance, as well as the interpretive and feminist methods of data collection and analysis I use to apply these concepts and answer the book's central questions in the remaining chapters.

CELEBRITY FEMINISM

As noted in the previous chapter, human trafficking has been framed as a feminist issue par excellence, and so I understand celebrity activism here a case of celebrity feminism. First introduced by Jennifer Wicke (1994), the term "celebrity feminism" refers to the locus for feminist discourse, politics, and conflicts in the "celebrity zone" of the public sphere. Celebrity feminists include those whose fame is "the product of their feminist enunciative practices; that is, they are famous *because* of their feminism" (Taylor 2016, 3, emphasis in original), *and,* for the purposes of this book, those who are typically already famous for something else but then deploy their celebrity capital to espouse and publicly articulate feminist ideologies and issue positions as part of their public persona (Brady 2016; Hamad and Taylor 2015; Taylor 2014). For example, when Beyoncé displayed a large screen emblazoned with the word "feminist" behind her during her 2014 Video Music Awards performance, she was engaging in this latter form of celebrity feminism (Cobb 2015)

Celebrity feminism emerged as media coverage of celebrity culture grew, and as celebrities took advantage of new social and other digital media platforms to engage in feminist political debates (Taylor 2016, Brady 2016). However, as scholars have documented, this phenomenon came to critical prominence after 2014, when luminaries such as Emma Watson, Jennifer Lawrence, Taylor Swift, and Beyoncé claimed a public and politicized feminist identity. In October 2017, celebrity feminism became even more globally visible after the *New York Times* published the sexual harassment and assault allegations against Harvey Weinstein, and actor Alyssa Milano tweeted a post inviting women who had withstood sexual assault to use the hashtag #MeToo. Responses snowballed, propelling a globally mediated movement, and in 2018, celebrities wore black at the Golden Globes as a collective and strong visual statement against sexual violence (Sue Jackson 2021).

Although scholars and feminist activists have identified celebrity feminism's ascent and potential power, there is little consensus about its meaning or utility for addressing gender inequality (Hamad and Taylor 2015). On the one hand, celebrity feminism has been criticized on a number of grounds, one of which is the celebrities' positionality. Given that the production of celebrity takes place within an extremely elite-driven political-economic environment, celebrity feminists are often "perched at the zenith of race, gendered, and economic hierarchies" (Hobson 2017, 1000). Even as women of color such as Beyoncé and Serena Williams are some of the most prominent celebrity feminists (particularly in the United States), individuals in this category are largely over-represented in the media by white, high socio-economic status, heterosexual, able-bodied women who meet Western beauty standards and are relatively safe and "palatable" to their fans and other entities that promote and endorse them (Casey and Watson 2017, 4). Roxane Gay thus terms celebrity feminism "fame-inism"—a form of feminism fronted by "pretty young women in the public eye" (Gay 2014), and, more recently, it also includes conventionally attractive, decidedly un-macho, and predominantly white men like actors Mark Ruffalo and Joseph Gordon-Levitt, who make vague statements about equality for women (Cobb 2015).

In addition to critiquing its practitioners, scholars and advocates also criticize celebrity feminism for furthering individualism over more collectivist politics (Chidgey 2021). Since the celebrity feminist is produced, extremely well-managed, commodified, and operates within the mainstream media industry, she will often claim a feminist identity and/or use feminism as a "cheer word" to capture media and public attention without specifying what it means politically (Gill 2017, 619; see also Evans and Riley 2013; Keller and Ringrose 2015). In so doing, she furthers a postfeminist, de-politicized popular feminist ideology that obscures critiques of patriarchal, racist, capitalist and other oppressive systems, while largely avoiding direct engagement with the grassroots, impacted communities fighting for gender and other equality (Chidgey 2021; Hopkins and Louw 2019; Banet-Weiser, Gill, and Rottenberg 2019). In short, celebrity feminism tends to avoid the actual work of feminism (Gay 2014).

But on the other hand, while these criticisms are indeed astute and valid, they tend to reduce celebrity feminism to what Hobson (2017, 1000) terms a "gateway feminism" or "feminism lite" that downplays a number of important realities of celebrity feminism. For one, as Anthea Taylor (2016, 7) indicates in her study of so-called "blockbuster feminist authors," mechanisms of celebrity such as self-branding, media-savvy, and commodification "have long been integral to public feminist performances." Critics routinely dismissed authors such as Germaine Greer and Gloria Steinem for deploying these strategies, claiming they were "'selling out' the movement and selfishly privileging the individual over the collective," even as they publicized the women, and their books, *and* feminism itself (4–7). Second, by extension, by emphasizing celebrity feminism's individualistic and commercial orientation, critics tend to downplay its variety, "collapsing often diverse political positions and obscuring the work" of women like transgender actor and activist Laverne Cox, who starred in *Orange is the New Black* and challenges the often white and cisgendered feminism that dominates mainstream media (Taylor 2016, 280). This collapsing also ignores celebrities who have publicly *rejected* feminism such as *Big Bang Theory* star Kaley Cucuo, who did so on the grounds that it "exists in opposition to femininity, and the traditional gendered position she chooses to adopt in her marriage" (Taylor 2016, 282).

Altogether, while celebrity feminism does indeed represent and reinforce many privileges and hierarchies that are figured as problematic and antithetical to feminist goals and modes of activism, celebrities remain powerfully positioned "to speak to, for, and with those who have fewer outlets for public discourse" (Hobson 2017, 1000; see also Taylor 2014). As such, they use their high profiles to make issues of gender inequality visible in the Western mediasphere (Taylor 2014; Casey and Watson 2017; Banet-Weiser, Gill, and Rottenberg 2019). In so doing, celebrity feminism is, as Taylor (2016) argues, a feminist practice, and not something that is always distinct from or extraneous to other forms of feminist activism, including grassroots activism. In just one example, as Red Chidgey (2021) shows in her study of Amber Rose—the model, actress, entrepreneur, and former sex worker who organized an explicitly branded and monetized annual SlutWalk between 2015 and 2018—Rose did indeed marshal the unpaid labor of activists and fans and others and drew corporate sponsors to suggest "an ardently postfeminist, capitalist appropriation of a grassroots movement" (1063). However, a closer examination reveals that the event was more nuanced, thought-provoking, and resolutely intersectional than previously assumed. In fact, Rose's "embodied position as a woman of colour and former sex worker could open up feminism for new constituencies" and her fanbase includes a strong constituency of young people of color "who attended her marches in the tens of thousands" (1063).

Therefore, whether we judge it as regressive, positive, or something in between, celebrity feminism clearly matters for contemporary feminist politics by generating collective conversations about what counts as feminism and who counts as a legitimate feminist, while also challenging and reinforcing gendered practices and expectations for the broader public (Lilburn, Magarey, and Sheridan 2000; Hobson 2017; Brady 2016; Chidgey 2021; Sue Jackson 2021). But while scholarship about celebrity feminism has provided essential definitions and raised important criticisms of this phenomenon, it has focused mainly on single case studies, with less attention to its variation over time (Taylor 2016 is an exception). To further this research, I understand celebrity feminism as "multiple" (Taylor 2016, 288)—as "a complex, internally variated assemblage of representations and political claims" (Chidgey 2021, 1057)—to better understand how celebrity feminists may serve as political representatives and present issues and populations to the broader public.

REPRESENTATION

At first glance, representation theory may seem irrelevant for understanding celebrities' political advocacy, especially in feminist politics. Even as political representation has long been a subject of scholarly analysis, much contemporary political science research extends Hannah Pitkin's (1969) so-called standard account, which focuses on *elected* representatives, where individuals are chosen by principals (constituencies formed on a territorial bases) through a set of procedural standards of authorization and accountability, namely free and fair elections. Once chosen, a representative has substantive obligations to act on behalf of others' interests, and these others hold their representatives accountable in subsequent elections (Rehfeld 2006; Urbinati and Warren 2008; Montanaro 2012). But in the 1990s, scholars began questioning the adequacy of the standard account in light of the continued exclusion and under-representation of so many groups from electoral politics based on their gender, race, and ethnicity, among other categories of identity (see, e.g. Urbinati and Warren 2008; Mansbridge 1999; Young 2000; Philipps 1998; Guinier 2000; Dovi 2002). In response, they proposed, among other things, re-thinking how legislators relate to constituents (Mansbridge 2003), promoting the special representation of marginalized groups through more pluralized, descriptive representation in political and associational institutions (Young 2000; Hawkesworth 2003), and limiting the participation and access of over-represented and privileged groups (Dovi 2009). Some even went as far as arguing that "the process of authorization and accountability that constitutes the representative function, finally, should not be confined to official government bodies" (Young 2000, 153).

These calls to consider political representation beyond the standard account were amplified further as political-participatory patterns in the United States shifted away from electoral/party politics and traditional civic groups like the Kiwanis Club (Stolle and Hooghe 2009). Instead, organized advocacy groups and nonprofits representing a range of communities and interests, from racial minority groups to gun owners to LGBTQ+ persons, to name just some examples, grew exponentially (see, e.g., Crowder 2020; Skocpol 2003; Strolovitch 2007). And in the wake of *Citizens United v. FEC* (2010)—which held that the free speech clause in the US Constitution prohibits the government from restricting communication expenditures by corporate entities—large, well-resourced, member-less pressure groups representing the interests of the advantaged (especially business) now constitute the lion's share of politically involved organizations in Washington, DC (Schlozman et al. 2015).

As these participatory patterns shifted, the *sites* of political engagement also expanded beyond those formed on a geographic/territorial basis as technological developments in travel, computing, and communication, alongside processes of economic globalization and the rise of migration in response to wars and environmental disasters, lessened the significance of national borders (Urbinati and Warren 2008; Saward 2009). Especially for marginalized groups, who have long engaged in protests, coalition building, and other actions to fight for justice and equality beyond the territorial boundaries of electoral politics, developments in communications and other technologies helped them organize and mobilize further across regions, nations, and cultures. As a result, the range of non-geographical constituencies concerned with gender, race, the environment, global trade, etc., increased exponentially, forming organizations and alliances to represent their own interests, while a wide array of groups such as the United Nations and NGOs also began responding to their non-residential/geographical concerns (Saward 2009). Certainly, these issue-based and policy driven networks of organizations and stakeholders have drawn attention to various groups' needs and interests, and while they often move more quickly than bureaucracies accountable to legislatures, they also lack the traditional electoral representative accountability to those affected by their decisions (Urbinati and Warren 2008).

So, as the political terrain has grown increasingly complex and decentralized, and as professionalized advocacy groups, non-territorial governing bodies, and wealthy and powerful individuals are increasingly visible in global and national politics, celebrities have increased their political visibility. But as unelected figures who are not territorially bound or accountable, they do not fit within the standard account of representation. Therefore, for the purposes of this analysis, I do not understand political representation as a fixed and rigid activity, but as a dynamic, variable, protean, contingent, and productive practice in context (Rai and Reinelt 2014a; Rai 2014). I also view celebrities who engage in politics (and feminist politics specifically) as "self-appointed representatives." As Laura Montanaro (2012) writes, these individuals' claims to represent occur apart from electoral and other forms of state-centric representation and consist of four elements: their self-identification as one who provides political presence for a constituency to an audience (Ashley Judd representing human trafficking victims before the UN audience); identification of a constituency potentially affected if the claim and actions were successful (human trafficking victims); identification of a constituency that is empowered by the claim to authorize the representative and demand accountability (anti-trafficking NGOs); and finally, the identification of a group whose recognition is required in order for the self-appointed actor to function as a representative (leaders of countries concerned with human trafficking).

At first glance, it seems challenging to assess the self-appointed representative's work, as her authority is not derived from and evaluated through the blunt verdict of an election. However, Michael Saward (2006, 298) offers a useful intervention here, arguing that since elections and legislatures are no longer all that matters for representation, it is worth looking instead at *what is going on in* representation—its dynamics, if you like—rather than what its (old or new) forms may be." To do this, he proposes "the representative claim"—that is, seeing representation in terms of claims to represent made by *a variety of political actors,* from electoral candidates to NGO figures to rock stars, rather than something to be achieved. The self-appointed representative may base her claims on, among other options, "deeper roots," where the individual has a profound interest in giving a voice to a group based on core aspects of its identity and their attachments thereto; "expertise and special credentials"; and finally, "wider interests and new voices," which emerge from the belief that an important perspective is not being voiced and heard due to the structural limitations and configurations of conventional representative government. These claims suggest to a potential audience that 1) you are part of the audience; 2) you should accept this representation of yourselves; and 3) you should accept me as speaking and acting for you.

Celebrities, as self-appointed representatives, may not have these same bases for their claims. Certainly, they may claim "deeper roots," as Ashley Judd did when she connected her anti-sex trafficking activism to her own experience with sexual abuse (see chapter 3). But generally, celebrities rarely have the expertise or special credentials to support their representative claims, and they are not inclined to offer "new voices," given their tendency to adhere to the status quo for fear of alienating their fans (Meyer and Gamson 1995; Bynoe 2004). What celebrities do have, however, is the dramatic authority to present themseleves as concerned spokespeople through the media (Demaine 2009). In so doing, they appear connected the broader public: as proxies for the masses who embody "the will of the people," they may convince audiences that they have answers to the problems they face (Brockington 2014b, 9).

As a result, as John Street (2004) argues, celebrities often have other bases for their representative claims. First, they are "in touch" with popular sentiment. For example, singer Bruce Springsteen's calls for blue-collar solidarity and actor Clint Eastwood's outlaw hero persona helped each amass legions of fans and ground their claims to represent "the people" (Nolan and Brookes 2013). Second, certain performers or genres of performance offer more conventions and opportunities for political engagement and representation: rap and folk music, for example, are often more politically attuned than teen pop and easy listening music. Third, celebrities may base their representative claims on the state. Whether it was willing to authorize airtime for the Live Aid concerts in the 1980s, or acting oppressively in ways that unintentionally create platforms and opportunities for performers, the state enables celebrities to assume leadership roles, which are legitimated by their success in their fields. Finally, Street writes that celebrities may also base their representative claims on the affective bonds they develop with their admirers. The strength of this bond rests, uniquely, in celebrities' capacity to offer audiences fantasies—imaginary, dream-like scenarios—on stages, screens, and in stadiums, among other venues. Supported by the entertainment industry, which is one of the greatest forces behind the production and consumption of fantasies in the United States and internationally (Hozic 2001), celebrities may link the activities that fuel their celebrity to their capacity to address complex socio-political issues. In short, even as they may not be superheroes, crusaders, or moral leaders "in real life," their fantastical performances on stages, screens, or in stadiums often convince audiences that they have the power to change the world. It is not surprising, then, for people to believe that since Ashley Judd tackles feminist issues like human trafficking in her movies, she may also do something about them in real life.

PERFORMANCE

To better understand the meaning of celebrities' political activism for movements fighting marginalization and oppression, and for democratic politics more broadly, I examine the aesthetic dimension of their representative work. In so doing, I do not simply understand political representation as an instrumental act; instead, I understand it as an *art*—a cultural act that draws on the skills and resources necessary to capture the attention of and communicate with people in a mass-mediated culture (Street 2004). Specifically, for the purposes of this book, then, I analyze Judd's and her peers' anti-human trafficking activism as *performances*—particularly involved, dramatized acts that are embodied, located in a specific site or sites, and witnessed by others (Diamond 2000; Langellier 1999). While we may think of performances as confined to theater and television and thus not relevant to the study of politics, Shirin Rai (2014, 1179) argues that "performance matters in and to politics."

In fact, there is a long history of performance in politics, reaching back to when the Assembly of Athenian citizens moved from Pyr to the Theater of Dionysus (Parkinson 2014). Since then, performance has pervaded everything from election rituals (for example, the highly staged and dramatized US presidential debates), to protests, to pundits' use of theatrical metaphors to describe the actions and drama in contemporary politics (Chou, Bleiker, and Premaratna 2017). In feminist politics specifically there is also a long history of performance. For example, with the rise of the popular press and its attendant coverage of theater, British suffragettes staged plays for wider audiences, which claimed that women's rights and influence should no longer be confined to the home. Through these performances, suffragettes gained national attention and eventually converted the public to their cause (Hill 2000). Similarly, struggles for racial justice have also involved performances. To name just one example, Cedric Robinson's (2007) seminal analysis of early twentieth century theater and film shows how silent films and early "talkies" (namely plantation and jungle films) firmly entrenched limited representations of African Americans, while also highlighting Black resistance to these practices and the linkages between racial beliefs and capitalism more broadly.

Considering performance in politics, then, draws our attention to how myriad political messages, opinions, and claims are not merely narrated but staged and dramatized to capture public attention and sway political opinions (Parkinson 2014; Hajer 2005). Yet while performances may be integral to politics, they have not been a major focus of analysis in mainstream political science, especially as the rise and dominance of quantitative positivism here has tended to prize "rationality," to the extent that drama and any analysis thereof is disparaged (Yanow and Schwartz-Shea 2010; Parkinson 2014). As a result, much political science research has often minimized the fact that democratic struggles for power are not solely determined by demography or even substantive issues, but by the symbolic and cultural constructs performed to voters and other audiences (Corner 2000; Alexander 2010).

However, scholars of Black politics in the United States have *not* ignored the role and importance of performance in politics. Examples here range from Robinson's aforementioned work on early-twentieth-century theater and films, to Yvonne Bynoe's (2004) study of rap artists' role and impact in politics, to Melissa Harris-Perry's (2004) analysis of orality and political deliberation in popular cultural spaces like Black Entertainment Television, to Brandon Wallace and David L. Andrews's (2021) examination of how television shows like *The Shop* deploy Black celebrities as mechanisms to depathologize Blackness, to Nikol Alexander-Floyd's (2021) Black feminist exploration of various television shows and movies to understand how they further and reproduce racist and sexist ideologies. While this is definitely not an exhaustive list of work in this field, it indicates the various ways in which performances—especially those in spaces *outside of electoral politics*—may appeal to audiences, advance policy frames and political ideologies, mobilize constituencies, and represent issues to capture broader public and political attention.

For the purposes of this book's analysis, Black politics scholarship offers critical interrogations of and insights into the role of what Erica Edwards

(2012) terms the "charismatic scenario" in politics and political performance. Defined as a "performative technology for African American mass mobilization that has structured public desires for black political leadership from Reconstruction to the present" (ix), examples of charismatics scenarios include, but are not limited to, religious ceremonies, United Negro Improvement Parades, and the Million Man March. These scenarios are led by singular, often male figures and commonly involve a series of bodily, spiritual, musical, and rhetorical affections, as well as "the performance of an idealized narrative of liberation" (18). Offering examples such as Marcus Garvey's visceral rhetoric to the working class, and Frederick Douglass's political performance at the World's Fair, among others, Edwards argues that the charismatic scenario has furthered a "central fiction of Black American politics: that freedom is best achieved under the direction of a single charismatic leader" (7).

In relating Edwards's analysis to the study of celebrity and politics, I am *not* claiming that a charismatic scenario like Ashley Judd's speech at the United Nations is analogous to Frederick Douglass's speech at the World's Fair. After all, as Edwards meticulously documents, the charismatic scenario in Black politics is a product of a very particular history—namely the post-Reconstruction segregated South, where the principal social institution in every community was the church, whose mix of democratic vision, religious devotion, and gender hierarchy cultivated Black leaders in political organizations that often mimicked the ecclesial. As former captives who were now becoming citizens in a liberal society defined by possessive individualism, whereby sovereignty was a "gendered function of property and manly self-possession," the nomination of singular, often-middle class Black men as leaders also served as a safeguard against white supremacist ideological and physical violence (6).

Instead, Edwards's analysis is important for studying celebrities' political performances because it draws attention to and critically interrogates singular, charismatic leadership in movements for social change, and the ways in which our focus on this may hide and repress their heterogeneity. As Edwards writes, the tendency to focus on singular, charismatic leaders and scenarios is part of "a larger cultural problematic that informs scholarly and popular historiographies and defines the conceptual limits of collective political desire" (11). Indeed, we may understand the celebrity engaged in anti-trafficking (or other) politics as part of this cultural problematic. When celebrities like Judd speak against human trafficking at the United Nations, it is easy to focus on these exceptionally gifted individuals and their impeccably produced performances over the often more complicated cacophony of grassroots and other voices in the anti-trafficking movement.

Yet, as Edwards argues, we need not assume that the singular charismatic figure is a static, natural structure of human sociality. Instead, these figures emerge out of particular cultural contexts and must be historicized and deconstructed as such. Theater and performance studies are particularly useful for this deconstructive analysis of celebrities' oft-charismatic performances, as they draw our attention here to "questions of subjectivity (who is speaking/acting?), location (in what sites/spaces?), audience (who is watching?), commodification (who is in control?), conventionality (how are meanings produced?), and politics (what ideological or social positions are being reinforced or contested?)" (Diamond 1996, 4). For my specific analysis of celebrities' engagement in anti-trafficking politics, this area of study is especially useful, revealing representations of trafficked victims and critiquing hegemonic distinctions between, for example, coercion and choice (Reinelt 2016).

To conduct this analysis, I apply Shirin Rai's (2014) political performance framework (PPF). Defining a political performance as that which seeks "to communicate to an audience meaning-making related to state institutions, policies, and discourses" (1180), Rai's PPF draws our attention to the shared grammars of politics and performance. This is the common language base and set of recognizable rules or codifications that facilitate communication and offer complex modes through which performances are both constructed and construed as effective or ineffective (Rai and Reinelt 2014b). Specifically, her PPF maps the elements of a political performance on two axes. The first axis—its *markers*—includes the actors who occupy the space of popular imagination and their words/scripts/speech, as well as the space/place of the performance. It also includes performative labor—that is, how political performances constitute identities and experiences within and through various discursive and institutional forces to potentially reflect, resist, or re-work existing and shifting power relations (Drake and Higgins 2012; Langellier 1999; Butler 1997; Rai 2014; Saward 2014a). Returning to Judd's UN speech, attending to these markers allows us to query how, for example, her tendency to "speak for" women and children in Thailand and Cambodia, in a highly emotional way, reinforces her power as a celebrity and their status as victims.

The second axis of Rai's PPF maps the political performance's various *effects,* one of which is authenticity of representation—that is, whether the audience accepts the performance's representative claims. Considering the audience in this way reminds us that a performance is ultimately a transaction of meaning—a continuous negotiation between the performers and the spectators or recipients of the act (Parkinson 2014; Kershaw 2000; Rai and Reinelt 2014b). Since the audience's reception of the performance is *part of* the performance, we must consider both the claims made on stage *and* how the audience negotiates, receives, and responds to them (Finlayson 2014; Chou, Bleiker, and Premaratna 2017). In addition to audience responses, other performance effects include modes of representation, which are conveyed through words and speech and framed within recognizable cultural narratives and symbols; the moment of liminality, when political actors are in a space/place/time when "disruption of the stable is possible"; and resistance to claims-making, which accounts for how audiences accept some claims made through a performance while mocking or rejecting others outright through (to name just some ways) demonstrations, mimicry, and humor (Rai 2014, 1186). Continuing with Judd's performance at the United Nations, one may query, for example, the extent to which she disrupted dominant cultural narratives and images of women and girls in the Global South for the assembled audience.

REPRESENTATION-AT-A-DISTANCE

From this scholarship on celebrity feminism, representation, and performance, I understand celebrities who engage in anti-trafficking and other politics as powerful individuals who represent issues and their impacted populations through charismatic political performances that are staged to capture public attention. But even as celebrities increasingly present themselves as sovereigns who stand for social justice and speak for disenfranchised, marginalized groups, they remain extremely distant—physically, socially, and economically—from these constituencies and the issues they face (Kapoor 2012; Richey and Ponte 2008). In this position, they offer what I term representation-at-a-distance, by which I mean that they operate above the fray of electoral, grassroots, collective, and/or other political struggles to define important issues, change public opinion, and shape laws and policies, and they circumvent these structures and processes through direct appeals to a broader audience (Partzch 2015; Marshall 2014).[1]

Here I am not claiming that celebrities never engage directly with elected officials or the communities for whom they claim to speak. Instead, I would like to blur the often sharp and binaristic distinction that one may easily make between politically active celebrities and the elected officials who populate the standard account of representation. While the latter is understood to be more authoritative, capable, and legitimate than the former because she is selected through election and, presumably, working in public service, the former commands less authority because she is self-selected and working in the service of her own individual, commercial interests. Yet even as this may be the case, elected officials and celebrities engaged in politics parallel each other in many ways. After all, as P. David Marshall (1997, 203) writes, in politics, an elected leader "must somehow embody the sentiments of the party, the people, and the state. In the realm of entertainment, a celebrity must somehow embody the sentiments of an audience."

These parallels are especially apparent when we look at national-level politics in the United States. Similar to celebrities, those elected to Congress must be "known," and they require significant media profiles to attain this status. Hence, it is unsurprising that entertainment celebrities such as Ronald Reagan and Arnold Schwarzenegger successfully transitioned to electoral politics (Street 2004, 2012). As well, elected officials, like celebrities, are not always descriptively representative of the US general population. At the time of writing, the demographic make-up of the US Congress was the most diverse yet in terms of race and gender, but unlike the US population writ large, its members remain overwhelmingly male (73 percent), white (73 percent), and socioeconomically advantaged (94 percent of House members and all one hundred senators have a bachelor's degree or more) (Schaeffer 2021). Regarding issue knowledge, members of Congress also parallel celebrities. While they may have more direct experience and familiarity with their constituents' concerns, they also have knowledge gaps that they rely on "experts"—oftentimes, lobbyists—to fill. Furthermore, both elected officials' and celebrities' political performances offer their audiences various fantasies by promoting ideal ways to imagine addressing issues and improving society. In so doing, elected officials and celebrities often offer multiple and even contradictory (and uninformed!) performances to both sustain and expand their popular bases. Finally, although elected officials' power is definitely different from celebrities' in that it derives from an election *and* it enables them to actually propose and pass legislation, it is also difficult in practice for voters to hold them accountable and remove them from office, as indicated by the incumbency advantage in the US Congress (Praino and Stockemer 2012; Mayhew 2008).

Yet even as celebrities and elected officials may parallel each other in many ways, celebrities' distance from those they claim to represent often grants them greater discretion in how they portray an issue and its impacted communities. As public figures who are unelected and often disconnected from those they speak for, celebrities may be freer to develop their own takes on various issues, especially given their capacity and need to reach and appeal to a wide audience. Certainly, this may mean that their political performances will offer sensational and attention-grabbing issue representations (and, by extension, policy proposals and ideologies) over those that may better align with impacted communities' experiences and desires on the ground. However, as the previously cited research on celebrity feminism suggests, they also may offer more nuanced and complex issue representations to expand their appeal to other audiences.

All of this raises questions about what celebrities' representation-at-a-distance means for democracy, especially since, as Sarah Steele and Tyler Shores (2014) so trenchantly observe, state authority is now shared with celebrities, who use their fame, notoriety, and media savvy to draw public and political attention to important issues in ways that elected politicians cannot. On the one hand, this potentially threatens the principles of representative democracy: by thriving on admiring fans over discerning citizens, privileging style over substance, and marginalizing relevant expertise, celebrities "enable a form of leadership that is driven by fame, admiration, and dramaturgy, rather than election, representation, and accountability" (Jeffreys 2015, 27). But on the other hand, even as these critiques may ring true, it is important to note that political representation *of all kinds* is steeped within power relations of domination, exploitation, and subordination (Alcoff 1991). As a result, it may include some people while excluding others (Celis and Childs 2018), privilege the political identities of some groups at the expense of others (Lombardo and Meier 2018), co-opt and silence marginalized groups (Holm and Castro 2018), maintain systems of domination (Strolovitch and Crowder 2018), and exert pressures to conform (Severs and de Jong 2018). Therefore, to consider whether and to what extent celebrities' representative actions further such unequal power arrangements, the remaining pages of this chapter outline the interpretive feminist methods I use to answer the questions guiding this book, which I introduced in the previous chapter. These questions and methods help us understand how celebrities represent human trafficking *and* the implications of granting and sustaining celebrities' political power for democratic engagement and accountability more broadly.

To answer the book's first question—how and to what extent do US-based celebrities raise awareness about human trafficking?—I first searched for the markers of celebrities' political performances, per Rai's (2014) PPF. To find these across the widest possible range of celebrities, my research assistants conducted online searches using Google and Looktothestars.com (a database of celebrities' charitable activities) for instances of celebrities' anti-trafficking activity since 2000, when the TVPA became law, to 2016, the end of the Obama administration. Here, an "instance" refers to celebrities' engagement in a discrete activity; for example, Ashley Judd's testimony before the United Nations counts as one instance.

To search for these instances as extensively as possible in the US context, my research assistants and I began with Dina Haynes's article "The Celebritization of Human Trafficking" (2014), which focuses on celebrities who testified about this issue before the US Congress since 2000, and offers the most comprehensive overview of US celebrities' anti-trafficking activity to date. From there, we "snowballed" our searches to capture these *and other* (ideally, all) instances of celebrity engagement with the issue that were *not* discussed in Haynes's article. Specifically, this involved searching online for the celebrities mentioned in Haynes's article with the term "trafficking." For example, Haynes writes about Ricky Martin's testimony before the US Congress; my research assistants searched for "Ricky Martin" and "trafficking" in other settings. Then, to find celebrities who engaged in anti-trafficking activity beyond that which was presented in Haynes's article, my research assistants employed a number of strategies including, but not limited to, reviewing major anti-trafficking campaigns (such as Rock Against Trafficking) to find the celebrities involved, and then searching for any of their activities beyond these. We also logged the URLs for the news stories and other online sources documenting these activities, many of which are cited in this book's reference list (we also saved their respective web pages as PDFs). However, as I wrote this book, many of these URLs have disappeared or ceased to function; while I updated them as much as possible when this manuscript went into production, readers may still find that some no longer work.

To catalogue and quantify the different markers of performance contained in each instance of celebrity anti-trafficking activity—the actors, settings, and words/script/speech—I entered the following information about each instance into an Excel spreadsheet: personal data about the celebrities involved such as their names, gender, and race/ethnicity; type of celebrity (actor, musician, athlete, band, director/producer, other); a description of their anti-trafficking activity to capture the setting where it took place (for example, "appeared in PSA for Department of Homeland Security"); the year of the activity; and the type of trafficking they focus on in this instance (such as sex trafficking). From there, I worked inductively, immersing myself in the data to group the celebrities by their gender, race, and celebrity type. To determine the settings of their work, I individually grouped their instances of activity into categories, which are summarized in table 1. A documentary (DOC) is one example of a performance setting.

This categorical grouping drew my attention to the particular words/script/speech I would analyze in different performance settings. For example, a documentary requires one to consider words and images, whereas a PAC may only offer visual images for analysis. With these materials, I turned to the second question guiding this book—how do celebrities represent and propose solutions to human trafficking, and what feminist interests and ideologies may we read from these?—to consider the effects of celebrities' political performances. To answer this question, I used interpretive and feminist methods of analysis. Interpretive methods of analysis (IMA) place human actors' meaning-making practices at the center of the examination and assume that social phenomena do not have any "real existence" independent of how people think of them (Schaffer 2016; IPIA 2015). As Lee Ann Fujii (2018, 2) writes, "the world is what people make of it," and so an interpretive methodology assumes that explaining any empirical phenomenon must begin with "an investigation into the meanings that people give" to social actions and the social worlds and cultural forms these actions help to constitute. Understood this way, an event or action's occurrence, like human trafficking and celebrities' related activism, is not reducible to a single truth, but is instead "a matter of how people understand and make sense of them" (2). As a result, IMA appreciates that multiple interpretations of a phenomenon under study are possible (Yanow and Schwartz-Shea 2006; Schwartz-Shea and Yanow 2012).

In addition to IMA, I used feminist methods of analysis (FMA). Broadly speaking, FMA do not deploy a specific set of techniques, per se, but are best understand as a research sensibility that centers non-dominant voices and is concerned with power, social change and justice (Kournay 2009; Rouse 2009; hooks 1999; Weldon 2019). With these commitments, intersectionality

TABLE I Settings of Celebrity Anti-Trafficking Activity (2000–2016)

Setting*	Definition	Example
Amnesty	Supporting or responding to work done by Amnesty International	Meryl Streep signs a letter opposing Amnesty International's support for decriminalizing prostitution
Award	Receiving/giving award or other recognition for anti-trafficking work	AnnaLynne McCord is honored at Variety's third annual Power of Youth event for working to raise awareness and improve the quality of life for sex-trafficking victims
Campaign	Featured in a public awareness campaign (PAC) to inform or educate the public, most commonly through a public service announcement (or series thereof)	"End Slavery Now" (ILO)
Doc/Docu-Drama	Appeared in documentary/ dramatic documentary	Half the Sky (Chermayeff 2012)
Donation	Donating to anti-trafficking causes	Beyoncé donates to the nonprofit Girls Education and Mentoring Service (GEMS)
Interview	Being interviewed about human trafficking, most often in the news media	Larry King interviews Julia Ormond on Larry King Live
Legislative	Engaging with legislatures to promote anti-trafficking laws, raise awareness, etc.	Jada Pinkett Smith testifies to the Senate Foreign Relations Committee
Misc	Miscellaneous	
Music	Creating music/supporting musical events related to human trafficking	Benefit concert for Free the Slaves in New York City
Org–Found	Founding an anti-trafficking organization	The Ricky Martin Foundation
Org–Support	Supporting an anti-trafficking organization	Demi Moore attends the From Slavery to Freedom Gala for CAST-LA
Panel/Forum	Participating on a panel or forum related to human trafficking	Emma Thompson attends the Vienna Forum to Fight Human Trafficking
Protest	Publicly protesting human trafficking	Alicia Keys leads protest against Backpage.com
Research	Supporting/producing human trafficking-related research	The Ricky Martin Foundation collaborates with the University of Puerto Rico and the Protection Project at Johns Hopkins University to study trafficking in Puerto Rico

Tech	Supporting/promoting technological solutions to human trafficking	Thorn Digital Defenders sponsors a forty-eight-hour "hackathon" to fight child exploitation and underage pornography online
Theater/Art	Appearing in theatrical/artistic productions related to human trafficking	Emma Thompson's traveling art exhibition "Journey" about sex trafficking
UN Ambsdr	Serving as a UN Ambassador	Liam Neeson as UNICEF ambassador
Witness	Witnessing human trafficking	Baseball star Adam LaRoche went undercover to brothels in Southeast Asia as part of an a rescue mission with Exodus Road

*I use the term setting to describe the general "realm" of these performances; many different examples may fall within those listed in this column.

is integral to FMA. Rooted in Black feminist theory and activism, and developed by Kimberlé Crenshaw in 1989, intersectionality is often used as a catch-all term for a broad body of scholarship seeking to examine and redress the oppressive and mutually constitutive forces (such as racism, classism, sexism, and others) that constrain Black women and women of color more generally (Alexander-Floyd 2012; Crenshaw 1995). Scholars have since scrutinized and debated the term's definition and application (see, e.g., Alexander-Floyd 2013, 2012; McCall 2005; Hancock 2007). For the purposes of this book, I follow Julia Jordan-Zachery (2017) and understand intersectionality not as a standardized mode of analysis, per se, but as a standpoint theory that seeks to unmask and understand power relations by centering the lived experiences of research participants. These participants include the celebrities under study, and the human trafficking victims they claim to represent. As well, given FMA's attention to standpoint and reflexivity in the research process (Doucet and Mauthner 2007), I am also aware of how my own standpoint as a white woman scholar from the Global North, who has never been a victim of trafficking *or* a celebrity, may shape my process of data collection and interpretation.

It bears noting that IMA and FMA may not seem applicable or useful for my project at first glance. For one, contra FMA, this book centers *dominant* voices—predominantly white celebrities from the United States—and their *individual* actions, all of which, one may reasonably assume, would reify rather than challenge gender (and other) power structures and injustices.

Furthermore, contra IMA, I could not ask these celebrities about their interest in human trafficking and how they made sense of it over the course of their activism. Certainly, developments in media technologies have collapsed the distance between celebrities and ordinary life, to the point that intimacy-at-a-distance (or, a para-social relationship) now characterizes the relationship between celebrities and their fan-like audiences. However, it still remains difficult for researchers to access celebrities directly, shielded as they are by legions of publicists, managers, corporate sponsors, and consultants, among others (Driessens 2014; van Elteren 2013; Bystrom 2011).

In fact, I experienced this difficulty firsthand when I attempted to contact the most active anti-trafficking celebrities (featured in chapters 3–5) from September 2017 to August 2018. At the time, I was living in Los Angeles, California, the center of the US entertainment industry, for my sabbatical year, while my husband John Rasmussen, a film and television editor, worked on a number of reality television shows in the city. Unfortunately, his work in "the industry" (as it's called in LA) offered me no special connections to any of the celebrities with whom I wished to speak, and so I resorted to IMDB.com, "an online database of information related to films, television programs, home videos, video games, and streaming content online—including cast, production crew and personal biographies, plot summaries, trivia, ratings, and fan and critical reviews." Through this site I found the contact information for the celebrities' managers, publicists, and other staff, and over the course of twelve months I emailed and called these individuals repeatedly, only to find that none were willing to speak with me. I was, however, able to secure interviews with representatives from two NGOs that celebrities have supported (The Polaris Project and End Child Prostitution and Trafficking [ECPAT]) and four philanthropic consultants who advise celebrities on their charitable and political activities.

To operationalize IMA and FMA in light of these challenges, I followed scholars who study celebrities such as P. David Marshall (2006) and Renée Cramer (2016) and used the celebrities as texts that, as Cramer writes, offer a lens through which to interpret and/or investigate complex questions. Understood as such, texts do not simply represent the world. Instead, they operate as a system of signs that are ideologically driven and thus linked to and reflective of systems power. As such, they may normalize what are human constructions (Jordan-Zachery 2017; Barthes 1972). In my case, I used my materials documenting celebrities' anti-trafficking activities, such as their public awareness campaigns, as texts for analyzing celebrities' political performances and what they signified about human trafficking and gender inequality.

In my analysis of these texts, I was especially attentive to their discourse. Understood as a set of "categories and concepts embodying specific assumptions, judgments, contentions, and capabilities" (Dryzek and Niemeyer 2008, 481) that are articulated through both images and verbal text to structure "the way a thing is thought, and the way we act on the basis of that thinking" (Rose 2012, 190), discourse makes issues and constituencies visible and audible. Yet, as Jordan-Zachery (2017) reminds us in her study of various platforms for Black women's speech, while a discursive analysis draws our attention to what we hear and see, we also must look for silences, which operate as another form of discourse that discloses ideologies of power with their own meanings and interpretive values. Therefore, to account for what celebrities' discourse illuminates *and* silences, I employ a critical analytic approach to reveal its assumptions and prejudices by, among other things, looking at how celebrities construct subjects and present inequalities (Kogen 2014). Furthermore, I did not examine celebrities' discourse in isolation. Following Wendy Hesford (2011, 10), my discourse analysis is inter-contextual in that it foregrounds both the textual *and* contextual dimensions of celebrities' representational practices and their attendant discourse to see "why an image [and/or text] and the meanings attributed to it are persuasive, culturally resonant, and politically viable at any given historical moment."

My analysis of how celebrities represent human trafficking thus assesses celebrities' discourse and its attendant power in the following ways. First, I draw from the political representation literature, discussed earlier, to consider the language, stories, and other ideas they use to *appoint and authorize* themselves as representatives who speak about human trafficking and advocate for its impacted populations. Second, to *interpret the meanings celebrities give to human trafficking,* I considered what their discourse makes visible *and* silences about the issue through the scripts it follows and the narratives it produces. Following Jordan-Zachery (2017), I understand scripts as mechanisms that define roles and how we/others should play them; repeated over time, they highlight and value certain identities and experiences over others. Furthermore, scripts offer narratives. Created by people conversing and arguing with others within their wider environment, narratives (and counternarratives) generally have a "beginning, middle and end," involve heroes and villains, and often end with a transformation of sorts (Stone 2002). Identifying a narrative ultimately helps us understand an issue's definition, causes, and potential policy responses, and from this narrative we may also read broader social, political (and other) values and beliefs, and the frameworks through which we may conceive of and galvanize political action (Alexander-Floyd 2013, 2021; Jordan-Zachery 2017; Fischer 2003).

To draw out and keep track of celebrities' narratives of human trafficking from their performances, I used ATLAS.ti software to code each instance regarding the following: a) type of trafficking (is the celebrity focused predominantly on sex trafficking, labor trafficking, or both?), b) victims (how they are portrayed in terms of sex, gender, race, ethnicity, immigration and economic status, physical/mental capacities, etc.), c) causes (do celebrities explain that human trafficking is caused by criminal individuals, poverty, economic displacement, or other factors?), and d) solutions to human trafficking (crime control-oriented, structurally-oriented, private sector-focused, etc.)

Third, I *interpreted the feminist ideologies* that celebrities conveyed through their performances and their attendant narratives. Following bell hooks (1999), I understand feminism broadly as a movement to end sexism, sexist exploitation, and oppression, as well gender inequality and oppression. As noted in the introduction, I understand feminist ideologies as sets of beliefs about and solutions for achieving gender and sex equality and justice. Over many decades, feminist scholars and activists have identified a wide range of feminist ideologies, ranging from liberal to post-modern, among many others (Tong and Botts 2017). However, given my interpretive orientation, I did not use a pre-determined list of feminist ideologies and then test the extent to which celebrities promote each of them. Rather, my analysis was inductive and interpretive, in that I looked to see which ideologies emerged from their anti-trafficking efforts—namely, in the solutions they promoted to end human trafficking.

To read these solutions and their related ideologies from celebrities' human trafficking narratives, two key works were especially instructive. First, Brooke Ackerly's *Just Responsibility: A Human Rights Theory of Global Justice* (2018) calls on us to ask whether those engaged in struggles for justice are offering solutions that respond to harms by alleviating individual suffering, or by making visible and addressing the actual sources of injustice—that is, the systems of power (colonialism, racism, imperialism, etc.) that *create* the conditions for harms. Second, Nikol Alexander-Floyd's *Re-Imagining Black Women: A Critique of Post-Feminist and Post-Racial Melodrama in Culture and Politics* (2021) draws our attention to melodrama, which she conceptualizes as an optimal mode for quelling or resolving social anxiety. Grounded in pathos and embodied in "good and evil" characters, melodramatic narratives serve to direct attention towards individual attitudes and away from structural inequality. With these works in mind, I considered whether celebrities' narratives of human trafficking represent this issue by focusing on individual subjects, or on the systems of power that render them vulnerable to human trafficking, and I read various feminist ideological interests from there. For example, the dominant narrative, which roots human trafficking in networks of criminal men and promotes punishing traffickers as a key solution, is clearly melodramatic and focused on subjects over conditions. As such, it offers a carceral feminist ideology that does little to challenge the systems of power that leave individuals vulnerable to trafficking in the first place (Limoncelli 2009; Bernstein 2012).

It is reasonable to expect that celebrities' anti-trafficking activism would promote the dominant, melodramatic narrative and its attendant feminist ideologies. After all, as an extensive body of scholarship by women of color and/or from the Global South clearly indicates, privileged white women from the Global North have long *spoken for* other women in national and global feminist debates, promoted Western ways of seeing, and elevated certain issues and concerns over others (Narayan 1997; Spivak 1988; Minh-ha 1989; Alcoff 1991). In the process, they tend to portray women—particularly those from the Global South—as victims who must be saved, while also minimizing the historical and global-economic complexities of their experiences and their capacity to resist and change the conditions under which they live and work (Abu-Lughod 2013; Mohanty 2003; Hua and Nigorizawa 2010; Allam 2018; Ali 2018). And certainly, as many scholars have shown, the global anti-trafficking movement, which is often dominated by feminists from the Global North, has evinced these tendencies (see, e.g., Bernstein 2018). Since celebrities, and celebrity feminists in particular, are often privileged, skilled at communicating with the public, and often averse to complex understandings of political challenges and systematic inequalities regarding a range of issues (Casey and Watson 2017; Jeffreys 2016; Kogen 2014), it is reasonable to assume that their anti-trafficking activism would be similarly myopic. However, feminist scholarship has long emphasized that "women" are not a monolithic group, and so I also do not assume that celebrity feminists are a homogenous community either. Following Anthea Taylor (2016), I instead understand celebrities who engage in anti-trafficking work as an internally variegated group whose work merits critical interrogation.

As I show in the following chapters, celebrities' political performances may exist along a spectrum, ranging from those that reinforce the dominant narrative and its attendant ideologies, to those that resist these (and all points in between).[2] Given this, my book asks a third question: how may we account for variation among these activities and representations? Answering this question is essential for understanding celebrities' roles as political representatives, feminist or otherwise. After all, as Saward writes, representative claims are never fully redeemed and always contain ambiguities and instabilities; they may operate differently in various cultural contexts, and representatives may strategically (re)shape their personas in an effort to represent groups and policy positions (Saward 2014b, 2006, 2010). Therefore, examining celebrities' anti-human trafficking activism may offer various issue representations and help us understand the conditions under which we may engage with and challenge these performances. To account for this variation, then, my interpretive analysis in chapters 2–5 reveals how celebrities' own motivations and positionality ("the personal") and the settings of their performances ("the contextual") shape their anti-trafficking activism and its representations of the issue.

The Personal

Motivation. Since I was unable to interview any celebrities (or their managers or publicists), I interpreted their motivations for engaging in anti-trafficking activism from their statements in the media, the materials they produce (for example, their memoirs), and from my interviews with consultants from four philanthropic advisory firms in Los Angeles. Broadly speaking, these consultants advise celebrities about their choice of philanthropic and other awareness-raising activities, help them learn about the issues they take on, and work with them to develop and implement their awareness raising strategies. Indeed, four consultants are in no way a large or representative sample of individuals in this profession, and so I do not claim that they speak for all celebrities. However, in line with other scholars (Van den Bulck 2018), my interviews with them reveal that a strong personal interest in an issue motivates celebrities' related activism. I discuss this motivation and how it may shape celebrities' representations of human trafficking and its impacted populations more in the following chapters.

Positionality. In this book, I also interpret how celebrities' positionality— personal factors including, but not limited to, their childhood experiences, gender, race, and wealth—motivated them to learn about human trafficking and shape how they represent this issue and its impacted populations to broader audiences. In so doing, I did *not* assume that, to put it crudely, positionality is destiny (for example, that all white women actors will position themselves as saviors and speak condescendingly about women of color trafficking victims). But I also did not ignore how race, gender, and other markers of experience and identity may shape their performances in various ways. After all, celebrities' humanitarian and other political work is not "presented as separate or add-on roles . . . but profoundly interwoven" (Littler 2008, 238) with furthering their careers. This is particularly true for women in Hollywood, where sexism, racism, and ageism, among other things, are well documented (see, e.g., Yuen 2017). Therefore, it is important to consider whether and how, for example, an "aging" woman actor in Hollywood may take on anti-trafficking activism to maintain her visibility and secure other acting work, or how a white male celebrity who has faced charges of sexism may begin to speak out against sex trafficking to show his concern about and respect for women. Altogether, bringing celebrities' personal/positional factors into this analysis helps us understand their interests in and representations of human trafficking.

The Contextual

Social, cultural, economic, and political factors have long shaped celebrities' fame and capacity to engage in political life and make representative claims. Similarly, these contextual factors shape their anti-trafficking work, and in my analysis, I am particularly attentive to its time period, settings, and audiences.

Time Period of Their Engagement. When did the celebrities become active around the issue? Considering this is important because debates in the United States about the extent of human trafficking and how to address it go back to at least the "white slavery" panics of the late 1800s and early 1900s. Knowledge about the extent of human trafficking and its forms, victims, and causes also remains incomplete and contested, especially as the public has been exposed to various human trafficking narratives through popular movies, documentaries, and news stories. In addition, the policy-scape of celebrities' anti-human trafficking activism—defined as "a landscape densely laden with policies created in the past that have themselves become established institutions, bearing consequences for governing operations, the policy agenda, and political behavior" (Mettler 2016, 369)—has also shifted over time. Governing bodies and law enforcement agencies are constantly creating, passing, and implementing laws, programs, and policies that understand and address human trafficking in different ways. In light of all of this, my analysis considers how, if at all, dominant discourses, knowledge, and policy-scapes shape and are reflected in celebrities' anti-trafficking performances. Are, for example, some celebrities focused more on law-and-order approaches to human trafficking when lawmakers are focused on passing related legislation, whereas others are more interested in labor law reforms at other times?

Settings. As noted in table 1, celebrities' anti-trafficking performances span a range of settings, from fundraisers to public awareness campaigns, and so I consider how and to what extent these settings shape celebrities' representations of human trafficking. A public awareness campaign (PAC), for example, must be simple and direct to engage a wide audience, whereas a celebrity's interview for a news program may be longer and more in-depth. Furthermore, since the media may be more attentive to performances in some settings more than others, celebrities may shape their advocacy efforts to capture its attention accordingly.

Audiences. Given their fame, celebrities—unlike many other activists concerned with human trafficking—have massive, diverse, and overlapping audiences for their performances. At the broadest level, these audiences include *the general public,* namely fans and non-fans who may encounter media coverage of these celebrities. More specific audiences may also shape how celebrities develop and deliver their performances, including what Michael Saward (2009) terms *authorizing audiences*—those empowered by the claims to exercise authorization and demand accountability (such as the UN representatives and other dignitaries who were present for Judd's 2008 speech). As well, what I term *beneficiary audiences*—those who may gain value from the celebrities' performances in some way, such as NGOs that partner with celebrities—may also monitor celebrities' performances to evaluate how they are serving their organizations' interests. And finally, I consider what I term *represented audiences*—those for whom the celebrity claims to speak (in this case, victims of human trafficking). In sketching these audiences, I am not claiming that they are finite in number; instead, I want to demonstrate how vast and diverse they may be so we may better understand their responses to celebrities' performances *and* how celebrities reflect, engage, and respond to their preferences and interests.

TO WHAT END? ASSESSING CELEBRITIES' POLITICAL POWER

This chapter opened with Ashley Judd addressing the United Nations about sex trafficking, and it has offered a broad framework and method for documenting and analyzing this and other celebrity anti-human trafficking work. What, then, as this book's fourth question asks, does this all mean for how we understand celebrities' political power and responsibility, particularly in broader movements to end oppression and marginalization? Answering this question is important because celebrities are influential figures: they serve a high-profile pedagogical function that grants them the epistemic power to influence what people think, believe, and know, and to enable and disable others from exerting similar influence (Marshall 2010; Archer et al. 2019). While they may use this power to raise awareness about more marginalized communities and fight injustices, I noted in this book's introductory chapter that they most reliably draw attention to themselves, thereby furthering the neoliberal ethos of individualism. The remaining pages thus outline how I assess celebrities' political power. Given this book's interpretive orientation, my analysis here largely avoids a normative approach that applies particular standards to clarify representatives' (in this case, celebrities') power relationships and identify their violations and misuses of power (see, for example, Severs and Dovi 2018). Instead, I propose a more radical, diagnostic approach that evaluates the extent to which celebrity advocacy reproduces inequalities and Western dominance (Brockington 2014a). To this end, I suggest and explain below some guiding ideas for how we may interrogate and assess celebrities' representative work in ways that reveal and situate the power dynamics of a given performance.[3]

First, I consider the *power dynamics* between the celebrities and the communities for whom they claim to speak. In their position as unelected representatives-at-a-distance, celebrities occupy a privileged location, where, as charismatic leaders, they have the power to interpret and convey a (marginalized) constituency's situation and wishes to wider audiences (Alcoff 1991). However, as feminist scholars have long argued, those from the constituency are best positioned to illuminate the conditions of inequality that shape their lives, and therefore they should have the ability to accept and authorize particular representations (hooks 1999; Saward 2020). Given this, I consider the capacity of the celebrity's constituency to contribute, respond to, and authorize what she is saying.

Judd's example, which opened this book, illustrates these capacities and their related power dynamics. Judd, a wealthy, white actor, is representing the interests and experiences of impoverished Thai and Cambodian women to an audience of world leaders. While she is aware that her celebrity capital affords her access to this setting and the power to engage in representative work, she contests this power by reframing it. By stating that she is at the United Nations as an earnest witness, she recasts herself as "ordinary"— a decent individual who has witnessed something terrible and cannot stay silent about it. Put differently, she is claiming to act in a way that *all* of us would act ("Stars—they're just like us!," to quote the popular section in *Us Weekly*). But what about the Thai and Cambodian women's power to respond to Judd's representation of their needs and experiences? Clearly, their inability to attend a UN meeting indicates that they have very little power here, and so one may argue that Judd's representative work ultimately perpetuates inequality, especially as in the process she reifies her own fame and the power and authority this grants her.

Second, in assessing the power dynamics between celebrities and those they represent, I consider the *effects of their representative work*. As noted previously, celebrities' political activities writ large have not gone very far in terms of changing public opinion or policy on a range of issues; however, a wide range of constituencies, from NGOs to the United Nations, still call upon them to represent various issues and interests. Given this, I assess the effects of celebrities' activism *beyond* the realm of law and policy, specifically by considering how celebrities make issues and populations *visible and invisible,* and the extent to which this reifies and/or challenges existing power arrangements that sustain inequality.

In feminist scholarship, Black feminists and others have long endeavored to "render the invisible visible" in order to reveal interlocking system of oppression and how they construct and perpetuate marginalized identities and experiences *and* foster opportunities for resistance (Jordan-Zachery 2017, 19). Yet scholars also indicate that visibility is not without risks and limits, and so we must remember, as Monica Casper and Lisa Jean Moore (2009, 15) state so succinctly, that "seeing [does] not necessarily lead to [progressive] social change," especially in an age when more bodies than ever are illuminated and seen by a range of powerful, globalized entities such as media and internet technologies, medical research, street security cameras, and customs and border tracking procedures, among many others (see also Fukushima 2019).

Regarding human trafficking, since victims are often mostly invisible, missing, and/or silent to the general public, representations of them reveal their lived experiences and conditions of marginalization (Reinelt 2016). However, this visibility may only serve to sustain power arrangements that further victims' marginalization and vulnerability. As critical scholars and activists have long noted, the dominant sex trafficking narrative has certainly captured public and political attention through a "spectacular representation" of women as passive and naïve victims who are tricked a lured into the sex industry by dangerous men and criminal networks (Hesford 2011). But this representation also reinforces racial and gender stereotypes, promotes a crime control agenda that may actually re-victimize women and girls, and furthers repressive cultural and political agendas that do little to address the conditions that create vulnerabilities to trafficking, let alone provide victims with housing, job training, and other much needed social supports (Hesford 2011, 125–30; see also Lutnick 2016, Gira Grant 2014).

Third, in addition to assessing the power dynamics and effects of celebrities' representative political work, I also consider how their power is *unstable and contested*. As Laurel Weldon (2019, 130) writes, a feminist analysis acknowledges that "some bodies will be perceived as exercising more authority and as commanding more status regardless of whether anyone chooses to exercise that power." Although it is reasonable to perceive celebrities as such bodies, Weldon indicates that power is not a thing given to certain sets of people (like celebrities) but a set of relationships present throughout society. Therefore, even as celebrities may seem all powerful—distinguished as they are from the general population by their charisma, beauty, and exceptional talents—their power as political representatives is in fact subject to contestation.

Judd's United Nations speech is illustrative here. On the one hand, she uses her celebrity capital to stake her representative claim, despite her lack of special expertise or particular experience. But on the other hand, as I show in the following chapters, performances like these are not a *fait accompli*. Even with their resources and power, celebrities' representative claims are often mediated by their positionality and by the broader socio-political contexts in which they act. Certainly, attempts to challenge celebrities and their statements about any issue may draw further attention to the celebrity and bolster, rather than check, their epistemic power (Archer et al. 2019). Yet, as the following chapters also show, such challenges also indicate that celebrities' power—like the phenomenon of celebrity itself—is always and inherently unstable.

TWO

Performing Feminism

CELEBRITIES' ANTI-TRAFFICKING
ACTIVISM, 2000–2016

> Celebrities would not be given the platform to make recommendations about human trafficking without the acceptance and complicity of an audience.
>
> DINA HAYNES (2014, 34)

REFERENCES TO CELEBRITIES' ACTIVISM PUNCTUATE our daily conversations, and as I wrote this book, friends and colleagues would routinely tell me when a celebrity said something about human trafficking. "Did you hear that Kanye West just equated strip clubs with sex traffickers?," a friend asked about the rapper's claim that posters advertising strip clubs promoted sex trafficking (Mahadevan 2019). Or, "did you see Amy Schumer and Seth Meyers's pro-SESTA/FOSTA ads?" another friend asked, referring to the comedians' support for the Stop Enabling Sex Trafficking Act (SESTA) and the Fight Online Sex Trafficking Act (FOSTA). Passed in 2018, these laws open online platforms to state and federal criminal and civil liability for promoting sex trafficking.

Oftentimes, our conversations would turn to the utility of these celebrity efforts. Did Kanye know that strip club advertising is not, by any legal definition, the same as coercing someone to engage in sex work? And if Schumer and Meyers listened to sex workers, they would know that SESTA/FOSTA could force the closure of social media sites and online message boards where they advertised services *and* communicated with their peers to screen clients (A. Arnold 2018). Regardless of our conclusions here, the fact that we were having these conversations shows how celebrity activism *works*. Even if we were skeptical about Kanye West's, Amy Schumer's and Seth Meyers's actions and knowledge, we were talking about sex trafficking *and* we were talking about *them*. In short, celebrities' activism depends on our attention: as the epigraph indicates, they and their actions would not be possible without an audience watching, sharing, and commenting on them.

From 2000–2016, celebrities who engaged in anti-trafficking activism offered their audiences many performances, and this chapter provides a broad overview of their markers and effects—namely, how celebrities represent human trafficking's forms, victims, causes, and solutions over time to communicate various feminist interests and ideologies. Specifically, while a range of celebrities perform anti-trafficking activism, a closer analysis reveals that these performances are more concentrated among particular performers—namely, white women actors—in a relatively narrow range of high-profile, media-friendly settings. However, when we look at the most popular activities across all celebrities, we see that they offer more diverse representations of human trafficking and, consequently, a wider range of feminist ideologies than one may expect. Various personal and contextual factors help us account for this variation. As a result, it is difficult to definitively evaluate the effects of celebrity activism across this decade and a half. While it is certainly challenging to engage with and hold them directly accountable for their actions, celebrities make human trafficking visible to the public in a range of ways and they are not immune to contestation.

MARKERS OF PERFORMANCE

Since 2000, US-based celebrities have joined the contemporary anti-trafficking movement en masse. According to my research, at least 282 unique celebrities from a range of fields engaged in at least one instance of anti-trafficking activity that was captured in the media. Whether they were addressing the United Nations, advocating for anti-trafficking legislation in Congress, or speaking about victims' experiences in a documentary (to name just some examples), they were making representative claims that they wanted their audiences to accept (Saward 2014b). Yet when celebrities authorize themselves as spokespeople and raise awareness about human trafficking—an issue where information remains scarce, fragmented, and often highly controversial—they risk mischaracterizing or exaggerating it to the public and policymakers alike. Certainly, participants in the anti-trafficking movement with much more experience and expertise face similar challenges, but since celebrities often reach significantly larger audiences, the ways in which they may (mis)represent the issue and its impacted populations merits close

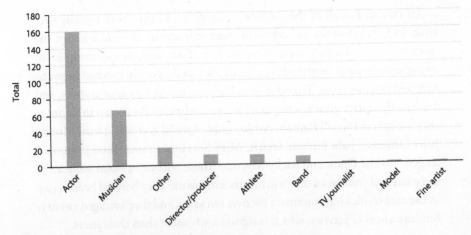

FIGURE 1. Celebrities engaged in anti-trafficking activity (by type).

attention. So, to parse out how celebrities authorize themselves as anti-trafficking advocates and represent the issue to the public, this section analyzes their activities through Rai's (2014) PPF, illustrating here the markers of their performances (the performers, settings, and performative labor) and then sketching broadly the personal and contextual factors that motivate and shape these.

The Performers

From 2000–2016, a fairly narrow range of celebrity "types" engaged in anti-trafficking activism. As figure 1 indicates, actors were the most likely to be involved, followed by musicians.

In line with celebrity feminist activism across a range of issues, women celebrities were the most likely to do anti-trafficking work (151 women versus 131 men), and the majority were white. Specifically, across celebrity types, I found 112 white women celebrities (78 of whom were actors) had at least one instance of activity, followed by 19 Black and 10 Hispanic women celebrities. The remaining women celebrities were variously Asian or mixed race. Among men, white men were the next most engaged group: 89 white male celebrities (44 of whom were actors) had at least one instance of anti-trafficking awareness work, followed by 24 Black and 10 Hispanic male celebrities. Again, the remaining male celebrities were variously Asian and mixed race.

Of course, not all of these celebrities engaged in this work equally over time. In fact, 216 of the 282 celebrities had only one instance of activity, the most common of which were relatively low-effort, such as appearing in an awareness campaign or attending a fundraiser. Only 9 celebrities had between four and ten instances. Ten celebrities had over ten instances of activity, and I define this latter group as the most active celebrities. As shown in figure 2, they are actors Daryl Hannah, Ashley Judd, Ashton Kutcher, Demi Moore, Julia Ormond, Jada Pinkett Smith, Mira Sorvino, Emma Thompson, and singers Natalie Grant and Ricky Martin.[1] These celebrities stood out for the duration and volume of their anti-trafficking work: they have all been active in the anti-trafficking movement for over ten years, and they averaged twenty-four instances of activity, which is significantly more than their peers.

Settings

Over time, celebrities performed their anti-trafficking activism in a range of settings, as outlined in table 1 in the previous chapter, the majority of which were (unsurprisingly) high-profile, media-friendly, and visible to vast audiences, such as PACs, documentaries, legislatures, and the United Nations. However, these settings were not equally popular with all celebrities over time. As figure 3 shows, their activity was concentrated in a particular time period. Namely, the years 2008–2012 had the most instances of activity in the time period studied (2000–2016), peaking in 2011 and 2012 and again in 2015.

As figure 4 indicates, between 2000 and 2016, the following four settings were the most popular with celebrities over all: Amnesty International (Amnesty), awareness campaigns and/or documentaries (Campaign, Doc/Docu-drama), and working with anti-trafficking organizations (Org-support). Within these four most popular settings, the following specific examples (many of which are described in more detail later in this book) were especially popular with celebrities. I define "popular" as being supported by and/or featuring ten or more unique celebrities.

The first is signing the Coalition Against Trafficking Women's (CATW) 2015 letter to oppose Amnesty's support for decriminalizing prostitution. Founded in 1961 by British lawyer Peter Berenson, Amnesty International is a "global movement of more than 7 million people who take injustice personally" (Amnesty International 2021), working from a popular base of individuals, networks, and community and regional groups to address human rights

FIGURE 2. The ten most active celebrities in the anti-trafficking movement (2000-2016). Left to right, top row: Demi Moore, Julia Ormond, Jada Pinkett Smith, Natalie Grant, Ashley Judd. Left to right, bottom row: Ricky Martin, Mira Sorvino, Ashton Kutcher, Emma Thompson, Darryl Hannah. All images are available through Wikimedia Commons.

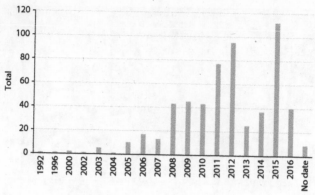

FIGURE 3. Celebrity activities over time.

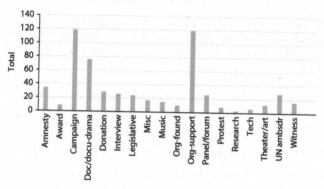

FIGURE 4. Instances of activity per setting category.

(Clark 2001). In the summer of 2015, Amnesty issued a "Draft Policy on the Protection of Human Rights of Sex Workers" (Amnesty International 2015) in advance of its International Council Meeting, which was scheduled for August 7–11, 2015 in Dublin. This document proposed that Amnesty would oppose "the criminalisation or punishment of activities relating to the buying or selling of consensual sex between adults" while maintaining "Amnesty International's longstanding position that trafficking into forced prostitution should be criminalised as a matter of international law." Amnesty based its proposal on consultations, a review of substantive evidence and international human rights standards, and first-hand research, all of which indicated how criminalization has done little to keep sex workers safe and healthy. In response, the Coalition Against Trafficking in Women, "a worldwide network against trafficking and prostitution" (CATW 2011), published an open letter on July 17, 2005, opposing Amnesty's proposal (CATW et al. 2015). Thirty-three celebrities ranging from Meryl Streep to Lena Dunham signed in support, alongside a range of service providers, advocates, and government officials from across the globe.

A second example is the International Labour Organization's (ILO) "End Slavery Now!" campaign. Originally formed in 1919 in response to the Treaty of Versailles, the ILO is now a tripartite UN agency that "brings together governments, employers and workers of 187 member states to set labour standards, develop policies and devise programmes promoting decent work for all women and men" (ILO 2021a). As part of their work, the ILO created the "End Slavery Now" campaign, which ran between 2012 and 2014. At an event to raise awareness about and recruit celebrities for the campaign, which was held in Oscar-winning composer Hans Zimmer's studio, Beate Andrees, the head of the ILO's Special Action Programme to Combat Forced Labour (SAP-FL), presented facts, figures, and trends about forced labor and human trafficking, and explained how the ILO works. She told the assembled crowd that "artists have a special role in raising awareness about forced labour," and she "urged the guests to use their talent, be it music, photography or written work, to support the campaign" (ILO 2013). Altogether, at least twenty-five celebrities including Mila Kunis, Ron Howard, Oliver Stone, Jada Pinkett Smith, and Pharrell, among many other prominent artists, athletes, and activists, are featured in photos holding placards that state "End Slavery Now" (see figure 5). Pinkett Smith also recorded a short video for the campaign (discussed more in the following chapter) that explains the importance of addressing forced labor.

My third example is Ashton Kutcher and Demi Moore's "Real Men Don't Buy Girls" campaign. On the advice of the Global Philanthropy Group, a consulting firm that advises celebrities and other prominent people and organizations about their philanthropic endeavors, Kutcher and Moore created the DNA Foundation to address the sex trafficking of children. They launched a campaign on YouTube (hereafter referred to as Real Men) as their foundation's first anti-trafficking awareness effort at a Clinton Global Initiative event on April 11, 2011. As I describe in more detail later in this chapter, Real Men featured at least seven male celebrities, including Bradley Cooper, Drake, Kutcher, Isaiah Mustafa, Sean Penn, and Justin Timberlake performing domestic tasks incorrectly.

My fourth example is a documentary created by Christian rock musician and filmmaker Justin Dillon. *Call + Response* "seeks to raise awareness about

FIGURE 5. Pharrell, for the ILO's End Slavery Now campaign, November 16, 2012. © ILO. Available at *https://www.flickr.com/photos /ilopictures/8190960982/in/album-72157631999021053*.

the 27 million slaves in the world today" (Dillon 2008). The documentary, which follows what Bernstein (2010, 45) terms a "rockumentary" format, is largely comprised of musical performances by critically acclaimed artists like Natasha Bedingfield, Moby, and Talib Kweli. Their performances are intercut with interview snippets from luminaries such as Madeleine Albright, Nicholas Kristof, Julia Ormond, Ashley Judd, Dr. Cornel West, "and many other prominent political and cultural figures who weigh in on the 21st century slave trade" (Dillon 2008).

Fifth is a set of documentary works: *Half the Sky: Turning Oppression into Opportunity for Women* and *A Path Appears*. Inspired by *New York Times* columnist Nicholas Kristof and his wife Sheryl WuDunn's book of the same title, *Half the Sky* "introduces women and girls who are living under some of the most difficult circumstances imaginable—and fighting bravely to change them" (Chermayeff 2012). In this documentary, Kristof travels with A-list celebrity advocates America Ferrera, Diane Lane, Eva Mendes, Meg Ryan, Gabrielle Union and Olivia Wilde to cover sex trafficking, as well as gender-based violence, education, inter-generational prostitution, maternal mortality, and economic empowerment in selected countries. *A Path Appears* (Chermayeff 2015) is a three-part PBS series that continues with many of the themes developed in *Half the Sky* by following "intrepid reporters Nicholas Kristof and Sheryl WuDunn and actor/advocates Malin Akerman, Mia Farrow, Ronan Farrow, Jennifer Garner, Regina Hall, Ashley Judd, Blake Lively, Eva Longoria, and Alfre Woodard to Colombia, Haiti, Kenya, and throughout the United States as they uncover the harshest forms of gender-based oppression and human rights violations, as well as the effective solutions being implemented to combat them." Much like *Half the Sky,* this series does not focus exclusively on human trafficking, but it does devote an entire segment to sex trafficking.

Finally, I give two examples of organizational support. In 1998, Dr. Kathryn McMahon, the Thai Community Development Center, and a group of community activists founded The Coalition to Abolish Slavery and Trafficking in Los Angeles (CAST-LA), in response to the discovery that seventy-two Thai workers had been kept for seven years in slavery and debt bondage in LA County. According to their website, CAST-LA works to "put an end to modern slavery and human trafficking through comprehensive, life-transforming services to survivors and a platform to advocate for groundbreaking policies and legislation" (CAST-LA 2021c). To raise funds for their work, CAST-LA has hosted its annual From Slavery to Freedom gala benefit since at least 2008. At least twenty-six celebrities ranging from Ashton Kutcher to Russell Simmons have supported the organization, often more than once, by attending this benefit, donating funds, and/or by joining its organizing committee (the main goal of which is to sell tickets and raise money).

Many celebrities also supported the (now defunct) Somaly Mam Foundation, formerly the fundraising arm of AFESIP (the French acronym for Acting for Women in Distressing Situations). Founded by Somaly Mam, who claimed to be a former sex slave, AFESIP rescued girls from Cambodian brothels and offered them rehabilitative services. Nicholas Kristof featured AFESIP in *Half the Sky,* and with this attention, the Somaly Mam Foundation became very popular with celebrities and raised millions of dollars. According to journalist Pat Joseph (2014), "The foundation's annual fundraising galas [were] star-studded, red-carpet events featuring supermodels, Hollywood actors, Silicon Valley financiers, and high-profile journalists, including Kristof and news anchor Katie Couric." At least thirty celebrities, ranging from Susan Sarandon to Seth Meyers to Oprah Winfrey, supported the organization in some way between 2000 and 2016. (I discuss the organization's decline in more detail in the following chapter.)

Performative Labor

According to Rai (2014), political performances are marked by their performative labor—that is, the identities and experiences the performers (and performances) draw from and produce. When celebrities do anti-trafficking work, they are using their fame capital to draw media and public attention to the issue; in so doing, they also draw attention to themselves and further their own celebrity status and power. But celebrities' performative labor here also produces and constitutes them in a number of other roles including, but not limited to, the following.

Various NGOs and governing bodies will invite celebrities to serve as *ambassadors* for their anti-trafficking efforts. In this capacity, celebrities constitute themselves as spokespeople for organizations such as the United Nations and for the issues they champion. Similar to their endorsements of various goods and services, celebrities also become the "face" of anti-trafficking efforts as *endorsers*. Here, by associating their highly recognizable images with campaigns such as the ILO's "End Slavery Now," they draw the public's attention to an issue, inform them about it, and ultimately motivate them to act (by making a donation, for example). And various governing bodies often call upon celebrities to testify about human trafficking as *experts*, often despite their lack of personal or other experience with the issue. For example, Jada Pinkett Smith, Ricky Martin, and Ashton Kutcher have testified before the US Congress about human trafficking.

Celebrities are well known, and so they may use their fame and other resources to draw attention to and raise money for various causes, thereby constituting themselves as *fundraisers* and *philanthropists*. However, it is important to note that celebrities are not often philanthropists in the traditional sense, donating their own fortunes to their causes. As Marc Pollick, who heads the Giving Back Fund (a philanthropic advisory firm that works with many celebrities) informed me, "About 97 percent of celebrities who create foundations do not donate any of their own money to their foundation because the public will donate money—the public won't think twice because it's a celebrity."[2]

Many celebrities play *heroes* in films and on television, and they may also further constitute themselves as such in their anti-trafficking work. For example, when they partner with an anti-trafficking nonprofit and attempt to "rescue" girls from a sex business (as Mira Sorvino aimed to do in Cambodia, for example; see chapter 5), this "plays into the celebrity-as-rescuer-of-victim ideal that receives a huge amount of attention from the media and the public" (Haynes 2014, 25). Celebrities also appear at and engage in public protests. One example of a celebrity *protestor* is the singer Alicia Keys, who constituted herself in this role when she sponsored a protest in front of Village Voice Media in New York City in January 2013 to oppose their site, Backpage.com, where adults could advertise escort and other commercial sexual services.

Finally, celebrities sometimes appear as *witnesses* and *journalists*. As noted previously, human trafficking is a "made for TV" issue. Celebrities, with their penchant for dramatization and large fanbases, are uniquely positioned to capture attention about this issue in the contemporary media-scape, and they often do this as what I term "witness journalists," partnering with a journalist such as Nicholas Kristof to "witness" the horrors of trafficking and show how they are called to action (Heynen and van der Meulen 2021; Fukushima 2019).

Motivation and Context

Celebrities' performances of anti-trafficking activism from 2000–2016 are marked by a range of actors, settings, and performative labor. Yet these performances did not emerge and appear in a vacuum, and so we must consider the factors that motivated and shaped them because celebrities are commercial products whose value depends on their continued visibility and popularity with their fans. Although no reasonable or decent person would argue that human trafficking is an acceptable practice, it is a controversial issue for many reasons discussed throughout this book. So what, then, motivates celebrities to wade into this risky and divisive issue arena? Since I was not able to obtain any answers to this question directly from any celebrities, I rely here on my interviews with the philanthropic consultants introduced in the previous chapter. It is worth noting that procuring their services requires significant resources. For example, a Global Philanthropy Group (GPG) representative informed me that the cost of their services "varies based on scope and duration of work," and they offer their clients a "multi-person, multi-skilled team for about what it costs to hire an executive director."[3] As a 2010 article about GPG reported (Holson 2010), this cost would be about

$150–200,000 per year of consulting work (or approximately $183–245,000 per year in 2021).

These consultants strongly indicated that celebrities authorize their engagement in anti-trafficking (and other political) issues by claiming "deeper roots," per Saward (2009, 10)—that is, some kind of personal connection to the issue. Here the consultants informed me that celebrities engaged with an issue like human trafficking out of genuine personal interest. According to a representative from the Artemis Agency, celebrities' motivation to take on an issue, including human trafficking, most often comes from "a personal place; even if they have not been personally impacted by the issue, they may have worked somewhere where they witnessed this issue."[4] As Kyle, another philanthropic consultant, explained, they do this because it is "often some part of their life story—they have encountered an issue that is close to home or they have been awakened by some chance encounter."[5]

Certainly, many scholars and critics argue that these claims to a personal connection are fundamentally self-serving: they help the celebrity justify her engagement with an issue, which in turn draws attention to the issue *and* the celebrity herself, thereby furthering her status (Haynes 2014). However, philanthropic consultants tended to disagree with this assessment. As a representative from the GPG wrote to me in an email, "Frankly I have never seen this [self-serving interest] up close and find [these] criticisms to be small and not worth my time to comment. If most people put the energy they do into criticism into actual activity, they could be part of solutions rather than problems. And I've yet to see critics who are actually doing anything themselves."[6]

Of course, celebrities were not solely driven by personal connections to the issue. A range of contextual factors—namely, changing political priorities and technological developments—facilitated celebrities' anti-human trafficking activities, particularly, per figure 3, as they peaked in 2011–2012 and again in 2015. For one, the federal policy context created more opportunities for celebrity engagement, albeit indirectly. Namely, as I document elsewhere (Majic 2022), in January 2010, President Obama issued a proclamation declaring January National Slavery and Human Trafficking month. His administration took other actions that expanded the range of advocates engaged in anti-trafficking efforts by adding a fourth "P"—partnerships—to the federal government's anti-trafficking strategy, which previously focused on "3 Ps"—prosecution, protection, and prevention. Although the federal government had partnered with various anti-trafficking stakeholders since the passage of the TVPA, under the Bush administration these partners were predominantly anti-prostitution and faith-based groups (Weitzer 2007). Now, under Obama, these partnerships would expand to include a wider range of government, nonprofit, private sector, and other NGO stakeholders with a range of perspectives about human trafficking.

These new partners included celebrities such as Demi Moore and Ashton Kutcher, who were developing a reputation for anti-human trafficking advocacy through technological novelties such as YouTube and Twitter. Kutcher, who was the first Twitter user to amass 1 million followers, met with Rachel Lloyd, the founder of Girls Education and Mentoring Services (GEMS, discussed below) and then tweeted about the organization in 2009 (*The Guardian* 2009). He and Moore released Real Men in 2011, and they also created a human trafficking PSA for the DHS's Blue Campaign, which was established "to harness the authorities and resources of the Department of Homeland Security (DHS) to deter human trafficking by increasing awareness, protecting victims, and contributing to a robust criminal justice response" (DHS 2010).

Illustrating how state authority is now often shared with celebrities (Steele and Shores 2014), Kutcher and Moore's PSA reflected the DHS/Blue Campaign priorities. Their one-minute PSA opens with Kutcher and Moore stating that the United States welcomes millions of people each year, but thousands (especially women and children) arrive full of hope, only to find themselves living in slavery. In line with the dominant narrative, the PSA also maintains that bad individuals and criminal networks cause human trafficking, as indicated by a number of "have you . . ." questions Kutcher and Moore then pose to the viewer. Voiced over various photos of individuals in compromised positions, these questions include: have you "had ID or travel documents taken?," "been told what to say to immigration officials or law enforcement?," "been forced against your will to work without pay, pay off debt, or engage in sex?," and "been threatened with violence or had your family threatened?" Then the camera shows Kutcher and Moore, who ask the viewer, "Are you a slave?"

Kutcher and Moore's instructions for viewers who answer "yes" to these questions show the celebrities promoting state-oriented solutions to human trafficking. However, instead of arguing for policies that will improve labor conditions or reduce poverty, which researchers and advocates have long argued will reduce vulnerabilities to human trafficking (see, e.g., Limoncelli 2009; O'Brien 2015), Kutcher and Moore reinforce neoliberal and neoconservative political rationalities by emphasizing the importance of individual action and law enforcement responses (Brown 2015). Specifically, they do this by telling viewers to get help by contacting the police, visiting the DHS website, or calling the DHS trafficking hotline, adding that the "US is determined to stop trafficking" and "law enforcement officers and agencies are tracking down and prosecuting traffickers and protecting victims." Panning to Moore's and Kutcher's faces, the PSA tells viewers to "do your part. Be alert. Take action," and to "make a difference in someone's life by helping to end human trafficking."

This PSA reached a potentially large audience. It was featured on CNN's Airport Network in 2011, and according to their marketing materials, ads and PSAs that appear here may be in forty-five airports and twenty-seven club rooms annually, nationwide, reaching an estimated 234.9 million viewers, an "upscale and influential" audience whose median age is forty-five, and average income is $101,400 per year (CNN Airport Network 2011).[7] Although there is no data about the impact of Kutcher and Moore's PSA on this audience, soon after it aired more government and NGO entities began working with celebrities as key anti-trafficking partners, inviting them to, among other things, testify before Congress and the National Council of State Legislatures, and appear in major public awareness campaigns such as the ILO's "End Slavery Now" initiative, which ran from 2012–2014. By 2015, when celebrity anti-trafficking activity peaked again, celebrities were well-established anti-trafficking activists, and so it is not surprising that various NGOs such as the CATW and journalists like Nicholas Kristof again drew on their fame in their response to Amnesty International and in *A Path Appears,* respectively.

PERFORMANCE EFFECTS: NARRATIVES AND IDEOLOGIES

In this section, I draw from the most popular examples of celebrities' anti-trafficking activism, noted above, to discuss their broader discursive effects—that is, the extent to which personal and contextual factors shape how these performances resist or reaffirm dominant narratives of the issue to promote various feminist interests like gender and racial equality. Taken together, these examples indicate that while celebrities do offer and reinforce the dominant narrative's representation of human trafficking, they also offer other, more complex narratives that promote multiple (and, at times, conflicting) feminist ideologies, thereby challenging the notion that celebrity feminism eschews controversial topics and complex issue positions to avoid alienating fans (see, e.g. Cobb 2015).

What's the Story? Celebrity Narratives of Human Trafficking

Celebrities' anti-trafficking activism offers a range of narratives, some of which "interact with dominant framings" (Budabin and Richey 2018, 261)— namely the dominant, melodramatic, made-for-TV story where dark, dangerous men capture innocent girls, who are then rescued by heroic law enforcement officers or NGO representatives (Vance 2011). Among the activities that were especially popular with celebrities, the Real Men campaign and the CATW's letter to Amnesty International are particularly illustrative of this narrative and the and personal contextual factors shaping its promotion.

The Dominant Narrative. Launched on YouTube at a Clinton Global Initiative event on April 11, 2011, Real Men was comprised of videos that follow a similar format to the most widely viewed video, starring Sean Penn and featuring Ed Norton (InboxMag 2011; see also Majic 2018). This video opens in a dimly lit wood-paneled living room, where Penn is hunched over an ironing board. Jazzy music plays in the background, and the viewer can hear a hissing sound and see the steam from the iron. The camera turns to Penn, and text on the screen appears, read by a deep masculine voice: "Real men know how to use an iron." A pull away shot reveals that Penn is in fact ironing a cheese sandwich, followed by the same deeply masculine voice stating, "real men don't buy girls." Penn reappears, taking a bite out of a grilled cheese sandwich; his face then fades in to a picture frame with the title "Real Man." Next, another framed picture of Burt Reynolds appears with the same text, followed by two more pictures of Bruce Willis and Harrison Ford. Jessica Biel appears next, standing beside a framed picture of Edward Norton, and says to the camera, "Edward is a real man. Are you?" The screen reads, "Take a stand against child sex slavery," and two textboxes below this state, "I am a real man" and "I prefer a real man." A (now defunct) link to "demiandashton.org" encourages the viewer to "click here to create and share your own Real Men video now!"

An interpretive analysis reveals this campaign's promotion of the dominant narrative and its attendant gender role stereotypes to its audience (Majic 2018). By stating that "real men don't buy girls," the campaign emphasizes that sex trafficking is the most egregious form of human trafficking, and it frames it as a heterosexual phenomenon, where girls are the victims, while individual men and their non-normative behavior are the main cause. By casting men who purchase sexual services as predators who endanger young girls, Real Men reifies dominative masculinity—a point that the campaign underscores further by casting men as incapable of (feminized) domestic tasks such as making a cheese sandwich. The campaign also emphasizes diminutive femininity by objectifying girls and rendering them innocent, silent and invisible objects for purchase, as opposed to animate human beings. At the same time, by stating that "real men" do not "buy girls," the ads also indicate that "real girls" do not sell sex. This indirect reference to "real girls" signals that even those who exhibit a modicum of (constrained) agency in their decision to trade sex (for example, in exchange for a place to stay) are deviant or damaged in some way, while also minimizing the fact that boys and transgender youth also may trade sex (Showden and Majic 2018; Lutnick 2016).

A combination of personal-relational and contextual factors shaped Real Men's (strange) conveyance of the dominant narrative. One was Kutcher and Moore's partnership with Trevor Neilson, a prominent "philanthropic advisor" who once worked in the Clinton White House's travel office and later partnered with his wife, Maggie, a former technology executive, to found GPG (Holson 2010). It is unclear how GPG worked with Kutcher and Moore, specifically, to help them learn about a complex issue like human trafficking and develop their own awareness-raising strategies and messages. As a GPG representative explained to me, they are "unable to discuss specific client engagements due to contract [non-disclosure agreements]." However, in general terms, to help clients learn about issues, they "provide research and analysis services. We typically cull from many primary and secondary sources into digestible, concise content." To then develop their client's particular approach to the issue, GPG considers "what it would it take to eliminate the issue and who is doing what ([government], nonprofits, corporate, [high net worth individuals], celeb[rities], otherwise) in order to find where there are engagement opportunities that match our clients' assets."[8]

In 2010, with GPG's assistance, Kutcher and Moore decided that an NGO might help to eliminate the issue, and so they established the Demi and Ashton Foundation (DNA Foundation), a 501c3 nonprofit that would become the main setting for their anti-trafficking efforts. I interpret GPG as drawing from two particular "client assets" to shape how Kutcher and Moore justified their interest in human trafficking and represented the issue to the public through Real Men. First, Kutcher and Moore showed that their decision to focus on the sex trafficking of women and girls was based on deep personal interest. As Kutcher declared in a 2011 press release, he developed this interest after watching *Children for Sale,* a 2004 Dateline documentary about sex trafficking in Cambodia that sparked his empathy and altruism for victims. As he explained, "I was watching six and seven year-old girls be raped for profit. . . . I don't want to live in a world where these things are happening and I'm not doing anything about them" (Kavner 2011). Kutcher's recounting of the documentary exaggerates what it shows (viewers did not see children raped), but this introduction to human trafficking, and to sex trafficking more specifically, informed his understanding of it going forward.

Second, GPG and DNA drew from Kutcher's celebrity persona as a goofy "bro," which he established through his acting in shows such as *Punk'd* and *Dude, Where's My Car?* Real Men's format, with its bizarre emphasis on men performing domestic tasks incorrectly, also used similarly goofy humor to capture the attention of a presumably reluctant audience (men who may purchase sex). Since many of the male celebrities featured in the campaign were already inter-textually known for playing uber-masculine roles, the "irony" of them performing domestic tasks in the ads made them funny and, in theory, would engage (male) viewers with the campaign. According to data obtained from the DNA Foundation (now Thorn Digital Defenders), "1.6 million people participated in Real Men; traffic to demiandashton.org increased 2,117% in the first week of the campaign; and online mentions of the terms "child sex slavery" and "real men don't buy girls" increased 1,120% and 2,738%, respectively, in the first month of the campaign."[9] While it is unclear how or to what extent participation in Real Men reduced sex trafficking, the campaign certainly ensured that viewers saw the celebrities while also teaching them that individuals and their behavior—and not states, institutions, or other structural conditions—are both the cause of and solution to sex trafficking.

Celebrities also promote the dominant narrative through their partnerships *with* organizations that support this story, such as when they signed the CATW's letter to Amnesty International (CATW et al, 2015). As noted elsewhere in this book, the CATW explicitly opposes all forms of sex work and views sex trafficking as the worst manifestation of human trafficking *and* patriarchal oppression writ large. Therefore, when Amnesty International announced that it would support decriminalizing prostitution in 2015, the CATW opposed this, and in their letter to Amnesty they offered the dominant narrative by conflating sex work (specifically prostitution) with sex trafficking, and by casting women and girls as the predominant victims.

The CATW letter opens by stating that Amnesty's support for decriminalizing prostitution "flies in the face of [its] historical reputation" for defending human rights, and women's rights more specifically, by noting that "human beings bought and sold in the sex trade . . . are mostly women." Like the Real Men campaign, the letter also emphasizes that men are the main cause of sex trafficking. Regarding solutions, the CATW's letter—and the celebrity signatories, by extension—claim that support for decriminalizing prostitution is akin to supporting sex trafficking and gender inequality. This is the case even as Amnesty clearly stated that their support for decriminalizing prostitution does *not* preclude their support for criminalizing sex trafficking. In the CATW's letter, this claim is especially apparent in the proposition that decriminalizing prostitution would "support a system of *gender apartheid,* in which one category of women may gain protection from sexual violence and sexual harassment, and be offered economic and educational opportunities; while another category of women, whose lives are shaped by absence of choice, are instead set apart for consumption by men and for the profit of their pimps, traffickers and brothel owners" (emphasis in original). In terms of solutions, then, the CATW continues the dominant narrative by proposing *other* forms of criminalization. Here, while the CATW agreed with Amnesty in their letter that "human beings bought and sold in the sex trade, who are mostly women, must . . . be respected and protected to the fullest extent," the letter ultimately supported carceral solutions, such as "laws that decriminalize solely those who sell sex and criminalize solely those who purchase it."

In the absence of direct statements, one cannot state for certain *why* each individual celebrity signed this letter and, in turn, endorsed the dominant narrative and its representation of human trafficking. However, it seems that the dominant narrative's enduring popularity may help us understand celebrity support for the CATW's letter to Amnesty. Although numerous critical trafficking scholars and activists have long criticized this narrative and supported decriminalizing prostitution, it remained in strong circulation in 2015, when Amnesty declared its support for decriminalizing prostitution. Therefore, it is not surprising that Amnesty's action provoked a strong backlash from *many* sectors of society, as indicated by the range of *non-celebrity* signatories to the CATW letter, and by the disagreements within Amnesty's membership (see, e.g. Lieberman 2018). Celebrities' support for the CATW's letter, then, may be read as yet another example of them taking popular and/or status quo positions in order to maintain their stature with their fans and signal their virtue.

Challenging the Dominant Narrative. Yet even as celebrities' support for Real Men and the CATW's letter confirms many of the trends in and criticisms of celebrity feminism, and celebrity anti-trafficking activism specifically, other celebrity activism challenges these tendencies. Namely, through their support for the ILO and CAST-LA, celebrities draw attention to more complex representations of human trafficking's forms, victims, causes, and solutions.

Unlike Real Men and the CATW, the ILO and CAST-LA do not believe that sex trafficking is the most common and egregious form of human trafficking. The ILO understands human trafficking as a form of forced labor, which it defines broadly as "work that is performed involuntarily and under the menace of any penalty." This may include situations where "persons are coerced to work through the use of violence or intimidation, or by more subtle means such as manipulated debt, retention of identity papers or threats of denunciation to immigration authorities" (ILO 2021c). CAST-LA also defines human trafficking as including many types of labor, although given its location in the United States, its specific definition aligns with the TVPA. Its website explains: "Human Trafficking is the exploitation of human beings through force, fraud or coercion for the purposes of commercial sex or forced labor." It specifies that all persons under the age of eighteen who engage in commercial sex are considered "victim[s] of human trafficking, regardless of whether force, fraud, or coercion was present" (CAST-LA 2021b).

The ILO and CAST-LA understand human trafficking's victims and causes broadly. Regarding victims, both organizations recognize that human trafficking impacts (cis and transgender) women and girls *and* boys and men throughout the United States and internationally. The ILO simply refers to "persons" or "any person" when discussing victims, and CAST-LA is similarly gender-neutral, writing that "Any survivor of human trafficking, whether it's labor or sex trafficking, a foreign national or a U.S. citizen, or an adult, youth, or a child can receive CAST's services at no charge" (CAST-LA 2021a). Regarding causes, while these organizations acknowledge the role of individual traffickers, this is not as simple as "men buying girls" (per Real Men). In fact, these organizations' websites state that broader structural factors, such as immigration systems that marginalize minority groups, foster vulnerability to human trafficking. Here the ILO indicates that "migrant workers and indigenous people are particularly vulnerable to forced labour" (ILO 2021b), and CAST-LA (2021b) explains that in "today's global economy, workers can be enslaved by threats of deportation, debt bondage or merely a lack of viable alternatives." With this broader understanding of the issue, both the ILO and CAST-LA reject carcerally-oriented solutions, with CAST-LA's CEO, Kay Buck (2017), calling on the Trump administration to "place more weight and thought on the diverse forms of justice that victims need as well as on prevention of this crime in the United States and abroad." The prevention CAST-LA supports includes public awareness, services for victims, and legislative reform.

I interpret celebrities' support for the ILO and CAST-LA—and the more complex human trafficking narratives they convey—as shaped by personal factors such as their reputations. Here celebrities may support organizations that challenge the dominant narrative to show that they are serious about learning about the issue. As regular tabloid fodder, for example, Kutcher and Moore had to establish their sincere engagement with the issue: after all, why should the public view the stars of *Punk'd* and *GI Jane* as credible anti-trafficking advocates? We could argue that it was to change this impression that they began to support CAST-LA, serving as honorary co-chairs at the organization's annual From Slavery to Freedom Gala, which was held on May 12, 2011 at the Skirball Center in Los Angeles.

Contextual factors such as a geographical location may also explain celebrities' support for the ILO's and CAST-LA's more complex narrative of human trafficking. Since the "End Slavery Now" launch and the CAST-LA annual gala were and are located in Los Angeles, the heart of the American entertainment/celebrity industry, it was easy, cynically speaking, for many celebrities to attend and get some publicity for their efforts. However, celebrities' engagement with the ILO and CAST-LA also indicates that they are aware of multiple issue positions, including debates about and challenges to the dominant human trafficking narrative. As I show in the following chapters, celebrities do acknowledge the growing body of evidence that trafficking involves multi-gendered victims in many industries, and that criminal justice solutions do little to address the issue's root causes.

Feminist Ideologies

Celebrities' anti-trafficking activism offers diverse feminist ideologies—sets of beliefs and values about gender and sex equality and justice and the goals and objectives for achieving this—and I interpret these ideologies from the solutions they promote to human trafficking. As noted in chapter 1, my reading here considers whether the celebrities offer solutions that respond to harms by alleviating individual suffering, or by making visible and addressing the actual sources of injustice—that is, the systems of power (colonialism, racism, imperialism, etc.) that *create* the conditions of injustice (Ackerly 2018; Alexander-Floyd 2021). Drawing from the celebrity performances enumerated in this chapter, I show in the following pages how celebrities' anti-trafficking activism conveys a wider range of overlapping (and even contradictory) feminist ideologies than scholars and critics might anticipate.

Carceral Feminism. When celebrities' anti-trafficking activism conveys the dominant narrative, they tend to emphasize criminal justice solutions to human trafficking, thereby communicating a carceral feminist ideology. Coined by Elizabeth Bernstein (2007a), the term "carceral feminism" refers broadly to the use of criminal justice measures to address gender inequality. As Lorna Bracewell (2016; 2021) documents, carceral feminism is often portrayed as primarily emerging from a confluence of feminist and conservative energies, where radical feminists were the most ardent supporters. Emerging in the 1970s through the pioneering works of Andrea Dworkin, Catherine MacKinnon, and Susan Brownmiller, among others, radical feminists focused on women's oppression through patriarchy, and they have long situated the sex industry as a site of women's subordination in society that reinforces misogyny and violence against women. However, as Bracewell carefully documents, many radical feminists in fact *opposed* the use of the carceral state to address sex work and any related exploitation it perpetuates, because they viewed it as an extension of the patriarchal rape culture they sought to dismantle. Instead, as Bracewell shows, liberal legal scholars and feminists contributed to the ascendance of carceral feminism, particularly in the context of feminist debates about pornography throughout the 1980s. "Wary of the sweeping regulations on speech that broad and deeply politicized conceptions of pornography's harms like 'silencing' and 'objectification' could be used to justify," these liberals opted to describe pornography's harms in terms of "violence," "crime," and "illegal conduct" (Bracewell 2016, 183).

As human trafficking—and sex trafficking specifically—captured public and political attention by the late 1990s, feminists of all stripes shifted their energies to address this issue. Liberal feminists, particularly those working through the National Organization for Women (NOW), argued in favor of increased criminal penalties for prostitutes' customers in an effort to stop sex trafficking through prostitution (Bernstein 2010). Radical feminists also took a carceral turn when it came to sex trafficking, arguing that patriarchy, manifested through men's demand for and access to commercial sex, is its root cause. But instead of promoting structural solutions that would address the conditions of injustice such as the abolition of patriarchy, they promoted carceral policies that would expand and employ the state's criminal justice systems alongside other governmental programs capable of surveillance (Hinton 2016; Kinney 2013). Today, prominent examples of carceral feminist policies include but are not limited to increasing arrests of men who purchase sexual services, waging public awareness campaigns, and implementing "john schools," where men arrested for prostitution solicitation pay a fine and attend a day of classes to learn about the consequences of their actions, in lieu of prosecution (Majic 2014c, 2015; Bernstein 2010; see also demandforum .net).

By supporting organizations that adhere to the dominant narrative and promote carceral policy solutions, celebrities promote carceral feminism, and this is especially apparent in their support for the CATW's letter to Amnesty International, which called for criminally punishing those who purchase and facilitate the sale of sexual services. They also promote this in the documentary *A Path Appears*, when Kristof (arguably a celebrity journalist) visits the Cook County, IL, sheriff's department to illustrate a "better" law enforcement approach to prostitution and sex trafficking. (Cook County is the Chicago metro region). Kristof and actor Malin Akerman praise the sheriff's office for pioneering a "national johns day," where the police specifically target clients through a false Craigslist ad. The documentary shows Kristof participating in the raid, where multiple men are arrested in a hotel room, and afterwards, Akerman declares that targeting johns is "inspiring," stating that "the more men we can involve [in the fight against prostitution], the better."

Variations of Liberal Feminism. Celebrities' anti-human trafficking efforts also emphasize that individuals and NGOs are a solution to human trafficking, and in so doing they variously reflect liberal feminist ideologies. Rooted in the pioneering philosophies of Elizabeth Cady Stanton and John Stuart Mill, among others, liberal feminism is arguably the most well-known and influential feminism in the West. Understanding gender inequality as rooted in unequal access to state, market, and other institutions, liberal feminists argue for reforming these institutions to enhance women's freedom and promote gender equality, as opposed to radically restructuring society. Liberal feminism's impact is most evident in changes to property rights, women's suffrage, and addressing equal pay discrimination, among other equality-oriented measures (Epure 2014).

While feminists have long debated the relative merits of liberal feminism, more recent debates have considered the presence and prominence of *neo*liberal feminism (Ferguson 2017). Broadly speaking, neoliberalism is a political rationality that casts citizens as individualized, active subjects, and it is generally associated with preferences for a marketized organization of the economy and society, and for a minimal state that is oriented towards the deregulation and privatization of services (Brown 2015). Some scholars argue that feminism, too, has been tarnished by a neoliberal devotion to market principles, privatization, and individualism as its mainstream has shifted away from a critique of political economy and the belief that the state could facilitate women's equality (Brown 2015; Fraser 2013). The result—a so-called neoliberal feminism—is apparent in works like Sheryl Sandberg's *Lean In* (2013), which calls on women to simply work harder for their liberation, with little regard for how structural factors such as racism and low wages can create barriers to their success (Sitkin 2017; Rottenberg 2018).

Celebrities' anti-trafficking activism illustrates elements of liberalism and neoliberalism, which I refer to as "variations of liberal feminism." These variations are particularly evident in their support for philanthropic/nonprofit organizations, or what Chris Rojek (2013) terms "celanthropy" (celebrity philanthropy)—that is, celebrity engagement in humanitarian and charitable causes that may have formerly been the job of the state (see also Littler 2015). Anti-human trafficking celanthropy occurs through celebrities' support for NGOs of all stripes—from the DNA Foundation to CAST-LA—and it promotes a combination of individual, market-based, and philanthropic/nonprofit solutions to human trafficking.

Celebrities' support for GEMS illustrates how celanthropic anti-trafficking activism promotes individual victims' empowerment. Founded in 1998 in New York City by Rachel Lloyd, GEMS stresses that all girls can take charge of their lives, even if they have been trafficked. In line with (neo)liberal feminist principles, GEMS provides a non-governmental means by which young women are supported and given "viable opportunities for positive change" (GEMS 2021). To this end, GEMS serves girls and young women at risk for commercial sexual exploitation and domestic trafficking "who were being ignored by traditional social service agencies." Victims are generally directed to GEMS through law enforcement and social service agencies. According to its website, the group's programming is "gender responsive, trauma informed, developmentally grounded, strengths based, social justice oriented, and culturally competent." Additionally, GEMS emphasizes "survivor leadership and transformational relationships" through services that are based on "survivors' ideas, input, and expertise." Celebrities such as Beyoncé have donated money to support their efforts.

However, through their celanthropy, celebrities may also promote varied feminist practices and ideologies, as indicated by their support for socially entrepreneurial initiatives to fight human trafficking. One of the most popular examples here is Shoerevolt.com, which was created by Ateba Crocker around 2011, after she read that shelters for victims of trafficking were closing because they lacked funding.[10] Although she was unemployed at the time, she wanted to help because the issue resonated with her as a survivor of childhood sexual abuse, and as a woman who had worked at an escort agency to support her first son, which, she claimed, eventually made her "feel dead inside" (cited in Fong 2010). As Crocker recounts, she eventually left the escort agency when "through her faith and family, [she] found the strength to return to school, to graduate college with a Master's Degree, and to publish her first book, *Rescued: A Testimony of God's Saving Power*" (Austin Smith 2013).

To help victims of sex trafficking, Crocker began selling some of her shoes online, and she realized that if "she had shoes to donate, surely others did as well! And Shoe Revolt was born" (Herd 2011). Shoe Revolt soon became a "social enterprise that would produce a steady revenue stream through the sale of new and used donated shoes" (Newport News 2010). The organization's net profits were dedicated to fighting human trafficking through donations to charitable partners (such as GEMS) and through educational scholarship and public advocacy for survivors. Crocker later created a partner program, Teen Revolt, which aimed to "educate, engage, and empower youth to take the lead in the fight against domestic sex trafficking through peer-to-peer education" (Austin Smith 2013). While both programs are no longer operating (it is unclear when they closed), Shoe Revolt received extensive celebrity support. At least fifteen celebrities, including *Sex and the City* shoe icon Sarah Jessica Parker, joined this effort by donating their shoes to the virtual shoe boutique and tweeting and providing interviews about their participation (Mitzeliotis 2011). These (used) shoes sold online for considerable sums—actor Kristen Stewart's black Keds sneakers sold for over $1,300 (Herd 2011).

On the one hand, we may read Crocker and Shoe Revolt, with their emphasis on individual initiative and marked-based solutions to social problems, as exemplars of neoliberal feminism. However, we may also read Crocker—a Black woman who once engaged in sex work and identifies with sex trafficking victims—as engaging in what scholars like Jessica Gordon Nembhard (2014a, 2014b) and Caroline Hossein (2018) refer to as Black community-based asset building, and/or solidarity economies, respectively. Developed in the face of harsh and exclusionary political and economic conditions, these socially entrepreneurial and mutual-aid-oriented efforts have operated separately from the state and business sectors in an effort to engage, empower, and economically uplift the community.

Celebrities' engagement with Shoe Revolt indicates how their advocacy may also promote a range of competing feminist interests and ideologies. By donating their shoes, the celebrities arguably acted in solidarity with Crocker to support and empower victims of sex trafficking—many of whom, as noted previously, are Black girls, who are often over-policed and under-served in anti-trafficking efforts. But celebrities' engagement with Shoe Revolt also amplified a neoliberal feminist ideology by promoting individually-oriented, marked-based action (namely, the donation and purchase of shoes) as a solution to human trafficking. Certainly, the revenue from these shoe sales helped to fund organizations that provide services for victims, but ultimately these individually-oriented, market-based actions do little to destabilize the broader structural conditions such as racial and economic inequality—a key focus of Black solidaristic social and economic efforts—that also create vulnerabilities to human trafficking and other exploitative labor practices.

Structurally Intersectional Feminism. Celebrities' promotion of carceral and liberal feminist approaches to human trafficking make sense because they convey often melodramatic, audience friendly messages ("Real Men Don't Buy Girls!") and feel-good individualism (buy shoes to help sex trafficking victims!). But what about more nuanced representations of and solutions to human trafficking and gender inequality? Socialist feminists, through the pioneering works of Heather Booth and colleagues (1972) and many others, have drawn attention to how structures of capitalism and patriarchy intersect to disadvantage women, while post-colonial and anti-racist feminists such as bell hooks (1999), Audre Lorde (1984), and Chandra Talpade Mohanty (1991), among others, were among the first to indicate how structures such as racism and colonialism also oppress women in the Global North and South (Epure 2014). These feminists offer a structurally intersectional feminist ideology that "centers the operation of systems and structures in society that result in the marginalization of individuals," particularly regarding their social needs and legal status (Jordan-Zachery 2017, 26).

Many feminist scholars and activists have applied this structural analysis to human trafficking, arguing that a confluence of factors including, but not limited to, state actions, unemployment, and/or displacement by environmental disasters have increased women's vulnerability to exploitative labor situations, and this vulnerability is particularly acute for women of color (Limoncelli 2009; Kempadoo, Sanghera, and Pattanaik 2012; Milivojevic and Pickering 2013; Sharma 2003). While these and other critical trafficking scholars and advocates do see a role for individuals and NGOs in the fight against human trafficking, they promote economic and other policy solutions that grant all workers (including sex workers) structural protections alongside autonomy and labor rights (see, e.g., Zheng 2010; Limoncelli 2009). In theory, this structurally intersectional approach to human trafficking should not appeal to celebrities who, as scholars and critics argue, tend towards neoliberal, post-feminist ideologies glorifying individualism and market-based solutions while also muting discussions of structural inequalities in furtherance of the celebrity brand (Gill 2017; McRobbie 2009).

However, a closer look at celebrities' anti-trafficking activism does, in some cases, offer and/or support more complex, structural responses to this issue (and, by extension, gender inequality), such as when actor Julia Ormond identified economic globalization as a cause of human trafficking. As she states in the documentary *Call + Response*, economic globalization has allowed businesses to move for cheap labor that lowers the price of goods for Western consumers. Human trafficking is "the dark underside of globalization," she says, "and we've been enjoying the benefits." Certainly, some data exists to support this point. In addition to offering (Western) consumers cheaper goods, globalizing labor markets have also increased corporate profits and exploitation. As the ILO indicates, millions of victims are exploited by private individuals or enterprises, and forced labor in the private economy generates an estimated US$150 billion in illegal profits per year (ILO 2022).

Other celebrities have also promoted structurally intersectional analyses of human trafficking through their support for organizations like the ILO and CAST-LA. Although one may argue that NGO support furthers a neoliberal feminist ideology (as I just did), it is also true that these organizations work to ameliorate how various structures create vulnerabilities to human trafficking. For example, the ILO emphasizes the state's role in promoting forced labor, and its Abolition of Forced Labour Convention No. 105 opposes the state's use of forced labor as punishment for the expression of political views or for the purposes of economic development (ILO 2021c). Similarly, CAST-LA states that structural factors in the Los Angeles area such as the "proximity to international borders, numerous ports and airports, significant immigrant populations and large economies that include industries that attract forced labor" create vulnerabilities to human trafficking, and they work to shape public policies and raise awareness to address these (CAST-LA 2021b). By supporting and promoting these NGOs, then, celebrities indicate that ending human trafficking and gender inequality involves more than simply ending men's demand for prostitution and/or donating to NGOs. In so doing, they convey a more complicated narrative of human trafficking that furthers a structurally intersectional feminist ideology.

TO WHAT EFFECT?

When we look at celebrities' anti-trafficking activism over time, across a range of settings, we see that they represent human trafficking in many ways, and different personal and contextual factors help us understand this varia-tion. But what does their anti-trafficking-activism-as-feminist-activism *mean* for how we understand celebrities' political power and responsibility, par-ticularly in broader movements to end oppression and marginalization? Is this just high-profile virtue signaling, or is it something else? To explore this question, the remainder of this chapter assesses celebrities' anti-trafficking work with regards to its visibility effects and the extent to which celebrities are held accountable for their actions.

Visibility

The anti-trafficking and feminist movements value celebrities for their power to capture attention and teach the public about various issues. But when they shine their light on an issue like human trafficking, celebrities illuminate some elements of it while also, following Jordan-Zachery (2017), relegating others to the shadows. Therefore, it is important to unpack what celebrities' fame may illuminate *and* obscure about human trafficking so we better understand their capacity to promote feminist interests such as gender and racial justice. Two particular examples illustrate these possibilities: celebri-ties' tendency to refer to human trafficking as "slavery" and/or "modern-day slavery," and the ways in which their efforts may center the celebrity over other stakeholders and impacted communities.

Celebrities frequently use the term "slavery" to describe human trafficking. To name just some examples from the most active celebrities, Julia Ormond (2008b) defines human trafficking as "the process of moving a person into slavery." As she told the audience at the USC Price School of Social Policy, she believed slavery was something that was "over." "I used to believe that I was in this very privileged position, that I was living in a country that respected human rights," she said, "and that I was free" (Ormond 2017b). However, when she learned that slavery still existed, she was motivated to fight it because "it threatens the freedom of individuals, the legitimacy of free markets and free governance worldwide" (ASSET 2018). Similarly, Mira Sorvino (2011b) described human trafficking as "the latest incarnation of slavery ... a relatively new concept," and in later speeches, she explained how her discovery of this "new" form of slavery motivated her to get involved with the issue. As she told an audience at Sonoma State University (Sorvino 2016), "I had naively thought that slavery was a thing of the past, that Lincoln freed the slaves." But, she realized, "I was very, very wrong. And I think all of us have a huge wake-up call that slavery is very much a thing of the present, not the past."

Of course, celebrities are not the only activists who refer to human trafficking as slavery; this has long been part of the anti-trafficking movement's repertoire. As Allison Page (2017, 51) writes, this is a powerful strategy for "creating shock value (that is, the shock a reader might feel that slavery is not, in fact, abolished)." In fact, as Kamala Kempadoo (2015) documents, human trafficking's conflation with slavery emerged in the late 1990s from the work of Kevin Bales, who published the book *Disposable People: New Slavery in the Global Economy* (1999, 2004). Bales founded the US organization Free the Slaves (an offspring of the group British Anti-Slavery International, which was established in 1839 to end the enslavement of Africans). Since then, he has created the Walk Free Foundation, which developed the "Global Slavery Index," an internationally recognized system that ranks nations according to their estimated prevalence of slavery. Through these efforts, Bales has disseminated the rhetoric of "modern day slavery" to describe human trafficking through a global network of religious groups, academics, business people, and journalists.

Given the prevalence of the term "slavery," it is unsurprising that celebrities have also adopted it, but since they may convey this term to very large audiences, we must critically scrutinize it for a number of reasons. First, celebrities (like many others in the anti-trafficking movement) tend to offer a "reductive understanding of slavery" (Heynen and van der Meulen 2021, 14). By claiming that human-trafficking-as-slavery is a "modern" phenomenon, celebrities present the chattel slavery of Africans and African Americans as a foil for the "real" slavery (human trafficking) that exists today on an allegedly larger scale (Page 2017). In so doing, celebrities position themselves leaders of a moral crusade against an "unconscionable evil"—namely, a crusade that proudly claims to be following in the footsteps of the British and American nineteenth-century evangelical-inspired movements to abolish the enslavement and trade of Africans (Kempadoo 2015, 15).

However, according to historians such as Dale Tomich (2018, 2004), this conception of slavery as something that was abolished—and then re-emerged later, in a new and "modern" form—furthers the assumption that "slavery" is an anachronistic, time-bound, nation-specific phenomenon that disappeared with the emergence of liberal, capitalist modernity. Instead, as Tomich writes, slavery is but one of many ongoing forms of economic and exploitation and social domination that were and are integral to the development and reformation of the capitalist world economy. For example, he documents how after the vigorous liberal and anti-slavery movements transformed the Atlantic world and pushed Britain to abolish slavery, a "second slavery" developed in the nineteenth century to meet the growing world demand for cotton, coffee, and sugar. This second slavery accounts for "the extraordinary expansion of new frontiers of slave commodity production—cotton in the US South, sugar in Cuba, and coffee in Brazil—during the nineteenth century and their role in the economic and political transformations of the nineteenth-century world-economy" (Tomich 2018, 479).

Second, in addition to ignoring the long history of slavery in the world economy, celebrities' deployment of the terms "slavery" and "modern-day slavery" mis-represents how human trafficking typically impacts people today. For one, contemporary human trafficking is not state-sanctioned in the same way as chattel slavery was in the United States, and thus it is not visible in the same way it was earlier in the nation's history (Merry 2016; Kempadoo 2015). Rather, as Kempadoo and others write, many incidents of so-called "modern-day slavery" may occur in legal work situations, and/or look more like debt bondage or forced migration, as they do not necessarily involve the physical restraints or violence that held African slaves in bondage (O'Connell-Davidson 2006; Chuang 2010; Kempadoo 2015). Furthermore, by implying that one iteration of slavery (chattel slavery) is "over," celebrities also ignore what Saidiya Hartman (2007) terms the "afterlife" of slavery. This term refers to the fact that the Emancipation Proclamation barely reconfigured life for ex-slaves into something that resembled freedom, to the extent that the persistence of slavery remains a salient issue that implicates the biopolitics of everyday life in the contemporary United States (see also Page 2017). By sidestepping how the legacy of slavery continues to pervade so many *other* aspects of daily life for many Black Americans, including those who are not victims of human trafficking, celebrities "provide gravity and moral import while simultaneously expunging the afterlife of slavery, a maneuver that is prevalent within the larger anti-trafficking movement" (Page 2017, 54).

In addition to often ignoring and obscuring the historical and contemporary realities of slavery and human trafficking, celebrities tend to center their own perspectives on these issues over those of the impacted communities. Here, the CATW's letter to Amnesty International is instructive: while the letter listed the celebrity signatories, it ignored many sex workers' experiences and perspectives. Like any other community, sex workers hold diverse views about the best legal and policy approaches to sex work and human trafficking, and many have long expressed support for decriminalizing prostitution, arguing that this would help them reduce violence and other exploitation in their work (Majic 2014a, 2014b; Lutnick and Cohan 2009; Chateauvert 2013). Consequently, when Amnesty announced its support for decriminalizing all sex work, many sex workers expressed their support for this position (Albright and D'Adamo 2017). The celebrities who signed the CATW's letter to Amnesty may not have been aware of this, or they may not have agreed with the sex workers who supported Amnesty's view. But whatever their reasons may have been, the CATW's letter indicated how celebrities, as self-appointed representatives, may overshadow and sideline the voices of those for whom they claim to speak.

The actor Lena Dunham, who signed the CATW's letter and was one of the only celebrities to publicly explain why she did this, offers an illustrative case here. As she stated in a series of tweets soon after the letter was published, she signed it "after much careful research and consideration" because she did "not believe [Amnesty's] proposal protects the exploited or properly punishes the exploiters" (Schwiegershausen 2015). This "careful research" seemed to involve reading Nicholas Kristof's (2015) column (which she tweeted), where he stated the following about Amnesty's proposal: "Nice theory, but a failed one. It has been tried repeatedly and it invariably benefited johns while exacerbating abuse of women and girls: A parallel underground market emerges for underage girls." Amnesty did in fact call for punishments for those exploiting underage girls, and Kristof provided no evidence to support his claims, while also ignoring research showing that sex workers' health and safety has in fact improved in countries that decriminalize prostitution (see, e.g., Sweetman 2017). Dunham ignored all of this, holding instead that her celebrity status trumps both peer-reviewed research *and* sex workers' support for Amnesty's proposal. As she added in a later tweet, "I'm not a sex worker or a trafficking survivor. But I'm blessed to have a platform that many close to this issue do not." In so doing, she shows how, as Hobson (2017, 1001) writes about the celebrities who signed the CATW's letter, "The privileges of beauty, fame, and finance that accompany such celebrities still impose restrictions on whose voices and whose feminisms matter. When celebrity feminists . . . frame the commercial sex trade through the lens of victimhood, they effectively silence the voices of actual sex workers who seek to decriminalize their profession."

Accountability, Instability, and Contestation

At first glance, celebrities' anti-trafficking advocacy illuminates their lack of accountability in their roles as unelected political representatives. Because they often do this work in high-profile, media-friendly settings such as documentaries and Hollywood fundraisers that are largely inaccessible to the public, human trafficking victims—the constituency that celebrities claim to represent—have few opportunities to shape, engage with, and respond to their performances. As a result, celebrity anti-trafficking activism, like other celebrity political engagement, appears to reflect and perpetuate unequal power relations. But while celebrities may seem all-powerful and unaccountable, their audiences may in fact contest and destabilize their actions and issue positions. As previously mentioned, social media has increased celebrities' ubiquity, but it has also made it possible for fans and other observers to question and call them out. Journalists and other members of the media often investigate, review, and challenge celebrities' claims. As well, as I show in later chapters, celebrities' beneficiary audiences—the nonprofits, NGOs, and other organizations that rely on celebrities to draw attention to and raise funds for their work—may offer counter-narratives and constrain the celebrities, in a sense, by educating them about issues and ensuring that their advocacy aligns with the organizational mission. Furthermore, organizations may also reject celebrities' actions and issue positions: even though Lena Dunham and other high-profile celebrities rejected Amnesty's position on decriminalizing sex work, Amnesty supported this policy anyway, officially adopting it on May 26, 2016.

At the same time, fans, journalists, and beneficiary audiences are also limited sources of accountability for celebrities. The case of the Somaly Mam Foundation is particularly instructive here. Because the organization was receiving so much media attention and raising so much money, Simon Marks, a *Newsweek* journalist, investigated Mam and her organization. He found that Mam had fabricated much of her personal story of sex trafficking, recounted in her memoir *The Road of Lost Innocence* (Mam and Marshall 2008), and she coached the girls at AFESIP to lie about their backgrounds as well (Marks 2014). In fact, Long Pross, the girl who Kristof wrote about as a trafficking victim in the *New York Times,* had her eye disfigured from a tumor removal surgery and not by the actions of a brutal pimp (Marks 2014). In response, the Somaly Mam Foundation's board hired the law firm Goodwin and Proctor to conduct its own investigation of Mam and AFESIP, and four months later Mam resigned from her position and the foundation shut down. Although *Marie Claire* magazine found witnesses who supported Mam's story and challenged Marks's account in *Newsweek,* evidence continued to emerge that Mam had largely fabricated her story (Hoefinger 2016).

The celebrities who drew money and other resources to AFESIP were not held accountable for supporting an organization with demonstrably questionable bona fides. Nicholas Kristof only offered a tepid apology for promoting Mam, despite calls from the *New York Times* Public Editor that Kristof "owes it to his readers to explain, to the best of his ability and at length, what happened and why" (Sullivan 2014). On his blog (and *not* in his main column in the *Times*), he barely confirmed or denied the veracity of Mam's story and his reporting failures as a journalist (Kristof 2014b). Instead, he wrote that "I thought [Mam] was a hero and, in fairness, so did lots of others," and then he proceeded to list the many other journalistic outlets that covered her story before he did this. He minimized his past engagement with and support for Mam, writing, "One irony: This post is longer than the column I wrote on Somaly, and I've now written more about her for the *Times* post-scandal than pre-scandal." This claim should strike many readers as odd, given that he featured Mam in *Half the Sky* and even penned the foreword to *The Road to Lost Innocence.* He then reminds readers to "not lose sight of the larger issue"—human trafficking—and he ultimately concludes that "I now wish I had never written about her." Yet, ultimately, Kristof's significant failure as a journalist was of little consequence: indicating his white male privilege, he continued to hold a prominent role on the *Times*'s opinion page until 2021, when he left to run for Governor of Oregon.

Certainly Mam, and not celebrities like Kristof, may be regarded as being at fault here. After all, Mam misled journalists and the public about her story and her organization, while the celebrities were merely there to support her. However, as a woman from the Global South, Mam was in a less powerful position to begin with, and so while her story merited scrutiny, the onus for vetting it was arguably on powerful journalists like Kristof and the celebrities who promoted her work. Focusing on Mam ultimately detracts from the celebrities' role in amplifying questionable causes without accountability for their actions. Prominent anti-trafficking celebrities who supported Mam, like Ashley Judd and Meg Ryan, never retracted their support for her, and other celebrities even continued promoting her. After she was forced to step down from her foundation, she ultimately re-branded as "The New Somaly Mam Fund," which maintains the support of celebrities such as Susan Sarandon and worked through the organization "Together 1 Heart" to fight sex trafficking in Cambodia.[11]

Celebrities' lack of accountability is even more pronounced when the organizations they support are their own, and here the DNA Foundation and Real Men are especially instructive. After its release, scholars, journalists and activists alike subjected Real Men to a barrage of condemnation for, among other things, treating the serious issue of sex trafficking in a way that "reek[s] of frat boy humor" (Cizmar, Conklin, and Hinman 2011), and for promoting a "tired and harmful trope" of innocent girls and predatory men (Auguston 2014). Furthermore, Kutcher circulated misinformation by claiming that the average age of entry into prostitution is thirteen years of age. (This statistic is routinely reported by government officials and the news media). However, this is a mathematical impossibility that appears to have originated as a misrepresentation of "the average age of first *noncommercial* sexual contact (which could include kissing, petting, etc.) that was reported by *underage* girls in one study" (McNeill 2014). When the *Village Voice* confronted Kutcher about his inaccurate statistics (Cizmar, Conklin, and Hinman 2011), Kutcher responded angrily that they were only questioning him because their parent company, Village Voice Media, owned Backpage. com. This site advertised adult sexual services and had long been accused of promoting the commercial sexual exploitation of children.[12] Although Kutcher never explicitly took responsibility for these (mis)representations of human trafficking, he did eventually shift his tactics and narrative after his divorce from Moore, as I discuss in chapter 4. The Real Men videos are no longer widespread, and he has since changed his foundation's focus to preventing children's sexual exploitation online.

CONCLUSION

This chapter provided a broad overview of celebrities anti-trafficking activism from 2000–2016 to illustrate the possibilities and limits of celebrity feminism. At first glance, celebrity anti-trafficking activism confirms what many scholars and activists suspect about celebrity feminism writ large: it is dominated by white women celebrities, and many of their actions promote the dramatic, attention-grabbing dominant narrative of human trafficking. Yet when we examine this activism over time, across a range of cases, a more complicated picture emerges. Celebrities in fact promote a range of issue representations and feminist ideologies, and various personal and contextual factors help us account for this variation. As a result, we cannot simply dismiss celebrity anti-trafficking activism as a case of high-profile virtue signaling. While it is certainly true that many celebrities may appear just once at an anti-trafficking fundraiser, for example, and get some easy media coverage as a result, a number of celebrities also expend significant fame, financial, and other capital for their anti-trafficking endeavors.

The following chapters offer comparative case studies of the most active celebrities to illustrate the complex dynamics of their celebrity feminism in more depth. Specifically, I focus here on Ashley Judd, Jada Pinkett Smith, Ashton Kutcher, Ricky Martin, Mira Sorvino, and Julia Ormond.[13] These individual comparisons illuminate celebrities' power as feminist political representatives and the possibilities and limits of their advocacy more broadly. While we may think of celebrities as a collective entity, they are in fact individual agents whose particular brand of fame serves as a personal source of power by allowing them to draw significant attention to an issue and shape how the public understands it (Partzsch 2017). Yet these individual cases also show that while celebrity feminists may appear powerful, their performances are not unchecked and absolute; as such, they offer insights about how we may challenge and contest celebrity power going forward.

THREE

White Saviors and Activist Mothers

ASHLEY JUDD, JADA PINKETT SMITH, AND THE SEX TRAFFICKING OF WOMEN AND GIRLS

IF ACCOLADES AND AWARDS SIGNAL excellence in activism, and feminist activism in particular, then 2016 was a good year for Ashley Judd and Jada Pinkett Smith.[1] Citing her global advocacy for survivors of human trafficking, both the United Nations Population Fund, which focuses on sexual and reproductive health, and the Polaris Project, which leads "a data-driven social justice movement to fight sex and labor trafficking" (Polaris 2021a), named Judd an Ambassador for their organizations. And in New York, Girls Education and Mentoring Services (GEMS), a nationally recognized nonprofit committed to "empowering commercially sexually exploited and domestically trafficked girls and young women" (GEMS 2021), bestowed upon Pinkett Smith its first "Revolutionary Award" for her commitment to girls' empowerment and anti-trafficking advocacy.

Given their lack of scholarly, policy, or other expertise, what have Judd and Pinkett Smith done to earn this recognition? The answer rests, in part, on their celebrity: these women are notable among their peers for expending significant fame capital to draw attention to human trafficking, which has long been framed as a feminist issue. Yet celebrity alone does not explain their ascendance in this activist space. This chapter argues broadly that to "self-appoint" (Montanaro 2012) as representatives who speak about human trafficking and for its impacted populations, Judd and Pinkett Smith each developed and demonstrated "deeper roots" (Saward 2006) that connected them to the issue, namely, a personal, familial connection.

To understand why and how individual celebrities may draw from their personal experiences to this end, and to what effect, this chapter comparatively analyzes Judd's and Pinkett Smith's anti-trafficking activism as political performances, focusing on settings where they are highly visible and play a central role. For Judd, this includes her 2008 speech at the United Nations, her memoir *All That Is Bitter and Sweet* (2011), her work with Population Services International (PSI), and her appearance with *New York Times* journalist Nicholas Kristof in the documentary *A Path Appears* (Chermayeff 2015). For Pinkett Smith, I consider her music video *Nada Se Compara* (Nothing Compares), her Congressional testimony, her performance in the CNN documentary *Children For Sale* (Coorlim 2014), and her work with and support for NGOs, namely her web-based group Don't Sell Bodies (DSB).

My analysis of these performances reveals how celebrities' personal stories and the temporal and organizational contexts of their activism shape how they represent issues and their impacted populations to broader audiences. Specifically, Judd bases her interest in human trafficking on her experience with familial abuse, whereas Pinkett Smith links hers to familial love. These personal connections, combined with the time periods in which they became active and the organizations with which they affiliated, shaped how they represent the issue to the broader public. I show that in their roles as, respectively, a "white savior" (Judd) and an "activist mother" (Pinkett Smith), both women consolidate and challenge the dominant human trafficking narrative about the sex trafficking of women and girls, thereby circulating a range of feminist ideologies that both challenge and reinforce race and gender hierarchies. The effects of their activism, then, are mixed: while they draw attention to important issues and challenge various Hollywood norms and stereotypes, their celebrity status and power sustains their distance from the issue and its impacted communities, leaving them only minimally accountable for their actions.

PERFORMERS AND SETTINGS

As two of the most active anti-trafficking celebrities from the most active sub-category (women actors), Ashley Judd and Jada Pinkett Smith derive their power from their significant stocks of fame capital, which has afforded them opportunities to engage in a range of high profile anti-trafficking activities. Yet these women differ in key ways: in addition to race (Judd is white, while Pinkett Smith is Black and the only woman of color among the most active celebrities), their familial backgrounds differ, and these differences have motivated and are reflected in their anti-trafficking work over time.

Ashley Judd

Ashley Judd was born in 1968 in Los Angeles. She had an itinerant upbringing, moving between family members' homes in California, Kentucky, and Florida as her parents divorced and her sister, Naomi Judd, and her mother, the late Wynonna Judd, pursued a country music career, becoming superstars when Ashley was a teenager. In 1990, she left the University of Kentucky and moved to Los Angeles, where she started auditioning and working immediately. Her first film, *Ruby in Paradise,* won a Sundance Award in 1993, and she was later nominated for two Golden Globes and two Primetime Emmy Awards. In 2001 she married Dario Franchitti, a racecar driver (they divorced in 2013). She does not have children.

Judd first learned about human trafficking, and sex trafficking more specifically, in the early 2000s, through her work with Population Services International (PSI), a US-based charitable NGO that works predominantly in the Global South with governments, the private sector, and community leaders to address issues including family planning, gender-based violence, and access to clean water. Taking a "business approach to saving lives," (PSI 2022b) PSI provides information, products, and services related to contraception access, HIV prevention, and gender-based violence. As part of their work, PSI enlists celebrity "ambassadors" who "use their stage to give voices to the many people in need, and help us reach a wider audience" (PSI 2022a). In 2002, PSI asked Judd to be an ambassador, and the timing was fortuitous for her. As she documents in her memoir (Judd and Vollers 2011; see figure 6), which describes her "odyssey" from lost child to fiercely dedicated advocate, she had always felt passionate about many social justice causes and was torn between pursuing an acting career and saving the world.

When she received a letter from PSI asking her to be a Youth AIDS Ambassador, her career was at "a frenzied peak": she had starred in six movies in the past four years, and she was currently filming *Twisted,* a film noir where she played "a depressed homicide detective with a nasty temper" (Judd and Vollers 2011, 42). The shoot was grueling, and she was plagued by insomnia and anxiety (afterwards, she spent time in the hospital), and so she did not believe that she had any energy to advocate for a cause. But from working in the entertainment industry, she was well aware of the scourge of HIV/AIDS, and she wanted to do something to help the impacted populations. "Could this be what I was looking for, the opportunity to connect with my latent passion? A chance to bring a voice to the voiceless, to address injustices

FIGURE 6. Cover of *All that Is Bitter and Sweet* (2011). Courtesy of Penguin Random House LLC.

I had witnessed throughout my childhood?" (58) she asked in her memoir, where she also discussed her experience with neglect and sexual abuse as a young person.

She accepted PSI's invitation, and while this was no doubt driven by her commitment to activism on behalf of the less fortunate, the opportunity was well-timed. Despite having a star-studded cast and an experienced director, *Twisted* received almost universally negative reviews (an average critic score of 2.9/10 on the website *Rotten Tomatoes* (n.d.) rendered it one of their lowest rated movies). Some even went further to argue that *Twisted* marked the end of Judd's career doing the highly-paid, high-concept thrillers she had starred in since the 1990s (*Bomb Report* 2004). Working with PSI offered Judd a break from acting and, as I describe below, it set her on a course of advocacy work. This took her first to the Global South and then to various places in the United States, where she met the individuals who worked in the sex industry for whom she wanted to advocate.

Jada Pinkett Smith

Jada Pinkett Smith was born in 1971 in Baltimore, and she lacked Judd's celebrity pedigree: her mother was a nurse and her father worked in construction. Her parents divorced shortly after she was born, and her mother and grandmother raised her. After a year at the University of North Carolina School for the Arts, she began acting in 1990, starring in an episode of *True Colors*. She ascended to fame through her performances in many TV series and big budget films such as *The Matrix Reloaded* (2003), *The Matrix Revolutions* (2003), and *Girls Trip* (2017). In 1997 she married actor Will Smith, and she has three children: a stepson, Trey, from Smith's previous marriage, and Jaden and Willow, who were born in 1998 and 2000, respectively, and are well-known actor-musicians and fashion icons.

Pinkett Smith began to raise awareness about human trafficking later, in 2012, and unlike Judd, her acting career was progressing well when she began this work. But like Judd, she had no scholarly or other expertise about human trafficking, and she had mainly engaged in philanthropic work through the Will and Jada Smith Family Foundation (WJSFF). Created in 1996, this foundation is focused on "Investing in innovative solutions that make the world better" (WJSFF 2021a), namely by contributing to work in arts and education, empowerment, health and wellness, and sustainability (WJSFF 2021b). At the time of writing in 2021, their current projects were geared towards increasing gender and racial/ethnic diversity in film and television production (WJSFF 2021b), and their previous projects seem to cover a range of issues. For example, the *Philanthropy News Digest* (2006) reported that the WJSFF gave $1 million to Pinkett Smith's alma mater, the Baltimore School of the Arts (which she attended with the late Tupac Shakur), to fund part of their $30 million expansion program. Past WJSFF grantees also include the University of California-Los Angeles, Children's Hospital of Los Angeles, and the American Red Cross, among others.

Given the focus of her previous philanthropic ventures, Pinkett Smith's 2012 entrance into the anti-human trafficking movement seemed somewhat out of the blue, and so, like Judd, she used her personal, familial experiences to explain and justify her motivation. As media accounts describe it, when Pinkett Smith's daughter, Willow, was eleven years old, she told her mother that she had learned in school about young girls sold for sex in the United States and wanted to do something about it. As Pinkett Smith told ABC News,

> I was actually really quite ashamed that I didn't know about this particular situation in our country, because when you think about human trafficking, you think about it 'over there.' Wherever 'there' is. . . . When you talk about modern-day slavery, you don't see chains. It's all about the mind. . . . So, it's a very layered, complex issue that's going to take some time for us to figure out how to pull apart. . . . Right now, we just have to get aware (Allin 2012).

To help the public and political leaders "get aware," Pinkett Smith leveraged her fame capital to learn and raise awareness about human trafficking, and she was soon the face of various PSAs and formed the web-based group Don't Sell Bodies, among other activities.

NARRATIVES OF HUMAN TRAFFICKING

Given their stocks of fame capital, Judd and Pinkett Smith were well positioned to engage in anti-trafficking activism, and they have offered, per Edwards (2012), charismatic political performances that tended to center themselves and their experiences in their efforts to promote social change. In the following pages I illustrate how their performances' representations of human trafficking (and, as I show later, the solutions they promote for it) variously reflect their personal connections to the issue and the temporal and organizational contexts in which they worked.

Ashley Judd: Constituting the Dominant Narrative

In 2008, as I recounted in chapter 1, the United Nations invited Judd to address the General Assembly about the issue of human trafficking. Speaking passionately to the audience, she described what she had witnessed in her travels with PSI to "brothels in Kenya, Madagascar, El Salvador, Guatemala,

Cambodia, and the Democratic Republic of Congo." She declared that, in each place,

> I have made one keening vow: I will never forget you, and I will tell your stories. I will tell your stories. I will tell your stories. To quote the effervescent light that is Marianne Williamson, 'My greatest fear is not that we are inadequate, but that we are powerful beyond measure.' Ms Williamson adds, 'We are, all of us, not just some of us, children of God, and our playing small does not serve the world.' So I am here at the United Nations because when it comes to human dignity and rights, I refuse to play small and I am going to tell you those stories. How dare I not (Judd 2008).[2]

In stating this, Judd appointed herself as a representative for trafficking victims: she would speak *for* them and use her celebrity capital to illuminate their stories; however, she did not initially believe that she was qualified to do this. Therefore, she drew on her personal, familial experience to demonstrate her connection with and commitment to them, particularly those she believed were sex trafficking victims.

In the foreword to her memoir, *New York Times* columnist Nicholas Kristof (2011, xvi) affirmed Judd's personal connection to this advocacy, writing that when he opened her memoir, he was surprised to find the "abuse and neglect described as closer to home, swirling around Ashley herself as a young girl." He goes on to describe how her experiences with sexual abuse and childhood neglect shaped her commitment to issues like sex trafficking because they "armed her with unusual empathy" so that her "antennae were always out for other little Ashleys" (xvi). As Judd confirms later in her memoir, she always had "an insane sensitivity to sexual exploitation of any kind" (Judd and Vollers 2011, 279), which she attributed to her personal experience with sexual abuse. To Judd, this experience placed her on a continuum with sex trafficking victims. Here, she writes, "my own background modestly qualified me for this mission [to work with PSI and raise awareness about sex trafficking]—not just the fame that accompanied my acting career, but more meaningfully, my very own righteous anger, my very own journey as an abused and neglected girl" (68). As the following pages indicate, in her anti-trafficking work in the United States and internationally, Judd would draw on her personal experiences with and anger about sexual abuse (particularly that perpetuated by men and families), her organizational affiliations, and the information available at the time to mainly represent human trafficking as the *sex* trafficking of women and girls.

As noted in previous chapters, knowledge about the extent and scope of human trafficking remains fragmented at best, and scholarly research and journalistic reporting about this issue has long been riddled with challenges and inconsistencies, often emphasizing that the majority of victims are women and girls coerced into the sex industry. In the early 2000s, when Judd began to work with PSI, Congress had recently passed the TVPA and the Bush administration was directing the bulk of research funding to scholars and organizations who conflated sex work with sex trafficking, and all other human trafficking with sex trafficking, while the media was also reporting extensively about sex trafficking (Weitzer 2007). In this context, and in light of her personal experiences, since she partnered with PSI in 2003, Judd has largely represented human trafficking's forms, victims, causes, and solutions in ways that consolidate and promote this dominant sex trafficking narrative.

Working predominantly within a communicative structure that Lili Chouliaraki (2012, 1) terms a "theater of pity" that circulates images and stories of suffering to propose dispositions of emotion and action to largely Western audiences, Judd tends to describe the women and girls she meets in the sex industry through what Claudia Cojocaru (2015) calls the trope of the girl (or woman) who is duped and naïvely tricked and trafficked into sex work. This trope is particularly apparent in Judd's descriptions of the women and girls she encountered in the Global South. For example, in Cambodia, she was struck by the brothels, describing what she saw there as sex trafficking (i.e., sex work under conditions of force, fraud, and coercion). "Many women, devoid of alternatives, succumbed to prostituted sex work to survive or were lured to the city in search of factory jobs, only to be tricked, forced, coerced, and outright kidnapped into brothels, from which there was usually no escape" (Judd and Vollers 2011, 75). She proceeds to describe them as "trapped in prostitution" (93), and engaged in "exploited sex" (93) or "economically forced prostitution" (94). When she does acknowledge their agency, she still emphasizes their constraints. Writing about her trip to Kenya with PSI, she states that although the women she met at a brothel "were admittedly illiterate . . . they were no fools, I will say that, and their exploitation was by their own desperate decision making in the absence of other choices, unlike many of the women I met in Thailand and Cambodia who had been coerced and kidnapped" (125). In the rare instances when she acknowledges that men and boys may also be victims of trafficking, she does so in the same terms. For example, when she addressed the United Nations, she shared the story of a "male sex slave" who recounted a story of being raped as a dog mauled his face.

Regarding human trafficking's causes, scholars have long indicated that structural factors such as unemployment and migration for labor, among others, increase vulnerability to exploitative labor situations (Milivojevic and Pickering 2013); however, the dominant human trafficking narrative has instead emphasized the role of "bad" men and cultures. Judd is aware of more structural causes, which she mentions in her appearance in the 2008 documentary *Call + Response* (Dillon 2008). In one of her appearances here, Judd discusses how human trafficking occurs in the garment industry, concluding "I don't want to wear someone's despair" in order to alert viewers to the fact that the production of cheap clothing often involves trafficked labor. In her memoir, she is also critical of the United States government, writing that the "Americans had destroyed Cambodia with bombs, then abandoned the country to murderers," which left women especially vulnerable to coercive labor. The country was "colonized by the French, bombed by the Americans, and savaged by a dictator named Pol Pot and his psychotic Khmer Rouge, until finally returning to self-rule as a constitutional monarchy in 1993." As a result, "all lives in Cambodia have been touched by genocide." She notes that in addition to the at least 1.7 million people slaughtered, the country's infrastructure and social fabric were destroyed. The "years of war, genocide, and mass migration had turned Cambodia into one of the world's poorest countries and a nation of orphans and widows" (Judd and Vollers 2011, 72–75).

Although she may acknowledge structural factors, Judd predominantly emphasizes that men and patriarchal cultural-familial practices cause human trafficking. A typical example of this occurred in *Call + Response* (Dillon 2008), where Judd describes men's gang rape of women and girls in the brothels in India as a "distinctly Indian form of torture." And in her memoir, she discusses how in Cambodia, the patriarchal Khmer culture left women vulnerable to sexual exploitation. She further emphasizes this link between men, patriarchal cultures, and sexual exploitation when she recalls her PSI-sponsored visit to the Democratic Republic of Congo. Describing its capital, Goma, as a "shithole" (Judd and Vollers 2011, 345), she emphasizes that women here are in fact agentic and resourceful, while the men are lazy and wasteful, noting that women "save and invest every pittance, [while] men waste money at shocking rates" (346). She goes further to recount an interaction with a man who she meets and chastises for purchasing a mobile phone instead of a mosquito net for his family. When he dismissed her comments, she assumed that this meant that he was abusive, violent, and prone to sexually exploiting women, writing that after this interaction she walked to her car wondering "not if but how many women and girls that man raped" (347).

As her anti-trafficking work progressed, Judd began to publicly acknowledge human trafficking in the United States around 2015, when Nicholas Kristof invited her to participate in *A Path Appears* (Chermayeff 2015). Prior to this, as many have written (see, e.g. Fisher 2016; Mathers 2012), Kristof has long peddled the dominant narrative of human trafficking through his column in the *New York Times* and in documentaries such as *Half the Sky* (Chermayeff 2012), where the women and girls who engage in the sex industry are not active characters in the narrative but repeatedly referred to as individuals who are "bought and sold." *A Path Appears* continues this narrative, as noted in chapter 2. Sex trafficking in the United States is among the gender-based oppressions Kristof covers in the documentary, and he covers it with Judd.

In line with her international work, Judd draws on her personal experiences and organizational affiliations (in this case, Kristof's documentary production team) to promote the dominant narrative about human trafficking in the United States. In Judd's portion of *A Path Appears,* she and Kristof visit Nashville, Tennessee, and talk with women engaged in street-based sex work. As they drive around the city, Judd likens what she sees in Nashville to sex *trafficking,* noting that after years of international advocacy, "there is a reluctance to admit we have our own problem [in the United States]." To better understand this problem and how to address it, Judd and Kristof visit Magdalene House, which is run by Becca Stevens, a white woman who is also an Episcopal priest. Magdalene House provides housing and support to former sex workers (it refers to them as survivors) through what Stevens calls a "Benedictine model of hospitality." While there, Judd laughs and chats amiably with the women as they all serve themselves lunch from dishes laid out in the kitchen.

Judd is also aware of her position as a wealthy white celebrity, and so to relate to the women at Magdalene House, who (at least as shown in the film) are predominantly Black, she draws on her personal experience to connect with the women and amplify their stories. Sitting down with them, she introduces herself and describes the abuse she experienced growing up, which many of the women gathered there had also experienced, noting later that she is "lucky she did not end up in the same situation" as they did (that is, engaged in sex work). She uses her personal experience to emphasize that women and girls who trade sex are victims of sex trafficking, which is predominantly caused by bad men

FIGURE 7. Jada Pinkett Smith, right, accompanied by her actor husband Will Smith, and their daughter Willow Camille Reign Smith, left, testifies before the Senate Foreign Relations Committee during a hearing on "The Next Ten Years in the Fight Against Human Trafficking: Attacking the Problem with the Right Tools" on Capitol Hill in Washington Tuesday, July 17, 2012. AP Photo/Manuel Balce Ceneta.

and neglectful families. This is especially apparent in the portion of *A Path Appears* where Judd listens as a white woman named Shana tells her story of sexual abuse by her grandfather. Shana refers to this man as her trafficker, and she claims that his abuse led her to drugs and sex work. Declaring that "Shana is my hero" for surviving the abuse and eventually leaving sex work, Judd goes on to characterize sex work as universally dangerous and exploitative, paraphrasing Andrea Dworkin's statement that "Incest is boot camp for prostitution," and adding that "Shana's story is a universal story."

Jada Pinkett Smith: Complicating the Dominant Narrative

Few would describe Congressional hearings as star-studded events, but the Senate Foreign Relations Committee meeting on July 17, 2012 was different. That day, Jada Pinkett Smith sat before the senators to support the reauthorization of the Trafficking Victims Protection Act (TVPA), and Will Smith and their children Jaden and Willow sat behind her, wearing t-shirts that read "Free Slaves" (see figure 7).

As the *Associated Press* (2012) described the event, "The hearing room was filled mostly with young people, some trying to take photos of the famous family. With her father's arm around her, Willow remained attentive to her mother's testimony and often whispered to her father." Here, in a forum that is rarely available to seasoned advocates and experts who have worked on this issue for many years, Pinkett Smith established herself publicly as an anti-trafficking activist, at a time when the anti-trafficking movement was well developed and evidence had emerged showing that human trafficking was not confined to sex trafficking in the Global South. As the following pages indicate, Pinkett Smith drew on her familial experiences and the knowledge available at this time to establish her connection to the issue and inform her representations of it. Compared to Judd, Pinkett Smith has more frequently represented human trafficking beyond the dominant narrative, namely by emphasizing both sex and other labor trafficking of persons of many genders, but like Judd, she also tends to root its causes in the family.

Pinkett Smith's broader representation of human trafficking was first evident in her speech to the US Congress in 2012. Holding the chamber's full attention, Pinkett Smith opened her remarks by quoting Frederick Douglass's 1865 speech to the American Anti-Slavery society, delivered just three months after Congress approved the Thirteenth Amendment abolishing slavery. Pinkett Smith told the audience that Douglass urged the Society not to disband because "Slavery has been fruitful in giving itself names . . . and you and I and all of us had better wait and see . . . in what new skin this old snake will come forth." According to Pinkett Smith, this "old snake" of slavery has re-emerged today as human trafficking, and she explained that,

> Douglass was right, this old monster is still with us. Today there are an esti-
> mated 27 million slaves worldwide—more than at any point in history. We
> call these men, women, and children the victims of human trafficking. They
> represent every nationality, ethnicity and age group, and they can be found
> everywhere, including here in the United States.

Indeed, as I noted in the previous chapter, using the terms "slavery" or "modern-day slavery" to describe contemporary human trafficking is problematic for many reasons. However, when Pinkett Smith described human trafficking as slavery, we also see how rhetorically powerful these words may be when a wealthy and famous Black woman (with her famous and successful family in tow) delivers them to the US Congress in 2012, almost two hundred years after it ratified the Thirteenth Amendment, to support a law (the TVPA) that would ostensibly help to prevent slavery in the future.

To further her personal connection to and motivation for engaging with the issue, in her speech she went on to explain how she, like many Americans, did not know about this "ugly, and too often invisible, problem" until "my 11 year old daughter Willow, who is here with us today, [brought] it to my attention." To show her significant commitment, she then explained how she educated herself about the issue by "reading, travelling, meeting survivors and service providers, law enforcement and public officials, and everyday citizens fighting against slavery." She then introduced three trafficking survivors—Minn, Monica, and Jamm—all of whom were commercially sexually exploited by family members and would testify before Congress that day. "[T]hey remind us of why we are here today," she said, namely to reauthorize the TVPA.

Following her testimony in July 2012, Pinkett Smith became a spokesperson for the ILO's "End Slavery Now" campaign, for which she created a PSA (ILO 2022b, 2022c). Wearing a silky yellow blouse and standing in front of a black background covered with ILO and "Art Works" logos, Pinkett Smith begins the PSA, which runs just over one minute in length, by stating, "I'm Jada Pinkett Smith and I am proud to help the ILO in the fight against slavery." As noted previously, the ILO understands human trafficking as a labor and economics issue that impacts a range of people internationally, and in her PSA for the ILO's campaign (ILO 2022c), Pinkett Smith conveys this message.

> Now when we think of slavery, we think of the past, but the truth is that three out of every thousand people in today's world, that is, more than 20 million people are in forced labor, have been trafficked, or work in slave like conditions. Most of this is happening in Asia, Africa, and Latin America but even in western industrialized countries, 1.5 million people are being exploited in these ways. Women, men, and children toil every day in cotton fields, cutting sugar cane, making bricks, clothes, sporting goods in bad conditions and without proper pay. This is wrong. And it has to stop. The ILO is the UN agency responsible for the world of work and has been helping people out of poverty and exploitation for more than ninety years. And with our help, they can do even more. So, if you feel like I do, that slavery has no place in today's world, help put an end to it.

Although these estimates of human trafficking are impossible to confirm, they are repeated often in the media, and they do complicate the dominant narrative by emphasizing that trafficking occurs in a range of industries.

Having used her own experience to establish herself very publicly as an anti-trafficking activist, in 2012 Pinkett Smith also proceeded to launch a web-based organization, Don't Sell Bodies (DSB). Created with assistance from the communications firm Change Creation, DSB was launched through Pinkett Smith's production company, Overbrook Entertainment (the music, film, and television production company founded by Will Smith and James Lassiter), and it also offered broad definitions of human trafficking, beyond the dominant narrative. As the DSB website (now defunct) noted, quoting an article from *Refinery 29* (Petersen 2018),

> When we think of human trafficking, more often than not we think of people who have been bought, sold, and forced to perform sexual acts. But while sexual slavery is a horrifying form of exploitation that is all too prevalent around the world, forced labour may in fact be a more common form of human trafficking. And it could be happening right outside your window.

Reflecting this perspective, the DSB website also listed a number of resources, including links to thirty-nine different anti-trafficking NGOs, ranging from CAST-LA, discussed in the previous chapter, to ECPAT, which focuses exclusively on eradicating the commercial sexual exploitation of children. However, seemingly aware of the different perspectives these NGOs may offer—and, hence, the minefield of debates about the ways to define and solve human trafficking—the website stated that "these resources are listed here as a public service. Inclusion on our website does not constitute an endorsement by Don't Sell Bodies, Overbrook Entertainment or Jada Pinkett Smith." For visitors who wanted to learn or do more, the website connected them to the national human trafficking hotline number, as well as pages for "stories," "news," "facts," and "actions" regarding human trafficking. A link to a "store" once connected visitors to DSB merchandise; however, what this included is unclear because, at the time of writing, the website stated, "We're sorry. This store is closed" (DSB 2021). The site also linked to "bsafe," a "personal and public safety technology" to help individuals "never walk alone again" (BSafe 2021).

While Pinkett Smith has represented human trafficking as a more diverse phenomenon than Judd, overall, she also does focus specifically on the sex trafficking of women and girls. This was particularly evident in her 2012 music video *Nada Se Compara* (Nothing Compares), which she created and released with her friend and fellow actor Salma Hayek (Pinkett Smith and Hayek 2012). In the video, Pinkett Smith sings while inexplicably writhing naked on a mattress and against a wall. In the video's main story line, a some-what older (presumably Latino) man seduces a (presumably Latina) girl. After she falls in love with him, he forces her and a seemingly ethnically and racially diverse group of other young women into sexual slavery. These scenes are intercut with others where the girl's mother cries in front of crucifixes and candles. At the end of the video, Pinkett Smith stops writhing and singing to put on a white t-shirt that says "STOP," in English and Spanish, and the video then offers statistics about sex trafficking.

Later, in *Children For Sale,* where "Jada Pinkett Smith and the CNN Freedom Project reveal the human trafficking in the heart of America" (Coorlim 2014), she also focused on sex trafficking of girls and young women.[3] The film opens with Pinkett Smith dressed casually; her hair is pulled back and she is wearing a red hooded sweatshirt under a black coat. "I'm Jada Pinkett Smith," she says, by way of introduction, and "for the next hour, we're going to investigate something deeply disturbing and uncomfort-able. We're going to take a hard look at the lives of girls and women trafficked in the sex trade and explore the roots that lured them into the life I could never have imagined." The film then offers a montage of men in handcuffs, dark city streets, and various law enforcement officials and girls saying things like "human trafficking is real" and "I had sex with almost forty guys in one day." The camera then comes back to Pinkett Smith, who says, "As a mother, as a human being, this is something that is simply unacceptable. I want to show you traffickers, girls affected, and the people fighting back against mod-ern day slavery." To show all of these things, the film is set in Atlanta, GA, which some have argued is a hotbed for sex trafficking in the United States (Boxill and Richardson 2007). Over the course of the next forty or so min-utes, we meet law enforcement officers as they work on sex trafficking cases, nonprofit service providers who work with trafficking victims, a former traf-ficker, and a psychologist who explains what makes young people (and girls in particular) vulnerable to trafficking.

In *Children for Sale* we also meet various young women who entered the sex industry and were trafficked, and their stories often align with the domi-nant narrative, albeit in ways that challenge its racialized tendency to center white girls (Brooks 2021). One of the most prominent featured victims is Sasha, a young Black woman who was raised in Florida, where she was "picked on a lot" for "being Black." She tells the viewers that she felt lonely and socially isolated, so when an older classmate asked her to be a friend, she "jumped for it," and this friend led her to the man who would eventually become her trafficker. Pinkett Smith talks to Sasha about the "grooming process" and how she came to work for a "pimp working out of a barber shop." Sasha cries as she tells Pinkett Smith that he told her to have sex with his friends, and she did it as because it made her feel "special." She was drugged and forced to have sex with multiple men—once up to "forty guys in one day"— and she was in great pain. However, Sasha tells Pinkett Smith through tears, the trafficker made it clear that "leaving was not an option" because she would have nowhere to go, and so she stayed with him.

But while Pinkett Smith and *Children for Sale* challenge the notion that sex trafficking is something that only happens to white girls in the United States (or to women and girls "over there," in the Global South), her ideas about the causes of human trafficking are fairly mainstream. Like Judd, Pinkett Smith acknowledges that structural factors fuel human trafficking through her support for organizations like ILO and CAST-LA, and she also communicates through a "theater of pity" (Chouliaraki 2012) to emphasize how individual men and a lack of a familial love and support may create vulnerabilities to human trafficking. We see this emphasis on individual causes in *Nada Se Compara,* where she signals that a lack of familial love is the predominant cause of human trafficking, a theme that runs through much of her subsequent anti-trafficking work. At the end of the video, a quote from the then-US Ambassador-At-Large to Monitor and Combat Trafficking in Persons, Luis C. deBaca, appears on the screen: "The most common way to recruit trafficking victims is not kidnapping, but love" (Pinkett Smith and Hayek 2012).

This notion that a lack of love (or an offer of love) causes sex trafficking is similarly apparent in *Children for Sale,* most notably in Sasha's story, which, according to Pinkett Smith, teaches us about "falling prey to false love" and being "saved by the real thing." In the film, we learn that Sasha felt a lack of love early in her life: her father abandoned her when she was young, and when she begged her mother to meet him, her mother told her that she was "setting herself up for heartbreak." The camera then turns to a psychologist, Anique Whitmore, who tells Pinkett Smith that "heartbreak at home can provide the perfect setup for a trafficker looking to exploit a child." To explain this connection, Whitmore tells Pinkett Smith that children like Sasha "become vulnerable because [they] are looking for attention" and oftentimes girls in this position with low self-esteem "use their body to attract that [attention]." Over footage of Sasha on a swing, we hear Whitmore say that, "broken and hurting," these girls are "easy prey" for a person waiting and lurking in the background, who will "give them clothes," and "offer to do their nails." That is the "exact tactic Sasha Ray's exploiter used on her." Sasha then explains how there was "a feeling from him I got from no one else," and Pinkett Smith asks, "what was that feeling?" Sasha responds tearfully, "It was a love feeling, I guess, from a man. I was missing that part from my dad, that's what I think." Sasha's story is not the last time we hear from Pinkett Smith about the relationship between familial love and vulnerability to human trafficking. As she explains later, in an interview with *Ebony* magazine, "Sometimes we have to watch how we communicate with each other and what we call love because when people in these streets violate us we mistake those actions for love too because it looks familiar" (Hubbard 2016). In short, a lack of familial love, per Pinkett Smith, drives young people away from their homes, which renders them vulnerable to sexual and other exploitation.

SOLUTIONS AND FEMINIST IDEOLOGIES

In different settings, Judd's and Pinkett Smith's charismatic political performances offer varied representations of human trafficking's forms, victims, and causes. In the following pages, I interpret the feminist interests and ideologies they circulate through their solutions to human trafficking. Specifically, I show that both women support criminal justice and NGO-related solutions, but their familial experiences set them apart: Judd minimizes families as a solution to human trafficking, whereas Pinkett Smith centers familial love. Positioned, then, in roles as a "white savior" and an "activist mother," respectively, their performances variously circulate carceral, (neo)liberal, and familial ideologies in ways that both challenge and reinforce race and gender hierarchies.

Judd and Pinkett Smith: Carceral and Liberal Commitments

As noted in earlier chapters, criminal justice solutions to human trafficking are part of mainstream discourse, and Judd and Pinkett Smith have publicly endorsed them. Judd has done so, most notably, through her long-standing promotion of efforts to "end demand" for prostitution. Broadly defined, these efforts include law and policy initiatives that aim to deter, if not explicitly punish, (male) purchasers of sexual services, and they are based on the belief that reducing this demand for sexual services will also help to eliminate sex *trafficking* (Majic 2014c, 2015). In her memoir, Judd expresses her support for these initiatives: "As long as there is demand for prostituted sex, people will find a way to sell girls and women. Demand abolition is essential" (Judd and Vollers 2011, 80). Judd has maintained this position through her work. Even though she was a member of Amnesty International in college, she signed the CATW's letter, which opposed Amnesty's support for decriminalizing prostitution and called for measures to target the demand for prostitution.

Similar to Judd, Pinkett Smith has also used her fame and wide reach to endorse carceral solutions to human trafficking. In addition to testifying in support of the TVPA's reauthorization (this law mainly authorizes and funds law enforcement to arrest and prosecute people for trafficking crimes), in 2012 she also spoke at the Moms on a Mission "Vote Yes on 35" event in support of Proposition 35 in California, which passed in November of that year. This proposition increased penalties against human traffickers in the state by, among other things, creating higher prison terms and requiring convicted human traffickers to register as sex offenders, disclose their internet accounts to authorities, and pay fines for victims' services (Reinelt 2016; Halperin 2017). However, even as she supported these criminal justice solutions, Pinkett Smith did not sign the CATW's letter to Amnesty International.

In addition to promoting criminal justice solutions, Judd and Pinkett Smith also engage in celanthropy by creating, promoting, and fundraising for various NGOs. One example here occurred in *A Path Appears*, when Judd visited and expressed support for Thistle Farms Bath and Body Care. This Tennessee-based NGO is affiliated with Magdalene House, described above, and hires former sex workers to make and sell coffee and bath products. As noted previously, Pinkett Smith also created her own online organization, DSB, and has supported many others, such as the ILO and CAST-LA. Furthermore, in *Children for Sale*, Pinkett Smith praises the efforts of two Atlanta-area nonprofits, Living Water for Girls, which provides safe housing for victims of trafficking, and For Sarah, which conducts outreach to women working in strip clubs and other sectors of the sex industry.

Through *Children For Sale*, Pinkett Smith also indicates how a combination of law enforcement *and* NGO efforts may stop trafficking. As she states in an interview towards the end of the film, "Now we as citizens of America, we all have a part to play in this. And we all have to take responsibility, and it starts in our homes and it starts in our communities." To illustrate this responsibility, we see Casey, a blonde white woman and former exotic dancer who founded For Sarah, running a bus tour of Atlanta's trafficking "hotspots." The local news covered this tour, and a viewer who was worried about her missing fourteen-year-old granddaughter saw this news story and called the For Sarah hotline. The volunteer who answered her call contacted Sergeant Kennedy, a police officer in charge of vice and trafficking investigations, who is featured in the documentary. We learn that Kennedy and his team searched for days until they stopped a car near the airport; inside, they found a man with many arrest warrants and the missing granddaughter (and another fifteen-year-old girl), who said she was on the way to meet her first "john." The grandmother (blurred out) was ecstatic to find her granddaughter, who was connected with Living Water for Girls. We then hear Pinkett Smith conclude the story: "two girls, saved, when a community comes together: law enforcement, advocates, and eventually, caregivers like Lisa Williams [the founder of Living Water for Girls]."

Indeed, these carceral and celanthropic solutions merit criticism as feminist projects. While it is difficult to argue against punishing individuals who commit trafficking crimes, celebrity feminism that favors punishment-oriented and ending-demand approaches circulates a carceral feminist ideology that often, inadvertently, *harms* women and girls. Namely, by detracting attention and resources from victim services and preventative efforts such as anti-poverty initiatives, this ideology marshals support for criminalizing policies and practices that actually *exacerbate* sex workers' and trafficking victims' vulnerability (Andrijasevic and Mai 2016). In so doing, this feminist ideology may actually reinforce gender and racial hierarchies. For example, the criminalization of demand, which Judd supports, ignores how law enforcement in the United States often targets Black men and boys, who are also the least likely group to be seen as "innocent" and therefore quite vulnerable to being arrested on trafficking charges (Bernstein 2012).

In the case of Judd and Pinkett Smith's celanthropic efforts, while the NGOs they created and/or support may further anti-trafficking efforts, prioritizing their role here circulates a neoliberally-inflected feminist ideology that may also reinforce race and gender hierarchies. By centering individual efforts and Western philanthropy as solutions to human trafficking—a global problem of structural injustice—these efforts and their attendant neoliberal ideologies detract attention from the role that states, institutions, and structural conditions play in promoting human trafficking and its attendant inequalities (Ackerly 2018; Vance 2011). To illustrate, while Thistle Farms (the NGO Judd visited with Kristof) offers skills training and employment to former sex workers by showing them how to make beauty products and serve coffee, it also endorses highly gendered notions of work for a group of predominantly non-white women, while doing little to address the racism, sexism, and other discrimination they face in the labor market. Similarly, as Robert Heynen and Emily van der Meulen (2021, 6) write, DSB's emphasis on "empowerment" and capitalism as a solution to human trafficking (as indicated by the site's now-defunct "online store") promotes "the power of business and social enterprise to create viable alternatives to slavery," which also, ultimately, does little to address structural conditions that create vulnerabilities to forced labor. By focusing on "building awareness rather than providing services" DSB mirrored "the larger neo-liberal logic of branded activism" that has become so typical in celebrity activism writ large (6).

Focus on the Family?

Even as Pinkett Smith and Judd support many similar solutions to human trafficking and circulate similar feminist ideologies, their view of the family sets them apart here. As a result, their anti-trafficking advocacy indicates how celebrities may draw on their personal experiences to *distinctly* represent an issue in ways that reinforce and challenge gender and racial hierarchies. As a woman with few connections to and little faith in her own family as a site of safety and security, Judd does not endorse the family as a solution to human trafficking, hence her emphasis on carceral and NGO-related solutions. Indeed, many of her fans and other members of the public with negative familial experiences will relate to and agree with her. Moreover, beyond her personal experience, a growing body of evidence supports Judd's position on the family, especially for young people: familial poverty, abuse, and homo and trans phobia can leave them vulnerable to homelessness, food insecurity, and coercive sexual and labor situations (Showden and Majic 2018).

However, Judd's distrust of families, combined with her support for criminal justice and NGO approaches to human trafficking, has led her to see *herself* as the solution to human trafficking, as indicated by the many "rescue fantasies" she describes in her memoir. These stories reinforce racial hierarchies by positioning her among the "white saviors" who enact Western humanitarian rescue fantasies, where they raid, capture, and rescue and return home suffering, non-white bodies (Kempadoo 2015). An example of this white saviorhood occurred when Judd was in Thailand with PSI, where she met six young women working in brothels and other sex-related businesses. Appalled by their situation and feeling a deep personal connection to their plight, she states in her memoir that she "knew I couldn't rescue every woman and child from every bar, karaoke club, beer garden, and other place of slavery . . . [but] [t]hese six, however, I could. And I would" (Judd and Vollers 2011, 95). She decided that she would provide money to send the young women back to their homes, or to Denmark, and ensure they had enough for food, housing, and finishing school. (As I discuss later, PSI thwarted her efforts here).

In contrast, Pinkett Smith draws from her own *positive* familial experiences to position herself as an activist mother who believes that familial love is the ultimate solution to human trafficking. As she explained to *Ebony* magazine,

> To me, I think one of the biggest ways to combat trafficking (especially with our youth) on the micro-level is to look at how we show love in our homes. We have to pay attention to how we are actually loving our children so when they come across somebody that is manipulative, abusive, and violent, it's not the norm. . . . This is why we need to have conversations in our homes about sex and violence. . . . If we are willing to share our testimony, it's powerful (cited in Hubbard 2016).

To Pinkett Smith, her personal experience is proof that familial love—particularly love from a man who is a good father—can prevent exploitation. As she explains in *Children For Sale,* she grew up with a single mom and "didn't have a father" and "I've suffered because of it. I've had to learn a lot." But then she adds,

> Thank god I came across a man like Will who didn't take advantage of me. Because let me tell you something: when I look at these girls, I look at myself, I see myself. And that's . . . when I hear their stories, it affects me so much, because I go, man, that could have been me, that was me at one time. I know what that is.

Altogether, according to Pinkett Smith, a loving and supportive family helped her avoid exploitation (vaguely defined) *and* it helped her become a successful actor and attentive mother who offers a loving home to her own children. In fact, her home is so loving and open that her daughter, Willow, felt comfortable enough to discuss sex trafficking with her, and when Pinkett Smith decided to take on the issue, her whole family came to Congress to support her advocacy.

At first glance, Pinkett Smith's argument that the family can solve human trafficking seems unrealistic, if not actively anti-feminist. As scholars and activists have long held, the devolution of social problems to the family privatizes them, placing an undue burden on women, and ignoring the structural supports that families need to thrive (Fraser 2013; Moller Okin 1989). Pinkett Smith is, arguably, removed from these concerns: her wealthy family has the resources to ensure a safe, stable, and openly communicative home for her children. Moreover, she has a vested interest in this familial ideal. Although she claims Will is a good man who "didn't take advantage" of her, she has long contended with rumors about marital infidelity, and speaking publicly about how she and Will maintain their stable and successful marriage and family is part of her celebrity brand (Caramanica 2022). Altogether, Pinkett Smith indicates that even as celebrities may use their personal experiences to connect with their fans, they are ultimately living quite privileged lives.

However, Pinkett Smith's promotion of the family as a solution to human trafficking can also be interpreted as subverting racial and gender hierarchies by challenging (even to a limited extent) stereotypes of black mothers and families. As Cheryl Rodriguez (2016) writes, Black mothers have long been cast in popular discourse and social science research as angry, demeaning, and responsible for the supposedly dysfunctional Black family. But they have also challenged these brutal misrepresentations and their attendant policy implications through scholarship and activism, working to protect their children and promote the survival and progress of Black women everywhere. Jada Pinkett Smith is also a Black mother who is not immune to negative stereotypes, despite her wealth and celebrity. By using her considerable power—which she derives from her fame capital *and* from her long-married, wealthy, famous Black family—to draw attention to human trafficking, she positions herself as a mother and as an activist who is engaged in the fight against the sexism, racism, and violence that undergirds human trafficking. In so doing, Pinkett Smith is challenging negative representations of Black mothers and families in public discourse.

TO WHAT EFFECT: POWER AND ACCOUNTABILITY?

Ashley Judd and Jada Pinkett Smith indicate how celebrities may draw from their personal experiences and temporal and organizational contexts to appoint themselves as political representatives who variously raise awareness about human trafficking. In so doing they are engaging in celebrity feminism to circulate a range of issue representations and feminist ideologies. The remaining pages in this chapter consider the broader effects of these performances, particularly regarding their power to challenge racial and gender stereotypes and hierarchies, and their capacity to account for their actions.

The "Personal" Is Powerful?

The notion that "the personal is political" has long been a solidaristic rallying cry for feminists, particularly in the West, and celebrities like Judd and Pinkett Smith are not the first to draw from their personal experiences to publicize issues of gender based violence and inequality (see, e.g., Htun and Weldon 2018; Weldon 2011). However, because of their high profiles and legions of fans, their personal stories reach wider audiences than those of the average "civilian" activist. As a result, when celebrities share their personal stories, they are establishing and maintaining their distinct status in a crowded activist field (the feminist and anti-trafficking movements), justifying and explaining their engagement with the issue, promoting unique issue representations, highlighting particular solutions, and circulating feminist ideologies. All of this raises broader questions about the power of the personal story *and* about celebrity feminist power more generally. Does this draw attention to core issues like gender and racial inequality, or does it ultimately serve the celebrity and further her fame and its attendant privileges?

The answer to this question is mixed. On the one hand, Judd and Pinkett Smith's anti-trafficking activism seems to illustrate the self-serving nature of celebrity advocacy. As "pretty women in the public eye" (Gay 2014), their fame and resources allowed them to enter rarefied spaces like the United Nations and the US Congress and reach vast and influential audiences in ways that survivors, advocates, academics, and feminist advocates—who have labored for decades to combat human trafficking and have far more knowledge about the issue—could only dream of doing. Furthermore, Judd and Pinkett Smith have managed to conduct their activism, in large part, without getting into the messy fray of grassroots, feminist politics. Aside from highly produced scenes in documentaries and NGO-organized trips, their interactions with activists and impacted communities appear minimal and intensively managed at best. Therefore, even as Judd's and Pinkett Smith's political performances may have drawn significant public and political attention to human trafficking, they have reliably drawn media and other attention to themselves, furthering their celebrity status and power.

But dismissing Judd and Pinkett Smith's anti-trafficking performances as self-serving, fame-sustaining exercises ignores how they may also, somewhat paradoxically, challenge gender and racial inequality more broadly. Certainly, mixing their personal, professional, and political actions may help celebrities promote themselves and further their livelihoods, but these actions may also challenge the well documented sexism, racism, and ageism in the entertainment industry (see, e.g., Hunt and Ramón 2021; Yuen 2017). As women actors in their late forties and early fifties (at the time of writing), Judd and Pinkett Smith are "old" for Hollywood, while Pinkett Smith is additionally disadvantaged by her race. For these "aging" Hollywood stars, then, drawing on their personal experiences to engage in anti-trafficking activism brought attention to human trafficking *and* it helped them further their careers.

However, their actions also challenge Hollywood's biases against who can work and remain in the public eye. In fact, both Judd and Pinkett Smith have parlayed their public personas as anti-trafficking advocates into more acting work. Judd appeared in the 2009 film *Crossing Over,* which was about labor trafficking in Mexico and California. In 2012, her TV series *Missing* featured a human trafficking sub-plot, and in 2017 she played a trafficker in the film *Trafficked.* Similarly, although Pinkett Smith has not had any parts related to human trafficking to date, she has parlayed her message about familial love into *Red Table Talk,* a show that premiered on Facebook Watch in 2018. In the series, "Pinkett Smith, her daughter Willow, and mother Adrienne—three generations of women—open their home for a series of candid conversations with family and friends" (Facebook Watch 2022). These conversations cover topics such as motherhood and surviving loss, among others.

But Judd and Pinkett Smith have not solely challenged Hollywood's biases by parlaying their activism into career advancement: they have also politicized the personal to raise awareness about and fight sexism in Hollywood. In 2017, as the #MeToo movement gathered steam, numerous celebrities shared personal stories of sexual abuse and harassment at the hands of (male) producers, network executives, and actors, among many of their other colleagues in the entertainment industry (see, e.g., Nyong'o 2017). Ashley Judd was one of the first celebrities to come out as a #MeToo victim, speak openly about the notorious Hollywood producer Harvey Weinstein, and file a lawsuit against him. Here she alleged that after she rejected his sexual advances in a hotel room in the 1990s, he spoke negatively about her to the director Peter Jackson, who was considering her for a major role in *Lord of the Rings* and then declined to cast her. Her lawsuit alleges that "with those baseless smears, Weinstein succeeded in blacklisting Ms. Judd and destroying her ability to work on what became a multibillion-dollar franchise with 17 Academy Award wins and many more nominations" (Berkowitz 2018). As I discuss in the concluding chapter of this book, Judd's and other celebrities' personal stories about sexual harassment in Hollywood quickly drew national and international attention, forcing the removal of many alleged rapists and sexual assaulters such as Harvey Weinstein from positions of power, and raised money for direct services.

While Pinkett Smith has not been vocal as a #MeToo victim, she has challenged gender and racial stereotypes in Hollywood by speaking openly about her struggles with alopecia since 2018, when she addressed the issue on *Red Table Talk,* and then later, in 2021, through a story on Instagram. "Female pattern hair loss" (or female androgenetic alopecia) is the main form of hair loss in adult women, and it especially impacts Black women. Although there are many types of alopecia (for example, "traction alopecia" is caused by hair-styling practices such as straightening, whereas Pinkett Smith's alopecia is linked to an auto-immune disorder), it does not typically have other symptoms. However, alopecia can be extremely challenging, lowering one's self-esteem and quality of life, and few dermatologists are trained to understand and treat the condition (Edelson 2018; Ramos and Miot 2015). By openly addressing her own struggle with alopecia in the media, Pinkett Smith is raising awareness about the issue and challenging racialized societal beauty standards, especially those that valorize particular qualities and quantities of hair (straight, plentiful, and blonde). Of course, one may argue that Pinkett Smith, who is conventionally beautiful and has the resources to access the best treatments, may not be a very relatable spokesperson here. However, many sympathized with Pinkett Smith when the comedian Chris Rock made a joke about her hair loss at the 2022 Oscars, while she was in the audience. While her husband's response captured significant media coverage (Will Smith hit Rock on stage after he made the joke) and rekindled gossip about the strength of their marriage, this incident also drew attention to Pinkett Smith's condition *and* to the mockery and other societal scrutiny that many *non-celebrity* women face for their alopecia, thereby increasing awareness about how it impacts women's—and Black women's especially—self-esteem.

Even if readers may still, understandably, dismiss Judd's and Pinkett Smith's anti-trafficking activism as fundamentally self-serving, we cannot deny that they have drawn significant attention to human trafficking and, potentially, increased the public's related engagement and knowledge. After all, would swarms of people normally attend a Congressional hearing if the Smiths were not sitting in the audience and testifying before the Senate? Although there is currently no data to prove this, one may reasonably speculate that some of those who witnessed Pinkett Smith's and Judd's performances went on to learn more about human trafficking and related issues of gender inequality in one way or another. Put simply, Judd's and Pinkett Smith's activism against human trafficking indicates that, whether we like it or not, "Celebrities are key conduits through which feminism is mediated to larger audiences" (Casey and Watson 2017, 3).

But what, exactly, does the public learn about feminism through celebrities? This question merits investigation because celebrities' lack of expertise may also lead them to promote problematic issue representations that may undermine feminist goals, as indicated by the carceral and neoliberally-inflected solutions and ideologies Judd and Pinkett Smith have promoted (to name just some examples). How, then, do we hold celebrities responsible for their political performances, especially when they are often self-appointed representatives who are not subject to elections or directly accountable to grassroots or other constituencies? Answering this question is challenging, especially since many of the audiences that are best positioned to hold celebrities accountable—the individuals and organizations they speak for and represent—also benefit from their fame capital.

To understand the limits and possibilities of celebrity power and accountability in this regard, Judd's experience with PSI and Pinkett Smith's support for DSB are instructive. Judd's example illustrates how organizations that appoint celebrities (their beneficiary audiences) may hold them accountable by curbing their potentially harmful actions. As noted earlier, when Judd was in Cambodia with PSI, she wanted to rescue the young women she met at a brothel and send them to Denmark. When Judd explained this to PSI, they stopped her by explaining that her plan could harm the organization's work in the region. As Judd writes, PSI told her that they needed brothel owners' cooperation to hand out condoms and continue their HIV/AIDS prevention work, and that there were other organizations in the region that help women leave the sex industry and/or find other work to "reduce the number of clients they are forced to take" (Judd and Vollers 2011, 97). PSI's pushback here indicates how NGOs may hold celebrities accountable—in this case, by mitigating their white savior impulses—even as they benefit from their fame capital.

At the same time, relying on NGOs to hold celebrities accountable for their actions is also a precarious strategy, especially if the NGOs themselves misrepresent issues and the populations that they claim to help. After PSI thwarted Judd's rescue effort in Cambodia, they told her about AFESIP, an organization doing the rescue work that she wanted to do. However, as we learned in chapter 2, AFESIP was not entirely honest about its founder, Somaly Mam, and the scope of its work. As a result, when journalists discovered and exposed AFESIP's misrepresentations, there was very little in the way of accountability. While AFESIP did shut down, none of the celebrities and others who supported the organization, including Ashley Judd, took any responsibility for its actions.

When celebrities create their own organizations, opportunities to question and hold them accountable for their work are fewer still; DSB is an instructive example here. The site's creators claimed that DSB received 50,000 viewers in its first month (Change Creation 2022). However, there is no accounting for how these viewers engaged with and learned about human trafficking. Certainly, DSB was under no obligation to provide this information: because it was part of her private company, Overbrook Entertainment, Pinkett Smith and others affiliated with DSB did not have to explain its actions and their effects. Instead, it was and is up to the media, advocacy organizations, and scholars to question them and learn more about their work.

Certainly, this reliance on "outside" scrutiny may yield information and accountability in some instances, but this was not the case for DSB and its first major "product" for public consumption, *Nada Se Compara*. The video very clearly reinforced racial and gendered stereotypes by portraying young Latina girls as victims and Latino men as predators, while promoting love as the solution to human trafficking, even as this phenomenon very clearly requires a much more complex response. However, media scrutiny and commentary did not focus on these problematic representations and solutions (at least in the materials available online). Instead, the media mainly questioned why Pinkett Smith was naked, discussing here Salma Hayek's explanation that she would only direct the video if Pinkett Smith appeared this way, to show trafficking victims' vulnerability. "[I]t's important that you are as vulnerable as these women, because the obsession that men have with women's bodies, it's really threatening for us," Hayek explained (Nolfi 2021). While Pinkett Smith's nakedness was certainly a curious artistic choice, and trafficking victims are indeed vulnerable in many ways, the media focus and commentary centers the celebrity, and not the video's stereotypes of victims and its narrow solutions to human trafficking. However, since the DSB website is no longer extant, and no one from the organization ever returned my requests for interviews and other information, it is difficult to determine DSB's rationale for its materials and messages, to say nothing of the extent to which these influenced policy and other discussions of human trafficking more generally.

CONCLUSION

This chapter has shown the varying ways in which celebrities' personal stories and the contexts of their work may shape their performances of anti-human trafficking activism and the issue representations and feminist interests and ideologies they convey to their audiences. In this case, Judd's and Pinkett Smith's personal, familial experiences and the organizational and temporal contexts in which they worked set the stage for them to offer both the dominant narrative *and* more complex stories of human trafficking, thereby circulating a range of feminist ideologies that variously challenge and reinforce race and gender hierarchies. Yet their work also shows the limits of celebrities' self-appointed representation. While they have certainly drawn attention to human trafficking and used their activism to further their careers and challenge race and gender stereotypes in Hollywood, it has been difficult, if not impossible, to hold them accountable for their actions.

Ashley Judd and Jada Pinkett Smith thus illustrate the "mixed blessing" that celebrities offer the anti-trafficking and feminist movements. They have drawn significant public attention to human trafficking and gender inequality in many high profile venues. Yet in charismatically centering themselves and their stories to justify and inform their engagement with these issues, they have, in large part, framed human trafficking as a public problem that is ultimately caused by bad individuals and solved by good ones, like loving family members in partnership with nonprofits and law enforcement. While both women have, at times, acknowledged how broader structural forces such as the legacy of slavery and American imperialism have furthered human trafficking, raising awareness about these factors has not been the central thrust of their work.

In stating all of this, I am not claiming that we must disregard celebrities and/or chastise the public for caring about issues—feminist or otherwise—when a bright and shiny celebrity talks about them. Instead, we must remain attuned to the broader cultural, institutional, and other socio-political factors that have led celebrities to ascend in the public sphere and serve as feminist political representatives. These factors include the expanded and fragmented mediascape and shifting political-participatory patterns that foster elite dominance. The following chapter further illuminates how such factors, along with personal experiences, networks of consultants, technological initiatives, and NGO structures, shape male celebrities' anti-human trafficking activism.

FOUR

Latin Lovers and Tech Guys

RICKY MARTIN, ASHTON KUTCHER, AND
VARIATIONS OF MALE CELEBRITY FEMINISM

[A]lthough I could easily spend my days walking through the streets of Calcutta looking for girls to rescue, the fact of my being a person in the public eye creates a whole other dimension of work I can do to help, which isn't something everyone can do. . . . The fact that as an artist I can have the power to convince and create some type of awareness is amazing.

RICKY MARTIN (2010, 204–5)

I was just so appalled. If you can't do something about it, then who are you?

ASHTON KUTCHER,
in response to CBS News correspondent Michelle Miller's
question, "Why this cause [sex trafficking]?" (2018)

LIKE OTHER CELEBRITIES, singer Ricky Martin and actor Ashton Kutcher have harnessed and deployed their considerable fame capital to raise awareness about human trafficking. But among the ten most active celebrities that I identified in this arena, they are the only two who identify as men. Together, their gender identity and issue advocacy situates them as "male celebrity feminists" (MCF)—a small but growing number of men from the entertainment and sports industries who appear with frequency and regularity on popular media listicles to speak openly about their interest in gender equality (Dionne 2014, Cobb 2015). Commercially successful and conventionally handsome, these men almost never refer to themselves as feminists, nor do they actively campaign as part of the feminist movement. However, their public discussions of and efforts to raise awareness about a myriad of issues that have long concerned feminists, such as childcare and sexual harassment, combined with their decidedly un-macho heterosexuality, "creates a personal identity of a male celebrity who 'loves' and respects women, even as his on-screen roles may contribute to mediated hegemonic masculinity" (Cobb 2015, 137; see also Feasey 2017).

Even as the MCF is a relatively recent phenomenon, scholarly and other discussions are highly critical, characterizing and critiquing him as "a post-feminist figure [who] takes 'feminism into account' and simultaneously undermines women's claims on it" (Cobb 2015, 138; see also McRobbie 2009). While these are certainly valid criticisms, to date there is little scholarship analyzing and comparing examples of MCFs in depth. This chapter addresses this gap in research by comparing Ricky Martin's and Ashton Kutcher's anti-trafficking work as performances of male celebrity feminism, arguing that by offering different narrative representations of human trafficking and, by extension, feminist ideologies, they indicate its variations, limits, and possibilities for promoting gender equality.

Focusing on the primary settings for their political performances—The Ricky Martin Foundation and Kutcher's Thorn Digital Defenders—I show how personal and contextual factors shape Martin's and Kutcher's interests in and representations of human trafficking, and the sex trafficking of children in particular. Namely, even as both men are positioned differently across a range of identity categories and had distinct trajectories to fame, they both came to the issue by "witnessing" sex trafficking, and they used their extensive resources to establish their own foundations to address it. These personal experiences, combined with the timing of their engagement and their organizational affiliations has, consequently, shaped the extent to which they promote the dominant narrative of human trafficking. Specifically, Martin's longstanding interest in helping vulnerable children in Puerto Rico and his partnerships with international NGOs have informed his somewhat complex narrative of the issue, whereas Kutcher's more recent introduction to and engagement with the issue through celebrity philanthropic consultants and technology investments has contributed to his reification of the dominant narrative.

As a result, Martin and Kutcher promote different solutions to human trafficking from which we may interpret various feminist interests and ideologies and evaluate MCFs' potential for promoting gender equality more broadly. As I show in the chapter's final section, Martin and Kutcher follow their women-identified celebrity feminist peers by operating above the fray of grassroots anti-trafficking activism. With access to venues such as the United Nations and the US Congress, they have promoted various legal, NGO, and service-oriented solutions to human trafficking and circulated carceral, liberal and structurally intersectional feminist ideologies as a result. However, as prominent men in a women-dominated movement, Kutcher's and Martin's celebrity power also complicates traditional gender ideologies. Namely, by focusing on children, who have long been collectively constructed as a "women's concern," Martin and Kutcher variously reify and challenge hegemonic masculinity through their positions as sexual and ethnic minorities (Martin), and their emphasis on technological solutions (Kutcher) that promote a cyber-feminist ideology celebrating internet and other digital technologies as inherently liberatory for women (Wajcman 2007).

PERFORMERS AND SETTINGS

Ricky Martin and Ashton Kutcher amassed significant stocks of celebrity capital before engaging in anti-human trafficking activism. In the following pages I introduce each performer, showing here that "witnessing" trafficking motivated their engagement with the issue through their philanthropic foundations.

Ricky Martin

Enrique (Ricky) Jose Martin Morales was born in 1971 in San Juan, Puerto Rico, to a Catholic family. His mother, an accountant, and his father, a psychologist, divorced when he was two years old, remarrying and expanding their families. Martin has two older maternal half-brothers, two younger paternal half-brothers, and a younger paternal half-sister. Although Martin was partnered with Rebecca D'Alba (a TV presenter and model in Mexico) from 1994 to 2005, his sexual orientation was long a subject of tabloid speculation. In 2010, he came out as gay on his website and on the Oprah Winfrey Show, where he stated that he was in a relationship. He married Jwan Yosef, a painter, in 2018, and they have four children, twins Valentino and Matteo Martin (born to Martin via gestational surrogate in 2008), and Lucia Martin-Yosef and Renn Martin-Yosef, also by gestational surrogate, born in 2018 and 2019, respectively.

In his memoir, Martin (2010) describes a close and loving relationship with his family, and his desire to perform from an early age. With his parents' support, he began singing and taking acting lessons, going on to appear in eleven Puerto Rican television commercials for soft drinks, toothpaste, and restaurants. However, his big break came at the age of twelve, when he auditioned for and joined the boy band Menudo in 1984. Created by the producer Edgardo Diaz in 1977, and comprised of five young Puerto Rican boys (who "retired" by age 16), Menudo preceded the Backstreet Boys and New Kids on the Block, among other major North American boy bands, and it was the first Latin American boy band to reach international fame, filling stadiums across the globe. Martin left his family to tour with Menudo, and traveling the world in private jets and mobbed by fans at every stop, he "leaped into the world of fame, luxury and worship" (36). Yet members of the band have also alleged that Menudo was also a world of exploitation and abuse. In *Subete a mi Moto* (Get Off My Motorcycle), the 2020 Amazon Prime series about the band, former Menudo member Roy Roselló (whose time in the band overlapped with Martin's) and others alleged that they were subject to humiliation, mistreatment and sexual abuse at the hands of Diaz and other managers (Peña 2020).[1]

While Martin acknowledged in his memoir that being part of Menudo "cost me my childhood" (2010, 28), he has yet to respond to Roselló's allegations of abuse in Menudo (including Roselló's allegation that, at a party, Diaz once forced Martin to dress up as a woman (Simon 2014)). Instead, Martin wrote that being in Menudo instilled in him a sense of discipline and offered him professional growth that would serve him well throughout his career. After he left Menudo in 1989, Martin returning to Puerto Rico to finish high school and reconnect with his family. He moved to New York City when he was eighteen and lived modestly, saw friends, and traveled with his Menudo earnings. But this break was short-lived: during a trip to Mexico, he saw the musical *Mama ama el Rock,* which needed to replace a cast member. Martin auditioned and got the part, and from there he went on to star in the Mexican soap opera *Alcanzar una estrella II,* and then in a film loosely based on it (*Más que alcanzar una estrella*), for which he won a Heraldo, the Mexican equivalent of an Oscar, in 1992. He moved to Los Angeles in 1993 to pursue acting in the United States, appearing in the NBC sitcom *Getting By* and the soap opera *General Hospital.* Later in his career, he also appeared on the television show *Glee* (2012), as a coach on *The Voice Australia* (2012–2015), and as Antonio D'Amico, the partner of Gianni Versace, on the 2018 TV series *American Crime Story.*

Amidst his acting work, Martin returned to singing in 1991, quickly (re)ascending to global fame. His solo album *Ricky Martin* sold 500,000 copies (making it the highest-selling Latin album released by Sony in the previous ten years), followed by *Me Amaras,* which helped him earn a "Best New Artist" award at the Billboard Video Awards in 1993. In 1999, after releasing several albums in Spanish, he performed "The Cup of Life" at the Grammys, bringing Latin pop to the forefront of the US music scene. However, his hit song "La Vida Loca," which he released in 1999, marked his crossover into the English language music market when it hit number one in many countries, won a Grammy, and set the stage for other Latin artists like Jennifer Lopez and Enrique Iglesias to ascend in the American music industry. Declared the "King of Latin Pop," Martin has sold nearly 95 million albums over the course of his career.

Given his status as a barrier-breaking global superstar, questions arise about his motivations for anti-trafficking advocacy, as he did not need a cause to maintain his celebrity, and his roles on screen and on the stage have had nothing to do with this issue. Instead, as Martin writes, he was introduced to the issue somewhat by chance, and he soon followed the "witness-rescuer-expert" trajectory of many celebrity and other prominent anti-trafficking activists (Heynen and van der Meulen 2021, 9). As Martin (2010, 178) documents in his memoir, after his world tour in the 1990s, a friend invited him to India to visit an orphanage "that offers care and education to helpless girls in Calcutta." Although Martin had visited India a number of times, his 2002 trip was different. With his friend, they immediately went to "rescue girls from the street" (178) until they found what they were looking for: "a group of beggars, exactly the type of girls who were at risk of falling into child prostitution" (179). Through a translator, they explained their concerns to the girls' mother; she agreed to their help and Martin and his friend rushed the girls, who were "bitten up by rats . . . dirty and very thin," to Martin's hotel. A doctor from the orphanage arrived and administered medicine, and the next day the girls moved to the orphanage and "live there to this day" (183). Upon returning from this trip to India, Martin "began to realize that performing on onstage was simply not enough" (189), and he turned his attention to human trafficking, and the sex trafficking of children specifically. Fighting this would become, as he describes it, "the role of my life" (187). He proceeded to "go online and . . . read everything I could about human trafficking" (190), and as he studied, he felt that even though the subject had been written about and discussed for some time, "a true awareness of the gravity of what is really going on was lacking" (192).

Martin became one of the first celebrities to take on human trafficking as his central cause, beginning this work in the early 2000s, when the contemporary anti-trafficking movement was ascending and, as noted in earlier chapters, emerging research focused mainly on sex trafficking. International organizations were quick to capitalize on his interest and global celebrity. In December 2003, UNICEF named Martin a Goodwill Ambassador. He and his Ricky Martin Foundation (RMF) would support "UNICEF's efforts in fighting for children's rights, especially in the area of child trafficking" (UNICEF 2011). Established in 2000 as a 501c3 nonprofit, the RMF was originally formed to help children with disabilities in Puerto Rico (and, later, increase access to musical instruments and help youth at risk for entering gangs). Within the RMF, Martin established People for Children in 2004 as the foundation's principal project, and its mission is to "denounce human trafficking and educate about its existence through research and community initiatives, anchored in the defense of children and youth rights" (RMF 2021). Focusing mainly on human trafficking in Central America, and working with a team of approximately ten staff, the RMF's Form 990 reported total revenues of $1.8 million in 2019 (primarily from contributions, grants, and program service revenue), which funds programs such as Centro Tau (a holistic center for youth), research and education, working to make online environments safer for children, and creating PSAs, among other work discussed later in this chapter.

Ashton Kutcher

Christopher Ashton Kutcher was born on February 7, 1978, in Cedar Rapids, Iowa, where his mother worked at Procter & Gamble and his father was a factory worker at General Mills. He grew up in a conservative Catholic family, and when his parents divorced when he was thirteen, he and his siblings (a fraternal twin brother, Michael, and an older sister, Tausha) moved with their mother to Homestead, Iowa. Kutcher married actor Demi Moore in 2005, and they divorced in 2013. In 2015 he married actor Mila Kunis, who he met on *That 70s Show*, and they have two children: a daughter, Wyatt Isabelle Kutcher, born in October 2014, and a son, Dimitri Portwood Kutcher, born in November 2016.

Even as they share somewhat similar family backgrounds, Kutcher's path to fame was much less intentional than Martin's. After attending Clear Creek Amana High School, Kutcher matriculated at the University of Iowa to study bio-chemical engineering in 1996. However, he never completed his degree. In 1997, while he was at a bar with his friends, a modeling scout discovered him (ABC News 2011). Kutcher signed with the Next Agency and was soon appearing in commercials for Calvin Klein and modeling in Paris and Milan. Following this success, Kutcher moved to Los Angeles and after his first audition, he won the role of Michael Kelso in *That '70s Show,* which he played from 1998 to 2006. Since then, he went on to star in and/or produce numerous TV series such as *Two and A Half Men* (2011–2015), *Punk'd* (2003–2012), and films such as *The Butterfly Effect* (2004), *What Happens in Vegas* (2008), and *New Year's Eve* (2011), among others.

In addition to his acting career, Kutcher has parlayed his fame and its attendant resources into media and technology investing. In 2000, he founded a production company, Katalyst Media, through which he connected to many Silicon Valley venture capital firms, and in 2009, at the request of billionaire venture capitalist Marc Andreessen, he invested $1 million in Skype, eighteen months before Microsoft bought the company (Hoffower 2020). In 2010, he co-founded the venture capital firm A-Grade Investments with talent manager Guy Oseary and businessman Ron Burkle, growing $30 million to $250 million over six years by investing in tech companies such as Skype, Spotify, Airbnb, Uber, and Foursquare (O'Malley Greenburg 2016). Kutcher became a regular feature on technology panels (see figure 8), and in 2015, he and Oseary took a more formal approach to investing, founding the venture capital firm Sound Ventures with $100 million from Liberty Media. As a result of these efforts, Kutcher has invested more than $3 billion into startups and participated in 177 funding rounds over the past decade (Uranga 2020).

Like Martin, Kutcher had no exposure to human trafficking through his entertainment career, and he was already quite famous when he decided to get involved. As I document in chapter 2 and elsewhere (Majic 2018), Kutcher began speaking out about human trafficking, and the sex trafficking of children, in 2008 with his then-wife Demi Moore, after "witnessing" this crime in the Dateline documentary *Children For Sale* and creating the Demi and Ashton Foundation (DNA). However, his anti-trafficking work shifted to reflect his technology interests after he and Moore separated in 2011. DNA was renamed Thorn Digital Defenders (hereafter referred to as Thorn) in 2012, and its goal became to "build technology to defend children from sexual abuse" (Thorn 2021e). With a team of staff and contractors working in twenty-one states, Thorn's 2019 Form 990 lists $61.8 million in total revenue (up from $7.8 million in 2018), primarily from contributions and grants. Thorn partners with law enforcement officers in the United States and

FIGURE 8. Charlie Rose and Ashton Kutcher during TechCrunch Disrupt, New York, May 2020. Photo by Joe Corrigan/Getty Images for AOL/CC-BY-2.0.

Canada as well as nonprofits, technology companies, and donors to develop and disseminate Spotlight, a technology that seeks "to improve the effectiveness and efficiency of domestic sex trafficking investigations and increase the number of children who are identified and connected with help resources" (Thorn 2021c). Thorn is also developing Safer, a technology they tout as "a complete solution to help stop child sexual abuse material from spreading across your platform" (Safer 2021). (I discuss these technologies in more detail below).

NARRATIVES OF HUMAN TRAFFICKING

Despite their distinct trajectories to fame, Martin and Kutcher were motivated to engage in anti-trafficking advocacy after witnessing it in various ways, and they performed the bulk of their work through their foundations, which they created with their considerable resources. In the following pages, I illustrate how personal and temporal-contextual factors variously shaped and are reflected in Martin's and Kutcher's representations of human trafficking, which reify and complicate the dominant narrative.

Martin's personal experiences, as well as the timing of his engagement and his organizational affiliations, shaped and are reflected in his anti-trafficking performances. When Martin first became aware of human trafficking in the early 2000s, topical research was only emerging and focused mainly on the sex trafficking of women and girls (Weitzer 2007, 2005). While Martin was likely exposed to this research in his initial online searches, he also encountered other information about the issue during his travels and engagement with international organizations such as UNICEF. As a result, Martin has largely defined and characterized human trafficking broadly, in line with the 2000 UN Protocol. In many of his reports and speeches, he often refers to it as he does in his memoir, as "a crime that happens on various levels: ... includ[ing] factories that exploit their workers, prostitution, forced labor, sexual exploitation of minors, servitude, and organ trafficking" (Martin 2010, 192). As such, human trafficking is not merely an American problem, but, according to Martin, "an epidemic that affects the whole world" (190). Although he acknowledges that the "precise magnitude of the problem is difficult to ascertain because definitions vary and trafficking is a clandestine business" (Martin 2012), he has characterized it as a "massive and powerful monster" (Martin 2010, 201) that is also extremely lucrative. Testifying before the House Committee on International Relations of the US Congress, sharply dressed in a dark suit with his hair slicked back, he claimed that "Human trafficking generates anywhere from $12 billion to $32 billion around the world every year, and is surpassed only by the trafficking of drugs and arms" (Martin 2006).

Even as Martin has promoted a broader understanding of human trafficking's forms and scope than the dominant narrative, he is most passionate about child victims. In his memoir, he roots this concern in his personal experience, namely his time with Menudo; however, the band's extreme working conditions and the alleged abuse its young members suffered—which, one could argue, placed them on a continuum with other children who experience labor trafficking—did not motivate this interest. Instead, Martin writes, Menudo introduced him to UNICEF, which named him and his fellow band members Ambassadors for the organization. In this role, they invited children who were orphans and living on the streets to their shows, and by seeing the hardships *they* faced, Martin "began to understand how many children live in other parts of the world" (Martin 2010, 38). As a result, when he turned his attention to human trafficking, he did not (contra the dominant narrative) focus solely on white, American-born girls who are trafficked into the sex industry. Instead, as he explained passionately to Congress in 2006, before the Committee on International Relations,

> Child trafficking is a global nightmare.... in Mexico City more than 5,000 children are involved in prostitution, pornography and sex tourism. In Thailand, there are about 200,000 children involved in the sex trade and 86 percent of the patrons are local. In Africa, 200,000 boys and girls are trafficked and forced to work on plantations, mines, fishing boats and brothels each year.

Martin has reified the dominant narrative by de-emphasizing their potential agency, as was evident in 2004, when his foundation, in partnership with the Inter-American Development Bank, launched "Slaves of A New Era," a series of thirty-second PSAs to "create awareness about of the existence of child exploitation" (RMF and Inter American Development Bank 2008). In one of the ads, dramatic piano music opens and shadowy pictures of children's faces flash by as Martin's voice says, in a serious tone, "children of endless nights, their faces devoid of hope, their voice can no longer be heard. These are the slaves of a new era." Martin then emerges against a background of dirty clothes hanging on a line (among other markers of a dingy space), looks to the camera, and says "To stop the sexual exploitation of children: it's time, we act." According to the RMF's YouTube link, this PSA reached a wide audience and was distributed "in a mass media campaign in Latin American and Puerto Rico." The RMF also claimed (without providing any specific evidence) that the campaign was effective, stating that three years after the release "the subject is no longer taboo. Education is Freedom" (RMF and Inter American Development Bank. 2008).

Regarding the causes of trafficking, Martin both reflects and complicates the dominant narrative's emphasis on bad individuals and organized crime. In his early anti-trafficking work, Martin claimed that both individuals *and* poverty created vulnerabilities to trafficking, particularly for girls. In his memoir, for example, he mentions a "fourteen year old girl who had been sold and raped" in Cambodia (Martin 2010, 198). According to Martin, her abductors told her that they could help her become a model so she could make money to help her ailing grandmother afford the medications and treatment she needed. As Martin described it, "They were offering her an opportunity of a lifetime and, on top of it, a solution for her grandmother's illness. How could she say no?" But instead, "they kidnapped her and put her in a brothel, where a disgusting man raped her, got her pregnant, and gave her HIV" (198). Claiming that "there are millions of children with similar stories" (198), Martin told Congress (2006), "Traffickers have many different faces. They are members of sophisticated networks of organized crime.... They are family members, they are friends of the victims, and very often they are former victims of trafficking themselves." In addition to implicating this combination of individual, economic, and criminal causes, Martin (2010, 201) has also implicated the government's failure to implement anti-human trafficking legislation, writing, "It doesn't matter how many laws and regulations are in place to control human trafficking; there are too many countries in which laws are simply not obeyed. In other countries, laws are outdated."

After a number of years raising awareness about human trafficking globally, Martin shifted his focus and, hence, narrative, to his home of Puerto Rico. Even as it is a territory of the United States, which collects data about human trafficking through annual Trafficking in Persons reports, "specific statistics about human trafficking in Puerto Rico do not exist" (Hernández and Hernández Angueira 2010, 1). However, Martin believed that various factors "suggest the high potential for trafficking and exploitation in Puerto Rico" (Hernández and Hernández Angueira 2010, 1). To explore this suggestion, since 2010 the RMF has collaborated with academic institutions, government agencies, and other nonprofit organizations to produce three research reports on the issue: *Human Trafficking in Puerto Rico: An Invisible Challenge* (Hernández and Hernández Angueira 2010), *Human Trafficking: Modern Slavery in Puerto Rico* (Hernández and Hernández Angueira 2014), and *Gender Violence and Trafficking* (Hernández Angueira and Hernández 2017). Relying largely on interviews with government officials, NGO leaders, and victims, and reviews of existing research, these reports represent human trafficking's forms, victims, and causes in Puerto Rico in ways that both reflect and complicate the dominant narrative.

The RMF's reports include a wide scope of activities under the term "domestic trafficking"—that is, trafficking within the territory and its neighboring regions—ranging from labor trafficking into domestic work to "purchased marriage," among others (Hernández Angueira and Hernández 2017; Hernández and Hernández Angueira 2010, 2014). The reports also show that, contra the dominant narrative, persons of all genders may be vulnerable to trafficking in Puerto Rico. However, the RMF also reinforces the dominant narrative through its reliance on the 2000 UN Protocol, whose ideological framework furthers "a paternalistic discourse that infantilizes women and deprives them of agency, reinforcing the image of young, innocent victims deceived into prostitution"—and by arguing that "all prostitution is sexual violence and exploitation of women and girls" (Cabezas and Alcázar Campos 2016, 44). In just one illustrative example, a RMF-funded report argues that "Although there are no statistics or official reports to corroborate this data, it is believed that many Dominican women connect with Dominican and/or Puerto Rican male partners, who turn them into easy prey for illicit activities including prostitution, forced labor, household services and others" (Hernández and Hernández Angueira 2010, 7).

Regarding the causes of human trafficking in Puerto Rico, while Martin and the RMF implicate Dominican and Puerto Rican men, their reports name family members and the foster care system as the most frequent cause, stating that "Often the exploiter is a family member, a member of a foster family or someone in charge of the foster home. The exploiter could also be a neighbor, particularly in cases of prostitution and other forms of sexual exploitation" (Hernández and Hernández Angueira 2010, 1). Additionally, even as tourism is not a large part of the territory's economy, the RMF's reports also emphasized that "sex tourism," broadly defined, is another significant cause of human trafficking.

> Puerto Rico is a destination for sex tourism and a transit point for women and children from other Caribbean islands and from the interior of the Island for the purpose of sexual exploitation. Cases have also been reported of foreigners, both men and women, who are trafficked into Puerto Rico for labor exploitation (Hernández and Hernández Angueira 2010, 1).

In addition to emphasizing that families, foster care, and tourism create vulnerabilities to human trafficking, the RMF's research also names a broader range of complex causes that include some combination of "social inequality, gender discrimination, poverty, lack of education, minimal government intervention, and other socio-economic factors" (Hernández and Hernández Angueira 2010, 8). Although Martin and the RMF never state this outright, these complex causes are rooted in Puerto Rico's colonial relationship to the United States, which, as I detail further below, has limited Puerto Rico's economic development and left many of its residents vulnerable to poverty and exploitative working conditions, including human trafficking.

Kutcher: First Girls, Then All Children

In contrast to Martin, Ashton Kutcher has offered a more limited representation of human trafficking. As I show in the following pages, a combination of temporal and contextual factors, including his technology interests and organizational affiliations, have shaped and are reflected in his reification of the dominant narrative, which has shifted from emphasizing girls to all children, and from implicating individual men to naming "internet technology" as the main cause.

As noted throughout this book, the timing of a celebrity's engagement with an issue often shapes his or her related activism. When Ashton Kutcher first began speaking out about sex trafficking, the global anti-trafficking movement was well established and the dominant narrative was circulating through everything from Congressional hearings to movies like *Taken*. Therefore, Kutcher and Moore also conveyed this narrative in their initial activism, most notably through the Real Men and DHS videos, discussed in chapter 2. However, changes in Kutcher's personal life and his technology interests coincided with and shaped his subsequent anti-trafficking performances. In 2011, rumors surfaced that Kutcher was cheating on Moore, and they separated that same year, divorcing in 2013 (Riley 2019). During this time, Kutcher's technology investments grew and he became the first person to amass one million Twitter followers, tweeting often about trafficking, which likely benefited his investment in the platform (Tiku 2013; Haynes 2014; *The Guardian* 2009). Soon, the DNA Foundation was renamed "Thorn Digital Defenders" (thereby removing Demi's and Ashton's names) and it expanded its mandate to "partner across the tech industry, government, and NGOs and leverage technology to combat predatory behavior, rescue victims, and protect vulnerable children" (Thorn 2021f). The Thorn website lists Demi Moore as a board member "emeritus."

Positioned as what Kelly Gates (2011) terms a tech solutionist moral entrepreneur—one who presents himself as a rescuer to humanitarian problems by framing them as technological ones—Kutcher's anti-trafficking performances soon moved beyond the dominant narrative of human trafficking.[2] The Thorn website now states that "depictions in films like *Taken* don't hold up when we start talking about what sex trafficking actually looks like" (Thorn 2020b). Instead, "the reality of this issue is that it's very, very complex," and so they now focus on the broader "intersection of child sexual abuse and technology" (Thorn 2020a). As a result, Kutcher and Thorn no longer solely emphasize girl victims, noting instead that that sex trafficking is something that can truly happen to anyone (Thorn 2020a).

Regarding the causes of trafficking, Kutcher and Thorn both reject and reinforce his earlier emphasis on individual, predatory men as the main cause of trafficking. On the one hand, the Thorn website indicates that "When the term "sex trafficking" is used, it's easy to conjure mental images of men in masks jumping out of an unmarked van and abducting victims in a dark alleyway . . . [but] it's actually a longer process of grooming and coercion that can last from months to years before a victim enters trafficking" (Thorn 2020a). Here Thorn cites their research, which found that "88% of victims say . . . their trafficker told them they would take care of them, 83% respond[ed] that the trafficker bought them things, and 73% not[ed] that the trafficker told them they loved them" (Thorn Digital Defenders and Boucher 2018; Thorn 2020a). But on the other hand, they do acknowledge that a range of intersecting structural factors *also* create vulnerabilities for youth, noting, for example, that "LGBTQ youth face higher rates of discrimination, violence, and economic instability than their non-LGBTQ peers," and that "family rejection, lack of support systems, and financial challenges each offer heightened opportunities for traffickers to step in and exploit LGBTQ+ youth" (Thorn 2020b).

Among these structural factors, however, Kutcher and Thorn ultimately emphasize a second, much narrower cause of human trafficking that aligns with his interests: internet technology. As I and others document elsewhere (Anti-Trafficking Review 2020; Majic 2020), while technological developments such as telephones, pagers, and mobile devices have expanded the avenues for sexual exploration and communication, the internet has had the most significant effect on the sex industry by lowering the cost of entry (for example, by reducing dependence on third parties to find clients), enhancing safety by providing sex workers with tools to screen their clients, and fostering sex workers' solidarity by helping them reach out to, network, and organize with other sex workers (Cunningham and Kendall 2011; Bernstein 2007b; MacPhail, Scott, and Minichiello 2015; Weitzer 2013; Smith 2011). However, according to some, these technological developments have also increased risks for sex trafficking. As anti-prostitution advocate Melissa Farley and her colleagues write, "Adapted by traffickers, pimps, and pornographers, the global reach of the internet has facilitated sex buyers' access to prostituted women and children, thereby increasing sex trafficking" (Farley, Franzblau, and Kennedy 2014, 1044). Although these claims have never been systematically verified, online technologies have "become the new battleground spaces upon which longstanding disagreements about sex work, human trafficking, and the sexual exploitation of youth are enacted" (Thakor and boyd 2013, 279).

Kutcher and Thorn have positioned themselves as key actors on this battleground, stating, "Technology is playing an increasing role in grooming and controlling victims of [domestic minor sex trafficking]" (Thorn Digital Defenders and Boucher 2018). With data from their own studies, Thorn claims that while "45% of [youth] entering the life in 2015 reported meeting their trafficker face to face, [t]he remaining 55% reported use of text, website, or app" (6). Furthermore, as Thorn added on its blog, after they meet their traffickers, technology remains a factor in victims' exploitation. "The majority of minor victims of sex trafficking (69%) had access to the Internet while being trafficked, and the vast majority of those with access (90%) used the same social media platforms we all visit every day—both due to being forced to write their own online trafficking ads, but also with access to the same social apps we all use to post pictures and connect with friends" (Thorn 2020a). In light of this, Thorn's website declares that, "Technology has made it easier to harm kids" (Thorn 2021d).

SOLUTIONS AND FEMINIST IDEOLOGIES

Below I examine Martin's and Kutcher's solutions to human trafficking, reading from them a range of feminist interests and ideologies. As noted at the outset of this chapter, scholars and other commentators have accused celebrity feminists, and MCFs in particular, of promoting a bland version of feminism that does little more than make vague statements about gender equality. However, Martin and Kutcher indicate something different: by offering individual, NGO, state, and technologically oriented solutions, Martin and Kutcher promote a range of neo-liberal, carceral, structurally intersectional, and cyber feminist ideologies.

Martin, Kutcher, and (Neo)Liberal Feminism

Despite taking on anti-trafficking activism at different times and focusing on children in different regions of the world, Martin and Kutcher offer many similar solutions to human trafficking that confirm scholarly and activist accusations that celebrity feminists—and MCFs in particular—are prone to promoting neoliberally-informed ideologies. Echoing the neoliberal logic that state failure necessitates such responses (Brown 2015), an RMF report declares that

> During the last decade, *the failure of the State* to bring people together has prompted an increased presence of NGOs in Puerto Rico. These organizations play a major role in defining solutions for citizens, sometimes complementing the actions of government institutions, and often becoming more effective than the governmental agencies themselves. Their closeness to the people and their ability to understand the psychology of the communities and the urgency of the actions of community leaders all add to the value of the work of NGOs (Hernández and Hernández Angueira 2010, 31, emphasis added).

The RMF is among the few NGOs in Puerto Rico responding to human trafficking through its programs such as Centro Tau, noted earlier. Reflecting neoliberal logics of individual motivation and improvement, Centro Tau participants "are in charge of their educational plans so they can create the world they aspire to live in," and in an implicit comparison to failed state-run efforts, the RMF asserts that "Centro TAU offers participants an inspiring oasis where they can be children. A friendly and professional staff provides a comprehensive and personalized education based on the belief that everyone can develop their natural abilities if they are given real opportunities founded on love and respect."[3]

Kutcher also circulates this neoliberally-inflected feminist ideology by emphasizing how Thorn, a lean and efficient nonprofit, will help children: "We are a small but mighty team. Thorn is a growing full-time team of staff and contractors, working from over 14 states to unleash the power of technology on behalf of vulnerable children" (Thorn 2021e). Like Martin, Kutcher sees his NGO as essential to improving the work of government agencies and actors, noting, "Our work doesn't exist in isolation. We partner across the tech industry, government and NGOs and leverage technology to combat predatory behavior, rescue victims, and protect vulnerable children" (Thorn 2021a).

Through their NGOs, Martin and Kutcher also promote individual and public issue awareness, thereby furthering a liberal feminist ideology, long promoted by Western feminists, that "seeing" leads to social change (Whittier 2017). Martin's most prominent effort here has included a combination of public engagement, research and education activities. As Martin

(2008) stated at the Vienna Forum, while "changing attitudes and human behavior … is very difficult … global awareness [is a way] to inform the world of this heinous crime and mobilize people." To this end, Martin and the RMF have sponsored numerous awareness campaigns including "Slaves of a New Era," described earlier, and "Llama y Vive" (Call and Live), a 2006 campaign that established and promoted human trafficking prevention and victim protection hotlines "in Costa Rica, Ecuador, Mexico, Nicaragua and Peru as well as in in the Hispanic community of Washington, DC" and the Dominican Republic (Martin 2012). As he turned his efforts to Puerto Rico, Martin also waged specific public awareness campaigns here such as "Contrata," a 2016 advertising initiative led by Arteria Publicidad and the RMF to "teach the Puerto Rican population and the rest of the world about the modalities of this crime" during Puerto Rico's first Human Trafficking Prevention and Awareness Month (RMF 2016).

Such efforts illustrate the ways in which celebrity feminists, and MCFs in particular, may promote individual awareness as a solution to human trafficking in regions across the globe. According to Martin, these awareness campaigns have sparked individuals to act. As Martin (2008) told the Vienna Forum, "Dozens of lives have been saved through [Llama y Vive] and we've received more than 12,000 phone calls fostered by a force of more than five dozen investigations. The toll free number offers a call to action that enables the public to provide valuable information about suspected traffickers." Since I was not able to speak with Martin or anyone else from the RMF, I have no information about what actually happened to those whose lives were allegedly saved.

Ashton Kutcher has also supported individual awareness as a solution to human trafficking, in furtherance of a (neo)liberally-inflected feminist ideology, especially since DNA became Thorn. For example, in its "Survivor Insights" report, Thorn indicates how schools may promote human trafficking awareness by quoting a survivor who stated that, "A teacher would have been the most helpful to either give me the number [of the helpline] or call for me" (Thorn Digital Defenders and Boucher 2018, 10). Similarly, Kutcher has also promoted individual awareness and action in families by encouraging parents to "talk to your kids about sextortion and grooming; report trafficking activity and abusive content; talk to your representatives about child sex trafficking legislation; [and] donate to organizations addressing child sex trafficking" (Thorn 2021a).

Beyond the neoliberally-oriented solutions that scholars predict of celebrities (Evans and Riley 2013; Kapoor 2012), Martin and Kutcher also support and promote state and technological responses to human trafficking, thereby promoting more structurally intersectional ideologies that seek to expose and address the power relations that further human trafficking and undermine gender equality. In Martin's case, even as he blamed state inaction for human trafficking, he also acknowledges that "governments and law enforcement also have a very important role to play to ensure that children are protected around the world from this from exploitation" (2008). In 2006, his Congressional testimony requested—even "begged"—for state action.

> At a Federal level, I beg the Congress to take action on establishing a Division on Child Trafficking. Number two, expanding Federal funding initiatives to prevent child exploitation on the Internet. The Internet is really good because we can educate, but at the same time pedophiles go in there and they enter your house without permission. And number three, increasing the funding for anti-trafficking assistance to foreign governments and nongovernmental organizations.

Later, based on the RMF's research, he also called on US government agencies to improve their anti-trafficking operations, calling for the establishment of a "clear relationship between the actions of federal authorities and the State government in terms of their respective jurisdictions and the limits of their actions, clearly defining [human trafficking] at the national level through a legal ordinance and thus empowering local authorities with a clear policy to better prosecute the crime" (Hernández and Hernández Angueira 2010, 34–35). Furthermore, the RMF recommended a "training and guidance program for federal authorities—particularly ICE and the State Department—and NGOs about the protocols to be followed to better detect and fight human trafficking its different forms" (Hernández and Hernández Angueira 2010, 35).

As Martin turned his attention to human trafficking in Puerto Rico, he also called for stronger government action here to define and address the problem. As the RMF declared, there is an "urgent need to define human trafficking in the specific context of Puerto Rico . . . [and] formal procedures must be established in the compilation of data and statistics regarding human trafficking that will enable us to propose adequate public policies to protect vulnerable populations, especially children" (Hernández and Hernández Angueira 2010, 34). In addition, the RMF has called for the creation of a "structured or defined governmental agency in Puerto Rico that is specifically charged with the issue of human trafficking" (Hernández and Hernández Angueira 2010, 34) that would coordinate with nonprofits and help direct public policy and assist in the coordination of governmental efforts to combat human trafficking. In addition to this agency, Martin has also advocated for a range of legal reforms in Puerto Rico specifically, noting in that "although the United States passed the Trafficking Victims Protection Act in 2000, there are no comprehensive local laws to combat this crime in Puerto Rico" (Martin 2012). Among the many possibly legal reforms to address structural vulnerabilities to human trafficking, the RMF has supported those targeting child welfare laws, namely the Comprehensive Child Welfare Law No. 276 of 2008, which states, "everyone ... aware or suspicious that a minor has been or is at risk of becoming a victim of mistreatment, institutional mistreatment, negligence or institutional negligence [is] under the obligation of fulfilling their duties and taking affirmative action." The RMF also notes the inadequacy of this law, writing that "while this legislation addresses corrective measures to address the problem [of children at risk], it still ignores one serious dimension of the crime: the trafficking of children" (Hernández and Hernández Angueira 2010, 19). Altogether, even as Martin supports carceral solutions to human trafficking, his calls to reform and restructure a wide range of state agencies and improve their work with other sectors of society indicates how celebrities may promote structurally-oriented feminist ideologies through their activism.

Kutcher's Cyberfeminism

Since DNA became Thorn, Kutcher has offered many technological solutions to human trafficking; in so doing, he conveys a cyberfeminist ideology that celebrates technology, and internet technology in particular, as liberatory for women and girls (Wajcman 2007, 2009). At first glance, Kutcher's support for technological solutions to human trafficking may seem counterintuitive: after all, Thorn identifies internet technologies as a major *cause* of this problem. However, internet technologies may also disrupt human trafficking. Online sites that advertise sexual services help law enforcement investigate trafficking cases through facial recognition software, predictive analytics, and mapping techniques, and anti-trafficking advocates also use connective technologies to mobilize their networks, disseminate anti-trafficking messages, and fundraise, among other activities (Dixon 2013; Musto and boyd 2014; Thakor and boyd 2013). Kutcher and Thorn have acknowledged and embraced technology's liberatory potential here, stating that "While technology has made it easier for traffickers to exploit these communities, it can also be pointed towards defending children from these crimes" (Thorn 2020b). Therefore, it is essential to "acknowledge[] the quickly shifting landscape in any area involving technology" and "continuously review how technology is used by traffickers, victims, and buyers" (Thorn Digital Defenders and Boucher 2018, 9).

Among the many ways to use technology here, Thorn has committed specifically to "building tools to eliminate child sex trafficking" (Thorn 2020b), and to date, its most notable project is "Spotlight," which it describes on its website (Thorn 2021b) as

> a free, industry leading tool available to any law enforcement agent working on human trafficking cases. It helps law enforcement prioritize leads by using machine learning algorithms and link analysis to surface connections and relationships between disparate data sources. With Spotlight, officers get greater insight into the full historical and geographical reach of a victim's trafficking situation. Spotlight is helping law enforcement find more kids faster and stop future abuse.

Yet indicating what Kelley Cotter (2021, 1) terms the "black box problem"—the opacity of algorithmic technologies resulting from corporate secrecy and technical complexity—it is difficult to understand how Spotlight works, exactly, to eliminate human trafficking and protect children. When I visited Thorn's "Learn about Spotlight" link on their website to sign up for an introduction, it told me that only law enforcement is eligible for this, and Thorn never replied to my specific inquiries about Spotlight's operation and efficacy.[4] Kutcher himself is also unwilling to explain the technology, even as he has promoted it to Congress, stating here that, "in an effort to protect [Spotlight's] capacity over time, I won't give much detail about what it does" (Kutcher 2017). However, Violet Blue, writing for the online publication *engadget* (2019), did find that Spotlight works by "scraping" websites and forums to build an archive of millions of escort ads that law enforcement can then search and filter "based on phone numbers, email, key words, age, location."[5] So, for example, if law enforcement officials found a number of escort ads featuring pictures of girls who appear to be under the age of eighteen, they could investigate these ads as potential sex trafficking cases.

Even if Spotlight's precise mechanics may be unclear, Kutcher and Thorn insist on its efficacy. As Kutcher told the US Senate Committee on Foreign Relations (2017),

> [Spotlight's] working. In six months, with 25% of our users reporting, we've identified over 6,000 trafficking victims, 2,000 of which are minors. This tool is in the hands of 4,000 law enforcement officials in 900 agencies, and we're reducing the investigation time by 60%. This tool is effective. It's efficient. It's nimble. It's better. It's smarter.

Kutcher illustrated Spotlight's cyber-feminist ideological orientation with a story of a young girl who was allegedly "freed" from her traffickers by this technology. "Amy" was "a fifteen-year-old girl in Oakland" who met a man online. Soon after meeting him in person, "Amy was abused, raped, and forced into trafficking. She was sold for sex." Sadly, Kutcher claimed, this is not an isolated incident: "[t]he only unusual thing is that Amy was found and returned to her family within three days using the software that we created, a tool called Spotlight." This story indicates how internet technology may increase children's vulnerabilities to exploitation and abuse, but in telling it, Kutcher also furthers the notion that technologies like Spotlight are "the agent of change" (Wajcman 2007, 288) and play a role in shaping a new form of society that is potentially liberating, especially for women and girls, while subordinating and apprehending the men who potentially harm them (Wajcman 2009; Plant 1997). However, as I discuss later in this chapter, many sex workers have challenged Spotlight's (and other related technologies') gender-liberationist claims.

TO WHAT EFFECT: MASCULINITIES IN PLAY

By spending their considerable celebrity capital on anti-trafficking activism, Ricky Martin and Ashton Kutcher have positioned themselves as MCFs—individuals who scholars have identified and critiqued as post-feminist figures who are well-resourced, conventionally attractive, and take feminism into account while also undermining claims to gender equality in various ways (Cobb 2015). Looking at Kutcher's and Martin's anti-trafficking activism over time indicates the range of ways in which they affirm and complicate this understanding of the MCF, and celebrity feminism more generally.

When we look at Martin's and Kutcher's anti-trafficking activism, we see that they often represent and promote solutions to human trafficking that potentially undermine gender equality, like many of their women-identified celebrity feminist peers. Both men have promoted the dominant narrative and focused on vulnerable children—the most sympathetic of victims—and they variously attribute their exploitation to bad men, criminal networks, state failure, and internet technology. In response, Martin and Kutcher have offered solutions that many scholars and activists argue are extremely limited for helping victims, regardless of their gender or age. For example, while NGOs like the RMF and Thorn have waged campaigns to raise awareness about human trafficking, these also offered simplistic solutions to a highly complex problem (Andrijasevic and Mai 2016). While it is certainly important for individuals to recognize a trafficking situation and know how to respond to it, placing the burden on the public to identify human trafficking victims is a limited solution at best. Among other problems, victims may be unwilling to speak with authorities or others about their experiences because of stigma, fear of deportation, or many other reasons (Chapkis 2003, 2005).

Yet while these criticisms are valid, they are also, for lack of better phrase, easy to make, and they have been leveled against celebrity and non-celebrity anti-trafficking efforts alike for decades now. What are some *other* limits and possibilities of their anti-trafficking efforts? To answer this question, in the following pages I examine how Martin and Kutcher reify and complicate dominant gender ideologies. By taking on human trafficking and the trafficking of children, specifically, which has long been viewed in public discourse as a "women's concern," both men variously reify and complicate hegemonic masculinity. In the contemporary United States, this masculinity is "associated with military heroism, corporate power, sports achievement, action-adventure movie stars, and being tough, aggressive, and macho," and it is reproduced in Hollywood films, video games, and other forms of media culture (Kellner 2008, 18; see also Johnson 2014).

As Anna Szörényi and Penelope Eate (2014) argue, hegemonic masculinity, embodied by the middle-class white American man, is in crisis, and human trafficking is the means for rescuing it. Namely, "this [hegemonically masculine] man, his privilege confronted by assertive women, sexual liberation, and racial and ethnic others, appears as a metaphor for the endangered global superiority of the USA in the age of postcolonialism, and trafficking emerges as an occasion for managing this crisis by offering an easily defined enemy which can be punished with impunity" (619–20). Indeed, we see this (re)assertion of masculinity everywhere, from films such as *Taken,* to Gary Haugen and the International Justice Mission's efforts to locate, raid, and rescue trafficking victims (see CNN 2017). As the following pages show, while Martin's and Kutcher's high-profile anti-human trafficking efforts assert this hegemonic American masculinity, they also complicate it through their positions as sexual and ethnic minorities (Martin) and their emphasis on technological solutions (Kutcher).

Martin on the Margins

As an artist from Puerto Rico, Ricky Martin has long existed on the margins of masculinity,[6] including both American hegemonic masculinity and certain stereotypes of Latino masculinity. In particular, this means the "Latin lover," who is "is more sexually sophisticated, has more sexual allure, and more seductive power than do other men" and is also a "'hypersexual, aggressive, brutish, 'macho' Latino male" (Asencio and Acosta 2010, 1–2). One the one hand, Martin's engagement with these masculinities helped to establish him as a global celebrity. As an artist performing on stage, he and his production team deliberately worked to constitute his persona as the alluring "Latin Lover." Acting hunky and sexy, Martin wore tight clothes on stage and on screen and crooned lyrics such as "I wanna be your lover/your only Latin Lover" in hits such as "Shake Your Bon-Bon" (from his 1999 album *Ricky Martin*). These artistic choices fueled his ascension to global super-stardom, and he crossed over into the massive American music market with intergenerational and inter-ethnic appeal (Quiroga 2000; Quiroga and López Frank 2010). But on the other hand, Martin's rising global celebrity invoked questions about his sexuality. As Marysol Asencio and Katie Acosta (2010, 2) write, despite his talent and versatility as an entertainer, the media became "preoccupied with his sexuality on and offstage." By playing the "sexy Latin" pop star on stage while "refusing to display or discuss his conquests of women," Martin fueled suspicions about his sexuality in the media and popular culture more broadly (2).

Martin's entrance into the anti-trafficking space in the early 2000s could be read as a strategy to divert the media from his sexuality and assert his masculinity, and his *American* masculinity in particular, especially within the highly charged contours of identity discourses in the United States, which have long troped Latinx people as alien and/or threatening to the US national imaginary (Allatson 2015). Since at least the 1840s, following the Mexican-American War, and as American employers such as railroad companies recruited Mexicans as a source of cheap labor, Latinx people have been crucial to the American economy. Yet everything from their language to their skin color was a pretext for discrimination, and so they have faced mob violence, forced deportations (when Anglo-Americans accused Mexicans and other foreigners of stealing their jobs during the Great Depression), and school segregation, to name just some examples (Blakemore 2018). As Carmen Lugo-Lugo (2012, 69) writes, in the post 9/11 era, there existed "a general distrust of bodies deemed non- and un-American" and within that climate, Latino bodies were again "seen as immigrants and immigrants were seen as a threat to Americanness." Therefore, even as Martin, a Puerto Rican, was born a US citizen and has a primary residence in Miami, as a Latino he was also seen as "socially, culturally, and legally foreign to the country" (Lugo-Lugo 2012, 78–79). Furthermore, questions about his sexual orientation enhanced his "foreign-ness," particularly at a time when LGBTQ+ persons lacked access to full citizenship in many spheres of life (De Orio 2017). By taking on human trafficking as his celebrity cause, then, Martin arguably positioned himself as "the good Latino"—that is, the affluent, authentic, cosmopolitan consumer subject who embraces mainstream American values, as opposed to the "bad" Latino who is poor, marginal, unemployed, and/or politically active (Dávila 2001, 2008).

Martin thus asserted his masculine American-ness by engaging in what Elena Shih (2016, 66) terms "vigilante rescue," where he was empowered as a non-state actor "not through professional skills or legal authority, but rather through merging American concern with human trafficking with moral panics concerning race, class, and migration as markers of sex trafficking." Martin played this vigilante role in India in 2002, when he allegedly rescued girls from sex trafficking—an action that aligned with the broader narrative of "saving" women and girls from their "cultures," which was so popular among many American leaders in the post-9/11 era (Philips 2019, 957). In India, Martin further reified his role as the all-knowing American masculine vigilante by, as Robert Heynen and Emily van der Meulen (2021) write, seemingly ignoring the efforts of India's many sex worker rights groups such as the Durbar Mahila Samanwaya Committee, the largest sex worker-led organization in the world. Founded in 1992, this organization's extensive activities include "supporting children and youth living in poverty while challenging the criminalization of sex work." But, they add, "The Durbar Committee rejects the politics of rescue espoused by many anti-trafficking activists from the Global North" (9). The US government, however, affirmed Martin's vigilante rescue politics: he was one of the first celebrities invited to speak about human trafficking in front of Congress and be rewarded for his anti-trafficking work. In 2005, the State Department named Martin as one of its "Heroes Acting to End Modern Slavery." Praising his global awareness work and the efforts of the RMF, the 2005 Trafficking in Persons report described him as follows: "Lending a powerful voice to vulnerable children who are unable to speak for themselves, he's reaching tens of millions of people around the world" (US Department of State 2005, 39).

Martin's role as the "good Latino"—the independent, affluent male citizen who supports and helps to further the American government's anti-trafficking efforts—has thus limited his promotion of gender equality. In this role, he has advanced dominant institutional approaches—namely, carceral efforts to fight trafficking, such as increased support for anti-trafficking enforcement through ICE and through criminal and other laws to fight trafficking in Puerto Rico. By promoting these efforts, Martin ignores years of feminist activism and research showing that the immigration and criminal justice enforcement systems tend to respond poorly to problems like human trafficking and other issues of gender based violence, often *increasing* violence against children and women (and immigrant and women of color in particular) in the process (K. Arnold 2015).

Of course, Martin's support for carceral solutions is not unique among celebrities and others in the anti-trafficking movement. However, he advances these as what Ramón Grosfoguel (2003, 145) terms a "racialized/colonial subject . . . of the U.S. empire and of the U.S. domination of Latino Caribbean countries." In so doing, Martin draws our attention to Puerto Rico's colonial status—a deeper structural issue that has limited the region's capacity to develop and act to prevent and address human trafficking. In 1898, Spain ceded control of the territory to the United States after losing the Spanish-Cuban-American war, and despite the efforts of "dozens of movements, groups and organizations that have struggled for independence and . . . sought to challenge the colonial state of exception," Puerto Rico remains the world's oldest colony (Atiles-Osoria 2016, 224). As a result, Puerto Rico's power to create agencies and pass laws that respond to problems like human trafficking is extremely limited, due, in large part, to Public Law 600, which Congress passed in 1950 to establish The Commonwealth of Puerto Rico as a legal and political category. Since this law "did not transfer sovereignty to the people of Puerto Rico and its political institutions," it left the Island under some degree of political, military, economic, and other forms control by the United States (Atiles-Osoria

2016, 224). Here, for example, while the Jones Act of 1971 imposed US citizenship on Puerto Ricans, allowing them to move between the island and the US mainland, they cannot vote in presidential or congressional elections unless they reside on the mainland. And even though Puerto Rico has competed in the Olympics as an independent nation since the 1948 Summer Games, and the 2016 case *Puerto Rico v. Sánchez Valle* established that Puerto Rico has its own constitution, courts, government, and laws, the Double Jeopardy clause voids its status as a truly sovereign nation (Rodriguez-Coss 2020).

Puerto Rico's lack of sovereignty limits its capacity to develop economically. Traditionally, the region largely depended on sugarcane production, but by the middle of the twentieth century, it was one of the poorest places in the Caribbean. In response, the Puerto Rican legislature passed the Industrial Incentives Act. Known as "Operation Bootstraps," this law eliminated all corporate taxes and offered lower labor costs (among other incentives) to encourage US corporate investment on the island. Congress added to these efforts by passing Section 936 in 1976, which allowed US manufacturing companies to avoid corporate income taxes on profits made in US territories, including Puerto Rico (Schoen 2017). While these efforts drew some corporations to the Island, as Laura Briggs indicates, they "never contributed to the overall well-being and support of people (besides employing some people), because they never paid taxes" (cited in Durana 2017). In 1996, President Clinton signed a law that would phase out Section 936 over ten years, but as Zadia Feliciano and Andrew Green (2017) document, this decreased average manufacturing wages by 16.7 percent, and the number of manufacturing establishments by 18.7 percent to 28.0 percent. In response, Puerto Rico took on more debt, and by 2016 Congress placed it under fiscal oversight because it was unable to pay $72 billion owed to bond holders. Hurricane Maria, which devastated the Island in 2017, only increased the island's economic woes. As a result, many Puerto Ricans have left for the US mainland, and those who remain are largely poor. In 2017, the median household income on the island was $19,000 (compared to $60,000 on the mainland), and half the population of Puerto Rico is on Medicaid (Durana 2017; Federal Reserve Bank of New York 2020).

In light of all of this, Martin's anti-trafficking efforts are ultimately limited in the face of "the ongoing and deleterious effects of colonialism," which allows the colonizers to continually "define, control, regulate, marginalize, stigmatize, belittle, or in any other way devalue [colonized people] and their culture" (Tong and Botts 2017, 139). These effects of colonialism are dispro-portionately gendered: as Noralis Rodriguez-Coss (2020, 98) writes, "Puerto Rico's colonial history contributed to the feminization of poverty and une-qual access to resources, such as housing and employment, among other resources, causing havoc and an uncertain political and economic future." By extension, as scholars have long documented, poverty and resource depriva-tion enhances vulnerability to human trafficking, especially for women and young people (Showden and Majic 2018b; Lutnick 2016).

To my knowledge, Martin has not waged a deeper, more radical critique of American colonial power through his anti-trafficking work, and we may indeed criticize him for this. However, this omission also indicates how per-sonal and contextual factors constrain celebrities' advocacy, despite their resources and power. In Martin's case, these constraints are apparent in his own precarious position as a barrier-breaking Latino celebrity whose sexual-ity was under constant scrutiny. Wading into debates about human traffick-ing in the early 2000s, he risked making missteps and facing opprobrium from established activists, many of whom were promoting the dominant nar-rative, which was extremely popular with the US government at the time. Therefore he may have promoted carceral solutions to human trafficking—and avoided critiques of US colonialism—because he wanted to draw the US government's attention to human trafficking in Puerto Rico. If Martin were more critical of the US government, he might lose his "hero" award and sta-tus (a personal loss) *and* compromise any scraps the US government might throw at Puerto Rico to improve child welfare and fight human trafficking.

But while Martin may have avoided criticizing America's colonial power through his anti-trafficking work, he has acknowledged and criticized it else-where. For example, he critiqued the United States' use of the Puerto Rican island Vieques as a missile testing site until 2003, which many regarded as symptomatic of the island's fraught colonial relationship to the United States (Allatson 2015). Martin has also criticized the US government's deployment of power outside of the country through his opposition to the Iraq war in 2007. As Carmen Lugo-Lugo (2012, 69–73) recounts:

> In February 2007, on a warm Friday night, Ricky Martin gave a two-hour concert in San Juan, Puerto Rico. According to the local press, the concert was an average Ricky Martin show, nothing all that remarkable, with one particular exception: while singing the song "Asignatura Pendiente," . . . the usually well-behaved Martin proceeded to make an obscene gesture with his hand . . . during a specific line in the song about having his picture taken with

President Bush. To be more precise, Ricky Martin showed the middle finger of his left hand when he sang President Bush's last name.... When news about his uncharacteristic behavior at the February concert surfaced in the U.S., Martin released a statement to the press explaining that by flipping off the President he was condemning the war in Iraq. In his words: 'My convictions of peace and life go beyond any government and political agenda, and as long as I have a voice onstage and offstage, I will always condemn war and those who promulgate it.'

Certainly, celebrity disagreement with the Iraq war was not unique in 2007: on the eve of the invasion, Natalie Maines of the Dixie Chicks made her opposition loud and clear at a concert in London. But when Martin opposed the war, he did so as both an American and as a colonial subject; as such, he made "a gesture that somewhat challenges the very person/office that controls their lives from afar" (Lugo-Lugo 2012, 73–74). Furthermore, as a man whose sexuality was constantly under scrutiny in the post-9/11 era, Martin also threatened "a stars-and-stripes flag-waving, heterosexual Whiteness" with a gesture that many Americans read as expressing an anti-Bush *and* anti-American sentiment more broadly (77). Martin's gesture both reified and complicated American hegemonic masculinity by challenging a colonial power as a "feminized" (read: artistic, gay) subject.

In 2010, Martin engaged again in American sexual and colonial politics when he used his fame to reach a wider audience about LGBTQ+ equality. After he came out in 2010 on the Oprah Winfrey show, he appeared at the annual National Dinner in Washington, DC, for the Human Rights Campaign (HRC), the nation's largest LGBTQ+ rights organization (see figure 9). When he arrived at the podium, he said to the audience, "you heard I'm gay, right?" and they cheered and clapped loudly. In his brief remarks, Martin honored the HRC's commitment to "fighting for LGBT rights and equality," telling the audience, "I'm here; it took me awhile" (HRC 2010).

Martin proceeded to engage in LGBTQ+ rights advocacy on his own and in his capacity as a UNICEF Ambassador, and in 2019, nine years after he first addressed the HRC's audience, he received the HRC's National Visibility Award. This award was sparked, in part, by his protests against the former Governor of Puerto Rico, Ricardo Rosselló, who won the governor's seat in 2017. Rosselló, who is socially liberal, founded the advocacy group Boricua Ahora Es, which supports Puerto Rican statehood (Levine 2017). However, The Center for Investigative Journalism soon revealed 900 pages of text messages between Rosselló and various government officials and other

FIGURE 9. Ricky Martin at Human Rights Campaign dinner. (Human Rights Campaign), 2010. Photo by DB King/CC-BY-2.0.

elites that offered evidence of political corruption and shared crude, sexist, and homophobic messages. Soon after, nearly 40 percent of Puerto Ricans took to the streets for nearly two weeks in July 2019 to protest a corrupt and disconnected political class and demand Rosselló's resignation; he stepped down on August 2, 2009 (Sanchez 2019; Garcia-Navarro 2019).

As Andrés Besserer Rayas found, Ricky Martin's participation in the protests (alongside other moderate, "bourgeois," and pro-US Puerto Ricans) was central to Rosselló's downfall.[7] The chat messages revealed extremely negative comments about Martin's sexual orientation and his human trafficking activism. For example, Christian Sobrino, who was then the Chief Financial Officer for the Puerto Rican government, sent a tweet that said, "Given that you're talking of the daughter of Ricky Martin I will remind you all that surrogate pregnancy is another form of human trafficking, precisely what he is "trying" to combat." Sobrino also texted later, "Ricky Martin is such a machista [sexist] that he fucks men because women are no match for him. It is pure patriarchy." Elias Sanchez Sifonte, the former representative of Puerto Rico's government in the United States, responded to this message with stickers showing his approval of that comment about Ricky Martin. These messages motivated Martin to join the marches against Rosselló and call for his resignation. Here Martin stated publicly that "We cannot allow our Puerto Rico to be in the hands of such 'leaders'. . . . This is not the government we need. This is not the Puerto Rico that our grandparents and parents built and much less the one we want to leave our children" (*Intransigente* 2019). By making these statements and joining the protests, Martin reveals how celebrities who engage in anti-trafficking activism may be drawn into broader conflicts (in this case, regarding Puerto Rican politics and independence), where they may also deploy their celebrity capital to draw attention to issues such as homophobia that further marginalize sexual minorities, among others.

Kutcher in the Mainstream

Unlike Ricky Martin, Ashton Kutcher is, at first glance, very much in the mainstream of American masculinity. Straight, white, cisgender, conventionally attractive, and born in the nation's "heartland," Kutcher has long embodied the privileges of male celebrity—a status he ascended to seemingly without effort. As a result of his career in Hollywood (where, it is worth noting, there are always plenty of well-paying lead roles for men like him), Kutcher amassed significant connections and wealth, which he has parlayed into a very successful technology investing career. His personal life also seems equally "blessed" by his celebrity: he was married to Demi Moore, a famous and accomplished actor in her own right, and the tabloids and other media routinely featured him happily cavorting with her daughters and her ex-husband, the actor Bruce Willis. When that relationship ended, he married the also-famous and talented actor Mila Kunis, with whom he now has two children. We might conclude that while Kutcher has no doubt faced challenges in his personal and professional life, his trajectory renders him a celebrity feminist who is unlikely to challenge the dictates of hegemonic masculinity.

Yet a closer look at Kutcher's anti-trafficking activism, particularly within the technology sector, shows that he promotes a modified and more "modern" masculinity. Most notably, he focuses on children, long the purview of women-identified activists in the anti-trafficking and broader feminist movements. As a result, Kutcher's entrance into the anti-trafficking space was somewhat risky and made him vulnerable to criticism. As a model and actor known for playing clueless "dudes" on television and in the movies, he confronted a credibility gap when he began to speak out against trafficking. He took a considerable risk with the Real Men campaign, discussed in chapter 2, and although he did not seem to suffer personally or financially from the blowback against it, he changed the tone and focus of his anti-trafficking advocacy after his divorce from Moore. Instead of emphasizing that individual men and criminal networks are the main cause of human trafficking, he focused on technology.

At first glance, Kutcher's approach to human trafficking appears technologically and gender neutral. As Kutcher explained to Congress in 2017:

> Now there's often a misconception about technology: that in some way it is the generator of some evil; that it's creating job displacements; and that it enables violence and malice acts. But as an entrepreneur and as a venture capitalist in the technology field, I see technology as simply a tool—a tool without will. The will is the user of that technology, and I think it's an important distinction. An airplane is a tool. It's a piece of technology. And under the right hands it's used for mass global transit, and under the wrong hands it can be flown into buildings. Technology can be used to enable slavery but it can also be used to disable slavery, and that's what we're doing.

Because Kutcher's specific tool (Spotlight) relies on machine learning algorithms, which use a base model of sample data (such as online escort ads) to make decisions and predictions (for example, about who may be a victim of trafficking online) without explicit programming, it is in theory *gender* neutral too. Since it could draw from a wide range of sample data featuring escort ads for persons of many genders, for example, Spotlight therefore seems capable of avoiding many of the hegemonically masculine pitfalls of more traditional anti-trafficking efforts such as vice raids, where women police officers "act" like under-aged sex workers in order to arrest men who are trying to purchase sex.

However, as Blue (2019) documents, many sex workers challenge this characterization of Spotlight, arguing that by gathering and making escort ads searchable for law enforcement, it actually increases risks for consenting *adult* sex workers, many of whom are women. Not only could Spotlight subject sex workers to heightened surveillance by police and platform companies, it could drive them away from the forums and other online platforms they use to generate income, screen clients, and communicate with others in their community (see also Blunt et al 2020). But Kutcher and Thorn—whose other nonprofit partners largely reject the notion that anyone could choose sex work (Blue 2019)—minimized these concerns. As Thorn CEO Julie Cordua stated, "With our work on child sex trafficking, we recognize that this crime often presents itself within the broader field of sex work, which does include consensual adult sex work." However, she insisted, "Our programs are designed specifically to channel very limited resources on the recovery of children who are being exploited through sex trafficking, not on consenting adults" (cited in Blue 2019). Thorn has never, to my knowledge, provided evidence to support this contention.

By indicating that Spotlight is both neutral *and* discerning, Kutcher and Thorn inadvertently signal that—contra their cyber-feminist ideology—technology *does* have a will. This will is implemented through its developers, and thus it is deeply implicated in the destabilization and reification of existing gender power relations. By stressing that technology is simply a "tool," Kutcher minimizes how the wider gendered context of its development, design, and use often furthers hegemonic masculinity and gender inequality, both materially and symbolically (Faulkner 2001; Lohan and Faulkner 2016). As a result, Kutcher's portrayal of Spotlight as a simple, neutral tool-for-good side-steps a *techno*-feminist critique. As Maria Lohan and Wendy Faulkner (2016) write, techno-feminism rejects the *cyber*-feminist notion that technology is neutral or asocial in the process of social change. Instead, intersecting factors such as class, gender, and race may shape technology's possibilities and limits. For example, Jessie Daniels (2009) shows here that while computers and the internet have increased employment and other opportunities for women (a la cyber-feminism), those in industrialized nations are more likely to access and benefit from them than women in developing societies, who are also more likely to be employed in "low-skilled" (underpaid) microchip production to make the computers in the first place. All of this indicates that technology is not neutral but is in fact "shaped as a result of complex social processes" (Lohan and Faulkner 2016, 322).

Indeed, the technology industry and Kutcher's position therein is highly gendered as a result of various socio-economic and political processes. In the United States, gender role stereotypes and socialization have long diverted women from playing and tinkering with tools and technology, and from the STEM (science, technology, engineering, and math) disciplines that tend to "feed" the technology industry—namely, the more lucrative sectors such as investing, coding, engineering, and other aspects of product and application design and development (World Economic Forum 2018). Those women who do enter the industry are more likely to be paid less and leave it (Dice 2021). A recent study found that "50% of women abandon technology careers by the age of 35, and only 21% of women in the study said they believed the technology industry was a place they could thrive; sadly, that number falls precipitously to 8% for women of color" (Maynard 2021). These gender and racial disparities then trickle down to shape many of the technology industry's investments and other outputs. Women are unlikely to occupy influential positions in venture capital and other investment firms, and many technology products and applications are also often geared towards the needs and interests of dominant groups, namely white men (Tugend 2019).

By developing technologies to eradicate human trafficking, Kutcher may be challenging gender inequality in the technology industry and society writ large. However, a closer look at his technology development efforts reveal how he actually reifies hegemonic masculinity, albeit with a more modern, neoliberal sheen. Namely, by developing propriety machine learning software (Spotlight) and promoting other tech-oriented measures to fight trafficking, Kutcher's anti-trafficking efforts offer a variation of "vigilante abolitionism," per Shih (2016), a key feature of neoliberal governance that empowers citizens to police state order through their efforts to eradicate trafficking. To name just one example, we see a variation of this vigilante abolitionism in Thorn's 2014 "hackathon," where

> nearly 80 engineers, activists and data scientists joined Thorn and Formation 8 at Twilio's headquarters. . . . Over two days, twenty teams tackled a variety of challenges, ranging from helping Thorn obtain better insights from our data, to creating programs to deter abusive behavior and improve victim identification. . . . Ashton's stated goal for the weekend was for participants to take the issue of human trafficking with them in their hearts and in their minds and to let their work continue beyond the weekend's hackathon (Thorn 2014).

Among the projects created over the course of forty-eight hours, Thorn favored the following: "a data visualization approach to better understand the behavior patterns of those downloading child abuse material; an automated way to learn about new abuse language used online; and a new way to research the role of virtual currency in the trade of child abuse material" (Thorn 2014).

Created with the goal of eradicating sex trafficking, these initiatives, and others such as Spotlight, produce what scholars term techno-masculinity. Connected to a gendered ideological perspective that naturally associates men with highly skilled technological work and advanced knowledge of computers, and prioritizing rational calculus, technological prowess, and expertise, techno-masculinity departs from the traditional, hegemonic masculinity based on militarism, politics, and finance that is commonly enacted by governments, armies, banks, and religious institutions (Johnson 2014; Poster 2013). However, Kutcher's techno-masculinity both disrupts and continues the more hegemonically masculine orientation of traditional anti-trafficking efforts such as police raids. For one, Kutcher and Thorn's initiatives do not abandon the state. Spotlight is a tool *for* law enforcement, which may use it to capture traffickers and rescue victims, but also, potentially, to arrest consenting adults engaged in sex work. And for another, these initiatives, with their techno-masculine bent, do little to eradicate the structural conditions such as racism, sexism, and economic inequality that create vulnerabilities to trafficking and gender inequality more broadly.

Kutcher and Thorn acknowledge these limits, stating that, "While we're proud of the results of our tools to identify more victims faster, we know that the issue doesn't end there. Survivors need a wide array of services for a sustainable recovery—from basic needs to health care to job training" (Thorn Digital Defenders and Boucher 2018, 10). However, this acknowledgment is not the same as accountability. Technological responses to human trafficking (like Spotlight) may harm marginalized groups like sex workers, who have called for more transparency about these technologies, even as their proponents have remained surprisingly immune to their calls (Musto, Thakor, and Gerasimov 2020). Kutcher's money, investment relationships, and capacity to develop proprietary software grant him this immunity: he is under no legal or other obligation to show how his technology actually works and helps victims *or* how it may harm sex workers. Given his significant investments in the tech industry, Kutcher also has very little incentive to open Spotlight to scrutiny so more people may see it, question it, and potentially discover its flaws and limitations. Doing this could compromise his tech industry bona fides and Thorn's reputation as an organization that fights against child exploitation. As a result, Kutcher is ultimately benefitting from (and furthering) his white, techno-masculine privilege and, in the end, undermining gender equality.

As extremely famous and, in Martin's case, barrier-breaking celebrities, Ricky Martin and Ashton Kutcher could choose any issue as their central cause and use their celebrity to illuminate it to a wider audience; among these, they chose the trafficking of children. In so doing, at first glance, Martin and Kutcher embody MCFs' attendant power and privileges, which situate them as neoliberal political figures par excellence. Both men are cisgender, able-bodied, conventionally attractive, wealthy, and famous, all of which makes them appealing to the media and a wider audience. As a result, they easily, and individually, marshalled their fame and other resources to stake positions in the anti-trafficking movement and garner significant attention for their efforts. And almost instantly, both men secured invitations to address high-profile audiences, from the Clinton Global Initiative to the US Congress, thereby confirming the ways in which gender and celebrity grant MCFs vast (and, arguably, un-earned) power and privileges.

But on closer examination, Martin's and Kutcher's anti-trafficking advocacy is actually more complex and intriguing. By taking on the trafficking of children—an issue that is traditionally framed as a "women's concern"—Martin and Kutcher position themselves as male celebrity feminists and challenge notions of hegemonic masculinity. Aside from Martin's "rescue" of the young girls in India, their activism has largely been un-macho (at least in the more traditional sense), focusing instead on awareness raising and service provision (Martin) and technological causes and solutions (Kutcher). Taken as a whole, this might indicate how MCFs can challenge dominant gender norms.

At the same time, Martin's and Kutcher's anti-trafficking performances demonstrate the limited power of celebrity feminism to challenge gender and other inequality. Martin has worked to raise awareness about human trafficking globally and in Puerto Rico, which is admirable given the relative lack of knowledge about or attention to the issue in the region. However, he has remained relatively silent about US colonialism, a key driver of human trafficking, labor exploitation, and gender inequality more broadly in the territory. And while Kutcher changed his focus to technology, the solutions and feminist ideologies he offers here remain limited by his belief in technological neutrality. Furthermore, neither Martin nor Kutcher have ever really accounted for the omissions or outcomes of their efforts. Certainly, they are in the public eye, and they've both spoken to Congress about their anti-trafficking work, but they were and are under no obligation to offer deeper, more explanatory information about these efforts. To name just some examples, the RMF has not released the numbers of children it has assisted (Allatson 2014), and during Kutcher's testimony about Spotlight, he refused to provide information about the software.

As a result, both Martin and Kutcher indicate that even as MCFs may challenge hegemonic masculinity and take strong positions on controversial issues, they are extremely privileged and, often, deeply implicated in and indebted to the very patriarchal and capitalist structures—celebrity, philanthropy, technology, etc.—that sustain their own power and influence. Stated another way, the very structures that empower them to engage in feminist activism, such as the industries that created their fame and the media attention they attract, allowed them to create their own (independent) advocacy organizations and draw attention to human trafficking *and* to themselves, all of which bolstered their celebrity capital. In the following chapter, I show how actors Julia Ormond and Mira Sorvino draw from their personal experiences and organizational affiliations to indicate how celebrities may use their power and platforms to offer more nuanced analyses of human trafficking, further feminist goals, and account for their efforts.

FIVE

Anti-trafficking Ambassadors

JULIA ORMOND, MIRA SORVINO, AND THE UNODC

> I have witnessed first-hand, human trafficking does not comprise just prostitution, nor are the targets solely women and children. In fact, the largest group of victims fall into the category of forced labor, which can involve many trades—agriculture, child soldiering, fishing, textiles, domestic servitude, factory labor, and mining, just to name a few.
>
> JULIA ORMOND,
> *speech to the United Nations Security Council (Ormond 2007)*

> When news stories purport that sex trafficking is worse than labor, it creates an awkward dynamic among survivors; they don't want one to be weighed more heavily, neither from a treatment or an advocacy perspective; they feel the media is doing a disservice to the movement.
>
> MIRA SORVINO,
> *speech to the Georgetown University School of Foreign Service*
> *(Sorvino 2013)*

AMONG THE CELEBRITIES WHO RAISE awareness about human trafficking, actors Julia Ormond and Mira Sorvino stand out. Unlike their peers who, as detailed in previous chapters, were largely motivated to take on this issue by personal experiences, Ormond and Sorvino became anti-trafficking advocates at the invitation of the UN Office of Drugs and Crime (UNODC), where they would be Global Ambassadors for its work. Scholars and activists have long criticized this celebrity-international organizational nexus, particularly as it pertains to the promotion of gender equality. Many argue here that while celebrities in this position capture public attention and raise awareness about various issues globally, they are also drawing attention to themselves and furthering their careers while promoting Western, patriarchal capitalist values, with little accountability for their actions (Hopkins 2017; Chouliaraki

2012; Littler 2008; Yrjölä 2011b). Given this, we may reasonably assume that Ormond and Sorvino, in their ambassadorial positions, would give global purchase to the dominant, American-centric human trafficking narrative that was extremely salient in 2005, when they began speaking out about the issue.

However, as I show in this chapter, Ormond's and Sorvino's charismatic anti-trafficking performances challenge this logic. As a result of personal and contextual factors—namely, their willingness to receive new information and their travels with the United Nations—they variously *destabilize* the dominant narrative by rejecting the notion that sex trafficking merits special attention, and by highlighting a range of structural factors that create vulnerabilities to human trafficking, most notably poverty and criminal law enforcement. To mitigate these factors, they advocate for expanded economic opportunities (Sorvino), supply chain regulations (Ormond), and anti-trafficking law reform (Sorvino).

Yet even as their performances may challenge scholarly and activist expectations, a closer interpretive analysis of their activism reveals the limits of even the most structurally-intersectional celebrity feminism. By reinforcing American imperialism and failing to call for deeper market reforms, Ormond and Sorvino also uphold and reproduce the gendered and racialized power relations and structures embedded in Western patriarchal capitalism (Hopkins 2017). Of course, it is unrealistic to expect that any individual celebrity could mitigate these and other conditions that create vulnerabilities to human trafficking and sustain gender inequality more broadly. However, even as they may diverge from their peers, Ormond's and Sorvino's anti-trafficking activism still reveals the limits of celebrities' allegedly "peerless heroism" (Yrjölä 2011b, 370), particularly for addressing complex problems of gender, racial, and other inequality.

PERFORMERS AND SETTINGS

Like many of the celebrities discussed in this book, Ormond and Sorvino amassed their fame capital as actors in Hollywood films. But unlike their peers, personal experiences did not motivate their anti-trafficking activism. Instead, their fame captured the attention of international organizations—namely, Amnesty International and the UNODC—the latter of which has provided a significant setting for their anti-trafficking work.

Julia Karin Ormond was born on January 4, 1965 in Surrey, England. Her mother, Josephine, was a laboratory technician and her father, John, worked as a stockbroker and computer engineer (they divorced in 1969). The second of five siblings, Ormond attended independent schools in England, graduating from the Webber Douglas Academy of Dramatic Art in 1988. She was married to actor Rory Edwards from 1988 to 1994, and then to political activist John Rubin from 1999 to 2008. Based in Los Angeles, Ormond has a daughter, Sophie Rubin, who was born in 2004.

Ormond began her acting career shortly after graduating from the Webber Douglas Academy, starring in the 1989 British television series *Traffik,* where she played a drug addict. Her star quickly ascended and she transitioned to Hollywood, starring in numerous big budget, critically acclaimed films, including three blockbusters of the 1990s: *Legends of the Fall* (1994), *First Knight* (1995), and *Sabrina* (1995), where she reprised Audrey Hepburn's title role. But as she achieved great fame and success, she was subject to intense media criticism and scrutiny. Ignoring her ten-year career on the British stage and screen before coming to Hollywood, news outlets like the *New York Times* claimed she had not earned her celebrity (Das 2007). In response, Ormond retreated from Hollywood, taking roles in independent and foreign feature films and on stage. By the early 2000s she returned to the American film and television scene, appearing in films such as *Resistance* (2003), *The Curious Case of Benjamin Button* (2007), and *Temple Grandin* (2010) (for which she won a Primetime Emmy Award), and TV series such as *Mad Men* (2007) and *Law and Order: Criminal Intent* (2011), among others.

Given her success, Ormond's anti-human trafficking activism may seem like an unusual choice. She had no scholarly, personal, or other experience with the issue, and she did not need to engage in high-profile activism to draw attention to herself. As she told an audience assembled for the Skoll Foundation's World Forum (Ormond 2017a), her engagement with the human trafficking was somewhat "random," beginning when she was "supporting and celebrating NGOs through Vital Voices," an international NGO that invested in women's leadership. At the organization's annual event at the Kennedy Center, in Washington, DC, Melanne Verveer, Vital Voices co-founder and CEO, asked Ormond if she was interested in serving as a UNODC Ambassador against trafficking and slavery. Ormond initially rejected Verveer's invitation because she lacked a personal connection to the issue and had relatively little knowledge about it, except for what she had seen and interpreted as human trafficking while working. As she told the audience at Women*etics* (Ormond 2012), "as an actress, I did a lot of work in Eastern Europe, so I saw very early on ... what was happening in restaurants right behind me. Guys sitting down discussing setting up false marriages, businesses. ... I saw in particular how it was affecting women, and this was all women. ... " She explained further, to the Skoll Foundation (Ormond 2017a):

> And I said [no to Verveer] not because I'm an awful human being ... [but] because at the time, the picture that we were seeing was that the vast majority of this was sex trafficking. And ... I couldn't see solutions to it. And, and, and I felt that [having solutions] was vital. I saw it as a government and a police enforcement challenge.

However, she recounted that Verveer told her to "get over [her]self, and get out there, take on the role and use it to investigate and get a bigger and deeper picture" (Ormond 2017a). In response, Ormond declared, "I realized it wasn't good enough to make the excuse [that] I'm scared and that I'm going to look foolish in conversation, or I'm going to make a mistake. I've learned everything from the mistakes I've made" (cited in Oriel 2016).

In 2005 the UNODC appointed Ormond as its first Ambassador focused on trafficking. In this capacity, she traveled throughout California, Europe, Russia, and Asia to observe and learn more about the issue (UNTV 2005). In 2007, she founded a 501c3 nonprofit, ASSET (Alliance to Stop Slavery and End Trafficking), with funding from the Clinton Global Initiative. ASSET is "dedicated to reducing and stopping enslavement and trafficking before it starts, and delivering human rights" (ASSET 2021a). At the time of writing, ASSET had a board of directors and just one staff member beyond Ormond, who is listed as the Founder. Since I was unable to speak with Ormond (or anyone else from the organization), I could not find any details about ASSET's finances, with the exception of a recent (2017) IRS Form 990, which listed the organization's total revenue as $158,152. With these resources, ASSET's website says it works mainly to develop and deliver "innovative solutions to elaborate forced labor in our supply chains to deliver human rights and social impact" (ASSET 2021b).

Mira Sorvino

Mira Katherine Sorvino was born on September 28, 1967 in New York City. Her parents worked in the entertainment industry: her mother, Lorraine

Davis, as an actress and drama therapist, and her father, the late Paul Sorvino, as a character actor and director. Sorvino has two younger siblings, Michael and Amanda, and grew up in New Jersey, where she graduated from Englewood High School. She attended Harvard University, majoring in East Asian studies and graduating *magna cum laude* in 1989 (Nicol 2016). She married actor Christopher Backus in 2004 and they have four children, Mattea (born 2004), Johnny (born 2006), Holden (born 2009), and Lucia (born 2012).

Sorvino pursued an acting career after college, moving to New York City where she waitressed, auditioned, and worked for Robert De Niro's production company. She made her television debut in 1990 on an episode of *Law and Order*, and later, after working on set, was cast as the female lead in the independent gangster movie *Amongst Friends* (1993). Her performance caught Hollywood's attention, and she was soon cast in her first Hollywood feature, *Quiz Show* (1994), followed by Woody Allen's *Mighty Aphrodite* (1995), for which she won an Oscar for Best Supporting Actor in her role as a sex worker. Since then, Sorvino has worked steadily in a range of films and television series, including but not limited to *Norma Jean & Marilyn* (1996), for which she received Golden Globe and Emmy nominations, *Romy & Michelle's High School Reunion* (1997), *Human Trafficking* (2005), for which she received another Golden Globe nomination, *Attack on Leningrad* (2009), *Abandoned* (2011), *Space Warriors* (2013), the Netflix series *Lady Dynamite* (2016), and *Mothers and Daughters* (2016), for which she won a best supporting actress award at the Milano International Film Festival.

Sorvino brought a considerable amount of fame capital to her anti-trafficking work, but unlike Ormond, she had a longer history of social justice activism. As she told the audience assembled at Sonoma State University (SSU), she wrote her undergraduate thesis at Harvard on racial conflict in an effort to "get to the bottom of what allows people to treat different racial groups as other, something less than human, not worthy of empathy or equal treatment" (Sorvino 2016). She carried her passion for addressing inequality to other issues such as the genocide in Darfur, and in 2004 Amnesty International appointed her as an Ambassador for its "Stop Violence Against Women" campaign. Combining her advocacy with her film and television work, Sorvino appeared in the miniseries *Human Trafficking* (2005) for the Lifetime Network, and in 2007 she became the first face of CNN's "Hero's Campaign," appearing in *Every Day in Cambodia* (2013/2014), a documentary about sex trafficking for CNN's "Freedom Project."[1] In 2009, the

UNODC appointed her as a Goodwill Ambassador, and she took the position because she believed that it would allow her to "reach ears that have the power to affect change" (Sorvino 2016). Sorvino served here until 2017, traveling the world as part of the UN's "Blue Heart" Campaign and raising money and awareness for the UNODC's anti-trafficking work.

Setting the Stage: The UN's Celebrity Program

Since the United Nations provided a major setting for Ormond's and Sorvino's anti-trafficking work, the following pages contextualize its deployment of what Andrew Cooper (2008) terms celebrity diplomats and its involvement with human trafficking more specifically. In fact, the United Nations has long enlisted high-profile individuals from the worlds of entertainment, art, sports, and literature to "highlight priority issues and draw attention to its activities" (Wheeler 2011, 15). In 1946, following the failure of the League of Nations to prevent war, and the horrors of Nazi propaganda, the United Nations created its Department of Public Information (DPI) and tasked it with communicating the organization's ideals. The United Nations and the DPI viewed celebrities, with their broad appeal, as convenient tools for promoting UN projects (Alleyne 2005); however, this began by chance, in 1953, when actor Danny Kaye met UNICEF's then-Executive Director Maurice Pate on a flight between London and New York. Kaye was planning a trip to Asia and Pate asked him to visit UNICEF's health and nutrition projects in the region. Kaye agreed and was officially appointed as UNICEF's Ambassador-at-large; soon after, he was visiting UNICEF projects in Myanmar, India, Indonesia, Korea, Thailand, and Japan.

Following Kaye's appointment, other celebrities entered into similar relationships with the United Nations, which formally established its celebrity program in the late 1990s in response to its "image problem," after surveys from 1989–91 showed that wealthy countries rated it poorly for maintaining international peace and security (Alleyne 2005, 183). Many have questioned the extent to which celebrities, and American celebrities in particular, may promote the United Nations' global/universal values, especially given Hollywood's limited credibility in the realm of selfless advocacy (Volcic and Erjavec 2014). This criticism escalated as numerous UN celebrity ambassadors acted in insensitive and materialistic ways. To name just one example, in 1992 actor Sophia Loren arrived at a UN Refugee Agency ceremony—for an appointment related to Somali refugees—in a brown Rolls Royce and dressed in a matching fur coat (Wheeler 2011). As the United Nations' reputation fell further with the global conflicts in Bosnia and Somalia, it changed both its leadership and its celebrity program. After the Clinton administration pushed for Secretary General Boutros Boutros-Ghali's ouster in 1996, it endorsed Kofi Annan as Secretary General (Lim 2019).

As the first Secretary General to come through the organization's ranks, Annan was well aware of the United Nations' image problems *and* its limits as an international nonprofit organization with a restricted budget for advertising and public relations work, and so in March 1997 he announced that it would reorient many of its public information and relations activities (Lim 2019; Alleyne 2005). Most notably, it would formalize its celebrity program to better raise awareness about the suffering of others and shift public opinion in favor UN missions and activities (Volcic and Erjavec 2014). To this end, Annan expanded the Goodwill Ambassador program by creating three tiers of Ambassadors appointed by the heads of UN funds, programs, and agencies. These individuals included international ambassadors, consisting of film, music, and sports stars with global media recognition, and regional and national ambassadors from similar fields whose impact is conditioned by more local forms of fame. Annan also established the Messengers of Peace program in 1997. Appointed by the Secretary General, these messengers—"distinguished men and women of talent and passion"—would use their global fame to draw attention to and marshal public support for the aims of the UN Charter (Wheeler 2011, 14). Enrico Macias, an Algerian-French refugee turned singer and composer, was the first celebrity to hold this position. Consequently, the celebrity program expanded exponentially under Annan's watch: by the time he departed in 2007, there were more than four hundred UN Goodwill Ambassadors.

However, the United Nations was soon forced to rethink and revise its rapidly expanding celebrity program. A 2003 report by a UN communication group warned that many of the Ambassadors were named without regard for their stature and commitment to UN goals (cited in Lim 2019), and a 2006 report also argued that there were too many Ambassadors working under multiple titles and not enough resources to administer and monitor their activities (Fall and Tang 2006). Furthermore, these celebrities were not particularly diverse in terms of race and national origin, and since their terms of service were unlimited, they were often fatigued and difficult to replace. In response, Annan and his UN colleagues established the current guidelines and selection criteria for the Goodwill Ambassadors and

Messengers of Peace (United Nations 2021). Now, individuals may only represent one UN program, fund, etc. "for a period of two years, renewable, based on mutual agreement by the parties on the basis of satisfactory fulfillment of the role and their demonstrated interest in continuing the relationship" (3). They receive a symbolic payment of $1 per year or equivalent, along with "allowances when they are travelling on behalf of the UN" (3), and "their designation shall be terminated" (4) if the Head of the relevant UN Office, Fund or Programme determines that the designee is unable or unwilling to carry out his or her role and/or engages in activities that undermine the UN's reputation and goals.

Even with these changes, scholars and observers remain divided about celebrities' roles at the United Nations. As Andrew Cooper (2008) argues, while these "celebrity diplomats" may reinforce a top-down, elite politics and dumb down key issues at times, their broad appeal allows them to mobilize a form of soft power and generate interest in various international causes. For example, when Annan gathered celebrities in New York in 2000 and 2002, these meetings garnered extensive media attention, and soon the United Nations received some of its largest donations from entertainment and internet media moguls, including $1 billion from Ted Turner, and millions for health care projects from Bill Gates, the founder of Microsoft (Alleyne 2005). Yet, as Riina Yrjölä (2011b) reminds us, we must also question celebrities' supposedly universal appeal: whose possibilities do they create *and* invalidate? Indeed, even as Annan revived the UN celebrity program by appointing a French-Algerian celebrity, his clear preference for American and European celebrities betrayed a partiality for Western notions of universality, and for US interests and approaches to social status (Alleyne 2005).

The United Nations' preference for Western/US values and interests is apparent in its approach to human trafficking, which, as noted earlier in this book, became a priority issue for the organization as the geopolitical interests of developed countries aligned to police borders in the wake of economic globalization in the 1990s, and NGOs and other advocates concerned with the "trafficking in women" and human rights debated the extent to which sex trafficking was the predominant form of human trafficking (Kotiswaran 2019). Since then, its approach to human trafficking has largely reflected and reinforced the law and order interests of predominantly Western countries (Kotiswaran 2019), as indicated by the fact that the majority of the United Nations' anti-trafficking work is located in the UNODC, whose "mission is to contribute to global peace and security, human rights and development by making the world safer from drugs, crime, corruption and terrorism" (2021b). Although the UNODC defines human trafficking broadly, as a crime that appears in many forms and impacts persons of all genders, it reflects the dominant narrative by emphasizing that individual traffickers who "use violence or fraudulent employment agencies and fake promises of education and job opportunities to trick and coerce their victims" are a central cause. In response, they support other nations as they draft, develop and review laws, policies and action plans to "effectively combat human trafficking"—namely, criminal-legal approaches that treat and address human trafficking as a crime. As the UNODC (2021a) states, "Through the services we provide, authorities are better equipped to prevent human trafficking, identify and protect victims, and prosecute the perpetrators. Countries are able to dismantle the criminal networks behind human trafficking and seize the illegal proceeds."

NARRATIVES OF HUMAN TRAFFICKING

As white US-based actors and Ambassadors for the UNODC, one might reasonably expect that Ormond and Sorvino would promote the dominant narrative, which is reflected, in part, in the UNODC's approach to human trafficking. However, as the following sections indicate, their personal orientations and various contextual factors have led them to contest and even challenge this crime-centric representation of the issue.

Ormond: Structures from the Start

Julia Ormond is unique among celebrities in the anti-trafficking movement. Although she began engaging with the issue in 2005, when the dominant narrative ascended through films and news exposés, she has consistently resisted the notion that *sex* trafficking merits the most attention. As she told the Vienna Forum in 2006,

> Most of us have heard the stories of the trafficked women, for example from Eastern Europe, who believe that they are coming to the West for better opportunity and promises of decent salaries as perhaps household help, waitresses, teachers, that end up forced into prostitution. That is one horrific type of trafficking. In fact, forced prostitution accounts for less than half of all trafficking victims (Ormond 2006a).

Ormond's travels as a UNODC Ambassador shaped her understanding of human trafficking as a global problem that occurs in a range of industries, which she realized during her first UNODC trip to Lake Volta, Ghana, where she was appalled to learned that children were forced to work in the fishing industry. As a white woman celebrity, Ormond's reaction to this situation may be read as yet another case where "African childhoods [are portrayed] as realms of vulnerability," while failing to account for the social and cultural underpinnings of children's movement to fishing communities for work (Koomson and Abdulai 2021, 30). As Betty Nemsah and Samuel Okyere show (2019), allegations of child slavery in the Lake Volta region—made often by Western journalists and NGOs—reflect a limited understanding of the residents' lived realities. Here, fishing is one of the few guaranteed means of subsistence, and parents rightly teach their children this skill. As a result, "Outsiders or those unfamiliar with this fundamental social set-up can wrongly translate the sight of a child in a boat with an adult as a child being exploited or forced to work" (Nemsah and Okyere 2019).

Ormond did soon realize that forced labor was a more complex issue that was not confined to children in Lake Volta, but was in "pretty much in every part of the world in every product" (Strickland 2017). Reflecting on her work at the 2016 Benchmark Seminar, she said that she "felt like every product I was buying, or most of the products I was buying, whether it was my cell phone, or my computer, my car, my coffee, my sheets, my food, whatever—it was based on the oppression of someone else, and potentially putting a child at risk. And I found that unacceptable" (Ormond 2016). In stating this, Ormond challenged the notion of "Africa as the *dark continent* bereft of technological, economic, and political development that characterizes the *developed world*" (Koomson and Abdulai 2021, 31, emphasis in original).

Informed by her travels, Ormond also resisted the dominant narrative's assertion that human trafficking victims are predominantly women and girls. As she told the US House of Representatives in 2006, just one year into her term as a Goodwill Ambassador, "Trafficking is not just women and girls, there are many male victims, too" (Ormond 2006b). As she explained later, in her 2011 speech to the US Congress:

What keeps me up at night, what haunts me, are all of the victims' stories. I'll never forget the girl who crawled out of an eight-floor window for fear of her life in sex slavery. But I can equally never forget the ... footage of a Mayan agricultural slave in Florida picking my tomatoes. These people are no less deserving of all of our compassion than those forced into sex slavery. All victims of trafficking and slavery deserve our attention and our commitment (Ormond 2011).

Ormond has maintained this broad victim characterization through her nonprofit, ASSET, whose language about human trafficking is gender neutral, focusing on "every person" as opposed to only women and girls (ASSET 2021a).

Regarding causes, Ormond has consistently rejected the dominant claim that individual men and/or organized crime networks are primarily responsible for human trafficking. Instead, she has highlighted various structural causes, namely poverty. As she explained to the Vienna Forum, "It is certainly true that trafficking and modern-day slavery are intimately linked with poverty, corruption and an ever increasingly visible gap between rich and poor. Trafficking is the ugly face of globalization" (2006a). She also testified to Congress that "the lack of economic opportunity and lack of free education worldwide remain key contributory factors [to human trafficking" (Ormond 2006b). Yet in stating this, Ormond has not ignored the fact that individuals and organized crime do contribute to human trafficking]. Reflecting her engagement with the UNODC, she told the UN's Security Council's Arria-Formula Meeting that "crime has gone through its own globalization," and is now more sophisticated than ever (Ormond 2007). Her thirty-second radio spot for the UNODC that aired in 2008, and was broadcast in various languages globally, very much promotes the UNODC's understanding of the issue. In one of the ads, following pulsing dramatic music, Ormond (2008a) says

Every year, thousands of people are trafficked worldwide. In their search for a better life, they fall prey to criminal gangs, their freedom is taken away and they are forced to work for little or no money under appalling conditions. This exploitation is happening in your country; please don't ignore it. This is Julia Ormond, Goodwill Ambassador for the United Nation's Office of Drugs and Crime.

However, unlike other advocates and celebrities at the time who tended to emphasize that traffickers were predominantly non-Western and/or non-white men, she declared that "Smugglers and traffickers are of diverse ethnicities and operate on every continent, often in coordination with each other" (Ormond 2007). Furthermore, as she told the Global Philanthropy Forum in 2008, "I think it's instinctive for [UN] member states to reach for an isolated response and to clamp down on the borders" (Ormond 2008b). She then proceeded to describe how closed and/or restrictive borders and immigration policies actually *force* individuals in desperate circumstances to rely on "coyotes"—individuals who smuggle people across borders—leaving them at risk and in debt to these coyotes. In stating this, Ormond emphasized that poverty and crime do not cause human trafficking in a vacuum; instead, they are fueled by intersecting structures and power disparities.

Among the many causes of human trafficking that Ormond identifies, the bulk of her activism has focused on supply chains—the set of activities that process raw materials into finished goods for consumption, involving suppliers of products, component parts of products, and raw materials (Eckert 2013; Ma, Lee, and Goerlitz 2016). As her NGO, ASSET (2015b), states: because "enslavement is a global problem in supply chains, we understand it affects not just the men, women and children enslaved, but all of us who profit or benefit from their exploitation." Much of this profit and benefit comes from pressure to lower costs in what Harry Van Buren and colleagues term the labor supply chain, which "feeds into product supply chains at any point in the production process and replies to the demand for cost cutting" (Van Buren, Schrempf-Stirling, and Westermann-Behaylo 2019, 6). While this labor sourcing does not always bring forced (trafficked) labor into the supply chain, major brands', retailers', and buyers' capacities to set prices often constrain suppliers and labor contractors; in response, they increasingly source low-cost workers from desperately poor regions of the world.

Of course, cost-cutting and exploitation in the labor supply chain is not new. As Stephanie Barrientos (2011) writes, the transatlantic slave trade provides one of the earliest and most horrific examples of how labor was sourced and moved from parts of Africa to the "new world" for exploitation in colonial production. Labor contracting in the United States developed further as agricultural industries in the nineteenth century sourced 'gangs' of seasonal labor at harvest time, and again as economic globalization has accelerated since the 1980s. Aided by low-cost and abundant labor, improved infrastructure and communications, relatively cheap and accessible land, limited regulatory environments, free trade and production agreements, and technological advances, retailers and brand companies (predominantly from the Global North) have increasingly sourced labor from the Global South (Berg, Farbenblum, and Kintominas 2020; Van Buren, Schrempf-Stirling, and Westermann-Behaylo 2019; Rende Taylor and Shih 2019; Eckert 2013).

Because supply chains are now so internationally connected and highly outsourced, "the risk of using slave labour somewhere in the supply chain is present in almost all industries, from electronics, high-tech, automotive and steel to agriculture, seafood, mining, garment and textiles" (Gold, Trautrims, and Trodd 2015, 3).

Regulatory failures are also to blame here, and Ormond is especially concerned about these. As ASSET states, "insufficiently monitored and regulated legal supply chains" are a major cause of human trafficking (2015b). On the one hand, this regulatory failure is understandable: the bulk of contemporary supply chains are transnational, complex, diffuse, and opaque, and their layers are barely visible to firms, let alone to consumers and investors, all of which makes them difficult to trace, monitor, and regulate (Berg, Farbenblum, and Kintominas 2020; Sarfaty 2015). But on the other hand, this regulatory failure is entirely predictable: global corporations are powerful, and they have worked to ensure that supply chain regulations are largely *voluntary* and fall under the rubric of "corporate social responsibility" (CSR), defined as "instances where the company goes beyond compliance and engages in actions that appear to advance a social cause [like ending human trafficking]" (Rodriguez et al. 2006, 736). Even where governments have stepped in to regulate supply chains more directly, their efforts are insufficiently coercive. As Stephanie Limoncelli (2017) writes, legal approaches aimed at preventing human trafficking in supply chains have mainly emerged through transparency laws that require companies to report the measures they take to address the issue. However, she adds that most of these laws only require companies to *self-report*, and so they may not fully disclose their anti-trafficking efforts, if they report them at all. As we will see later in this chapter, Ormond's anti-trafficking work has focused on attaining better *mandated* corporate reporting.

Sorvino: A Shifting Narrative

Like Ormond, Sorvino began to speak against human trafficking in 2005, when Amnesty International appointed her as a Goodwill Ambassador for its Stop Violence Against Women (SVAW) Campaign. Launched in 2003 at the organization's International Council Meeting in Mexico and "breaking new ground" in the organization's work, the SVAW Campaign would investigate the "causes, forms and remedies [of VAW]" by exploring the "relationship between violence against women and poverty, discrimination and militarization" and by highlighting "the responsibility of the state, the community and individuals for taking action to end violence against women" (Amnesty International 2004, 1). Adopting a broad view of VAW as a phenomenon that occurs in the family, the community, and/or is perpetrated by the state, the SVAW Campaign included "trafficking, forced prostitution, and forced labor" under its purview (4), and Sorvino learned about these issues here.

But unlike Ormond, Sorvino's political performances initially reflected and conveyed the dominant narrative, most notably when she began her advocacy by playing a witness in the miniseries *Human Trafficking* (2005) (Heynen and van der Meulen 2021). The series was created for the Lifetime Network, which tended to favor stories with a melodramatic edge, where a strong (and usually white) female protagonist overcomes adversity to correct an injury without engaging in institutional or systemic challenges (Byers and Meehan 1994). In line with this brand, *Human Trafficking* is set in the Czech Republic and tells the story of Helena, a single mother who is seduced by a successful business man who moves her to New York City, where she becomes a sex slave for a powerful international ring of sex traffickers. After the third death of a young Eastern European sex worker in the city, Sorvino's character Kate, an ICE agent, investigates the case, eventually raiding and rescuing the women from the trafficker's clutches and dismantling the trafficking ring.

Human Trafficking informed Sorvino about human trafficking and solidified her position as a serious anti-trafficking advocate, even though the film is replete with tropes of helpless women victims, predatory male traffickers, and law enforcement raids and rescues, all of which anchored its sense of realism in timely political anxieties about women's migration and forced prostitution in the post-1989 period (de Villiers 2016). As Sorvino (2009) explained during an interview with UN Television, the miniseries gave her "a chance to combine my acting work and my social interest work, the advocacy I do as a sort of second career." She added here that it "would be a great way to raise awareness on this topic, and in doing the film, I really became greater acquainted with certain elements of the topic." In addition to earning a Golden Globe nomination for her performance in *Human Trafficking*, Amnesty awarded Sorvino an "Artist of Conscience" award in 2006.

However, Sorvino's receptivity to new information and exposure to the issue as a UNODC Goodwill Ambassador eventually led her to offer a more complex representation than she did in *Human Trafficking*. As she explained to an audience assembled at Georgetown University (Sorvino 2013), "In the four years I have had the immense honor of working as the United Nations

Office on Drugs and Crime's Goodwill Ambassador to combat Human Trafficking, so much has happened to the movement, and I have learned so much." As the remainder of this section illustrates, Sorvino (2012) learned that human trafficking does not only involve sex trafficking; instead, it is "an enormous, multi-tentacled crime." As she stated at Georgetown, human trafficking "can be found everywhere, under every rock you can turn over, even in the most unexpectedly innocuous-seeming of settings," and to illustrate, she offered the example of a case in California where men were trafficked to work on Christmas tree farms (Sorvino 2013).

As a UN Goodwill Ambassador, Sorvino also emphasized that girls and women in the Global South are not the only trafficking victims. As she implored the National Council of State Legislatures (NCSL), "Please do not neglect the labor trafficking victims, simply due to the overtly heinous nature of child sex trafficking, nor prioritize women and girls over men and boys, and the extant resources for aftercare for the latter almost nonexistent" (Sorvino 2012). Yet even as she emphasized that victims may hold a range of gender identities, she still often tended to characterize them as lacking agency and damaged by the experience. In fact, she regretted how her own acting career might have led audiences to believe that sex workers have agency, telling the audience at a briefing in support of the Domestic Minor Sex Trafficking Deterrence and Victims Support Act (S. 596) in Washington, DC, that "when we think of prostitution, the whole game has to change. Now, there's no such thing as the independent contractor anymore. There is no such thing as the myth of the happy hooker. And I'm sorry to say that *Mighty Aphrodite* may have led you to believe otherwise" (Sorvino 2011a).

As Sorvino expanded her representation of human trafficking's forms and victims, she also emphasized a wider range of causal factors, namely poverty. In 2013, she combined her role as a UNODC Ambassador with a performance in CNN's documentary *Every Day In Cambodia,* which was filmed in Svay Pak. Located north of Phnom Penh and primarily inhabited by Vietnamese families who work in fishing, farming, and other small businesses, Svay Pak has a well-known brothel district and has been at the forefront of debates about global HIV/AIDS prevention policy (Busza 2014). In the documentary, which was released in 2014, Sorvino tours Svay Pak with Dan Brewster, a white American former pastor who moved to the area from California in 2009 with his wife, Bridget; together, they run Agape International Missions, an American evangelical Christian NGO devoted to doing "whatever it takes to end the evil of child sex trafficking" (Agape

International Missions 2021). Over the course of the film, viewers see how poverty creates vulnerability to human trafficking through stories of young girls like Kieu, who Sorvino describes as having a "smile that lights up her face" that also "hides the sadness in her eyes." Sorvino visits Kieu's mother in her fishing village, which is crowded with houses teetering on stilts near murky water. About the residents, Sorvino says, "They are poor, desperate, and extremely vulnerable to the traffickers who come here, looking for little girls." Through a translator, Kieu's mother tells Sorvino that when her family could not earn enough money selling fish, they took out a loan with a high interest rate. "That's when the trafficker came calling," she said. To repay the loan, Kieu was sent to work in a brothel that she could not leave; three to six men raped her every day.

The film is replete with these horrifying stories about the relationship between poverty and girls' vulnerability to sexual exploitation; however, illustrating Alexander-Floyd's (2021, 4) insight that melodrama is "the privileged representational vehicle for reproducing racist and sexist ideologies," *Every Day In Cambodia* "positions poor women as objects of sight for the privileged gaze" (Hesford 2011, 148) while also promoting the "racist dehumanization of alleged perpetrators" (Heynen and van der Meulen 2021, 20). As Sorvino, a privileged white woman from the United States, tours Svay Pak, she also tries to introduce viewers to individuals who facilitate sex trafficking. The production team appears to identify a group of Thai men who are traffickers, and although there is no evidence to support these allegations, since the men "scatter like roaches exposed to light" when the cameras approach, this is proof enough for her to characterize them as traffickers and as vermin (cited in Heynen and van der Meulen 2021, 20).

Fortunately, Sorvino discussed how poverty creates vulnerability to human trafficking in an arguably less offensive and problematic way at the Catholic Bishops' Conference of England and Wales meeting on human trafficking, which took place in April 2014 in Vatican City. It is worth noting here that religious groups have long played a powerful role in the anti-trafficking movement, but mainstream Hollywood celebrities are not common fixtures at faith-based anti-trafficking gatherings. Sorvino, who is Catholic, is thus a "a relatively rare celebrity who invokes the role of faith in her own anti-trafficking work" (Heynen and van der Meulen 2021, 10). As she declared in her speech, "Personally speaking, as Christians, our call is clear. To stand with the oppressed, to fight for justice. I want to thank Pope Francis for making this issue a defining call to action in his papacy" (Sorvino 2014).

In her long and at times rambling speech, Sorvino (2014) told the audience that "We know that poverty is the number one cause of vulnerability to being trafficked." However, she did not solely attribute poverty to individual failings; instead, she rooted it in capitalism, stating, "Capitalism and free markets have a tendency to lionize the lowest bidder . . . as the profit margin's the widest. And then you are biting into a chocolate bar made with beans picked by tiny child slave hands, or soaking in a porcelain tub created with pig iron smelted by trafficked men." In stating this, Sorvino departs from other faith-based anti-trafficking advocates who, as critical trafficking scholars have shown, tend to focus less on addressing poverty as a root cause and more on promoting carcerally-oriented anti-sex trafficking laws (C. Jackson 2016; Bernstein 2010, 2012).

SOLUTIONS AND FEMINIST IDEOLOGIES

Drawing from post-colonial feminist scholarship, researchers have carefully documented how celebrities rarely challenge the logic of the modern global marketplace, which made them very wealthy and influential in the first place. As a result, celebrities are more likely to *reproduce* the gendered power relations that sustain Western patriarchal capitalism than they are to challenge them (Hopkins 2017). However, a closer, interpretive look at Ormond's and Sorvino's anti-trafficking work reveals other possibilities for celebrity feminists who are willing to learn from their experiences and the available research and evidence. In addition to calling for the eradication of poverty, Ormond and Sorvino offer solutions that challenge Western patriarchal capitalism and, by extension, the carceral and neoliberal feminist ideologies that have featured so prominently in anti-trafficking politics.

Solving Poverty by Redeeming Capitalism?

To solve human trafficking, both Ormond and Sorvino have promoted the eradication of poverty. As Ormond (2006a) told the Vienna Forum, "I have to join my voice to others around the world calling for the eradication of world poverty; indeed this is written into the anti-trafficking treaty as an underlying cause of trafficking, and we are therefore legally obligated to do what we can." Similarly, in her speech to UN General Assembly at end of her UN Goodwill Ambassadorial term, Sorvino (2017) told the audience that "a parallel vigorous attack on the root causes of vulnerability such as gender inequality, cultural discrimination, poverty, access to clean water, education and economic opportunity must occur" if trafficking is ever to end and, by extension, gender equality is to be achieved.

Given the challenges of quickly eradicating poverty on a global scale, Ormond and Sorvino have also supported other more immediate economic and criminal law-related solutions. Regarding the former, feminists and anti-trafficking activists have long called for stronger labor protections and higher wages, among other measures to reduce poverty and vulnerability to coercive labor. Recently, however, the media, policy makers, and other stakeholders have also emphasized what Elizabeth Bernstein (2016, 46) terms "socially entrepreneurial business ventures" to fight human trafficking such as "apps" and online games, among other market-based responses to the issue (see also Anti-Trafficking Review 2020). Locating these efforts within scholarship on so-called "new capitalism," Bernstein (2016, 55) labels these ventures as part of "redemptive capitalism"—that which "is understood by its proponents to be not only transforming of self but of world, and indeed, of markets themselves in a moment when the era of social entitlements is over." Proponents of these ventures also argue that they promote feminist values. For example, by allowing women to report trafficking and connect to NGOs through an app, these measures are empowering them and promoting gender equality.

Ormond and Sorvino have variously emphasized redemptive capitalist solutions to human trafficking and, by extension, promoted a neoliberally inflected feminist ideology. Sorvino's efforts here are especially evident in *Every Day In Cambodia* (2013/2014), where she promotes Agape's efforts to, as Brewster tells her, "reintegrate [girls who worked in Svay Pak's sex businesses] as loving, healthy women in Cambodian society," which sees them as "trash." To this end, Brewster opened a garment factory in 2012, and in the film, we see young Cambodian women laboring there on sewing machines. Brewster emphasizes the redemptive nature of this work, telling Sorvino that "these jobs are far more than employment: they are a place to restore honor to a girl! Not just in the eyes of people in the factory but in whole community—they become people of honor again." Furthermore, this work also redeems Brewster. In the film, viewers learn that making money is *not* the number one goal for his philanthro-capitalistic venture—the likes of which scholars have criticized for promoting feminized, low-waged labor for girls, individual agency and business acumen as solutions to gender-based oppression, and a "privatized politics" that endorses global capitalist values and the hegemony of neoliberalism (Hopkins 2017, 276; see also Kinney 2013). Instead, Brewster says in the film, "I am more concerned with making a difference than making money," explaining further to Sorvino that their products cost more to sell because they pay their workers three to four times the area's average wages and offer them childcare, healthcare, and other services.

Like Sorvino, Ormond has also identified how capitalism creates vulnerabilities to human trafficking, but in contrast to Sorvino's promotion of socially entrepreneurial responses, Ormond's NGO, ASSET, was founded to "work on systemic solutions and align with the UNODC mandate of Prevention, Prosecution and Protection" (ASSET 2015a). However, Ormond has also come to resist this UN approach, noting that while she initially thought it was "admirable and holistic" (Ormond 2008b), it was not sufficiently focused on addressing economic systems and structures, namely product supply chains. ASSET states that "product supply chains affect all of us and are a part of all of our daily lives, and therefore became ASSET's primary tactic to engage all consumers, all supply chain stake holders, and move the needle of engagement" (ASSET 2015b). To fix supply chains, Ormond has pursued legislation, most notably through the California Transparency in Supply Chains Act (CTSCA), which was signed into law by then-Governor Arnold Schwarzenegger on September 30, 2010.

Before discussing the CTSCA, it is important to recognize that efforts to reduce human trafficking and forced labor in supply chains are not new. As Lisa Rende Taylor and Elena Shih (2019, 136) document, "Worker rights and labour organising groups have worked directly with workers for hundreds of years, aiming to empower workers and drive responses from management through collective action and collective bargaining." In the twentieth century, the labor movement has worked specifically to address labor supply chain issues, expecting that "effective labour regulation would help to achieve more stable and direct employment relations, through which workers could be protected" (Barrientos 2011, 4). As Galit Sarfaty (2015) documents extensively, a number of laws have been passed since the 1930s to variously address labor and supply chain issues, such as Section 307 of the Smoot-Hawley Tariff Act, which prohibits the importation of products made with forced or convict labor, and the Foreign Corrupt Practices Act, which attached liability to a company through its supply chain vendors, to name just some examples. Since the early 2000s, many anti-trafficking organizations have worked with some of the most exploited workers in the world to provide protection, support, outreach, and empowerment through hotlines, awareness-raising, direct assistance, and policy advocacy and systems-capacity building (Rende Taylor and Shih 2019).

Among these efforts, Ormond's stand out because her fame allowed her to (relatively) quickly mobilize resources and support for the CTSCA. In 2007, she reached out to Darrell Steinberg, a Democratic politician who was elected to the California State Senate in 2006, asking him to be the principal author of a bill that would eventually become the CTSCA, and he readily agreed (Mattos 2012). In addition to its celebrity support, the bill was also well timed to complement existing legislation such as the California Trafficking Victims Protection Act, which passed in 2005. This law created the California Alliance to Combat Trafficking and Slavery (California ACTS) Task Force, which was charged with reviewing the state's response to human trafficking. California ACTS reported in 2007 that, among other things, the state must take further measures to address labor exploitation in supply chains (California ACTS Task Force 2007).

In 2008, Steinberg introduced Ormond's bill as SB1649, which would have required "retail sellers and manufacturers doing business in the state to develop, maintain, and implement policies related to their compliance with federal and state law regarding the eradication of slavery and human trafficking from its supply chain. . . ." (CA Assembly 2010a, 9). The law would apply to businesses with more than $2 million in annual sales, and it would require them to indicate to consumers on their website (or by other means) that all of the suppliers in their supply chain comply with the laws "regarding slavery and human trafficking of the country or countries in which they are doing business," and that they "will make a good faith effort to eradicate slavery and human trafficking in its existing supply chain rather than only stop doing business in the area where it discovers that its supply chain is tainted by slavery or human trafficking" (CA Assembly 2008).

A range of groups supported SB1649, including CAST-LA, the California Teamsters Public Affairs Council, the California Labor Federation, the American Federation of Labor, Planned Parenthood Affiliates of California, and many others; however, it did not receive final legislative approval (Mattos 2012). Indicating how collective corporate power may far outweigh celebrity power, a coalition of business groups opposed the bill, including the California Chamber of Commerce, the California Manufacturers and Technology Association, the National Federation of Independent Business, the California Retailers Association, the California Independent Grocers

Association, and the Grocery Manufacturers Association. While these opponents stated their opposition to trafficking and slavery (many large retail companies had already implemented environmental and ethical standards along their supply chains for a number of years), they also claimed that businesses cannot reasonably be expected to police supply chain practices (Mattos 2012; Pickles and Zhu 2013; Rao 2020).

In reality, the bill was not asking that much from businesses: SB1649 would have only required companies to develop and publicize a policy that, in large part, indicated their compliance with existing state and federal laws regarding trafficking in supply chains. Companies also did not have to reveal trade secrets, and the penalty for non-compliance was merely injunctive relief, whereby a court would issue an order for the defendant to stop committing one or more specified actions (in this case, not publicizing their policy, as the law would require). However, the business community still lobbied strongly against SB1649, leading Steinberg to revise and reintroduce it as SB657. Instead of requiring companies to develop policies targeting their supply chains and demonstrate compliance with various state and federal laws, SB657 would now apply only to retail sellers and manufacturers whose threshold revenue was $100 million (up from $2 million) in annual worldwide gross receipts (or 3.2% of the state's businesses), and they would only have to "disclose their efforts to eradicate slavery and human trafficking from their direct supply chains for tangible goods offered for sale" in five key areas (CA State Assembly 2010b).[2] The penalty for non-disclosure remained the same (injunctive relief).

Even in this watered-down form, SB657 exemplifies the power of celebrity to relatively quickly address human trafficking through measures that potentially redeem capitalism. When Schwarzenegger signed the bill into law on September 30, 2010 (just three years after Ormond reached out to Steinberg with her idea), media coverage featured him—a celebrity from the fitness and film worlds—happily shaking hands with Ormond (see figure 10). Together, their celebrity helped pass a law that offered "a rare example of mandated corporate social responsibility disclosure" (Birkey et al. 2016, 827) that would "harness the immense economic power" of California consumers to help tackle a "complex and challenging problem" by providing them with "access to basic information to aid their purchasing decisions" (CA Assembly 2010a, 3).

Speaking about the CTSCA in 2011, before the Congressional Commission on Security and Cooperation in Europe, Ormond declared that it would "for the first time enable consumers to choose to support businesses that are creating best practices, using their purchasing power to encourage

FIGURE 10. Julia Ormond and California's then governor, Arnold Schwarzenegger, signing the CTSCA. Photo by s_bukley (Ryan Born)/depositphotos.com

them to bring their expertise and knowledge of supply chains into the equation" (Ormond 2011). Furthermore, as Ormond explained, this law was actually *good* for business. Not only would it "elevate human rights and place them right at the heart of their strategy," it would also "educate companies unaware of a possible problem" *and* create a good public relations opportunity for them. In short, she stated, "Companies already doing the right thing can more robustly and publicly turn it into part of their brand identity" (Ormond 2011). Later in this chapter I consider the extent to which this law has lived up to its promise.

Fighting Trafficking Through Better Criminalization?

In addition to redeeming capitalism, both Ormond and Sorvino have promoted criminal justice-oriented solutions to human trafficking that further carcerally-oriented feminist ideologies; however, their emphasis here differs significantly. Reflecting and promoting the mission and goals of the UNODC, both Ormond and Sorvino have called for better education and training for criminal justice professionals and others who may be positioned to identify and assist victims. As a UN Ambassador, Sorvino (2014) told audiences about the need "to educate members of law enforcement, and members of the prosecutorial, defense and judiciary staff on modern day slavery." Similarly, Ormond (2006a) has called for "educating police on how to identify trafficking victims, be knowledgeable about victims' rights, [and] having them work with NGOs to be supportive." She also extended this call for training to border control and customs enforcement officers so that they may better help victims *and* protect national security interests. "It is the front-line of police, border control, and customs that need to be empowered and coordinated globally in order to assist the war against terrorism," Ormond (2007) told the UN Security Council. "Without sufficient prioritization and awareness-training globally to identify trafficking, leading to a sharing of criminal information, we are denying ourselves the opportunity to join the dots and see the emerging patterns." Failure to do this not only harms "the world's poor" but leaves "ourselves vulnerable."

While both celebrities have advocated for more law enforcement training, they have taken different positions in debates about decriminalizing sex work, which, as noted throughout this book, is one of the most hotly debated responses to human trafficking. Of the two, Ormond is more willing to consider non-criminalizing approaches to prostitution, telling the audience at Vienna Forum on human trafficking,

> The jury is still out on whether legalization has a positive or negative impact on the numbers of women and children trafficked into prostitution, and while one might argue that surely that depends on how it is done, we are living in an era where different governments are taking radically different approaches; from Sweden's criminalization of the client but legalization of the prostitute, to Holland's all out legalization, to other countries' total criminalization. This is fertile ground for unbiased research to determine which is the better policy. Such data will never be absolute in the links between causality and outcome, yet we must work with the best data we can get (Ormond 2006a).

Since Ormond made this speech (which, to my knowledge, is the only time she addressed prostitution-related policy and legislation specifically), researchers have found that decriminalization often does enhance sex workers' health and safety.[3] However, it was a considerable risk for Ormond to consider non-criminalizing approaches to prostitution in 2006, as these were not as popular with many audiences as they were by 2015, when Amnesty declared its support for decriminalization. Her 2006 statement thus indicates that celebrities do not always avoid controversial positions for fear of alienating their fans.

Yet even as sex workers themselves have argued for decriminalizing sex work and a growing body of evidence supports this position, Mira Sorvino has been much more reluctant to endorse it, especially in her state-level advocacy at the National Council of State Legislatures (NCSL). Founded in 1975 to represent "the legislatures in the states, territories and commonwealths of the U.S.," the NCSL's mission is to "advance the effectiveness, independence and integrity of legislatures and to foster interstate cooperation and facilitate the exchange of information among legislatures." The NCSL has examined human trafficking, and Sorvino addressed this topic at the 2011 NCSL Legislative Summit in San Antonio, TX, and at the 2012 NCSL Capital Forum in Washington, DC, which focused broadly on women's health and leadership.

In her position as a UN Ambassador, Sorvino emphasized at the NCSL meetings that states must improve their enforcement of existing trafficking-related laws. Regarding enforcement, Sorvino (2011b) told the NCSL audience that "Our and every other nation's assignment of priority to battling this ruthless scourge has thus far been fairly low, if judged by our discovery of victims, convictions of traffickers, or overall money spent," adding further that "Every month, the U.S. spends more on the War on Drugs than all the total budget ever expended fighting Human Trafficking since we designated it a crime over ten years ago!" Sorvino also drew attention to the problematic enforcement of existing laws, noting when she revisited the NCSL (Sorvino 2012) that victims are often not rescued, but arrested. Here she told the audience that "every day, vice squads make sweeps and arrest children and teenagers for the crime of prostitution, incarcerate them on occasion in adult jail, others in juvenile detention, sometimes with a misguided attempt at 'protecting' them, branding them with criminal records that will haunt them the rest of their lives."

To improve trafficking laws, then, Sorvino (2011b) reminded the NCSL that US states must align their legislative priorities with UN goals and protocols, because in this great nation, each state has been given the awesome power and responsibility to write its own laws, which govern the day to day operation of law enforcement, the judicial system, and the social services afforded its citizens. All of these areas, if brought up to date with the United Nations Palermo Protocol and the Federal Trafficking Victims Protection Act, have the power to discover thousands if not hundreds of thousands of trafficking victims within our borders, to punish the evil perpetrators profiting from the sale of human beings, and to save and uplift the lives of those currently living under the yoke of slavery.

To this end, Sorvino strongly emphasized two carcerally-oriented solutions at the NCSL meetings that were popular among anti-sex work carceral feminists and other anti-trafficking advocacy groups: safe harbor laws and so-called "end-demand" initiatives. The former, broadly speaking, would protect minors from prosecution for prostitution through some combination of decriminalizing their participation in prostitution, diverting them to social services, and reclassifying them as victims or sexually exploited children (Gies et al. 2018). Among the states that passed these laws, Sorvino (2011b) praised Illinois: "By now I think you know where I stand on the creation, passage, and implementation of robust Safe Harbor Laws in the 44 states which still do not have them," she said, adding that "Illinois currently has the strongest one that guarantees immunity from prosecution as a prostitute to any child under the age of eighteen and does not place the burden of proof of trafficking on the victim. The age is enough." As Sorvino told the audience, such safe harbor laws were "crucial to shattering the archaic public and law enforcement lens that perceives children under the age of 18 trafficked for sexual exploitation as criminals guilty of the crime of prostitution." More importantly, these laws would give young people "crucial social services necessary to reassume their rightful place in society, with a background unmarred by a criminal record."

In addition to safe harbor laws, Sorvino also promoted end-demand initiatives that target and penalize the *purchasers* of sexual services. For Sorvino these are important from a gender equality perspective because men are rarely punished in the United States for purchasing sex. "He is often sent home with a slap on the wrist," she told the NCSL, adding that police officers "on the scene have been known to say, 'Go home to your wife and kids, we don't want to ruin your life.' Or if he is brought in, he pays a $300 fine and attends 'John School' where he is lectured for a day" (Sorvino 2011b). To address these inconsistencies, Sorvino argued for harsher penalties for buyers, praising states that "have come up with some interesting antidotes to this leniency" and offering examples such as Hawaii, which made habitual solicitation of prostitution greater than two times a felony, and California, which "just passed legislation creating a mandatory $25,000 fine for johns who have solicited any minors, which will go directly into a fund to benefit child victims of sex trafficking" (Sorvino 2011b). In advocating for these end-demand initiatives at the 2012 NCSL meeting, Sorvino added that she was "happy to see so many men in the room today" because "they should be at the table ideating solutions. This is not women's business, it is everyone's, and the real generational shift will come from fathers teaching their sons to respect women and girls by not abusing and exploiting their bodies for commercial sex" (Sorvino 2012). Sorvino reiterated her support for ending demand in numerous other forums, telling the CNN Freedom Project, "The demand side really needs to be addressed," adding, "If people weren't trying to buy child sex it wouldn't be being sold" (cited in Cohen 2015).

Safe harbor laws and end-demand initiatives are not new, but Sorvino's advocacy helped to publicize and diffuse them across the nation, thereby furthering a carceral feminist ideology, albeit a kinder, gentler one that removes young people from the purview of punishment and, in theory, is more gender-equal. To date, the majority of US states have passed some version of a safe harbor law, and according to Demand Forum (2021), "a comprehensive online resource for people interested in ending sex trafficking and prostitution," more than 2,125 cities and counties in the United States have launched initiatives aimed at deterring men from purchasing sexual services.

TO WHAT EFFECT: STRUCTURAL CHALLENGES AND CELEBRITY ACCOUNTABILITY

Together, Ormond and Sorvino have used their fame capital to engage in anti-trafficking advocacy on behalf of international organizations, and in so doing, they have at times resisted many of their peers' tendencies to promote the dominant narrative of human trafficking. At the same time, they remain uber-privileged white women from the Global North, and as the following discussion indicates, their performances remain inextricably linked to and supportive of Western/US-centric norms and values.

In the global political realm, celebrities occupy privileged positions: they engage with grassroots, impacted communities at their discretion, and their fame secures access to the United Nations and other influential organizations and governing bodies in ways that other more experienced and knowledgeable advocates can only imagine. While their celebrity may indeed help these entities draw public and political attention to issues like human trafficking, scholars indicate how they also often reproduce "the colonial legacy in which western values are defined as universally ethical, while failing to remember that the highest values of western civilisation have been deeply complicit in the violent history of colonialism and its ideology" (Yrjölä 2011b, 362). As a result, "celebrity ambassadors on tour are also ambassadors of cultural imperialism, ruling not by direct imperial control, but through the 'soft power' of good PR and strategic image management" (Hopkins 2017, 286).

This exercise of soft power is evident in Sorvino's anti-trafficking activism, most notably in *Every Day in Cambodia,* where she positions herself as the American "(white) savior defending victims against the evils of . . . implicitly or explicitly racialized perpetrator[s]" of human trafficking (Heynen and van der Meulen 2021, 20), while largely ignoring how US and international governing bodies create vulnerabilities to trafficking in the first place. This tendency is particularly evident in the scene where Sorvino meets with Chou Bun Eng, one of the few women in the Cambodian government, and a high-ranking one at that. As a long-time member of the ruling Cambodian People's Party and Secretary of State for the Interior since 2008, Eng chairs the country's National Committee on Counter Trafficking, where she has worked to change Cambodian law so that the police and other officials may better investigate and prosecute trafficking crimes. In English, she tells Sorvino how they have been trying to get judges, police, and prosecutors to work together to improve their practices here "because so far it seems our law doesn't allow [surveillance of potential traffickers]." In response, Sorvino adopts the position of "the benevolent global citizen" (Engle 2012, 116) and, using what Lauren Kogen (2014) terms a discourse of condescension, challenges Eng by cutting her off. "Well, it doesn't seem that your law doesn't allow it, it just seems that it was not included as an explicit part of your human trafficking law," she says. Sorvino goes on to explain to Eng that "nothing in your legal code denies the use of surreptitious surveillance [of sex businesses]," stating here that if this surveillance is allowed for drug traffickers, "why wouldn't [it apply to] human traffickers who are arguably far more damaging to human people? Why aren't they worthy of the same level of scrutiny?"

Reflecting criticisms that celebrity feminists often speak confidently on behalf of other less privileged women, Sorvino proceeds to tell Eng that sex trafficking victims want more surveillance of sex businesses. "I've met with victims around the world," she says, "and I'll say to you that I met with children yesterday that broke my heart, and they don't have the time to wait for these discussions." Eng tries to respond, but Sorvino raises her voice and speaks over her again. "You really must act quickly! You really need to save their lives!" she cries, adding, "Every moment you waste, another child is being brutalized and raped in a brothel right now around us!" Eng keeps trying to interject her agreement and explain what her government is doing about these issues, but Sorvino only grows more agitated. "I beg you, as a mother, you can do it. I believe you have this power." Eng tries again to explain the challenges of the legal process, and how her government has been working on these issues for a long time. "Ok, I know," Sorvino concedes, and Eng tells her that they "are close to something." Sorvino is fed up and indignant in response: "If it's going to be a few days, I'm ok with that, but if it's going to be a few years, I'm not ok." Here Eng replies, "We need to do it, but we have to find a way how to do it." In presenting this exchange, I am not claiming that Sorvino was wrong to highlight a major discrepancy in Cambodia's anti-trafficking law: the fact that the police cannot and do not thoroughly investigate sex trafficking has left many women and girls vulnerable to exploitation. However, one cannot help but cringe at the optics of a white celebrity, flanked by a camera crew from a major American television network, lecturing one of Cambodia's few female political officials about how to do her job, all the while ignoring the realities of the legislative process in a country that is not her own.

While ignorance of how governing structures may impede the passage of adequate anti-trafficking legislation is not unique to celebrities, it highlights how celebrities from the United States (and elsewhere in the Global North) often act as global citizens who chastise other nations for their actions, while ignoring how their own governments and organizations may have created conditions of oppression and marginalization in the first place. Here, in the same way that Ricky Martin was largely silent about the linkages between American colonialism and vulnerabilities to human trafficking in Puerto Rico (see chapter 4), Sorvino fails to indicate how the United States and the United Nations have increased trafficking risks for the Vietnamese people (and others) in Svay Pak, Cambodia. Although French colonization in the late nineteenth and early twentieth centuries motivated Vietnamese migration to Cambodia (the French employed Vietnamese farmers in Cambodia), this movement escalated following the Vietnam War. As Yen Le Espiritu (2014) writes, as one of the most brutal and destructive wars between Western imperial powers and the people of Asia, the Vietnam war's destruction, coupled with twenty years of US trade and aid economic embargoes, shattered Vietnam's economy and society, leaving the country among the poorest in the world, while scattering its people to all corners of the globe. Many Vietnamese people moved to Cambodia in search of opportunities; however, they became especially vulnerable here following the Khmer Rouge's seizure of the country in 1975. While Vietnam eventually ousted the Khmer Rouge from Cambodia and helped many Vietnamese people return to Vietnam, by the 1980s at least 300,000 Vietnamese persons remained in Cambodia. Their living conditions worsened, especially post-1993, when many ethnic Vietnamese people in Cambodia were classified as "non-citizens" and denied access to identification documents that would afford them benefits of citizenship. According to the Minority Rights Group (2021), there are an estimated 400,000–700,000 ethnic Vietnamese in Cambodia, and around 90 percent of them do not have birth certificates and/or identity cards, which makes it difficult for them to find work and, consequently, increases their risk for exploitation.

The United Nations also fueled migration and, consequently, vulnerabilities to sex trafficking in the region. As Joanna Busza (2014) documents, Svay Pak's well-known brothel district actually flourished when peacekeepers from the UN Transitional Authority were stationed in Cambodia. When the UN authorities left, Svay Pak's economic fortunes declined as competing brothel and other sex businesses opened closer to the capital; in response, many sex workers left Svay Pak, but many also remained there. By the late 1990s, the town had roughly twenty operating brothels, staffed mainly by young Vietnamese women who had migrated from provinces adjacent to the Cambodian border with the specific aim of working in a brothel—a common livelihood strategy among poor rural households. Altogether, this research indicates how Vietnamese and Cambodian people engage in sex work for a range of personal and economic reasons, and their risks for sex trafficking result from globally interconnected issues (Monto 2014; Hoefinger 2014).

As a UN Ambassador, Sorvino may have been aware of how geopolitical factors create vulnerabilities to human trafficking in Cambodia. However, her performance with Minister Eng—excoriating her to change the law so the police can better investigate trafficking cases—ignores the fact that criminal law reforms alone will not end human trafficking. Here Sorvino displayed "the soft side of imperialism," where celebrities and others "embrace the spectacle of themselves rushing in to save miserable victims" (Kempadoo 2015, 14). These performances ignore the fact that the supposedly miserable victims may not need saving. Sex workers in Cambodia do not lack agency: there is a long history of sex worker organizing and empowerment in the region through groups such as the Women's Network for Unity (WNU), a five thousand-member-strong union of sex workers in Cambodia with members from all around the country (Ditmore 2014). However, the WNU is nowhere to be found in *Every Day in Cambodia,* and so, like many other celebrity anti-trafficking performances, the film centers Sorvino and her celebrity over the many diverse voices of sex workers in the region.

Fixing Capitalism: The Limits of the CTSCA

Ormond's support for the CTSCA indicates how celebrities' efforts to decenter themselves and draw attention to structural causes—in this case, corporate supply chains—may be limited by their fealty to the broader systems that sustain them (in this case, capitalism). While supply chains do create vulnerabilities to human trafficking, questions arise about whether fixing them—and thereby sustaining the current market economic system—offers a sufficient solution. After all, as Kempadoo (2015, 17) asks, "Is more capitalism really the panacea to the problem of modern slavery and human trafficking?" The remainder of this section indicates how, by leaving corporate capitalist power largely intact, the CTSCA has ultimately had little discernable impact on human trafficking and gender inequality to date.

Before illustrating this critique, however, it is important to note that the CTSCA was one of the first (rare) laws to institute a disclosure regime that required companies to scrutinize their supply chains for illegal labor practices (Prokopets 2014). Even if it lacks teeth, many corporations *do* comply with the law. For example, Rachel Birkey et al.'s study of 105 retail companies subject to the CTSCA found relatively high compliance: 82.9 percent provided a CTSCA disclosure of their efforts to eradicate human trafficking from their supply chains on their website as of the first ten days of January,

2012 (Birkey et al. 2016). However, in larger studies, this rate tended to fall, and the disclosures were often minimal, if not non-existent. Yoon Jin Ma and colleagues studied the website disclosures of 204 US retail and manufacturing companies, finding that "less than half of the apparel, retail, and manufacturing companies in California and in the rest of the United States complied with the Act" (Ma, Lee, and Goerlitz 2016, 312). When companies disclosed, this was more symbolic than substantive in nature: only thirteen companies from Birkey et al.'s (2016) sample included extensive information for more than one of the CTSCA's five areas of disclosure. Furthermore, as Stephanie Limoncelli (2017, 121) writes, since the legislation "requires only that a company provide a statement about what, if anything, it does to combat human trafficking in its supply chains, it may simply report that it does nothing at all," and indeed, a number of major manufacturing, energy, and agricultural companies provided such "no action" disclosures.

From all of this, one may conclude that the CTSCA, for all of its celebrity fanfare, has largely failed to fix supply chains and reduce human trafficking. Without full corporate disclosure, consumers have little information with which to hold corporations accountable and, in turn, force them to improve their labor supply chains. As a result, the CTSCA is yet another example of an anti-trafficking measure where "global capitalism is acknowledged as the economic context within which human trafficking occurs, but it is not identified as a problem from which people need to be freed" (Kempadoo 2015, 16). This maintenance of corporate, capitalist power is particularly evident in how the CTSCA asks little from the business community but much from the consuming public (Mattos 2012). Instead of forcing businesses to eradicate slavery in their supply chains, consumers must find (or request) information from businesses about their supply chains and make consumption decisions accordingly. In short, the CTSCA relies on consumer activism—that which is "taken by consumers through participating in the market such as through boycotts or ethical shopping" (Lightfoot 2019, 301)—to challenge and improve corporate supply chain practices.

However, the CTSCA's reliance on consumer activism is not entirely futile. As part of a broader movement that attempts to transform various elements of the social order surrounding consumption and marketing, consumer activism challenges the practices of powerful business elites and the public's consumption preferences and habits (Kozinets and Handelman 2004). This activism has a long history in the United States, dating back to the Boston Tea Party (which was essentially a boycott of British goods), and it has long been popular with those on the political margins, such as African Americans and women before they had the right to vote. For example, in the 1910s, African Americans boycotted companies that refused to hire African Americans, and the Montgomery bus system boycott in the 1950s emphasized African Americans' power to financially ruin the streetcar company (Lightfoot 2019). More recently, the internet has greatly influenced and expanded consumer activism by allowing for an explosion of niche consumer goods, activism, and charitable campaigns aimed at the so-called ethical consumer (Lightfoot 2019; Page 2017; Micheletti 2003).

Consumer activism has also targeted slavery and human trafficking. The Free Produce Movement was one of the most prominent consumer activist movements of the nineteenth century. Initiated by northern abolitionists, free African American slaves, and Quakers, this movement urged abstinence from slave-made products such as cotton and sugar (Lightfoot 2019; Reese 2020). Since then, groups such as the National Consumers League encouraged consumers to understand the working conditions of laborers worldwide in order to engage them in selective and ethical purchasing (Page 2017). Currently, the internet has spawned a range of online consumer activism through websites such as slaveryfootprint.org. Created by Justin Dillon, the man behind the celebrity-popular documentary *Call + Response* (discussed in chapter 2), the site purports to measure consumers' reliance on slave labor in the Global South through their consumption of popular goods like iPods, clothing, and coffee (Page 2017).

Yet for all of its promise, scholars and activists have long criticized consumer activism, particularly as it relates to mitigating human trafficking and, by extension, promoting gender equality. In its contemporary, mainstream, online forms (like slaveryfootprint.org), consumer activism often fails to critique or reject the moral foundations of the capitalist order/modes of production, where labor is never actually free. Instead, it works to sustain consumption, while corporations demonstrate their transparency as a marketing tool to appeal to consumers (Page 2017; Lightfoot 2019). As a result, capitalist modes of production—where businesses are motivated by profit and offer laborers the lowest possible wage—remains intact. As feminist economists have shown for eons, women, and women of color in particular, experience capitalism's downward pressure on wages most acutely. Therefore, celebrity efforts like Ormond's CTSCA, which rely largely on consumer efforts to fix supply chains, are limited solutions at best to human trafficking and gender equality more broadly.

Celebrity feminists, and celebrities in politics writ large, have long been criticized for their lack of accountability for their efforts. However, Ormond's and Sorvino's anti-trafficking work reveals how celebrities may at least acknowledge the limits of their activism and endeavor to improve it. Ormond's efforts to better understand the limits and possibilities of the CTSCA offer one example here. As noted earlier, the CTSCA ultimately did little to increase corporate disclosures and stop human trafficking, and Ormond did not ignore these facts. Instead, she conceded that the CTSCA was merely a "catalyst step" towards promoting greater corporate disclosure and creating a robust system of slavery-free production certification, stating here that critics' claims that the legislation was watered down and lacked teeth constituted a "legitimate opinion" (cited in Balch 2013).

However, Ormond did not merely pay lip service to the law's limits: she went on to study them, and among evaluations of the CTSCA to date, ASSET offered the most extensive study of its impact on corporate disclosure, the law's main goal. Partnering with iPoint, a consulting firm that "empowers companies to collect, analyze and report all necessary data to assess the environmental, social, and economic impacts of their products and related processes" (iPoint 2021), and Development International (DI), a nonprofit that seeks to "bring independent scientific scrutiny, clarity, and accuracy to bear on issues with an empirical deficit, thus enabling constructive discussions" (Development International 2021), their study reviewed *all* companies subject to the CTSCA over two years (2015 and 2016). As they document in their final report (Bayer and Hudson 2017), corporate disclosure improved since the law's passage. Of 2,126 eligible companies, 1,504 provided disclosure statements in 2015, while in 2016, this increased to 1,909 of 3,336 eligible companies. However, more disclosure did not exactly fuel other corporate efforts to reduce human trafficking. In line with other research noted above, the iPoint study found that relatively few eligible companies engaged in proactive anti-trafficking initiatives, and most had low levels of transparency regarding the methods and outcomes of their anti-trafficking programs.

Furthermore, Ormond's activism indicates how celebrities may be willing to learn and keep working on an issue. In the foreword to the report from ASSET's study of the CTSCA, Ormond wrote,

We still have a long way to go to reach the potential of transparency. ASSET ... continue[s] to work on that agenda, to ensure that we journey from transparency to transformation. However initially small these first steps, I believe that transparency is a powerful tool for our planet (Bayer and Hudson 2017).

Indeed, one may criticize Ormond for not going far enough; however, her anti-trafficking work highlights how celebrities may draw attention to structural causes of human trafficking, work to address them, and further struggles for equity and justice. To illustrate, the ASSET website now has a "Statement on Ending Systemic Racism" that declares:

As an advocacy organization on a mission to end systemic enslavement, we are keenly aware of the 40 million men, women and children whose lives are at risk and continue to suffer due to ongoing enslavement and society's complicity in it. The recent racist killings targeting the African Americans Ahmaud Arbery and Breonna Taylor follow centuries of racism and lynching in America. We have watched with sadness, horror and disgust the openly belligerent murder of George Floyd. We grieve with all the families and loved ones, recognize the face of racism, and that racism is a root cause and enabler of enslavement (ASSET 2021c).

The site then states that "ASSET is pledging to do more and to do it better," noting that they stand in solidarity with Black Lives Matter, and that they are committed to adding "critical systemic legislative agendas and solutions" to expand their supply chain transparency strategy to include federal and state legislation that will advance reparations for Africans and African Americans, and city and statewide police reform to tackle systemic racism (ASSET 2021c). Ormond's activism here indicates how celebrities may better link their work to contemporary struggles for racial justice in the United States when they are willing to acknowledge their positions of privilege *within* the nation's long history of racism.

Relatedly, a closer examination of Sorvino's evolving issue positions indicates how a celebrity's willingness to receive new information and listen to the audiences she claims to represent may moderate and hold her accountable for her actions. As previous chapters show, when faced with evidence of the harmful effects of their advocacy, celebrities tend to ignore this information or actively resist it (recall how Ashton Kutcher refused to correct the misleading statistics he proffered). However, Sorvino's evolving support for Safe Harbor and end-demand initiatives provides a different example. After nearly five years with the United Nations, Sorvino was invited to address an

FIGURE 11. Mira Sorvino speaking at the Anti-Human Trafficking Symposium, "Transforming the Coalition," Georgetown University, School of Foreign Service, January 30, 2013. Photo by School of Foreign Service Communications/CC-BY-2.0.

audience of students, government, nonprofit, and academic leaders at Georgetown University's School of Foreign Service on January 30, 2013 (see figure 11).

In her speech, titled "Beyond Awareness: Putting the Human Back in Human Trafficking" (Sorvino 2013), she reflected on her work as a UNODC Ambassador. Following a discussion of supply chains and the need for anti-trafficking activists to consider labor and sex trafficking equally, she said, "Above all, we must make sure that by what we are endorsing, we are not doing further harm." Here Sorvino acknowledged that some of the policies she supported have done more harm than good. "I have recently become aware that some of the solutions I have been vigorously advocating may be . . . harming the very individuals they are designed to help, and creating unintended targets of out of others," she said.

As Sorvino explained further to the audience, "some of the key pieces of legislation that I felt (and still feel with a caveat) were most important were the 'Safe Harbor' laws," which she believed were vital "to the wellbeing of children trafficked into commercial sex. Their intent in their best, most robust form, is to decriminalize the minor in commercial sex" and to "give these young people back their dignity, their right to choose the life they want." However, she went on to say, "I am very disturbed to report that some of those very laws which are meant to help, not only fail to do that, but actually harm survivors." Sorvino then offered the example of Illinois's safe harbor law, which she had praised fairly recently to the NCSL. Since the law passed, Cook County's State's Attorney's Office

> convicted 17 individuals of felony human trafficking, however, Chicago police reports show men (johns and pimp-traffickers) are even less likely to be arrested on prostitution related charges than they were in 2005, down 7 percent. Meanwhile prostitution charges are being almost exclusively levied against sex workers: 97% of the 1,266 prostitution related felony convictions in the past 4 years, some of them minors. Only 3 buyers have been charged with a felony (Sorvino 2013).

Sorvino concluded with dismay that "This attempt to focus on ending the demand side has actually escalated the number of arrests of those whom we consider to be the victims, and their charges have been bumped up from misdemeanors to felonies, criminal records which can and do haunt them for the rest of their lives."

Sorvino elaborated her new position about end-demand initiatives further to an audience at Sonoma State University in 2016. Here she stated that individuals and families—and not necessarily law enforcement—have a role to play in ending traffickers' demand for commercial sex workers:

> [I] implore all of you out there, men and women, to teach your sons that it's no longer a victimless crime, it's no longer really fun and games at the bachelor party to hire a hooker, you know, to go online and call an escort, you don't know what you are getting behind the smiles and the dance and whatever, you don't know if that person's going back and forking over their entire earnings to someone who if they don't do that . . . is going to beat them (Sorvino 2016).

She then tells the audience that "we have to stop buying sex and they will stop selling sex." But in an effort to disavow forced prostitution while also acknowledging sex workers' agency, she explains that "they" does not refer to sex workers. "I'm not talking about prostitutes," Sorvino explained, "I'm talking about the pimp traffickers. If no one is asking for it, if there is no demand for it, traffickers cannot sell children to men to sleep with. They cannot sell unwilling adults" (Sorvino 2016). Although her position on ending demand for commercial sex is somewhat convoluted, she does not insist that sex workers stop working. As she finished explaining, "I know it's very sensitive, and I know sometimes I get like hate mail from sex workers, and I really don't mean to upset them or make them feel I don't understand the difficulty of their lives." To emphasize her non-judgment and highlight how her views of sex workers' agency had shifted since 2012, she added, "far be it for me to tell a person who is an adult who has chosen sex work as their life that they are doing something wrong. It's their life and they can choose what they want to do" (Sorvino 2016). This example indicates how celebrities may be accountable to their audiences and change their issue positions if they are willing to learn.

Of course, Sorvino's revelations about safe harbor laws, end-demand initiatives, and sex workers' agency are not new or noteworthy to many sex workers, let alone to critical trafficking and sex worker rights scholars and advocates. Since Sorvino gave her speeches at the NCSL, extensive research shows the negative consequences of many of the laws she once supported. For example, while safe harbor laws across the United States encouraged more juvenile justice and court personnel to screen for trafficking and make more referrals to the child welfare system, a relatively low percentage of these cases were substantiated, confirmed, and/or resulted in criminal charges to the trafficker (Cole and Sprang 2020). My own studies of end-demand initiatives such as john schools and public awareness campaigns indicate that they tend to target men of color and their discourse is often highly problematic, circulating contradictory constructions of sex workers as both victims and criminals (Majic 2014c, 2015, 2017). And still others have shown that by increasing the police's presence, end-demand initiatives often end up with more arrests of women and girls (Dank, Yahner, and Yu 2017; Gruber, Cohen, and Mogulescu 2016).

However, Sorvino's changing positions on these issues are worth exploring for scholars and critics of celebrity, politics, and feminism. After all, it is exceptionally rare for a celebrity feminist to admit that her advocacy may have promoted gender *in*equality, especially in the anti-trafficking space, and it is rarer still for one to listen (or claim to listen) to sex workers *and* support their inclusion in the anti-trafficking movement. As Sorvino told the audience at Georgetown, "It must be made very clear that the anti-sex-trafficking movement is not an anti-sex worker movement." Sorvino has not explained why she was receptive to new information and to admitting the negative consequences of her advocacy. However, I read her 2016 Sonoma State University speech as illustrating how celebrities may be more willing to correct their positions over time when they are attentive to evidence and their audiences.

CONCLUSION

Among those engaged in the anti-trafficking movement, Julia Ormond and Mira Sorvino are rare celebrities: they draw attention to a complex issue without (entirely) relying on a melodramatic narrative that reifies women and girls as innocent victims and men as evil villains (Vance 2011). Instead, by highlighting structurally-oriented causes and solutions, Ormond's and Sorvino's anti-trafficking performances may be read as celebrity feminism that attempts to understand the deeper causes of a complex issue. It may be that Ormond and Sorvino do not deserve praise for improving on the usual celebrity fare: within the broader scope of the anti-trafficking and feminist movements, their ideas and insights are not particularly radical, and other activists have long shared their issue representations and supported similar solutions. However, the position from which Ormond and Sorvino offer their representations of and solutions to human trafficking merits special attention. Unlike "civilian" activists, Ormond and Sorvino have fame capital, which affords them direct access to high-profile audiences ranging from the United Nations to the NCSL. Fortunately, because of their personal characteristics—namely, their willingness to learn—they have drawn from their experiences and used their platforms to underscore human trafficking's complexity. Furthermore, unlike some of their peers, they are even willing (in Sorvino's case) to admit when their efforts may have contributed to harms against sex workers, and (in Ormond's case) to study whether their legislative efforts have succeeded.

At the same time, the fact that we must largely rely on celebrities' personal characteristics for even a modicum of accountability underscores the fact that "there is no democratic mechanism for the well-intended celebrity ambassador to be dismissed by the oppressed poor she supposedly represents" (Hopkins 2017, 276). As a result, celebrities may still position themselves as white saviors (as Sorvino did in Cambodia, to name just one example) and remain at a distance when scholars, activists, and the communities they claim to represent want to know more about their efforts or even challenge them. In short, as self-appointed representatives, Sorvino and Ormond indicate that no matter how "tuned in" or "informed" a celebrity feminist may be, she is under no obligation to respond to her audience, even if her fame depends on her attunement to her fans and their reactions to her performances. This book's next and final chapter therefore proposes various ways in which we may demand accountability from celebrities and challenge their power to remain at a distance.

Conclusion

CELEBRITY, POWER, AND POLITICAL
ACCOUNTABILITY

IF YOU HAVE NOT SEEN *Taken,* please brace yourself for a spoiler. After learning that he has ninety-six hours to rescue his daughter Kim from the Albanian prostitution ring, Liam Neeson's character, Bryan Mills, does everything possible to save her. He collects intelligence from his colleagues at the CIA, borrows a private jet from his ex-wife's new husband, and, once in Paris, finds and tortures Marko, the Albanian trafficker, until he admits that Kim has been sold to a man named St. Clair. Bryan finds St Clair at a party where Kim is being auctioned off as "an American, a pure virgin." He pulls a gun, but he is knocked unconscious; when he awakens, he steals a car, drives to the Pont des Arts, and jumps onto the ship where an Arab sheikh is holding Kim captive at knife point. Bryan aims his gun at him in a stand-off, and as the sheikh begins to say, "We can negotiate," Bryan shoots him in the head. *Taken* ends back in the United States, where Bryan reunites Kim with her mother *and* lives up to his promise to help Kim start her singing career. They drive up to pop star Sheerah's home, where she ushers Kim inside and says, "let's see what you've got."

Replete with themes of heroic American masculinity, vulnerable femininity, anti-Arab sentiments, and anxieties about Eastern European criminal networks, *Taken* is but one of the many cultural productions to circulate the dominant human trafficking narrative. Dramatic and attention-grabbing, we may expect that celebrities' anti-trafficking activism would overwhelmingly promote this made-for-the-big-screen story. However, this book has shown that celebrities in fact represent human trafficking in a variety of ways, and a range of personal and contextual factors explain this variation. What broader lessons, then, may we learn from their anti-trafficking work, particularly regarding celebrities' political power and responsibility in broader movements to end oppression and marginalization?

As this book has shown, celebrities' political power derives not from their election or expertise but from their fame, which they use to illuminate issues like human trafficking to the broader public. Even if we may disagree with their positions and find their capacity to concretely address these issues is quite limited, we cannot dismiss celebrities' contributions to public discourse and, potentially, other meaningful change. Therefore, this chapter turns to the broader lessons this book offers about celebrities' power and accountability in an increasingly elite-dominated polity. Focusing on how they may shape human trafficking and feminist politics going forward, I consider the limits of celebrities' power: while they may control the terms of their engagement and how they represent issues to the public, their circumstances and contexts constrain the outcomes of their actions. I therefore suggest that the best use of their power may be to highlight the voices of impacted communities and the structures that create vulnerabilities to exploitation and oppression. From all of this, I indicate a range of ways to better hold celebrities accountable for their actions and advance our understandings of their political activism and power going forward.

LESSONS FOR POLITICS: HUMAN TRAFFICKING AND FEMINISM

In this book, I've understood celebrities' anti-trafficking activism as political performances, and I engaged Shirin Rai's (2014) PPF to analyze them and their work in terms of actors, settings, and discursive effects. Since performances are meant to be seen, this framework underscores the role of visibility in politics, particularly for highlighting and addressing marginalization and injustice in our society. On the one hand, visibility is essential here. As Timothy Pachirat (2011, 15) writes, a "politics of sight" works to make visible what is hidden in order to bring about change. As scholars of the LGBTQ+, women's, and HIV/AIDS awareness movements have shown, their progress and success are due, in large part, to illuminating these communities, the challenges they face, and how various oppressions impact their daily lives (Whittier 2017; Ayoub 2016; Chambré 2006). But on the other hand, scholars and activists have also debated the extent to which visibility is necessary for mitigating oppression and promoting social change. After all, as Julia Jordan-Zachery (2017) so trenchantly notes, while shining a light on an issue or community may indeed highlight their struggles and garner public sympathy, it also leaves many other communities and experiences in the shadows.

As the preceding chapters demonstrate, celebrities' political performances have made human trafficking visible in a range of ways, illuminating some experiences and populations while leaving others in the shadows. Even if we cannot directly discern these performances' impact on related policy, public debates, and the lives of impacted communities, they offer insights about the actors and settings of contemporary democratic politics in the United States. Regarding the former, scholars have drawn critical attention to the growing range of *unelected* individuals and organizations that make claims to represent individuals and interests and influence policy regarding a wide range of issues (see, e.g., Strolovitch 2007; Partzsch 2017; Goss 2016; Crowder 2020). Philanthropists, social entrepreneurs, business leaders and, of course, celebrities are among these unelected representatives, and their advocacy work often highlights how individuals who claim to speak for a constituency may have little in common with or connection to them. In so doing, they offer what I termed representation-at-a-distance, which is endemic to our increasingly *un*equal and *un*representative late-democratic, elite-dominated polity.

Celebrities who engage in anti-trafficking activism illustrate the chasm that may exist between representative claims-makers and their constituents, and this is evident when we look at the actors and settings of their performances through Rai's (2014) PPF. Regarding the former, there is an experiential and socio-economic gap between celebrities and the human trafficking victims for whom they claim to speak. While there remains no definitive picture of a "typical" human trafficking victim, the extensive research cited throughout this book makes it clear that poverty is their greatest source of vulnerability, especially when they are already marginalized on the basis of their race, gender, sexual orientation, and/or immigration status, among other factors. Celebrities in the United States are positioned very differently, for the most part, from the human trafficking victims they claim to represent. Although women celebrities are the most likely to engage in anti-trafficking activism, and #MeToo revelations like Ashley Judd's indicate that coercion and abuse is often part of their jobs, they are anything but poor. Celebrities' experiential distance from human trafficking victims is also evident when they engage with them directly, often through highly managed and produced events such as documentary filming. Furthermore, human trafficking victims and other impacted constituencies often lack any formal way to influence and inform celebrities about their needs and to hold them accountable for their advocacy on their behalf.

Regarding the settings of their political performances, celebrities appear in front of formal governing bodies such as Congress and the United Nations, in documentaries, and at fundraisers and foundation galas (among other non-governmental settings), and the most active celebrities often moved between these settings. On some level, this wide variety of settings furthers feminists' and other scholars of political inequality's long-standing arguments for conceiving of and studying politics beyond the electoral realm (see, e.g., Young 2000; Zukin 2006; Berger 2004). But these settings also reflect the elite and exclusive nature of many spaces in contemporary political life: they are high-profile, media-friendly, and rarely accessible to many non-celebrity activists and impacted communities. Moreover, in these rarefied settings, celebrities are empowered to control how they represent issues. They bring particular talents and resources to their performances, which tend to be heavily scripted and produced to capture the audience's attention, often in ways that blur the boundaries between fiction and non-fiction. Mira Sorvino's example is particularly instructive here. As Nicholas de Villiers (2016) observes, Sorvino repeated her fictional performances in non-fictional settings when she reprised her on-screen role as an anti-trafficking crusader for her position as a UN Goodwill Ambassador, and again when she went on a karaoke bar raid with Agape in *Every Day in Cambodia*. As de Villiers writes, Sorvino appears to "repeat lines from *Human Trafficking*" in the documentary *Every Day in Cambodia* when she appears teary-eyed and tells local men, "It's not okay to sell children to pedophiles, it's not okay" (161–81).

While Sorvino is not the only celebrity (or other unelected representative) to blur the boundary between fiction and non-fiction, her example illustrates celebrities' power to determine and control how they represent an issue to capture attention, especially in a highly mediatized environment, which, as noted earlier in this book, is increasingly fragmented, spectacle-driven, and disinclined towards critical, in-depth issue coverage. But while we may reasonably predict that all of Sorvino's and other celebrities' anti-trafficking advocacy would be similarly high-profile, dramatic, and attention-grabbing, we also see variation in their performances over time and across a range of settings. Celebrities' anti-trafficking activism therefore offers insights about their roles, utility, and potential for shaping human trafficking and feminist politics going forward.

Human Trafficking

The findings in this book highlight celebrities' limited capacity to determine the course of anti-human trafficking politics post-2016, the final year for which I collected data for this project. The contextual and circumstantial constraints they face here are especially apparent when we consider celebrities who occupy positions of significant power such as Donald Trump, the reality television celebrity who was elected President of the United States. Human trafficking was among the many issues of feminist concern that would come under the purview of his administration, but as Elizabeth Bernstein (2018, 182) so trenchantly notes, "in the early days of the Trump Administration, the issue of trafficking would recede from prominence amid the daily chaos of travel bans and attempts to overturn the Affordable Care Act," among so many other issues. But those who kept the issue on their radar were justifiably concerned about this administration's anti-trafficking efforts. Would this celebrity president continue the Obama administration's efforts to understand human trafficking as encompassing a wide range of industries and activities, and to develop partnerships with impacted communities and organizations working with them, at least to some extent? Or would it revert to a more law-and-order approach emphasizing prosecution and punishment?

Some advocates were not entirely fatalistic about the future of anti-trafficking politics under the Trump administration. Anne Gallagher (2017), a practitioner and scholar in criminal justice and human rights who received a Trafficking in Persons Hero award from US Secretary of State Hillary Clinton in 2012, wrote for *Open Democracy* that even with the Trump administration's tendency to be "singularly cold on human rights issues," there were good reasons to remain optimistic that "human trafficking, the quintessential human rights issue of our time, might be an exception." She explained that there were strong signs that the Trump administration would continue, and perhaps even accelerate, the US war against trafficking that began in the late 1990s and continued through the Obama years. These signs included Congress's authorization of unprecedented levels of funding to fight human trafficking in late 2016, and the assignment of Trump's (celebrity) daughter, Ivanka, as his advisor on the issue. "A celebrated neoliberal feminist in her own right" (Bernstein 2018, 183), Ivanka was and is no expert about human trafficking, but when Gallagher was writing, many observers and pundits saw her as a voice of reason who might temper her father's impulses in office. They were cautiously encouraged by Ivanka's efforts to gather experts and lawmakers to discuss legislation to combat human trafficking, and by the 2017 Trafficking in Persons report, which was "launched at a high-profile event hosted by Secretary of State Rex Tillerson, with a guest appearance by Ivanka Trump." In his remarks, Tillerson emphasized that human trafficking, a "crime against basic human rights is, and will continue to be, a priority for the US government" (Gallagher 2017).

However, the Trump administration's policies and practices regarding myriad other issues soon called his anti-trafficking efforts into question, in turn revealing "both the durability *and malleability* of trafficking discourse, as well as the cultural formations that underpin it" (Bernstein 2018, 182, emphasis added). Given that Donald Trump developed his celebrity as a notoriously sexist and "tough" businessman, and that he continued to deploy this persona throughout his presidential campaign, it is no surprise that his administration's anti-trafficking and other related efforts soon reflected and conveyed the dominant narrative by emphasizing law-and-order, masculinist, and racially structured xenophobic neo-imperialist aggression, all of which, as scholars and activists have long argued, increase vulnerabilities to human trafficking and further gender and other forms of inequality (Szörényi and Eate 2014). To name just some examples, as Bernstein (2018) documents, his administration sought to overturn a wide array of policies pertaining to sexual and gender-based violence through actions like an executive order revoking President Obama's Fair Pay and Safe Workplaces executive order. In other examples, Trump also signed executive orders to enhance immigration control and law enforcement-oriented approaches to trafficking prevention, and to curtail the US resettlement of Syrian refugees. The Trump administration's anti-immigrant/refugee positions have been particularly harmful for trafficking victims. To name just two of many examples here, a $13.5 million grant that would provide housing for trafficking victims was held up without explanation after its initial funding announcement stated that it would support non-citizens, and the administration also increased its denial rate for the T-visas that allow trafficking victims to legalize their immigration status, access services, and seek punishment for their abusers (Rogers 2020; Superville 2020).

But the public's responses to these and other Trump administration actions indicate that celebrity (and other) power in politics is temporary at best. It goes without saying that Trump was and is no friend to feminism, and as the Women's March protests that erupted in the wake of his election made clear, the prospect of him leading the most powerful country in the world accelerated feminist organizing globally. As Bernstein (2018) documents, encouraging waves of feminist, anti-racist, immigrant rights, and many other forms of activism increased exponentially since Trump's ascension. Furthermore, this activism also mobilized voters against Donald Trump, who lost his bid for re-election in 2020. At the time of writing, it was too early to say whether the Biden administration's anti-trafficking efforts will improve on its predecessors', but the mobilization of anti-Trump opposition indicates that while celebrity power may help candidates win elections, their power and influence in politics is not fixed and will always be subject to contestation.

Celebrity Feminism

Celebrities' anti-trafficking activism illuminates celebrity feminism's constrained power *and* how this power may be deployed more productively when it is connected to impacted communities and focused on targeting structures over individuals. Here the #MeToo movement against sexual violence is instructive, especially given the parallels between #MeToo's central concerns and human (and especially sex) trafficking. While the research about sexual violence is much more defined and established than that regarding human trafficking, victims of both crimes are less likely to report them and/or be willing to participate in related research studies (Hamby 2014; Daigle 2021). As a result, although existing research indicates that rates of sexual violence remain consistently high globally, and that women are the most likely victims, the true extent of sexual violence remains unknown, much like with human trafficking (Borumandnia et al. 2020; Raphael, Rennison, and Jones 2019). Consequently, efforts to address these issues, whether through criminal justice, social welfare, educational or other measures, remain contested topics of feminist (and other) debate.

Celebrities' anti-trafficking activism also parallels their #MeToo activism (see figure 12). Not only have celebrities placed their personal experiences with sexual violence on a continuum with sex trafficking (as Ashley Judd did; see chapter 2), they also highlighted how this violence occurs in their workplaces. Since at least 2017, the public learned from celebrities, in an unprecedented way, that sexual harassment and assault occurs at alarming levels in the entertainment industry, behind the scenes and beyond the studios. In an op-ed in the *New York Times,* the Academy Award winning actor Lupita

FIGURE 12. Ashley Judd and Mira Sorvino at the 2018 Oscars. Photo by everett225 (Ron Harvey)/depositphotos.com

Nyong'o (2017) detailed a litany of disturbing encounters with the notoriously powerful producer Harvey Weinstein that began when she was a student at Yale's drama school, and many other actors also shared similar stories dating back to the 1990s (Real 2019). Among the celebrities featured in this book, Ashley Judd filed a lawsuit against Weinstein, alleging that she lost lucrative work because of him (see chapter 3), and Mira Sorvino was also among the first Hollywood stars to go on the record in 2017 about her experience with Weinstein, alleging that she was "blacklisted from Hollywood studio films for two decades—in spite of an Oscar win, three Golden Globe nominations and one win, and an Emmy nomination" for refusing Weinstein's advances in 1995 at a hotel room at the Toronto International Film Festival (Miller 2021). While Weinstein denied these allegations, they opened the floodgates and on a near daily basis women in the entertainment industry were exposing numerous other powerful men in the entertainment industry for committing acts of sexual violence, ranging from Les Moonves, to Kevin Spacey, to Jeffrey Tambor, to Louis CK.

Celebrities' individual #MeToo revelations quickly led to collective action, which reflected celebrities' anti-trafficking activism in at least two key ways. First, their #MeToo activism was also high-profile and media-friendly. In addition to placing op-eds in places like the *New York Times* and receiving coverage of their stories in major mainstream media outlets, celebrities used venues such as award shows to draw attention to sexual harassment and other forms of gender-based violence. Most notably, at the 2018 Golden Globes Awards, women wore black gowns and men wore pins that read "Time's Up" in an effort to draw attention to issues of sexual assault, harassment, and discrimination against women in Hollywood and all other sectors of society. Second, celebrities' #MeToo activism also drew on "the personal." Even as celebrities have long shared elements of their personal lives such as their workouts, eating habits, and glamorous vacations through social and other media, their public stories and declarations of "me, too" offered "a new celebrity formation in which the personal is both public and political" (Larabee 2018, 9). As Nyong'o (2017) wrote, "I share all of this now because I know now what I did not know then. I was part of a growing community of women who were secretly dealing with harassment by Harvey Weinstein. But I also did not know that there was a world in which anybody would care about my experience."

Celebrities' #MeToo activism also diverged from their anti-trafficking activism in a number of significant ways. First, many of the most vocal celebrities in #MeToo had first-hand *experience* with sexual violence—something they did *not* have with human trafficking. Of course, one need not have direct experience with an issue in order to care about and work to address it. After all, as Hannah Pitkin's (1969) discussion of descriptive versus substantive representation still holds, political representatives need not, in theory, mirror their constituents' identities and experiences in order to represent them effectively (and, as I discussed earlier, elected officials do not always mirror their constituents either). But celebrities were often much closer to the issues #MeToo engaged than they were to sex trafficking in Cambodia or labor trafficking in Ghana, for example, and so their #MeToo activism may be read as more genuine and less self-serving. That is, they are not just doing this to re-enter the public eye and revive a flagging career, for example.

Second, celebrities' #MeToo narratives focused more on structures over individuals than they did in much of their anti-trafficking activism, even if media coverage sidelined this focus. As Ann Larabee (2018, 8) writes, "It should be no surprise to popular culture scholars that the mainstream media organs have shaped these personal [#MeToo] accounts into popular melodra-mas of evil ogres and beset damsels, suitable to Hollywood conventions and emphasizing women's weakness and wounding. As Melissa Gira Grant has pointed out, these media stories have emphasized sex over labor conditions and are informed by 'false notions of virtue and victim-hood.'" In fact, if we look beyond the media's stories to the *celebrities'* #MeToo claims and their related actions, we see more structural narratives of sexual violence, thereby indicating the problematic ways in which the media and entertainment industries (like so many other industries) create conditions of vulnerability for their workers. For example, Judd's actions and claims against Weinstein show that she was *not* a weak damsel in distress: she managed to have a suc-cessful acting career despite his actions *and* she came forward to file a lawsuit against him. Moreover, her lawsuit (which remained unresolved at the time of writing)—and many others that followed in its wake—highlights how the media and entertainment industries are structured so that extremely power-ful individual men have significant control over a person's career. This struc-ture often forces actors—and women actors in particular, along with many others in the production chain, from directors, to editors, to set workers, and so forth—to endure harassment and abuse in order to sustain and succeed in their careers.

Third, compared to their anti-trafficking activism, celebrities' #MeToo activism seemed, at times, more cognizant of and connected to grassroots activists' longstanding efforts to fight sexual violence. For example, at the 2018 Golden Globes, numerous celebrities brought as their dates women who led organizing efforts with marginalized women for many years, such as Tarana Burke, who attended the awards show with actor Michelle Williams. Burke coined the phrase "Me, too" in 2006, through her community-based work with women and girls who were victims of sexual violence. But in 2017, the phrase was credited to the white actor Alyssa Milano, when she tweeted to her followers, "If you've been sexually harassed or assaulted write 'me too' as a reply to this tweet." By highlighting Burke's history of activism, celebri-ties at the Golden Globes may be read as correcting the attribution of #MeToo *and* responding to a longstanding tendency in mainstream femi-nism towards marginalizing, if not silencing, non-white women's contribu-tions to other era-defining feminist debates. However, Burke did not take these celebrity efforts at face value. As *E! Online* reported, her initial response to Williams's invitation was, "'Yeah, I'm not going to be the Black lady that you just drag down the red carpet. I can't be that person.'" Burke only changed her mind after she spoke in depth with Williams, who convinced her that she was genuinely committed to the issue (Crist 2020). And at the Golden Globes ceremony, the celebrities followed through on their commitment to highlighting Burke's work and that of other long-time grassroots activists such as Ai-jen Poo of the National Domestic Workers Alliance. These women received prominent introductions and opportunities to speak about their work, and their celebrity dates took every opportunity to draw attention to their efforts. In so doing, the celebrities offered a show of solidarity, signaling here that despite their wealth, fame, beauty, and other privileges, they too experienced sexual and gender-based violence and discrimination, and they needed support from their peers to speak openly about it.

Finally, celebrities' #MeToo feminism quickly secured a number of high-profile material and legal victories that would have been unthinkable even a decade ago. To name just some examples, by the time the Golden Globes aired, "Time's Up" had raised millions of dollars to fund legal services for individuals challenging workplace sexual harassment, and soon after, a range of powerful men lost their positions in the entertainment and media industries. Most notably, on June 15, 2021, a range of news outlets reported that Harvey Weinstein, the former Hollywood mogul found guilty of multiple counts of rape and sexual assault in New York, would be extradited to California, where he would face additional charges that he attacked five women in Los Angeles (BBC 2021). Then, in September 2021, the *New York Times* reported that the legendary R&B singer R. Kelly had been convicted of federal sex trafficking and racketeering charges for a decades-long scheme to recruit women and underage girls for sex. As Troy Closson (2021) wrote for the *New York Times,* Kelly's conviction was a "significant moment in the #MeToo movement for both Black women and for the music industry, ushering in a sense that, finally, justice had been served." Taken together, these events offered high-profile victories for the #MeToo movement, alongside the growing number of laws, sexual harassment complaints, and other socio-legal developments that have emerged in its wake (Bracewell 2021).

In recounting these gains, however, I am *not* stating that celebrities were solely responsible for #MeToo's (limited) success to date, and that the movement's work is "done." It is no secret that women continue to experience violence in all areas of society, and it will take much more than celebrity tweets and lawsuits to eradicate this. In short, contemporary feminist activists still have their work cut out for them and, as Susan Faludi (2022) cautions in the *New York Times,* they must remember that "pop feminism's Achilles' heel is a faith in the power of the individual star turn over communal action, the belief that a gold-plated influencer plus a subscription list plus some viral content can be alchemized into mass activism." In short, individual celebrities are no substitute for broad-based, grassroots collective action. However, if celebrities are going to be part of these efforts, and surely they will, their #MeToo and anti-trafficking activism indicates where they may be more useful, and the feminist movement should deploy, engage, and hold them accountable accordingly. Certainly, celebrities may draw attention to feminist issues, but their actions seem more likely to further struggles for gender and other equality when they are a) connected with and highlighting the voices of impacted communities, and b) focused on drawing attention to (and fixing) structures that create vulnerabilities to violence and other forms of exploitation.

ACCOUNTABILITY

In this book, I situated celebrities who engage in anti-trafficking activism as self-appointed political representatives, which raises questions about how to hold them accountable for their actions and statements about human trafficking, among many other issues. Before discussing how we may do this, however, it is important to note the challenges here. As Alfred Archer and colleagues (2019) write, celebrities' representative positions and the epistemic authority they carry do not derive from an election, and so there are no other formal mechanisms regulating or monitoring their political engagement. Furthermore, celebrities are well equipped to guard themselves from direct scrutiny: the foundations they create are often shielded from significant regulatory oversight; they often have ready access to public relations and communications consultants who advise them and speak on their behalf; and they are not subject to the monitoring techniques of the political realm such as Freedom of Information Act requests or sponsorship disclosure requirements, to name just some examples—in fact, they enjoy "certain protections explicitly against such monitoring" (36). Moreover, publicly available, online sources of information about celebrities' activism is often ephemeral. In fact, as I finalized this manuscript for publication, I found that many of the URLs I cited in the reference list for the websites, videos, and other materials featuring celebrities' anti-trafficking activism had disappeared or become inactive.

Even with these challenges, it is possible to track and hold celebrities accountable by individual, organizational, and systemic means. At the individual level, we all may act like consumers: after all, celebrities are commercial products whose status and livelihoods depend on our attention. So, in the same way that many of us may engage in consumer activism by refusing to buy a product because we oppose the producer's labor practices, we may, as Robert van Krieken notes (2012), withdraw our attention from a celebrity at any time if she fails to perform adequately in our view. Furthermore, we may also boycott and withdraw support from the organizations, elected representatives, and social movements that rely on and benefit from celebrities who promote problematic issue representations (among other things). For example, the CATW, a dominant force in the anti-trafficking movement, garnered many celebrity signatures on its letter to Amnesty International. Those who disagree with the CATW's anti-sex work carceral feminist approach to human trafficking could contact, protest, and take other measures to oppose the CATW and its celebrity supporters; these actions may, in turn, push the CATW to revise its positions and activism within the broader anti-trafficking movement.

We may also communicate directly with celebrities about their political activism, and there is some evidence that they may respond to this. For example, when Mira Sorvino received "hate mail" from sex workers who disagreed with her anti-trafficking work, she educated herself about their positions (Sorvino 2016). However, it may be more effective to contact and hold celebrities accountable through social media platforms such as Twitter, where many celebrities have large and growing presences. Emerging research indicates that although most fan-celebrity interactions on Twitter are largely para-social, celebrities will occasionally reply to their various interlocutors here (see, e.g., Zilinsky et al. 2019; Stever and Lawson 2013). So, while a large amount of Twitter (and other social media) feedback about a celebrity's political activity may draw *more* attention to the celebrity, thereby bolstering rather than checking her power, this feedback may also push the celebrity to educate herself and/or adjust her positions. To name but one recent example here, after the director Spike Lee stood up for fellow filmmaker Woody Allen, who has long faced allegations of sexual assault, the backlash against Lee was so strong that just one day later, Lee took back his support and apologized, tweeting "I Deeply Apologize. My Words Were WRONG. I Do Not And Will Not Tolerate Sexual Harassment, Assault Or Violence. Such Treatment Causes Real Damage That Can't Be Minimized" (Yang 2020).

In addition to individual actions, a number of organizational reforms may also help to monitor and hold celebrities accountable for their political activism. Here the news and other media organizations may be key targets for reform because they have significant power over how the public learns about and understands any number of issues (Kogen 2014). Since celebrities command significant attention through the media, we must, as Archer and colleagues (2019, 37) write, "hope that citizens, celebrities, or media companies, upon seeing [celebrities'] responsibility in creating [celebrity/epistemic] power, will help to control its use." However, they add, "it seems somewhat naïve to think that each or any of these groups will in fact do this." Archer et al.'s doubts are certainly justified. Regulating the media is challenging at best, especially in the United States, where First Amendment protections limit restrictions on the press and speech. However, as Archer et al. write, media companies have recognized and responded to misuses of epistemic power, even if only to a limited extent. For example, YouTube, Facebook, and Apple all banned the conspiracy theorist Alex Jones from their platforms in August 2018.

Given all of this, it seems reasonable for media organizations to consider how a wide range of celebrities may misuse their epistemic power in their productions and on their platforms. Indeed, this raises questions about "what counts as a misuse" (Archer et al. 2019, 37), and these questions are especially relevant in the context of celebrities' anti-trafficking and other feminist activism. For example, is a celebrity who promotes the dominant human trafficking narrative on a nightly news show misusing her power? The answer to this question is debatable, but it does highlight the media's responsibility, at least in theory, to ensure that their reporting involves adequate research and engages a range of perspectives. To this end, media organizations could require that celebrities do adequate research before they speak on a topic, and they could help them with this by connecting them to relevant, verified experts, as they did when Bono worked with Professor Jeffrey Sachs of Harvard to learn more about developing world economics (Archer et al. 2019). Such connections and partnerships may prevent celebrities from only seeking out research and perspectives they agree with and/or those that are hand-picked by their philanthropic and other consultants.

A non-governmental oversight body that assesses celebrities' issue advocacy and advises other organizations about engaging them may also hold celebrities accountable for their actions. As Andrew Cooper (2009) suggests, oversight tools of this sort already exist for monitoring G8 and G20 nations' work towards their goals, so why could there not be a similar assessment exercise for celebrities and the promises they make? These exercises would operate much like an annual review or ranking system that considers whether celebrities keep their promises (e.g. to raise money for a cause), the extent to which their advocacy reflects and considers developments in research and policy, and their engagement with impacted communities. How this organizational/evaluative body may be funded and structured is up for debate (for example, media and other entertainment companies may have conflicts of interest here), but it seems that scholars of celebrity, NGO representatives, and those who work for national and international governmental bodies may be useful partners here.

These are just some of the ways in which individuals and organizations may hold celebrities accountable for their political advocacy (or, at the very least, ensure that they are sufficiently informed about the issues they bring to large audiences). However, strategies such as consumer activism and establishing celebrity monitoring bodies ultimately do little to challenge, reform, or even reconstruct the broader systems and structures that have allowed celebrities—and other unelected elites, from social entrepreneurs to wealthy philanthropists (Partzsch 2017)—to ascend and assume highly influential positions in our society. Therefore, targeting these systems and structures is essential, because if we look at human trafficking and the ascendance of celebrities and politics in parallel, we see that many of the conditions that created vulnerabilities to the former are also intertwined with the latter.

As noted in the book's introductory chapters, the ascendance of a neoliberal political ideology emphasizing individual, NGO, and marketized solutions to social problems, reduced government spending and taxation, and increasingly deregulated and unfettered capitalism have driven economic inequality to unprecedented levels in the United States and globally (Piketty 2020). This inequality is furthered by, among other things, wars, ethnic conflicts and genocides, increasingly frequent environmental disasters, and the limited power of labor unions. As critical trafficking scholars have long documented, all of these factors that fuel social and economic inequality writ large also create vulnerabilities to human trafficking by rendering workers more susceptible to displacement and poverty, which in turn limits their capacity to refuse or resist precarious, dangerous, and coercive labor arrangements (Rende Taylor and Shih 2019; Limoncelli 2009; Chang 2013).

Celebrities did not singlehandedly create socioeconomic and political inequality, but as products of the profit-driven media and entertainment industries—and, indeed, of market capitalism—they are manifestations of it and, on some level, they depend on it. After all, if celebrity status and its attendant capital were available to everyone, it would lose its meaning and value! So, following the logic of the late feminist scholar Audre Lorde (1984), who wrote that the master's tools will never dismantle the master's house, celebrities have little incentive to critique or undermine the very structures that have created and sustained socioeconomic inequality, let alone their careers and success. At the same time, celebrities are humans in the world who often hail from more humble beginnings, and so they are not oblivious to inequality either, especially since a recent focus on the police killings of so many Black men and women in the United States and the Covid-19 pandemic brought into sharp relief the structural factors that foster inequality such as gender-based violence, poverty, racism, and inadequate labor protections. These events also mobilized more celebrities to act politically, as indicated by their many appearances at the Women's Marches and their tweets in support of Black Lives Matter, among many other examples.

However, it will take more than celebrity activism to address inequality writ large. Instead, this will require the difficult work of researching, critiquing, and fighting for policies and systemic reforms (and revolutions!) that foster a more equitable and just society. Actions to this end are not straightforward or immediately effective, and they will require us to work together, often at a grassroots level, to center and elevate the voices and experiences of marginalized communities, and *not* celebrities' voices. To this end, we may work within the realm of electoral politics by, for example, supporting (or running as) candidates who are from under-represented groups and/or are not beholden to corporate and other powerful interests. Other actions will fall outside of electoral politics, often in the realm of protest. To name just some examples here, we must oppose any measures that foster unequal political participation, from gerrymandering to restrictive voting laws (that, at the time of writing, were spreading throughout US states like wildfire), to Supreme Court decisions like *Citizens United,* to policies that sustain unequal social and economic arrangements such as tax loopholes for the wealthy, weak labor laws, and union busting. This is a short, incomplete, and, some will probably argue, idealistic and "pie in the sky" list of suggestions, but it underscores the fact that reducing human trafficking and the power of unelected elites in our polity will require us to address inequality more broadly.

We cannot fight inequality without sufficient knowledge about the conditions that create it and the actors that represent and sustain it. To this end, I offer some suggestions for how we may further celebrity and politics research. First, I encourage scholars to build on my research about celebrities' anti-trafficking activism beyond the Obama administration, so that we may more comprehensively understand the evolution and extent of their actions here. Second, research about celebrities' political activism must engage celebrities directly, through interviews, so we can learn more from them about their motivations and goals, among other things. This will be challenging: while celebrities may occasionally respond to their fans on social media, I and others (see also Driessens 2014) have found that they are difficult to access for research interviews. Furthermore, even if we do manage to interview celebrities, they may offer the "PR spin" on their political work, which may not be very critical or insightful in the end.

But while we can debate the merits of (expanded) celebrity and politics research, the challenges of this are worth discussing, as they are similar to those that arise when researching "elites" in the United States more broadly. While many scholars (including me) have conducted extensive observational and interview-based studies with members of marginalized communities in the United States, fewer scholars have accessed and engaged members of wealthier and more powerful groups for research. For example, as Rachel Sherman (2019) found in her study of the lives of wealthy New Yorkers, they were reluctant research participants who expressed a deep ambivalence about their affluence, and they were often unwilling to talk about it. Celebrities' unwillingness to sit down with researchers and account for their political advocacy reflects a similar elite reluctance. Finding some way to interview and learn from celebrities directly, then, may help us better understand their political actions and socio-economic inequality more broadly. After all, as Sherman (2019) argues, silence from and about the wealthy and privileged contributes to the broader American tradition, however misguided, of denying class privilege, while also obscuring and distracting us from debates about the morality of vastly unequal patterns of wealth accumulation and distribution.

Third, celebrity and politics researchers must expand their conception of celebrities. Many studies of celebrity and politics (including mine) have focused on "big name" celebrities—the predominantly US-based movie stars, singers, and professional athletes who feature so prominently in the mainstream media. However, social media platforms have expanded the scope of who or what counts as a celebrity to include Instagram "influencers," video game players on Twitch, and make-up artists on YouTube, to name just some examples. Even as these celebrities may only reach and cater to more fragmented fanbases than Hollywood stars like Brad Pitt, for example, they are well-known, prominent in the media, and their actions are often produced and commercialized. They may also take political stances and engage in advocacy, and so, given their growing prominence in our media-scape, we need more research about their actions, positions, and influence in our polity.

Fourth, in expanding the range of celebrities we consider in our research, we must go beyond individual case studies and also study more celebrities based in the Global South. While individual case studies provide important insights about celebrities' political engagement, this book has shown that examining celebrities' advocacy *over time* better illustrates its range and variation, and this may also be true for other "hot button" issues of the day. Do celebrities who engage in environmental advocacy, for example, also tend towards simplistic, dramatic narratives, or are they willing to learn about the issue and promote more complex issue representations? As well, expanding our studies to include more celebrities *outside* of the Global North will provide a wider range of insights about how they are defined and engaging in an increasingly global, interconnected polity. Here, Zainab Alam's (2019) research about the late Pakistani social media celebrity Qandeel Baloch is especially instructive. Alam's analysis reveals that Baloch's social media activism critiqued long-established norms governing gender, class, and sexuality, and she expanded the boundaries of national belonging in Pakistan to include culturally rebellious women of limited economic means. Baloch's case thus indicates the ways in which celebrities may reinforce hierarchies and elite politics *and* use their position to illuminate and politicize injustices.

Finally, we need more research about celebrities' *actual* effects on their audiences' political preferences, opinions, and behaviors. Celebrities reach large and often influential audiences, but "once they have captured public attention about an issue, celebrities' capacity to directly shape how people think or act is more difficult to discern" (Majic, Bernhard, and O'Neill 2020, 3). Extant research here indicates that celebrities' direct impact on the public's electoral and other political preferences and actions is limited at best, but these findings are often drawn from small-n, regionally specific studies (see, e.g., Sue Jackson 2021; Frizzell 2011; Pease and Brewer 2008). Therefore, expanding this type of research is important, especially since celebrities may be useful tools for promoting pro-social behavior. For example, basketball legend Kareem Abdul-Jabbar (2021) argued in a *New York Times* op-ed that if more Black sports celebrities publicly received the Covid 19 vaccine (as he did), they would encourage other Black Americans—who have been disproportionately impacted by Covid-19 *and* have good reasons to be skeptical of the medical system—to get vaccinated. A combination of interviews with and/or surveys of sports fans, then, may help us test whether Abdul-Jabbar's proposition is true *and* whether celebrities may influence their fans in other ways. In fact, emergent experimental research shows celebrities may positively shape individuals' behavior and opinions, as Ala' Alrababa'h and colleagues (2021) show in their study of Mohamed Salah, the visibly Muslim elite player for the Liverpool Football Club, one of England's most storied teams. In their study, they analyzed data from hate crimes reports throughout England and millions of tweets from British soccer fans to examine whether exposure to celebrities from stigmatized groups may reduce prejudices against them. They found that hate crimes in the Liverpool area *dropped* by 16 percent (compared with a synthetic control), and that Liverpool fans halved their rates of posting anti-Muslim tweets relative to fans of other top-flight football clubs. Furthermore, their "original survey experiment suggests that the salience of Salah's Muslim identity enabled positive feelings toward Salah to generalize to Muslims more broadly," thereby supporting the parasocial contact hypothesis, which posits that "positive exposure to out-group celebrities can spark real-world behavioral changes in prejudice" (1111). While we cannot necessarily generalize its findings to other areas of influence, this study suggests creative methods for studying and learning about celebrities' effects on their fans' (and broader audiences') beliefs and behaviors.

· · ·

Going forward, we must continue to debate and interrogate celebrities' engagement in feminist and other political struggles because celebrities are fixtures here. Whether we like it or not, they have the power to reach and teach large segments of the public. Dismissing their activism as a largely flashy, shallow, ineffective spectacle perpetuates a grave political mistake because it ignores a key source of information about myriad issues for the general public. Instead, we as scholars, activists, and concerned citizens must understand and continue examining celebrities as multi-level political actors who represent various issues, interests, and constituencies in a range of settings. Their political performances reveal broader political dynamics and power arrangements that we must engage with, intervene in, and challenge in our struggles against marginalization and oppression.

NOTES

INTRODUCTION

1. This summary is adapted from a more detailed plot summary at IMDB.com: https://www.imdb.com/title/tt0936501/plotsummary.

2. I also introduced and discussed these features and processes in Majic, Bernhard, and O'Neill (2020).

3. Pugliese relied on a number of sources to calculate the federal government's total spending on human trafficking (email correspondence, April 19, 2021). The 2001 funding information is from the President's Interagency Task Force to Combat Trafficking in Persons Declaration of Achievements: 2001–2008 from the State Department's archive. Since then, in most cases, the Attorney General's TIP Reports included the total dollar amounts allocated to each department. When the reports did not provide these total amounts, she totaled the grants that were individually listed for the departments at the end of the reports, and she searched agency websites. She also relied on the DOJ's grant announcements for the 2020 totals, since there was not a TIP Report for that year at the time of writing.

4. While the Thirteenth Amendment of the US Constitution abolished slavery, it still permits involuntary servitude, in the form of forced labor, "as punishment for crime whereof the party shall have been duly convicted, shall exist within the United States, or any place subject to their jurisdiction." The Fair Labor Standards Act also excludes incarcerated people from protection by classifying their work as penal, not economic.

CHAPTER 1

1. This representative distance and its effects are not solely a function of geography, per se, as they are in David Willumsen's (2018) formulation.

2. I thank Michael Saward for this insight about the spectrum of performances (personal communication, May 14, 2020).

3. Michael Saward, personal communication, May 14, 2020.

CHAPTER 2

1. Although Thompson is a British citizen, I included her because much of her anti-trafficking work has taken place in the United States, and she has worked and developed her celebrity extensively in the US entertainment industry.

2. Interview, March 5, 2018.

3. Email communication, January 12, 2018.

4. Interview, November 14, 2017.

5. Interview, July 3, 2018.

6. Email correspondence, January 12, 2018.

7. A CNN official informed me (email correspondence, September 18, 2015) that PSAs like Kutcher and Moore's run without charge. Since "they do not have revenue associated with them and are just run sporadically when unsold ad inventory is available," the network does not track the number of times that they air.

8. Email correspondence, January 12, 2018.

9. Interview, January 22, 2015. A representative from Thorn could not specify the nature of the 1.6 million people's "participation." See Majic 2018, 299–300.

10. Shoe Revolt's website http://www.shoerevolt.org no longer existed as I finished drafting this book manuscript, so it is difficult to discern its exact founding date.

11. This organization too is now defunct; its former website was http://www.together1heart.org. An associated twitter account, @together1heart, last tweeted in May 2020.

12. Backpage.com was spun off from Village Voice Media the following year, in 2012. After a long series of civil and criminal investigations, it shut down in 2018.

13. Emma Thompson, Darryl Hannah, and Demi Moore are also among the most active celebrities I identified, but I have not included them for individual case studies because their engagement with the issue is in fact quite limited. Thompson's activity has mainly centered around "Journey," a traveling art exhibit she created in partnership with the Helen Bamber Foundation in the early 2000s. The majority of Hannah's activism on the issue has come through media interviews; her most significant anti-trafficking activity, a documentary about trafficking in Cambodia, was never completed or released, to my knowledge. And finally, Demi Moore's anti-trafficking performances were predominantly in partnership with Kutcher, as described in this chapter. As we will see in chapter 4, she largely stepped away from this work after their divorce.

CHAPTER 3

1. This chapter is an expanded and reframed version of Majic (2019).

2. Marianne Williamson is an American self-help book author and spiritual advisor to many celebrities, most notably Oprah Winfrey. She sought the Democratic party's presidential nomination in 2020.

3. In 2012, Pinkett Smith also released a documentary titled *Rape for Profit* (Esau and Palmer 2012), for which she served as the executive producer. Offering viewers "an up-close look at the true nature of the sex trade," the film is set in Seattle and covers many of the same themes as *Children For Sale,* including young girls in the sex trade, and the efforts of various law enforcement and other stakeholders to address this. However, since Pinkett Smith did not appear in the film, and it lacked the same wide distribution as *Children for Sale* (it was only released on iTunes), I did not include it in this analysis.

CHAPTER 4

1. These allegations of abuse against Menudo date back to at least 1991, when the *New York Daily News* reported that several members of the band were sexually abused and regularly plied with alcohol and drugs by the men who ran the band, including promoter Edgardo Diaz, attorney Orlando Lopez, and José Antonio Jimenez, the president of Menudo's Panama-based holding company. The *News* reported that Diaz admitted there had been drugs, sex, and emotional problems in the group, but said he had not been directly involved (UPI Archives 1991).

2. I was unable to secure an interview with any representatives from Thorn. In an email on September 25, 2017, the executive director, Julie Cordua, directed me to Thorn's website, but then did not respond to any of my follow-up questions. As a result, my interpretations of Kutcher's work are based on Thorn's published reports and other information published on their website.

3. This quote was formerly available at rickymartinfoundation.org, but the site has changed and the English version was not available as of August 16, 2021.

4. Thorn 2021c gives their public statements about Spotlight. The link I followed is https://spotlight.thorn.org/about.

5. At the time of writing, the links Blue (2019) provided to Thorn's publicly available informational handout about Spotlight (https://assets.htspotlight.com /portal/Spotlight-Handout.pdf) no longer worked.

6. I thank Dr. Aisha Beliso-De Jésus for this term "margins of masculinity," which she offered when I presented a draft of this chapter at the American Studies Workshop at Princeton University (virtually) on September 28, 2020.

7. At the time of writing, Andrés Besserer Rayas was a PhD Candidate at the CUNY Graduate Center. Following my presentation of a draft of this chapter at the CUNY Graduate Center, he very generously provided me with background research about Rosselló's downfall, and he also compiled and translated the text messages about Ricky Martin for me. I am extremely grateful for his work on this portion of the project.

CHAPTER 5

1. Created in 2011, the Project's mission is "shining a light on modern-day slavery. Traveling the world to unravel the tangle of criminal enterprises trading in human life. Amplifying the voices of survivors. Holding governments and businesses accountable" (CNN 2021).

2. These five areas include the extent to which eligible companies a) verified product supply chains to evaluate and address risks of human trafficking and slavery; b) conducted independent and unannounced audits of suppliers to evaluate supplier compliance with company standards; c) required direct suppliers to certify that raw materials for their products complied with the laws regarding slavery and human trafficking; d) have internal accountability standards and procedures for employees or contractors who do not comply with company policies on slavery and human trafficking; and e) provide employees and management responsible for supply chain management with training on human trafficking.

3. To name just some examples, the journal *The Lancet* argued that from a medical perspective, decriminalization will enhance sex workers' health and safety (C. Cooper 2014; Decker et al. 2015). And researchers in New Zealand, which decriminalized prostitution in 2003, found that this did not increase sex trafficking; instead, it helped sex workers improve their health, safety, and overall working conditions (Healy, Wi-Hongi, and Hati 2017; Sweetman 2017).

REFERENCES

Allatson, Paul. 2015. "Shakira, Ricky Martin and Celanthropic Latinidad in the Americas." In *Celebrity Philanthropy,* edited by Elaine Jeffreys and Paul Allatson, 191–210. Bristol, UK: Intellect Books.

ABC News. 2011. "A Not So Glamorous Model Life." *Nightline,* September 14. https://www.youtube.com/watch?v=rHh2cpLGzIA.

Abdul-Jabbar, Kareem. 2021. "We Should Let Some N.B.A. Players Jump the Vaccine Queue." *The New York Times.* February 2, 2021. https://www.nytimes.com/2021/02/01/opinion/nba-covid-vaccine-kareem-abdul-jabbar.html.

Abu-Lughod, Lila. 2013. *Do Muslim Women Need Saving?* Cambridge, MA: Harvard University Press.

Ackerly, Brooke A. 2018. *Just Responsibility: A Human Rights Theory of Global Justice.* New York: Oxford University Press.

Agape International Missions. 2021. "Homepage." Accessed August 12, 2021. https://aimfree.org.

Alam, Zainab B. 2019. "Do-it-Yourself Activism in Pakistan: The Fatal Celebrity of Qandeel Baloch." *Perspectives on Politics* 18 (1): 76–90.

Albright, Erin, and Kate D'Adamo. 2017. "Decreasing Human Trafficking through Sex Work Decriminalization." *AMA Journal of Ethics* 19 (1): 122–26.

Alcoff, Linda. 1991. "The Problem of Speaking for Others." *Cultural Critique* (20): 5–32.

Alexander, Jeffrey C. 2010. *The Performance of Politics: Obama's Victory and the Democratic Struggle for Power.* New York: Oxford University Press.

Alexander-Floyd, Nikol. 2012. "Disappearing Acts: Reclaiming Intersectionality in the Social Sciences in a Post-Black Feminist Era." *Feminist Formations* 24 (1): 1–25.

———. 2013. "(Inter)disciplinary Trouble: Intersectionality, Narrative Analysis, and the Making of a New Political Science." *Politics & Gender* 9 (4): 470–74.

———. 2021. *Re-imagining Black Women: A Critique of Post-feminist and Post-racial Melodrama in Culture and Politics.* New York: New York University Press.

Ali, Zahra. 2018. *Women and Gender in Iraq: Between Nation-building and Fragmentation.* New York: Cambridge University Press.

Allam, Nermin. 2018. *Women and the Egyptian Revolution: Engagement and Activism during the 2011 Arab Uprisings.* New York: Cambridge University Press.

Alleyne, Mark. 2005. "The United Nations' Celebrity Diplomacy." *SAIS Review of International Affairs* 25 (1): 175–85.

Allin, Olivia. 2012. "OTRC: Jada Pinkett Smith Fights Human Trafficking for Daughter Willow." *Eyewitness News.* https://abc7.com/archive/8709811.

Alrababa'h, Ala', William Marble, Salma Mousa, and Alexandra A. Siegel. 2021. "Can Exposure to Celebrities Reduce Prejudice? The Effect of Mohamed Salah on Islamophobic Behaviors and Attitudes." *American Political Science Review* 115 (4): 1111–1128.

Amnesty International. 2004. "It's In Our Hands: Stop Violence Against Women." London, UK. Accessed October 14, 2022. https://www.amnesty.org/en/documents /act77/001/2004/en.

———. 2015. "Proposed Policy on Sex Work." Accessed October 14, 2022. https:// www.hivlawandpolicy.org/sites/default/files/Amnesty%20Prostitution%20 Policy%20document%C2%A0.pdf.

———. 2021. "Who We Are." Accessed August 10, 2022. https://www.amnesty .org/en/who-we-are/.

Andreas, Peter, and Kelly M. Greenhill. 2010. *Sex, Drugs, and Body Counts: The Politics of Numbers in Global Crime and Conflict.* Ithaca, NY: Cornell University Press.

Andrijasevic, Rutvica, and Nicola Mai. 2016. "Editorial: Trafficking (in) Representations: Understanding the Recurring Appeal of Victimhood and Slavery in Neoliberal Times." *Anti-Trafficking Review* (7): 1–10.

Anti-Trafficking Review. 2020. Special Issue—Technology, Anti-Trafficking, and Speculative Futures. Edited by Jennifer Musto and Mitali Thakor.

Archer, Alfred, Amanda Cawston, Benjamin Matheson, and Machteld Geuskens. 2019. "Celebrity, Democracy, and Epistemic Power." *Perspectives on Politics* 18 (1): 27–42.

Arnold, Amanda. 2018. "Here's What's Wrong With the So-Called Anti–Sex Trafficking Bill." *The Cut,* March 20. https://www.thecut.com/2018/03/sesta-anti-sex-trafficking-bill-fosta.html.

Arnold, Kathleen R. 2015. *Why Don't You Just Talk to Him? The Politics of Domestic Abuse.* New York: Oxford University Press.

Asencio, Marysol, and Katie Acosta. 2010. "Introduction: Mapping Latina/o Sexualities Research and Scholarship." In *Latina/o Sexualities: Probing Powers, Passions, Practices, and Policies,* edited by Marysol Asencio, 1–12. New Brunswick, NJ: Rutgers University Press.

ASSET. 2015a. "Advancing Systemic Solutions to End Enslavement and Trafficking." Accessed August 2. http://assetcampaign.org/about/.

———. 2015b. "The California Transparency in Supply Chains (TISC) Law passed in September of 2010 and Came into Effect in January of 2012." Accessed August 2, 2021. http://assetcampaign.org/about-slavery-3/.

———. 2018. "About: the issue." Accessed June 18, 2021. https://www.assetcampaign.org/issue.

———. 2021a. "ASSET Campaign: About." Accessed August 12, 2021. https://www.assetcampaign.org/what-we-do.

———. 2021b. "ASSET Campaign: Our Strategy." Accessed August 12, 2021. https://www.assetcampaign.org/our-strategy.

———. 2021c. "ASSET Statement on Ending Systemic Racism." Accessed August 12, 2021. https://assetcampaign.org/statement-on-race.

Associated Press. 2012. "Jada Pinkett Smith Testifies Against Human Trafficking, Husband Will and Daughter Willow Give Support." *New York Daily News,* July 17. https://www.nydailynews.com/news/politics/jada-pinkett-smith-testifies-human-trafficking-husband-daughter-willow-give-support-article-1.1116472.

Atiles-Osoria, Jose. 2016. "Colonial State Terror in Puerto Rico." *State Crime Journal* 5 (2): 220–41.

Auguston, Amy. 2014. "The Problem with 'Real Men Don't Buy Girls.'" *Huffington Post,* May 20. http://www.huffingtonpost.com/amy-auguston/the-problem-with-real-men-dont-buy-girls_b_5355052.html.

Austin Smith, Holly. 2013. "Teen Revolt: Activist Ateba Crocker Launches Program to Educate Teens." Accessed June 6. http://hollyaustinsmith.com/teen-revolt-activist-ateba-crocker-launches-program-to-educate-teens.

Avelino, Flor. 2021. "Theories of Power and Social Change. Power Contestations and Their Implications for Research on Social Change and Innovation." *Journal of Political Power* 14 (3): 425–48.

Ayoub, Phillip. 2016. *When States Come Out: Europe's Sexual Minorities and the Politics of Visibility.* New York: Cambridge University Press.

Baker, Carrie. 2013. "Moving Beyond 'Slaves, Sinners, and Saviors': An Intersectional Feminist Analysis of US Sex Trafficking Discourses, Law and Policy." *Journal of Feminist Scholarship* 4 (Spring): 1–23.

———. 2014. "An Intersectional Analysis of Sex Trafficking Films." *Meridians* 12 (1): 208–26.

———. 2018. *Fighting the U.S. Youth Sex Trade: Gender, Race, and Politics.* New York: Cambridge University Press.

———. 2019. "Racialized Rescue Narratives in Public Discourses on Youth Prostitution and Sex Trafficking in the United States." *Politics & Gender* 15 (4): 773–800.

Balch, Oliver. 2013. "Julia Ormond Calls on Businesses to Do More to Stamp Out Human Trafficking." *The Guardian,* September 10. https://www.theguardian.com/global-development-professionals-network/2013/sep/10/julia-ormond-hollywood-human-trafficking-slavery.

Bales, Kevin. 1999, 2004. *Disposable People: New Slavery in the Global Economy.* 1st and rev. ed. Berkeley: University of California Press.

Banet-Weiser, Sarah, Rosalind Gill, and Catherine Rottenberg. 2019. "Postfeminism, Popular Feminism and Neoliberal Feminism? Sarah Banet-Weiser, Rosalind Gill and Catherine Rottenberg in Conversation." *Feminist Theory* 21 (1): 3–24.

Barrientos, Stephanie. 2011. "'Labour Chains': Analysing the Role of Labour Contractors in Global Production Networks." Manchester, UK: Brooks World Poverty Institute.

Barthes, Roland. 1972. *Mythologies.* New York: Hill and Wang.

Bayer, Chris, and Jesse Hudson. 2017. "Corporate Compliance with the California Transparency in Supply Chains Act: Anti-Slavery Performance in 2016." Development International: iPoint Systems, March 7. https://www.ipoint-systems.com/fileadmin/media/resources/CA-TISCA.v.25_S.pdf.

BBC. 2021. "US Judge Rules Harvey Weinstein Can be Extradited to California to Stand Trial." June 15. https://www.bbc.com/news/world-us-canada-57491949.

Berg, Laurie, Bassina Farbenblum, and Angela Kintominas. 2020. "Addressing Exploitation in Supply Chains: Is Technology a Game Changer for Worker Voice?" *Anti-Trafficking Review* (14): 47–66.

Berger, Tracy Michele. 2004. *Workable Sisterhood: The Political Journey of Stigmatized Women with HIV/AIDS.* Princeton, NJ: Princeton University Press.

Berkowitz, Joe. 2018. "Ashley Judd is Suing Harvey Weinstein, Who 'Torpedoed' Her Career." *Fast Company,* May 1.

Bernstein, Elizabeth. 2007a. "The Sexual Politics of the 'New Abolitionism.'" *Differences* 18 (3): 128–51.

———. 2007b. *Temporarily Yours: Intimacy, Authenticity, and the Commerce of Sex.* Chicago: University of Chicago Press.

———. 2010. "Militarized Humanitarianism Meets Carceral Feminism: The Politics of Sex, Rights, and Freedom in Contemporary Antitrafficking Campaigns." *Signs* 36 (11): 45–71.

———. 2012. "Carceral Politics as Gender Justice? The "Traffic in Women" and Neoliberal Circuits of Crime, Sex, and Rights." *Theoretical Sociology* 41: 233–59.

———. 2016. "Redemptive Capitalism and Sexual Investability." *Political Power and Social Theory* 30: 45–80.

———. 2018. *Brokered Subjects: Sex, Trafficking, and the Politics of Freedom.* Chicago: The University of Chicago Press.

Biccum, April. 2011. "Marketing Development: Celebrity Politics and the 'New' Development Advocacy." *Third World Quarterly* 32 (7): 1331–46.

Birkey, Rachel N., Ronald P. Guidry, Mohammad Azizul Islam, and Dennis M. Patten. 2016. "Mandated Social Disclosure: An Analysis of the Response to the California Transparency in Supply Chains Act of 2010." *Journal of Business Ethics* 152 (3): 827–41.

Blakemore, Erin. 2018. "The Long History of Anti-Latino Discrimination in America." Accessed January 17. https://www.history.com/news/the-brutal-history-of-anti-latino-discrimination-in-america

Blue, Violet. 2019. "Sex, Lies, and Surveillance: Something's Wrong with the War on Sex Trafficking." *engadget,* May 31. https://www.engadget.com/2019-05-31-sex-lies-and-surveillance-fosta-privacy.html.

Blunt, Danielle, Emily Coombes, Shanelle Mullin, and Ariel Wolf. 2020. "Posting Into the Void." Accessed July 12, 2022. https://hackinghustling.org/posting-into-the-void-content-moderation.

Bomb Report. 2004. "Twisted: Rating and Review." Accessed August 2021. https://bombreport.com/yearly-breakdowns/2004-2/twisted/.

Boorstin, Daniel J. 2012 [1961]. *The Image: A Guide to Pseudo-events in America.* 50th Anniversary Edition. New York: Vintage Books.

Booth, Heather, Day Creamer, Susan Davis, Deb Dobbin, Robin Kaufman, and Toby Klass. 1972. "Socialist Feminism: a Strategy for the Women's Movement." Chicago: Women's Liberation Print Culture. https://repository.duke.edu/dc/wlmpc/wlmms01035.

Borumandnia, Nasrin, Naghmeh Khadembashi, Mohammed Tabatabaei, and Hamid Alavi Majd. 2020. "The Prevalence Rate of Sexual Violence Worldwide: A Trend Analysis." *BMC Public Health* 20 (1835): 1–7.

Boxill, Nancy A., and Deborah J. Richardson. 2007. "Ending Sex Trafficking of Children in Atlanta." *Affilia* 22 (2): 138–49.

Bracewell, Lorna N. 2021. *Why We Lost the Sex Wars: Sexual Freedom in the #Metoo Era.* Minneapolis: University of Minnesota Press.

———. 2016. "Beyond Barnard: Liberalism, Antipornography Feminism, and the Sex Wars." *Signs: Journal of Women in Culture and Society* 42 (1): 23–48.

Brady, Anita. 2016. "Taking Time between G-String Changes to Educate Ourselves: Sinéad O'Connor, Miley Cyrus, and Celebrity Feminism." *Feminist Media Studies* 16 (3): 429–44.

Brockington, Dan. 2014a. *Celebrity Advocacy and International Development, Rethinking Development.* London: Routledge.

———. 2014b. "The Production and Construction of Celebrity Advocacy in International Development." *Third World Quarterly* 35 (1): 88–108.

———. 2015. "Towards an International Understanding of the Power of Celebrity Persuasions: A Review and a Research Agenda." *Celebrity Studies* 6 (4): 486–504.

Brooks, Siobhan. 2021. "Innocent White Victims and Fallen Black Girls: Race, Sex Work, and the Limits of Anti–Sex Trafficking Laws." *Signs* 46 (2): 513–21.

Brown, Wendy. 2015. *Undoing the Demos: Neoliberalism's Stealth Revolution.* Cambridge, MA: Zone Books.

BSafe. 2021. "bsafe: never walk alone." Accessed October 25, 2021. https://getbsafe.com.

Buck, Kay. 2017. "Coalition to Abolish Slavery & Trafficking (CAST) Responds to 2017 Trafficking In Persons (TIP) Report." CAST-LA, July 7. Accessed October 25, 2022. https://www.castla.org/coalition-to-abolish-slavery-trafficking-cast-responds-to-2017-trafficking-in-persons-tip-report/.

Budabin, Alexandra Cosima. 2015. "Celebrities as Norm Entrepreneurs in International Politics: Mia Farrow and the 'Genocide Olympics' Campaign." *Celebrity Studies* 6 (4): 399–413.

Budabin, Alexandra, and Lisa Ann Richey. 2018. "Advocacy Narratives and Celebrity Engagement: The Case of Ben Affleck in Congo." *Human Rights Quarterly* 40: 260–86.

Busza, Joanna R. 2014. "Prostitution and the Politics of HIV Prevention in Cambodia: A Historical Case Study." *Studies in Gender and Sexuality* 15 (1): 44–53.

Butler, Judith. 1997. "Merely Cultural." *Social Text* 15 (3/4): 265–77.

Byers, Jackie, and Eileen R. Meehan. 1994. "Once in a Lifetime: Constructing 'The Working Woman' through Cable Narrowcasting." *Camera Obscura* 11–12 (3–1 (33–34)): 12–41.

Bynoe, Yvonne. 2004. *Stand and Deliver: Political Activism, Leadership, and Hip Hop Culture.* Brooklyn: Soft Skull Press.

Bystrom, Kerry. 2011. "On 'Humanitarian' Adoption (Madonna in Malawi)." *Humanity* 2 (2): 213–31.

CA Alliance to Combat Trafficking and Slavery Task Force. 2007. "Human Trafficking in California: Final Report of the California Alliance to Combat Trafficking and Slavery Task Force." California Attorney General's Office. October. https://oag.ca.gov/sites/all/files/agweb/pdfs/publications/Human_Trafficking_Final_Report.pdf.

CA Assembly. 2008. Assembly Committee on the Judiciary. *Bill Analysis: SB1649.* June 18.

———. 2010a. Assembly Committee on the Judiciary. *The California Transparency in Supply Chains Act of 2010: New Information to Aid Consumer Purchasing Decisions.* June 29.

———. 2010b. California Transparency in Supply Chains Act of 2010. SB65. California Civil Code, Section 1714.43, adopted September 30. https://oag.ca.gov/sites/all/files/agweb/pdfs/cybersafety/sb_657_bill_ch556.pdf.

Cabezas, Amalia, and Ana Alcázar Campos. 2016. "Trafficking Discourses of Dominican Women in Puerto Rico." *Social and Economic Studies* 65 (4): 33–56.

Caramanica, Jon. 2022. "Hollywood's First Family of Putting It Out There." *The New York Times,* Feburary 10. https://www.nytimes.com/2022/02/10/arts/music/will-jada-willow-jaden-smith.html.

Casey, Sarah, and Juliet Watson. 2017. "The Unpalatable-Palatable: Celebrity Feminism in the Australian Mainstream Media." *Outskirts* 37: 1–19.

Cashmore, E., and A. Parker. 2003. "One David Beckham? Celebrity, Masculinity, and the Soccerati." *Sociology of Sport Journal* 20: 214–31.

Casper, Monica J., and Lisa Jean Moore. 2009. *Missing Bodies: The Politics of Visibility.* New York: New York University Press.

CAST-LA. 2021a. "Are you a survivor of human trafficking?" Accessed August 10, 2022. https://www.castla.org/human-trafficking/identifying-survivors.

———. 2021b. "The Issue." Accessed August 10, 2022. https://www.castla.org/human-trafficking.

———. 2021c. "Our Mission." CAST-LA. Accessed June 1, 2022. https://www.castla.org/about.

CATW. 2011. "An Introduction to CATW." Accessed October 11, 2021. http://www.catwinternational.org/about.

CATW, et al. 2015. "Letter to Amnesty International: Opposition to Decriminalization." Accessed June 8, 2022. https://catwinternational.org/wp-content/uploads/2019/09/AI-Open-Letter-over-600-sigs.pdf.

CBS News. 2018. "Live to Tell: Trafficked." *48 Hours,* March 31. https://www.cbsnews.com/video/48-hours-live-to-tell-trafficked.

Celis, Karen, and Sarah Childs. 2018. "Good Representatives and Good Representation." *PS: Political Science & Politics* 51 (2): 314–17.

Chambré, Susan Maizel. 2006. *Fighting for Our Lives: New York's AIDS Community and the Politics of Disease.* New Brunswick, NJ: Rutgers University Press.

Chang, Grace. 2013. "This is what Trafficking Looks Like." In *Immigrant Women Workers in the Neoliberal Age,* edited by Nilda Flores-González, 56–77. Urbana: University of Illinois Press.

Change Creation. 2022. "Jada Pinkett Smith/Overbrook Entertainment: Design, Social Media, and Strategy for Don't Sell Bodies—2012–2016." Accessed June 13, 2022. https://www.thechangecreation.com/jada-pinkett-smith-overbrook-entertainment.

Chapkis, Wendy. 2003. "Trafficking, Migration, and the Law: Protecting Innocents, Punishing Immigrants." *Gender & Society* 17 (6): 923–37.

———. 2005. "Soft Glove, Punishing Fist: The Trafficking Victims Protection Act of 2000." In *Regulating Sex: The Politics of Intimacy and Identity,* edited by Elizabeth Bernstein and Laurie Shaffner, 51–66. New York: Routledge.

Chapman-Schmidt, Ben. 2019. "'Sex Trafficking' as Epistemic Violence." *Anti-Trafficking Review* 12: 172–87.

Chateauvert, Melinda. 2013. *Sex Workers Unite: A History of the Movement from Stonewall to Slutwalk.* Boston: Beacon Press.

Chermayeff, Maro, dir. 2012. *Half the Sky.* Blue Sky Films.

———. 2015. *A Path Appears.* Show of Force.

Chidgey, Red. 2021. "Postfeminism™: Celebrity Feminism, Branding and the Performance of Activist Capital." *Feminist Media Studies* 21 (7): 1055–71.

Chou, Mark, Roland Bleiker, and Nilanjana Premaratna. 2017. "Elections as Theater." *PS: Political Science & Politics* 49 (1): 43–47.

Chouliaraki, Lilie. 2012. "The Theatricality of Humanitarianism: A Critique of Celebrity Advocacy." *Communication and Critical/Cultural Studies* 9 (1): 1–21.

Chuang, Janie. 2010. "Rescuing Trafficking from Ideological Capture: Prostitution Reform and Anti-trafficking Law and Policy." *University of Pennsylvania Law Review* 158: 1656–1725.

Cizmar, Martin, Ellis Conklin, and Kristen Hinman. 2011. "Real Men Get Their Facts Straight." *Village Voice,* June 29. http://www.villagevoice.com/2011-06-29/news/real-men-get-their-facts-straight-sex-trafficking-ashton-kutcher-demi-moore.

Clark, Ann Marie. 2001. *Diplomacy of Conscience: Amnesty International and Changing Human Rights Norms.* Princeton: Princeton University Press.

Closson, Troy. 2021. "R. Kelly Is Going to Prison. Why Did It Take So Long?" *The New York Times,* October 20. https://www.nytimes.com/live/2021/09/27/nyregion/r-kelly-trial-news.

CNN. 2010. "CNN: Demi Moore and Ashton Kutcher Talk Modern Slavery." Clinton Global Initiative. September 23. Accessed October 22, 2022. https://www.youtube.com/watch?v=XrCYdypmdis.

———. 2017. "Anti-trafficking Activist on Stopping Slavery." February 24. Accessed October 22, 2022. https://www.cnn.com/videos/world/2017/02/24/gary-haugen-human-trafficking.cnn.

———. 2021. "The CNN Freedom Project." Accessed August 12, 2021. https://www.cnn.com/interactive/2018/specials/freedom-project/.

CNN Airport Network. 2011. "CNN Airport Network Media Kit." http://i.cdn.turner.com/cnn/CNN/Programs/airport.network/cnn.apn.2011.pdf

CNN Freedom Project. 2013/2014. *Every Day in Cambodia.* https://www.cnn.com/videos/intl_tv-shows/2015/04/28/spc-freedom-project-every-day-in-cambodia.cnn.

———. 2015. "Fight for Freedom: Confronting Modern-Day Slavery—Broadcast Taping by the CNN Freedom Project." Harvard University. November 19. Accessed October 22, 2022. https://www.youtube.com/watch?v=rR8tzV8948I.

Cobb, Shelley. 2015. "Is This What a Feminist Looks Like? Male Celebrity Feminists and the Postfeminist Politics of 'Equality.'" *Celebrity Studies* 6 (1): 136–39.

Cohen, Lisa. 2015. "Sold by Their Mothers: Shining a Light on the Child Sex Trade in Cambodia." CNN Freedom Project, April 3. Accessed August 12, 2022. https://www.cnn.com/2015/04/03/world/cambodia-child-sex-trafficking/index.html.

Cojocaru, Claudia. 2015. "Sex Trafficking, Captivity, and Narrative: Constructing Victimhood with the Goal of Salvation." *Dialectical Anthropology* 39 (2): 183–95.

Cole, Jennifer, and Ginny Sprang. 2020. "Post-Implementation of a Safe Harbor Law in the U.S.: Review of State Administrative Data." *Child Abuse & Neglect* 101: 104320.

Cooper, Andrew. 2009. Panel Discussion: "The Effectiveness and Value of Celebrity Diplomacy." USC Center on Public Diplomacy and the Norman Lear Center Workshop. University of Southern California, May 14. https://learcenter.org/event/usc-center-on-public-diplomacy-workshop-celebrity-diplomacy.

———. 2008. *Celebrity Diplomacy.* Boulder: Paradigm Publishers.

Cooper, Charlie. 2014. "Decriminalise Prostitution': Top Medical Journal Lancet Calls for Global Action to Protect Sex Workers from HIV." *The Independent,* July 22. http://www.independent.co.uk/life-style/health-and-families/decriminalise-prostitution-top-medical-journal-lancet-calls-for-global-action-to-protect-sex-workers-from-hiv-9620273.html.

Coorlim, Leif, dir. 2014. *Children For Sale: The Fight to End Human Trafficking.* CNN International and Overbrook Entertainment. https://www.cnn.com/specials/us/children-for-sale.

Copley, Lauren. 2014. "What Does Policy Have to Do With It? The Political Economy of Latino Sex Trafficking in the United States." *Crime, Law and Social Change* 62 (5): 571–84.

Corner, John. 2000. "Mediated Persona and Political Culture: Dimensions of Structure and Process." *Cultural Studies* 3 (3): 386–402.

Cotter, Kelley. 2021. "'Shadowbanning Is Not a Thing': Black Box Gaslighting and the Power to Independently Know and Credibly Critique Algorithms." *Information, Communication & Society:* 1–18.

Cramer, Renée Ann. 2016. *Pregnant with the Stars: Watching and Wanting the Celebrity Baby Bump.* Stanford, CA: Stanford Law Books.

Crenshaw, Kimberlé. 1995. *Critical Race Theory: The Key Writings That Formed the Movement.* New York: New Press.

Crist, Allison. 2020. "Why #MeToo Founder Tarana Burke Initially Turned Down Michelle Williams' Golden Globes Invite." *E! Online,* July 6. https://www .eonline.com/news/1167875/why-metoo-founder-tarana-burke-initially-turned-down-michelle-williams-golden-globes-invite.

Crouch, Colin. 2004. *Post-Democracy.* Cambridge, UK: Polity Press.

Crowder, Chaya. 2020. "Following Black Lives Matter and Mainstream African-American Interest Groups on Social Media: An Intersectional Analysis of Black Organizational Activism on Twitter." *National Review of Black Politics* 1 (4): 474–95.

Cunningham, Scott, and Todd D. Kendall. 2011. "Prostitution 2.0: The Changing Face of Sex Work." *Journal of Urban Economics* 69 (3): 273–87.

Daigle, Leah E. 2021. "Special Issue: Research on Sexual Violence in the #MeToo Era: Prevention and Innovative Methodologies." *American Journal of Criminal Justice* 46 (1): 2–5.

Daniels, Jessie. 2009. "Rethinking Cyberfeminism(s): Race, Gender, and Embodiment." *WSQ: Women's Studies Quarterly* 37 (1–2): 101–24.

Dank, Meredith, Jennifer Yahner, and Lilly Yu. 2017. *Consequences of Policing Prostitution: An Analysis of Individuals Arrested and Prosecuted for Commercial Sex in New York City.* New York, NY: Urban Institute. April. https://www.urban.org /sites/default/files/publication/89451/legal_aid_final_0.pdf

Das, Lina. 2007. "Julia Ormond: The Rise and Fall of a Hollywood Star." *Daily Mail Online,* September 29. https://www.dailymail.co.uk/home/you/article-484550 /Julia-Ormond-The-rise-fall-Hollywood-star.html.

Dávila, Arlene M. 2001. *Latinos, Inc.: The Marketing and Making of a People.* Berkeley: University of California Press.

———. 2008. *Latino Spin: Public Image and the Whitewashing of Race.* New York: New York University Press.

De Orio, Scott. 2017. "The Invention of Bad Gay Sex: Texas and the Creation of a Criminal Underclass of Gay People." *Journal of the History of Sexuality* 26 (1): 53–87.

de Villiers, Nicholas. 2016. "Rebooting Trafficking." *Anti-Trafficking Review* (7): 161–81.

Decker, Michele R., Anna-Louise Crago, Sandra K. H. Chu, Susan G. Sherman, Meena S. Seshu, Kholi Buthelezi, Mandeep Dhaliwal, and Chris Beyrer. 2015. "Human Rights Violations Against Sex Workers: Burden and Effect on HIV." *The Lancet* 385 (9963): 186–99.

Demaine, Linda. 2009. "Navigating Policy by the Stars: The Influence of Celebrity Entertainers on Federal Lawmaking." *The Journal of Law and Politics* 25 (2): 83–143.

Demand Forum. 2021. "Homepage." Accessed August 12, 2022. https://demand-forum.org.

Development International. 2021. "Homepage." Accessed August 12, 2022. https://www.developmentinternational.org/about.

Department of Homeland Security. 2010. "Executive Summary: Blue Campaign Stakeholder Meeting with Senior Counselor Alice Hill." Washington DC: DHS.

Diamond, Elin. 1996. *Performance and Cultural Politics.* London: Routledge.

———. 2000. "Performance and Cultural Politics." In *The Routledge Reader in Politics and Performance,* edited by Lizbeth Goodman and Jane De Gay, 66–69. London: Routledge.

Dice. 2021. "The Gender Pay Gap in Tech." DHI Group, Inc. https://techhub.dice.com/Gender-Pay-Gap-in-Tech-Report_TY.html.

Dillon, Justin, dir. 2008. *Call + Response.* Fair Trade Pictures.

Dionne, Evette. 2014. "9 Feminist Male Actors Who Speak Out For Equality: Ryan Gosling, Joseph Gordon-Levitt & More." *Bustle.com,* March 9. https://www.bustle.com/articles/18087-9-feminist-male-actors-who-speak-out-for-equality-ryan-gosling-joseph-gordon-levitt-more.

Ditmore, Melissa Hope. 2014. "'Caught Between the Tiger and the Crocodile': Cambodian Sex Workers' Experiences of Structural and Physical Violence." *Studies in Gender and Sexuality* 15 (1): 22–31.

Dixon, Herbert. 2013. "Human Trafficking and the Internet* (*and other technologies, too)." *The Judges' Journal* 52 (1): 36–39.

Doezema, Jo. 2005. "Now You See Her, Now You Don't: Sex Workers at the UN Trafficking Protocol Negotiation." *Social & Legal Studies* 14 (1): 61–89.

———. 2010. *Sex Slaves and Discourse Masters: The Construction of Trafficking.* London: Zed Books.

Doucet, Andrea, and Natasha Mauthner. 2007. "Feminist Methodologies and Epistemologies." In *21st Century Sociology,* edited by Clifton Bryant and D. Peck. Thousand Oak, CAs: Sage Publications, Inc.

Dovi, Suzanne. 2002. "Preferable Descriptive Representatives: Will Just Any Woman, Black, or Latino Do?" *American Political Science Review* 96 (4): 729–43.

———. 2009. "In Praise of Exclusion." *The Journal of Politics* 71 (3): 1172–86.

Drake, Philip, and Michael Higgins. 2012. "Lights, Camera, Election: Celebrity, Performance and the 2010 UK General Election Leadership Debates." *The British Journal of Politics and International Relations* 14 (3): 375–91.

Drake, Philip, and Andy Miah. 2010. "The Cultural Politics of Celebrity." *Cultural Politics* 6 (1): 49–64.

Driessens, Oliver. 2013. "Celebrity Capital: Redefining Celebrity Using Field Theory." *Theory and Society* 42 (5): 543–60.

———. 2014. "Expanding Celebrity Studies' Research Agenda: Theoretical Opportunities and Methodological Challenges in Interviewing Celebrities." *Celebrity Studies* 6 (2): 192–205.

Dryzek, John S., and Simon Niemeyer. 2008. "Discursive Representation." *American Political Science Review* 102 (4): 481–93.

DSB. 2021. "DSB Store." Accessed August 11, 2021. https://www.indiemerch.com/dontsellbodies.

Durana, Alieza. 2017. "Gender Inequality in Puerto Rico Is About to Get Worse." *Slate,* October 12. https://slate.com/human-interest/2017/10/gender-inequality-in-puerto-rico-is-going-to-get-worse-after-hurricane-maria.html.

Eckert, Sophia. 2013. "The Business Transparency on Trafficking and Slavery Act: Fighting Forced Labor in Complex Global Supply Chains." *Journal of International Business Law* 12 (2): 383–416.

Edwards, Erica R. 2012. *Charisma and the Fictions of Black Leadership.* Minneapolis: University of Minnesota Press.

Edelson, Matt. 2018. "Of Hair Loss and Heartbreak." *Johns Hopkins School of Medicine Magazine,* Spring/Summer. https://www.hopkinsmedicine.org/news/publications/hopkins_medicine_magazine/features/spring-summer-2018/of-hair-loss-and-heartbreak.

Engle, Karen. 2012. "Celebrity Diplomacy and Global Citizenship." *Celebrity Studies* 3 (1): 116–18.

Epure, Madalina. 2014. "Critically Assess: The Relative Merits of Liberal, Socialist and Radical Feminism." *Journal of Research in Gender Studies* 4 (2): 514–19.

Esau, Eric, and Jason Palmer, dirs. 2012. *Rape for Profit.* Liberty Road Foundation: Mew Films.

Espiritu, Yen Le. 2014. *Body Counts: The Vietnam War and Militarized Refuge(es).* Berkeley: University of California Press.

Evans, Adrienne, and Sarah Riley. 2013. "Immaculate Consumption: Negotiating the Sex Symbol in Postfeminist Celebrity Culture." Journal of Gender Studies 22 (3): 268–81.

Facebook Watch. 2022. "Red Table Talk." Accessed October 12, 2022. https://www.facebook.com/pg/redtabletalk/episodes/?ref=page_internal.

Faludi, Susan. 2022. "Feminism Made a Faustian Bargain With Celebrity Culture. Now It's Paying the Price." *The New York Times,* June 20. https://www.nytimes.com/2022/06/20/opinion/roe-heard-feminism-backlash.html.

Fall, Papa Louis, and Guangting Tang. 2006. *Goodwill Ambassadors in the United Nations System.* Geneva: United Nations.

Farley, Melissa, Kenneth Franzblau, and Alexis Kennedy. 2014. "Online Prostitution and Trafficking." *Albany Law Review* 77 (3): 1039–94.

Farrell, Nathan. 2019. "Introduction: 'Getting Busy with the Fizzy'—Johansson, SodaStream, and Oxfam: Exploring the Political Economics of Celebrity

Activism." In the Political Economy of Celebrity Activism, edited by Nathan Farrell, 1–18. Abingdon, UK: Routledge.

Fassin, Didier. 2012. *Humanitarian Reason: A Moral History of the Present Times.* Berkeley: University of California Press.

Faulkner, Wendy. 2001. "The Technology Question in Feminism: A View from Feminist Technology Studies." *Women's Studies International Forum* 24 (1): 79–95.

Feasey, Rebecca. 2017. "Masculinit(ies) and the Male Celebrity Feminist." *Men and Masculinities* 20 (3): 283–93.

Federal Reserve Bank of New York. 2020. "Puerto Rico Economic Indicators." April 20. Research and Statistics Group, Federal Reserve Bank of New York.

Feliciano, Zadia, and Andrew Green. 2017. "US Multinationals in Puerto Rico and the Repeal of Section 936 Tax Exemption for U.S. Corporations" (Working Paper 2368). : Cambridge, MA: National Bureau of Economic Research. https://www.nber.org/system/files/working_papers/w23681/w23681.pdf.

Ferguson, Michaele L. 2017. "Neoliberal Feminism as Political Ideology: Revitalizing the Study of Feminist Political Ideologies." *Journal of Political Ideologies* 22 (3): 221–35.

Finlayson, Alan. 2014. "Becoming a Democratic Audience." In Rai and Reinelt 2014a, 93–105.

Fischel, Joseph J. 2016. *Sex and Harm in the Age of Consent.* Minneapolis: University of Minnesota Press.

Fischer, Frank. 2003. *Reframing Public Policy: Discursive Politics and Deliberative Practices.* Oxford: Oxford University Press.

Fisher, Jolene. 2016. "Playing With Empowerment: The Half the Sky Movement, Female-Facebook-Gamers, and Neoliberal Development." *Journal of Communication Inquiry* 40 (4): 313–30.

Fong, Dominique. 2010. "Beaverton Resident Collects Shoe Donations to Help Victims of Human Trafficking." *The Oregonian,* December 9. https://www.oregonlive.com/beaverton/2010/12/beaverton_resident_collects_shoe_donations_to_help_victims_of_human_trafficking.html.

Fraser, Nancy. 2013. *Fortunes of Feminism: From State-Managed Capitalism to Neoliberal Crisis.* Brooklyn, NY: Verso Books.

Frizzell, Craig. 2011. "Public Opinion and Foreign Policy: The Effects of Celebrity Endorsements." *The Social Science Journal* 48 (2): 314–23.

Fujii, Lee Ann. 2018. *Interviewing in Social Science Research: A Relational Approach.* New York: Routledge.

Fukushima, Annie Isabel. 2019. *Migrant Crossings: Witnessing Human Trafficking in the U.S.* Stanford, CA: Stanford University Press.

Gallagher, Anne. 2017. "Could Trump Be an Ally in the Fight against Human Trafficking?" *OpenDemocracy,* July 4. https://www.opendemocracy.net/en/5050/could-trump-be-ally-fight-human-trafficking.

Gamson, Joshua. 1994. *Claims to Fame: Celebrity in Contemporary America.* Berkeley: University of California Press.

Garcia-Navarro, Lulu. 2019. "The Connection Between Gov. Rossello's Leaked Chats And Corruption In Puerto Rico." NPR, July 28. https://www.npr.org/2019/07/28/745990020/the-connection-between-gov-rossellos-leaked-chats-and-corruption-in-puerto-rico.

Gates, Kelly. 2011. *Our Biometric Future: Facial Recognition Technology and the Culture of Surveillance.* New York: New York University Press.

Gay, Roxane. 2014. "Emma Watson? Jennifer Lawrence? These Aren't the Feminists You're Looking For." *The Guardian,* April 19. https://www.theguardian.com/commentisfree/2014/oct/10/-sp-jennifer-lawrence-emma-watson-feminists-celebrity.

GEMS. 2021. "Our Mission." Accessed August 11, 2022. https://www.gems-girls.org/our-mission.

Gies, Stephen, Amanda Bobis, Marcia Cohen, and Matthew Malamud. 2018. "Safe Harbor Laws: Changing the Legal Response to Minors Involved in Commercial Sex, Phase 1." *The Legal Review,* U.S. Department of Justice.

Gill, Rosalind. 2017. "Post-postfeminism? New Feminist Visibilities in Postfeminist Times." *Feminist Media Studies* 16 (4): 610–30.

Gira Grant, Melissa. 2014. *Playing the Whore: The Work of Sex Work.* London: Verso.

Gold, Stefan, Alexander Trautrims, and Zoe Trodd. 2015. "Modern Slavery Challenges to Supply Chain Management." *Supply Chain Management: An International Journal* 20 (5): 485–94.

Gordon Nembhard, Jessica. 2014a. "Community-Based Asset Building and Community Wealth." *The Review of Black Political Economy* 41 (2): 101–17.

———. 2014b. *Collective Courage: A History of African American Cooperative Economic Thought and Practice.* University Park, PA: The Pennsylvania State University Press.

Grosfoguel, Ramón. 2003. *Colonial Subjects: Puerto Ricans in a Global Perspective.* Berkeley: University of California Press.

Goss, Kristin. 2016. "Policy Plutocrats: How America's Wealthy Seek to Influence Government." *PS: Political Science & Politics* 49 (3): 442–48.

Gozdziak, Elzbieta. 2015. "Data Matters: Issues and Challenges for Research on Trafficking." In *Global Issues in Crime and Justice,* edited by Molly Dragiewicz, 23–38. Abingdon, UK: Routledge.

Gozdziak, Elzbieta, and Elizabeth Collett. 2005. "Research on Human Trafficking in North America: A Review of the Literature." *International Migration* 43 (1/2): 99–128.

Gruber, Aya, Amy Cohen, and Kate Mogulescu. 2016. "Penal Welfare and the New Human Trafficking Intervention Courts." *Florida Law Review* 68 (5): 1333–1402.

The Guardian. 2009. "Inside Ashton Kutcher's World of Twitter." April 20. https://www.theguardian.com/lifeandstyle/2009/apr/21/ashton-kutcher-celebrity-twitter.

Guinier, Lani. 2000. "Groups, Representation, and Race Conscious Districting: A Case of the Emperor's Clothes." In *Contemplating the People's Branch: Legislative*

Dynamics in the Twenty-First Century, edited by Kelly Patterson and Daniel Shea, 33–56. Upper Saddle River, NJ: Prentice Hall.

Gunter, Barrie. 2014. *Celebrity Capital: Assessing the Value of Fame.* New York: Bloomsbury.

Hajer, Maarten. 2005. "Setting the Stage: A Dramaturgy of Policy Deliberation." *Administration and Society* 36 (6): 624–47.

Halperin, David M. 2017. "Introduction: The War on Sex." In *The War on Sex,* edited by David M. Halperin and Trevor Hoppe, 1–64. Durham, NC: Duke University Press.

Hamad, Hannah, and Anthea Taylor. 2015. "Introduction: Feminism and Contemporary Celebrity Culture." *Celebrity Studies* 6 (1): 124–27.

Hamby, Sherry. 2014. "Intimate Partner and Sexual Violence Research: Scientific Progress, Scientific Challenges, and Gender." *Trauma, Violence, & Abuse* 15 (3): 149–58.

Hancock, Ange-Marie. 2007. "When Multiplication Doesn't Equal Quick Addition: Examining Intersectionality as a Research Paradigm." *Perspectives on Politics* 5 (1): 63–79.

Harris-Perry, Melissa V. 2004. *Barbershops, Bibles, and BET: Everyday Talk and Black Political Thought.* Princeton, NJ: Princeton University Press.

Hartman, Saidiya V. 2007. *Lose Your Mother: A Journey along the Atlantic Slave Route.* New York: Farrar, Straus and Giroux.

Harvey, David. 2005. *A Brief History of Neoliberalism.* Oxford: Oxford University Press.

Hawkesworth, Mary. 2003. "Congressional Enactments of Race-Gender: Towards a Theory of Race-Gendered Institutions." *American Political Science Review* 97 (4): 529–50.

Haynes, Dina F. 2014. "The Celebritization of Human Trafficking." *The ANNALS of the American Academy of Political and Social Science* 653 (1): 25–45.

Healy, Catherine, Ahi Wi-Hongi, and Chanel Hati. 2017. "Reflection from the Field : It's Work, It's Working: The Integration of Sex Workers and Sex Work in Aotearoa/New Zealand." *Women's Studies Journal* 31 (2): 50–60.

Herd, Aimee. 2011. "Shoe Revolt's Creative Fight against Human Trafficking." *Breaking Christian News,* November 14. https://www.expertclick.com/NRWire/Releasedetails.aspx?id=38993

Hernández Angueira, Luisa, and Cesar Hernández. 2017. "Gender Violence and Trafficking." San Juan, PR: Ricky Martin Foundation.

Hernández, Cesar, and Luisa Hernández Angueira. 2010. "Human Trafficking in Puerto Rico: An Invisible Challenge." San Juan, PR: Ricky Martin Foundation–The Protection Project, University of Puerto Rico, Johns Hopkins University.

———. 2014. "Human Trafficking: Modern Slavery in Puerto Rico." San Juan, PR: Ricky Martin Foundation.

Hesford, Wendy S. 2011. *Spectacular Rhetorics: Human Rights Visions, Recognitions, Feminisms.* Durham, NC: Duke University Press.

Heynen, Robert, and Emily van der Meulen. 2021. "Anti-trafficking Saviors: Celebrity, Slavery, and Branded Activism." *Crime, Media, Culture* 18 (2): 301–23.

Hill, Leslie. 2000. "Suffragettes Invented Performance Art." In *The Routledge Reader in Politics and Performance*, edited by Lizbeth Goodman and Jane De Gay, 150–56. London: Routledge.

Hinton, Elizabeth Kai. 2016. *From the War on Poverty to the War on Crime: The Making of Mass Incarceration in America*. Cambridge, MA: Harvard University Press.

Hobson, Janell. 2017. "Celebrity Feminism: More than a Gateway." *Signs* 42 (4): 999–1007.

Hoefinger, Heidi. 2013. *Sex, Love and Money in Cambodia: Professional Girlfriends and Transactional Relationships*. New York: Routledge.

———. 2014. "Gendered Motivations, Sociocultural Constraints, and Psychobehavioral Consequences of Transnational Partnerships in Cambodia." *Studies in Gender and Sexuality* 15 (1): 54–72.

———. 2016. "Neoliberal Sexual Humanitarianism and Story-Telling: The Case of Somaly Mam." *Anti-Trafficking Review* (7): 56–78.

Hoffower, Hillary. 2020. "Ashton Kutcher Is Hollywood's Most Active Silicon Valley Investor." *Business Insider,* February 6. https://www.businessinsider.in /slideshows/miscellaneous/ashton-kutcher-is-hollywoods-most-active-silicon-valley-investor-heres-how-he-built-a-lucrative-investing-career-from-making-an-early-bet-on-uber-to-turning-a-30-million-fund-into-250-million-/slidelist /73991474.cms.

Holm, Malin, and Jorge Humberto Ojeda Castro. 2018. "#solidarityisforwhite-women: Exploring the Opportunities for Mobilizing Digital Counter Claims." *PS: Political Science & Politics* 51 (2): 331–34.

Holson, Laura. 2010. "Charity Fixer To the Stars: Seeing the 'Power of Personality' and 'How to Leverage It to Do Good.'" *The New York Times,* December 5. http:// www.nytimes.com/2010/12/05/fashion/05TREVORNEILSON.html.

hooks, bell. 1999. *Feminist Theory: From Margin to Center*. Cambridge: South End Press.

Hopkins, Susan. 2017. "UN Celebrity 'It' Girls as Public Relations-ised Humanitarianism." *International Communication Gazette* 80 (3): 273–92.

Hopkins, Susan, and Eric Louw. 2019. "'Bring Back Our Girls': Social Celebrity, Digital Activism, and New Femininity." In *The Political Economy of Celebrity Activism*, edited by Nathan Farrell, 66–84. Abingdon, UK: Routledge.

Hossein, Caroline Shenaz. 2018. *The Black Social Economy in the Americas: Exploring Diverse Community-Based Markets*. New York: Palgrave Macmillan.

Hoyle, C., M. Bosworth, and M. Dempsey. 2011. "Labelling the Victims of Sex Trafficking: Exploring the Borderland between Rhetoric and Reality." *Social & Legal Studies* 20 (3): 313–29.

Hozic, Aida A. 2001. *Hollyworld: Space, Power, and Fantasy in the American Economy*. Ithaca: Cornell University Press.

Hozic, Aida, Samantha Majic, and Ibrahim Yahaya. 2018. "'It is not about me . . . but it kind of is': Celebrity Humanitarianism in Late Modernity." In *Race, Gender, and Culture in International Relations: Postcolonial Perspectives,* edited by Raldolph Persaud and Alina Sajed, 180–99. London: Routledge.

HRC. 2010. "Ricky Martin at the 2010 HRC National Dinner." October 11. https://www.youtube.com/watch?v=gBUgtQ8j5hY.

Htun, Mala, and S. Laurel Weldon. 2018. *The Logics of Gender Justice: State Action on Women's Rights around the World.* Cambridge, UK: Cambridge University Press.

Hua, Julietta, and Holly Nigorizawa. 2010. "US Sex Trafficking, Women's Human Rights and the Politics of Representation." *International Feminist Journal of Politics* 12 (3–4): 401–23.

Hubbard, Shanita. 2016. "A Conversation with Jada Pinkett Smith About Black Girls and Human Trafficking." *Ebony,* October 27. https://www.ebony.com/jada-pinkett-smith-sex-trafficking.

Huliaras, Asteris, and Nikolaos Tzifakis. 2010. "Celebrity Activism in International Relations: In Search of a Framework for Analysis." *Global Society* 24 (2): 255–74.

Hume, Tim, Lisa Cohen, and Mira Sorvino. 2013. "The Women Who Sold Their Daughters into Sex Slavery." The CNN Freedom Project. Accessed October 24, 2022. https://www.cnn.com/interactive/2013/12/world/cambodia-child-sex-trade.

Hunt, Darnell, and Ana-Christina Ramón. 2021. "Hollywood Diversity Report." Los Angeles: UCLA. https://socialsciences.ucla.edu/wp-content/uploads/2021/10/UCLA-Hollywood-Diversity-Report-2021-Television-10-26-2021.pdf

International Labour Organization (ILO). 2013. "Artists gather their talent to fight forced labour." May 7. Accessed October 24, 2022. https://iloartworks.org/forced-labour/artists-gather-their-talents-to-fight-forced-labour.

———. 2021a. "About the ILO." Accessed August 10, 2022. https://www.ilo.org/global/about-the-ilo/lang—en/index.htm.

———. 2021b. "Forced Labour, Discrimination and Poverty Reduction among Indigenous Peoples in Bolivia, Peru and Paraguay." Accessed August 10, 2022. https://www.ilo.org/global/topics/forced-labour/WCMS_082040/lang—en/index.htm.

———. 2021c. "What Is Forced Labour, Modern Slavery and Human Trafficking." Accessed August 10, 2022. https://www.ilo.org/global/topics/forced-labour/definition/lang—en/index.htm.

———. 2022a. "Profits and Poverty: The Economics of Forced Labour." Accessed July 28, 2022. https://www.ilo.org/global/topics/forced-labour/publications/profits-of-forced-labour-2014/lang—en/index.htm.

———. 2022b. "End Slavery Now." Accessed October 10, 2022. https://www.ilo.org/global/about-the-ilo/artworks/topics/forced-labour/end-slavery-now/lang--en/index.htm.

———. 2022c. "Jada Pinkett Smith: End Slavery Now!." Accessed October 10, 2022. https://www.ilo.org/global/about-the-ilo/multimedia/video/public-service-announcements/WCMS_194724/lang--en/index.htm.

InboxMag. 2011. "Real Men Know How to Use an Iron, with Sean Penn featuring Edward Norton." April 13, 2011. https://www.youtube.com/watch?v= NWQRPdZzK-Y.

Intransigente. 2019. "Claves para entender el mensaje de Ricky Martin, ¿qué busca para Puerto Rico?" Accessed October 5, 2021. https://elintransigente .com/2019/07/claves-para-entender-el-mensaje-de-ricky-martin-que-busca-para-puerto-rico/.

Institute of Public and International Affairs (IPIA) at the University of Utah. 2015. "What is Interpretive Research?" Accessed December 7, 2021. http://www.ipia .utah.edu/imps/html/research.html.

iPoint. 2021. "Homepage." Accessed August 12, 2022. https://www.ipoint-systems .com.

Jackson, Crystal. 2016. "Framing Sex Worker Rights: How U.S. Sex Worker Rights Activists Perceive and Respond to Mainstream Anti-Sex Trafficking Advocacy." *Sociologial Perspectives* 59 (1): 27–45.

Jackson, Sarah J. 2014. *Black Celebrity, Racial Politics, and the Press: Framing Dissent.* New York: Routledge.

Jackson, Sue. 2021. "'A Very Basic View of Feminism': Feminist Girls and Meanings of (Celebrity) Feminism." *Feminist Media Studies* 21 (7): 1072–90.

Jeffreys, Elaine. 2015. "On Celebrity Philanthropy." In *Celebrity Philanthropy,* edited by Elaine Jeffreys and Paul Allatson, 22–39. Bristol, UK: Intellect Books.

———. 2016. "Translocal Celebrity Activism: Shark-Protection Campaigns in Mainland China." *Environmental Communication* 10 (6): 763–76.

Jeffreys, Elaine, and Paul Allatson. 2015. "Celebrity and Philanthropy: An Introduction." In *Celebrity Philanthropy,* edited by Elaine Jeffreys and Paul Allatson, 1–16. Bristol, UK: Intellect Books.

Johnson, Robin. 2014. "Hiding in Plain Sight: Reproducing Masculine Culture at a Video Game Studio." *Communication, Culture & Critique* 7 (4): 578–94.

Jones, Mydrim. 2009. "Liam in Bid to Fight Kid Sex Slavery; UNICEF." *Sunday Mirror,* February 15. https://www.thefreelibrary.com/LIAM+IN+BID+TO+FI GHT+KID+SEX+SLAVERY%3b+unisafe+United+Nations...-a0193749814.

Jordan-Zachery, Julia Sheron. 2017. *Shadow Bodies: Black Women, Ideology, Representation, and Politics.* New Brunswick: Rutgers University Press.

Joseph, Pat. 2014. "Victims Can Lie as Much as Other People." *The Atlantic,* June 5. https://www.theatlantic.com/international/archive/2014/06/somaly-mam-scandal-victims-can-lie/372188.

Judd, Ashley. 2008. Speech to the United Nations General Assembly. June 3.

Judd, Ashley, and Maryanne Vollers. 2011. *All That Is Bitter & Sweet: A Memoir.* New York: Ballantine Books.

Kapoor, Ilan. 2012. *Celebrity Humanitarianism: The Ideology of Global Charity.* New York: Routledge.

Kavner, Lucas. 2011. "Ashton Kutcher and Demi Moore Launch 'Real Men Don't Buy Girls' Campaign." *Huffington Post,* April 11. http://www.huffingtonpost .com/2011/04/11/ashton-kutcher-demi-moore-trafficking_n_847291.html.

Kaye, Julie. 2017. *Responding to Human Trafficking: Dispossession, Colonial Violence, and Resistance among Indigenous and Racialized Women.* Toronto: University of Toronto Press.

Keller, Jessalynn, and Jessica Ringrose. 2015. "'But Then Feminism Goes Out the Window!': Exploring Teenage Girls' Critical Response to Celebrity Feminism." *Celebrity Studies* 6 (1): 132–35.

Kelley, Judith G., and Beth A. Simmons. 2015. "Politics by Number: Indicators as Social Pressure in International Relations." *American Journal of Political Science* 59 (1): 55–70.

Kellner, Douglas. 2008. *Guys and Guns Amok: Domestic Terrorism and School Shootings from the Oklahoma City Bombing to the Virginia Tech Massacre.* Boulder, CO: Paradigm.

Kempadoo, Kamala. 2005. "From Moral Panic to Global Justice: Changing Perspectives on Trafficking." In *Trafficking and Prostitution Reconsidered: New Perspectives on Migration, Sex Work and Human Rights,* edited by Kamala Kempadoo, Jyoti Sanghera, and Barbara Pattanaik, vii–xxxiv. Boulder, CO: Paradigm.

———. 2015. "The Modern-Day White (Wo)Man's Burden: Trends in Anti-Trafficking and Anti-Slavery Campaigns." *Journal of Human Trafficking* 1 (1): 8–20.

Kempadoo, Kamala, Jyoti Sanghera, and Bandana Pattanaik. 2012. *Trafficking and Prostitution Reconsidered: New Perspectives on Migration, Sex Work and Human Rights.* 2nd ed. Boulder, CO: Paradigm.

Kershaw, Baz. 2000. "Performance, Community, Culture." In *The Routledge Reader in Politics and Performance,* edited by Lizbeth Goodman and Jane De Gay, 136–142. London: Routledge.

Kinney, Edi. 2013. "Securitizing Sex, Bodies, and Borders: The Resonance of Human Security Frames in Thailand's 'War against Human Trafficking.'" In *Gender, Violence, and Human Security: Critical Feminist Perspectives,* edited by Aili Mari Tripp, Myra Marx Ferree and Christina Ewig, 79–108. New York: New York University Press.

Kogen, Lauren. 2014. "For the Public Good or Just Good Publicity? Celebrity Diplomacy and the Ethics of Representation." *Mass Communication and Society* 18 (1): 37–57.

Koomson, Bernard, and Dawuda Abdulai. 2021. "Putting Childhood in Its Place: Rethinking Popular Discourses on the Conceptualisation of Child Trafficking in Ghana." *Anti-Trafficking Review* (16): 28–46.

Kotiswaran, Prabha. 2019. "Trafficking: A Development Approach." *Current Legal Problems* 72 (1): 375–416.

Kournay, Janet. 2009. "The Place of Standpoint Theory in Feminist Science Studies." *Hypatia* 24 (4): 209–18.

Kozinets, Robert, and Jay Handelman. 2004. "Adversaries of Consumption: Consumer Movements, Activism, and Ideology." *Journal of Consumer Research* 31 (December): 691–704.

Kristof, Nicholas. 2011. "Foreword." In Judd and Vollers, xi–xviii.

———. 2014a. "When Sources May Have Lied." *The New York Times,* June 7. https://archive.nytimes.com/kristof.blogs.nytimes.com/2014/06/07/when-sources-may-have-lied.

———. 2014b. "A Woman I Regarded as a Hero, and New Doubts." *The New York Times,* June 2. https://archive.nytimes.com/kristof.blogs.nytimes.com/2014/06/02/a-woman-i-regarded-as-a-hero-and-new-doubts.

———. 2015. "Making Life Harder for Pimps." *The New York Times,* August 6. https://www.nytimes.com/2015/08/06/opinion/nicholas-kristof-making-life-harder-for-pimps.html.

Krook, Mona Lena, and Jacqui True. 2012. "Rethinking the Life Cycles of International Norms: The United Nations and the Global Promotion of Gender Equality." *European Journal of International Relations* 18: 103–27.

Kutcher, Ashton. 2017. "Opening Statement: End It: The Fight to End Modern Slavery." United States Senate Foreign Relations Committee Hearing on Ending Modern Slavery and Human Trafficking. February 15. https://www.foreign.senate.gov/imo/media/doc/021517_Kutcher_Testimony.pdf

Lancaster, Roger N. 2011. *Sex Panic and the Punitive State.* Berkeley: University of California Press.

Langellier, Kristin. 1999. "Personal Narrative, Performance, Performativity: Two or Three Things I Know For Sure." *Text and Performance Quarterly* 19: 125–44.

Larabee, Ann. 2018. "Editorial-Celebrity Politics and the 'Me Too' Moment." *The Journal of Popular Culture* 51 (1): 7–9.

Larner, Wendy. 2000. "Neo-liberalism: Policy, Ideology, Governmentality." *Studies in Political Economy* 63: 5–25.

Lauger, Amy, and Matthew Durose. 2021. "Human Trafficking Data Collection Activities, 2021." Washington, DC: Office of Justice Programs. October. https://bjs.ojp.gov/content/pub/pdf/htdca21.pdf

Lee, Maggy. 2011. *Trafficking and Global Crime Control.* Thousand Oaks, CA: Sage.

Levine, Daniel. 2017. "Ricardo Rosselló: 5 Fast Facts You Need to Know." *Heavy,* September. https://heavy.com/news/2017/09/ricardo-rossello-puerto-rico-governor-maria-response-wife-age.

Lieberman, Marcia. 2018. "Decriminalization of Prostitution Policy: Amnesty International Punishes a Dissenting Member." *Dignity: A Journal of Analysis of Exploitation and Violence* 3 (3): n.p.

Lightfoot, Elizabeth Bradford. 2019. "Consumer Activism for Social Change." *Social Work* 64 (4): 301–9.

Lilburn, Sandra, Susan Magarey, and Susan Sheridan. 2000. "Celebrity Feminism as Synthesis: Germaine Greer, The Female Eunuch, and the Australian Print Media." *Continuum: Journal of Media & Cultural Studies* 14 (3): 335–48.

Lim, Young Joon. 2019. "Promoting the Image of the United Nations." *Journalism History* 40 (3): 187–96.

Limoncelli, Stephanie. 2009. "The Trouble with Trafficking: Conceptualizing Women's Sexual Labor and Economic Human Rights." *Women's Studies International Forum* 32 (4): 261–29.

————. 2010. *The Politics of Trafficking: The First International Movement to Combat the Sexual Exploitation of Women.* Stanford, CA: Stanford University Press.

————. 2017. "Legal Limits: Ending Human Trafficking in Supply Chains." *World Policy Journal* 34 (1): 119–23.

Lindenberg, S., J.F. Joly, and D.A. Stapel. 2011. "The Norm-Activating Power of Celebrity: The Dynamics of Success and Influence." *Social Psychology Quarterly* 74 (1): 98–120.

Lindquist, Johan. 2010. "Images and Evidence: Human Trafficking, Auditing, and the Production of Illicit Markets in Southeast Asia and Beyond." *Public Culture* 22 (2): 223–36.

Littler, Jo. 2008. "'I Feel Your Pain': Cosmopolitan Charity and the Public Fashioning of the Celebrity Soul." *Social Semiotics* 18 (2): 237–51.

————. 2015. "The New Victorians? Celebrity Charity and the Demise of the Welfare State." *Celebrity Studies* 6 (4): 471–85.

Lohan, Maria, and Wendy Faulkner. 2016. "Masculinities and Technologies." *Men and Masculinities* 6 (4): 319–29.

Lombardo, Emanuela, and Petra Meier. 2018. "Good Symbolic Representation: The Relevance of Inclusion." *PS: Political Science & Politics* 51 (2): 327–30.

Look to the Stars. 2011. "Liam Neeson Announced As UNICEF Goodwill Ambassador." March 29, 2011. https://www.looktothestars.org/news/6038-liam-neeson-announced-as-unicef-goodwill-ambassador.

Lorde, Audre. 1984. *Sister Outsider.* Berkeley, CA: Crossing Press.

Lugo-Lugo, Carmen. 2012. "'Ricky Martin Ain't No Dixie Chick': Or, How We Can Learn A Few Things About Citizenship And Invisibility From Popular Culture." *Centro Journal* XXIV (1): 68–89.

Lutnick, Alexandra. 2016. *Domestic Minor Sex Trafficking: Beyond Victims and Villains.* New York: Columbia University Press.

Lutnick, Alexandra, and Deb Cohan. 2009. "Criminalization, Legalization or Decriminalization of Sex Work: What Female Sex Workers Say." *Reproductive Health Matters* 17 (33): 38–46.

Ma, Yoon Jin, Hyun-Hwa Lee, and Kylie Goerlitz. 2016. "Transparency of Global Apparel Supply Chains: Quantitative Analysis of Corporate Disclosures." *Corporate Social Responsibility and Environmental Management* 23 (5): 308–18.

MacPhail, C., J. Scott, and V. Minichiello. 2015. "Technology, Normalisation and Male Sex Work." *Cult Health Sex* 17 (4): 483–95.

Mahadevan, Tara C. 2019. "Kanye West: 'If There's an Advertisement for a Strip Club, That Is Advertising Sex Trafficking.'" *Complex,* November 17. https://www.complex.com/music/2019/11/kanye-west-if-theres-an-ad-for-strip-club-that-is-ad-sex-trafficking.

Majic, Samantha. 2014a. "Political Participation Despite the Odds: Examining Sex Workers' Political Engagement." *New Political Science* 36 (1): 76–95.

————. 2014b. *Sex Work Politics: From Protest to Service Provision.* Philadelphia: University of Pennsylvania Press.

———. 2014c. "Teaching Equality? 'John Schools,' Gender, and Institutional Reform." *Polity* 46 (1): 5–30.

———. 2015. "Implementing 'New' Norms? Examining 'John School' Policies in the United States." *Critical Policy Studies* 9 (3): 278–96.

———. 2017. "Sending a Dear John Letter: Public Information Campaigns and the Movement to "End Demand" for Prostitution in Atlanta, GA." *Social Sciences* 6 (4): 138–60.

———. 2018. "Real Men Set Norms? Anti-trafficking Campaigns and the Limits of Celebrity Norm Entrepreneurship." *Crime, Media, Culture* 14 (2): 289–309.

———. 2019. "Publicizing the (In)visible? Celebrities, Anti-Human Trafficking Activism, and Feminist Ideologies." *Social Politics: International Studies in Gender, State & Society* 28 (1): 94–118.

———. 2020. "Same Same but Different? Gender, Sex Work, and Respectability Politics in the Myredbook and Rentboy Closures." *Anti-Trafficking Review* (14): 82–98.

———. 2022. "It's Blue and It's Up to You! Examining Federal Antitrafficking Awareness Campaigns in the United States." In *Citizenship on the Edge: Sex/Gender/Race,* edited by Nancy J. Hirschmann and Deborah A. Thomas, 186–27. Philadelphia: University of Pennsylvania Press.

Majic, Samantha, Michael Bernhard, and Daniel O'Neill. 2020. "From the Editors: Celebrity and Politics." *Perspectives on Politics* 18 (1): 1–9.

Malloch, Margaret S., and Paul Rigby. 2016. *Human Trafficking: The Complexities of Exploitation.* Edinburgh: Edinburgh University Press.

Mam, Somaly, and Ruth Marshall. 2008. *The Road of Lost Innocence.* New York: Spiegel & Grau.

Mansbridge, Jane. 1999. "Should Blacks Represent Blacks and Women Represent Women? A Contingent 'Yes.'" *Journal of Politics* 61 (3): 628–57.

———. 2003. "Rethinking Representation." *American Political Science Review* 97 (4): 515–28.

Marks, Simon. 2014. "Somaly Mam: The Holy Saint (and Sinner) of Sex Trafficking." *Newsweek,* May 21. https://www.newsweek.com/2014/05/30/somaly-mam-holy-saint-and-sinner-sex-trafficking-251642.html

Marshall, P. David. 1997. *Celebrity and Power: Fame in Contemporary Culture.* Minneapolis: University of Minnesota Press.

———. 2006. *The Celebrity Culture Reader.* London: Routledge.

———. 2010. "The Promotion and Presentation of the Self: Celebrity as Marker of Presentational Media." *Celebrity Studies* 1 (1): 35–48.

———. 2014. *Celebrity and Power: Fame in Contemporary Culture.* 2nd ed. Minneapolis: University of Minnesota Press.

———. 2019. "Celebrity, Politics, and New Media: an Essay on the Implications of Pandemic Fame and Persona." *International Journal of Politics, Culture, and Society* 33 (1): 89–104.

Martin, Ricky. 2006. Speech for the House of Representatives: Committee on International Relations briefing and hearing, "Enhancing the Global Fight

Against Human Trafficking." September 26. http://commdocs.house.gov /committees/intlrel/hfa30141.000/hfa30141_of.htm.

———. 2008. "React: It's Time." Speech at the Vienna Forum to Fight Human Trafficking. February 13.

———. 2010. Me. New York: New American Library.

———. 2012. "Trafficked Children in Our Cities: Protecting the Exploited in the Americas." In *State of the World's Children 2012: Children in an Urban World*, edited by UNICEF, 54. New York: UNICEF.

Martyn, Amy. 2021. "This Company Gives Formerly Incarcerated People a Second Chance, but Workers Face On-The-Job Dangers." *NBC News*, May 8. https:// www.nbcnews.com/news/us-news/company-gives-formerly-incarcerated-people-second-chance-workers-face-job-n1266718.

Marwick, Alice, and danah boyd. 2011. "To See and Be Seen: Celebrity Practice on Twitter." *Convergence: The International Journal of Research into New Media Technologies* 17 (2): 139–58.

Maslin Nir, Sarah. 2015. "The Price of Nice Nails." *The New York Times*, May 7. https://www.nytimes.com/2015/05/10/nyregion/at-nail-salons-in-nyc-manicurists-are-underpaid-and-unprotected.html.

Mathers, Kathryn. 2012. "Mr. Kristof, I Presume?" *Transition* (107): 15–31.

Mattos, Ed. 2012. "New California Law Takes Aim At Forced Labor—Labor is Not a Commodity." *Labor Rights Blog*, December 14. https://laborrightsblog .typepad.com.

Mayhew, David R. 2008. *Parties and Policies: How the American Government Works*. New Haven, CT: Yale University Press.

Maynard, Pamela. 2021. "Are We Really Closing the Gender Gap in Tech?" *Forbes*, March 3. https://www.forbes.com/sites/forbesbusinesscouncil/2021/03/03 /are-we-really-closing-the-gender-gap-in-tech/?sh=3df540bc5d71.

McCall, Leslie. 2005. "The Complexity of Intersectionality." *Signs* 30 (3): 1771–1800.

McGough, Maureen. 2013. "Ending Modern-Day Slavery: Using Research to Inform U.S. Anti-Human Trafficking Efforts." *NIJ Journal* (271): 26–32.

McNeill, Maggie. 2014. "Lies, Damn Lies, and Sex Work Statistics." *Washington Post*, March 27. http://www.washingtonpost.com/news/the-watch/wp/2014 /03/27/lies-damned-lies-and-sex-work-statistics.

McRobbie, Angela. 2009. *The Aftermath of Feminism: Gender, Culture and Social Change*. Thousand Oaks, CA: SAGE.

Merry, Sally Engle. 2016. *The Seductions of Quantification: Measuring Human Rights, Gender Violence, and Sex Trafficking*. Chicago: The University of Chicago Press.

Mettler, Suzanne. 2016. "The Policyscape and the Challenges of Contemporary Politics to Policy Maintenance." *Perspectives on Politics* 14 (2): 369–90.

Meyer, David, and Josh Gamson. 1995. "The Challenge of Cultural Elites: Celebrities and Social Movements." *Sociological Inquiry* 65 (2): 181–206.

Micheletti, Michele. 2003. *Political Virtue and Shopping: Individuals, Consumerism, and Collective Action*. New York: Palgrave Macmillan.

Milivojevic, Sanja, and Sharon Pickering. 2013. "Trafficking in People, 20 Years On: Sex, Migration and Crime in the Global Anti-Trafficking Discourse and the Rise of the 'Global Trafficking Complex.'" *Current Issues in Criminal Justice* 25 (2): 585–604.

Miller, Julie. 2021. "Mira Sorvino Is Ready for Her Next Act." *Vanity Fair,* November 9. https://www.vanityfair.com/hollywood/2021/11/mira-sorvino-impeachment-interview.

Miller-Young, Mireille. 2010. "Putting Hypersexuality to Work: Black Women and Illicit Eroticism in Pornography." *Sexualities* 13 (2): 219–235.

Minh-ha, Trinh T. 1989. *Women Native Other.* Bloomington: Indiana University Press.

Minority Rights Group. 2021. "Cambodia: Ethnic Vietnamese." Minority Rights Group: World Directory of Minorities and Indigenous Peoples. Accessed March 16, 2021. https://minorityrights.org/minorities/ethnic-vietnamese/.

Mitzeliotis, Katrina. 2011. "Sienna Miller & Sarah Jessica Parker Donate Shoes To Charity, Just Like Kristen Stewart!" *Hollywood Life,* August 19.

Mohanty, Chandra. 1991. "Under Western Eyes: Feminist Scholarship and Colonial Discourse." In *Third World Women and the Politics of Feminism,* edited by C. Mohanty et al., 51–80. Bloomington: Indiana University Press.

———. 2003. "'Under Western Eyes' Revisited: Feminist Solidarity through Anti-capitalist Struggles." *Signs* 28 (2): 499–535.

Molland, Sverre. 2013. "Tandem Ethnography: On Researching 'Trafficking' and 'Anti-trafficking.'" *Ethnography* 14 (3): 300–23.

Moller Okin, Susan. 1989. *Justice, Gender and the Family.* New York: Basic Books.

Montanaro, Laura. 2012. "The Democratic Legitimacy of Self-Appointed Representatives." *The Journal of Politics* 74 (4): 1094–1107.

Monto, Martin A. 2014. "Prostitution, Sex Work, and Violence: Lessons From the Cambodian Context." *Studies in Gender and Sexuality* 15 (1): 73–84.

Murray, Christine. 2020. "Victims and Villains: Anti-trafficking Movement Urged to Tackle Racial Bias." *Reuters,* June 25. https://www.reuters.com/article/us-usa-race-trafficking-trfn/victims-and-villains-anti-trafficking-movement-urged-to-tackle-racial-bias-idUSKBN23W30S.

Musto, Jennifer L., and danah boyd. 2014. "The Trafficking-Technology Nexus." *Social Politics: International Studies in Gender, State & Society* 21 (3): 461–83.

Musto, Jennifer, Mitali Thakor, and Borislav Gerasimov. 2020. "Editorial: Between Hope and Hype: Critical Evaluations of Technology's Role in Anti-trafficking." *Anti-Trafficking Review* (14): 1–14.

Narayan, U. 1997. *Dis/locating Cultures/Identitites, Traditions, and Third World Feminism.* New York: Routledge.

National Black Women's Justice Institute (NBWJI). 2022. "Sex Trafficking of Black Women & Girls," January. https://www.nbwji.org/_files/ugd/oc71ee_cd4d16e2b9ce4568be165co9a6badf53.pdf?utm_campaign=0258da63-6844-471f-89af-a41716e6de5e&utm_source=so&utm_medium=mail&cid=c4e5163e-30e4-4aab-a848-dc506cocf28f.

Mensah, Betty, and Samuel Okyere. 2019. "How CNN reported on 'child slaves' who were not really enslaved." *Al Jazeera,* March 18. https://www.aljazeera.com /opinions/2019/3/18/how-cnn-reported-on-child-slaves-who-were-not-really- enslaved.

Newport News. 2010. "Sarah Jessica Parker Partners With Social Enterprise Shoe Revolt to Help Fight Sex Trafficking." *Social Enterprise Scotland,* May 27. https:// socialenterprise.scot/sarah-jessica-parker-partners-with-social-enterprise-shoe- revolt-to-help-fight-sex-trafficking.

Nicol, Travis. 2016. "40 Famous Harvard Graduates and 10 Famous Harvard Drop- outs." *Mass Live,* September 22. https://www.masslive.com/entertainment /2016/09/celebrity_harvard_alumni.html.

Nolan, David, and Stephanie Brookes. 2013. "Populism In Theory and Practice: Analysing Celebrity Politics." *Media Asia* 40 (4): 373–83.

Nolfi, Joey. 2021. "Why Salma Hayek Insisted Jada Pinkett Smith be Naked for 'Nada Se Compara' Music Video." *Entertainment Weekly,* June 23. https:// ew.com/music/jada-pinkett-smith-naked-nada-se-compara-music-video- salma-hayek/.

Nyong'o, Lupita. 2017. "Lupita Nyong'o: Speaking Out About Harvey Weinstein." *The New York Times,* October 19. https://www.nytimes.com/2017/10/19/opinion /lupita-nyongo-harvey-weinstein.html.

O'Connell-Davison, Julia. 2006. "Will the Real Sex Slave Please Stand Up?" *Feminist Review* 83 (Sexual Moralities): 4–22.

O'Brien, Erin. 2011. "Fuelling Traffic: Abolitionist Claims of a Causal Nexus between Legalised Prostitution and Trafficking." *Crime, Law and Social Change* 56 (5): 547–65.

———. 2013. "Ideal Victims in Trafficking Awareness Campaigns." In *Crime, Justice and Social Democracy: International Perspectives,* edited by Kerry Carrington, Matthew Ball, Erin O'Brien and Juan Marcellus Tauri, 315–26. Basingstoke, UK: Palgrave Macmillan.

———. 2015. "Prostitution Ideology and Trafficking Policy: The Impact of Political Approaches to Domestic Sex Work on Human Trafficking Policy in Australia and the United States." *Journal of Women, Politics & Policy* 36 (2): 191–212.

O'Malley Greenburg, Zack. 2016. "How Ashton Kutcher And Guy Oseary Built A $250 Million Portfolio With Startups Like Uber And Airbnb." *Forbes,* April 18. https://www.forbes.com/sites/zackomalleygreenburg/2016/03/23/how-ashton- kutcher-and-guy-oseary-built-a-250-million-portfolio-with-startups-like-uber- and-airbnb/?sh=f777cf711753.

Oriel, Cat. 2016. "Activist, Survivor Present about Human Trafficking." *The Oracle,* October 28. https://archeroracle.org/26175/news/activist-survivor-present-about- human-trafficking/.

Ormond, Julia. 2006a. "Statement of UN Goodwill Ambassador Julia Ormond." United Nations Office of Drugs and Crime, Vienna, Austria, April 24. https:// www.unodc.org/pdf/Julia%20Ormond%20Vienna%20address%2022.4.06.pdf.

————. 2006b. Briefing for the United States House of Representatives: Committee on International Relations' Subcommittee on Africa, Global Human Rights and International Operations hearing, *Modern Day Slavery: Spotlight on the 2006 "Trafficking in Persons Report," Forced Labor and Sex Trafficking at the World Cup.* Washington, DC, June 14. https://digitalcommons.unl.edu/cgi/viewcontent.cgi?article=1032&context=humtraffdata.

————. 2007. Speech at the United National Security Council, "Implications of Human Trafficking for International Peace and Security," UN Arria-Formula Meeting. July 19.

————. 2008a. "Anti-trafficking Radio Spot #6." UNODC Public Service Announcement. Accessed October 1, 2022. https://www.unodc.org/documents/audio/julia_ormond/juliaormondpsa6_music.mp3.

————. 2008b. Speech at the Global Philanthropy Forum. Redwood City, CA. April 11. https://philanthropyforum.org/explore/past-speakers/200-julia-ormond.

————. 2011. Speech at the Commission on Security and Cooperation in Europe, "Labor Trafficking in Troubled Economic Times: Protecting American Jobs and Migrant Human Rights." Washington, DC, May 23. https://www.congress.gov/112/chrg/CHRG-112jhrg93956/CHRG-112jhrg93956.pdf.

————. 2012. Remarks on human trafficking for Women*etics* (in partnership with Porsche). "Actress Julia Ormond on Human Trafficking." February 8. https://www.youtube.com/watch?v=DrKkPywo6Lk

————. 2016. Benchmark Study Webinar. https://register.gotowebinar.com/recording/1208910118007706114.

————. 2017a. Speech at Skoll Foundation World Forum, "Aha! Moments: When I Changed Course #SkollWF 2017." Oxford, UK. April 7. https://www.youtube.com/watch?v=jlZOX1Hvqrw.

————. 2017b. Panelist for Ending Trafficking: A Discussion of Human Rights. USC Price School of Public Policy. Los Angeles, CA. May 8. https://www.youtube.com/watch?v=h-fMZFB5ehk.

Pachirat, Timothy. 2011. *Every Twelve Seconds: Industrialized Slaughter and the Politics of Sight.* New Haven, CT: Yale University Press.

Page, Allison. 2017. "'How Many Slaves Work for You?' Race, New Media, and Neoliberal Consumer Activism." *Journal of Consumer Culture* 17 (1): 46–61.

Parkinson, John. 2014. "Performing Democracy: Roles, Stages, Scripts." In Rai and Reinelt 2014a, 19–33.

Partzsch, Lena. 2017. "Powerful Individuals in a Globalized World." *Global Policy* 8 (1): 5–13.

Pease, A., and P. R. Brewer. 2008. "The Oprah Factor: The Effects of a Celebrity Endorsement in a Presidential Primary Campaign." *The International Journal of Press/Politics* 13 (4): 386–400.

Peksen, Dursun, Shannon Lindsey Blanton, and Robert G. Blanton. 2017. "Neoliberal Policies and Human Trafficking for Labor: Free Markets, Unfree Workers?" *Political Research Quarterly* 70 (3): 673–86.

Peña, Alejandro. 2020. "Other Former Menudo Make Strong Accusations about the Boy Band." *RNow,* October 15. https://rnow.today/celebrities/Other-former-Menudo-make-strong-accusations-about-the-boy-band-20201015-0011.html.

Peters, Alicia. 2015. *Responding to Human Trafficking: Sex, Gender, and Culture in the Law.* Philadelphia: University of Pennsylvania Press.

———. 2013. ""Things That Involve Sex are Just Different": US Anti-Trafficking Law and Policy on the Books, in Their Minds, and in Action." *Anthropological Quarterly* 86 (1): 221–55.

Petersen, Lilli. 2018. "11 Photos Of A Woman Who Escaped Slavery In America." *Refinery 29,* January 11. https://www.refinery29.com/en-gb/2016/03/107182/human-trafficking-modern-day-slavery-photos.

Philanthropy News Digest. 2006. "Jada Pinkett Smith Donates $1 Million to Baltimore School for the Arts." December 16. https://philanthropynewsdigest.org/news/jada-pinkett-smith-donates-1-million-to-baltimore-school-for-the-arts.

Philipps, Anne. 1998. "Democracy and Representation: Or, Why Should it Matter Who Our Representatives Are?" In *Feminism and Politics,* edited by Anne Phillips, 224–41. New York: Routledge.

Philips, Menaka. 2019. "Feminist Preoccupations: Liberalism as Method in Debates Concerning Gender and Culture." *Signs* 44 (1): 955–77.

Pickles, John, and Shengjun Zhu. 2013. "The California Transparency in Supply Chains Act." *Capturing the Gains Working Paper 15.* https://papers.ssrn.com/sol3/papers.cfm?abstract_id=2237437.

Piketty, Thomas. 2020. *Capital and Ideology.* Translated by Arthur Goldhammer. Cambridge, MA: Harvard University Press.

Pinkett Smith, Jada. 2012. Speech for the United States Senate: Foreign Relations Committee full committee hearing, "The Next Ten Years in the Fight Against Human Trafficking: Attacking the Problem with the Right Tools." July 17. https://www.foreign.senate.gov/hearings/the-next-ten-years-in-the-fight-against-human-trafficking-attacking-the-problem-with-the-right-tools.

Pinkett Smith, Jada, and Salma Hayek. 2012. "*Nada se Compara* (Nothing Compares)." Don't Sell Bodies and Wicked Evolution. https://www.youtube.com/watch?v=G_SdBiTIocA.

Pitkin, Hanna. 1969. "The Concept of Representation." In *Representation,* edited by Hanna Pitkin, 1–23. New York: Atherton.

Plant, Sadie. 1997. *Zeroes + Ones: Digital Women + the New Technoculture.* New York: Doubleday.

Polaris. 2021a. "Mission and Vision." Accessed October 25, 2022. https://polarisproject.org/about-us/.

———. 2021b. "Myths, Facts, and Statistics." https://polarisproject.org/myths-facts-and-statistics.

Poster, Winifred R. 2013. "Subversions of Techno-Masculinity: Indian ICT Professionals in the Global Economy." In *Rethinking Transnational Men: Beyond, Between and Within Nations,* edited by Jeff Hearn, Marina Blagojevic and Katherine Harrison, 113–33. New York: Routledge.

Praino, Rodrigo, and Daniel Stockemer. 2012. "Tempus Fugit, Incumbency Stays: Measuring the Incumbency Advantage in the U.S. Senate." *Congress & the Presidency* 39 (2): 160–76.

Prokopets, Alexandra. 2014. "Trafficking in Information: Evaluating the Efficacy of the California Transparency in Supply Chains Act of 2010." *Hastings International Comparative Law Journal* 37 (2): 351–75.

PSI. 2022a. "Global Ambassadors." Accessed October 11, 2022. https://www.psi .org/staff/global-ambassador.

———. 2022b. "Our Approaches." Accessed October 11, 2022. https://www.psi .org/approaches.

Quiroga, José. 2000. *Tropics of Desire: Interventions from Queer Latino America*. New York: New York University Press.

Quiroga, José, and Melanie López Frank. 2010. "Cultural Production of Knowledge on Latina/o Sexualities." In *Latina/o Sexualities: Probing Powers, Passions, Practices, and Policies,* edited by Marysol Asencio, 137–49. New Brunswick, NJ: Rutgers University Press.

Rai, Shirin M. 2014. "Political Performance: A Framework for Analysing Democratic Politics." *Political Studies* 63 (5): 1179–97.

Rai, Shirin, and Janelle G. Reinelt. 2014a. *The Grammar of Politics and Performance*. London: Routledge.

———. 2014b. "Introduction." In Rai and Reinelt, 1–18.

Ramos, Paulo Müller, and Hélio Amante Miot. 2015. "Female Pattern Hair Loss: A Clinical and Pathophysiological Review." *Anais brasileiros de dermatologia* 90 (4): 529–43.

Rao, Sunil Salankey. 2020. *Modern Slavery Legislation: Drafting History and Comparisons between Australia, UK and the USA*. Abingdon, UK: Routledge.

Raphael, J., C. M. Rennison, and N. Jones. 2019. "Twenty-Five Years of Research and Advocacy on Violence Against Women: What Have We Accomplished, and Where Do We Go From Here? A Conversation." *Violence Against Women* 25 (16): 2024–46.

Real, Evan. 2019. "Rose McGowan Rips N.Y. Times, Claims She Was the First to Speak Out in #MeToo Movement." *Hollywood Reporter,* July 1. https://www .hollywoodreporter.com/lifestyle/lifestyle-news/rose-mcgowan-rips-ny-times-claims-she-spoke-first-metoo-movement-1221985.

Redmond, Shana L. 2020. *Everything Man: The Form and Function of Paul Robeson*. Durham, NC: Duke University Press.

Reese, Jacy. 2020. "Institutional Change and the Limitations of Consumer Activism." *Palgrave Communications* 6 (26): 1–8.

Rehfeld, Andrew. 2006. "Towards a General Theory of Political Representation." *Journal of Politics* 68 (1): 1–21.

Reinelt, Janelle. 2016. "Coerced Performances? Trafficking, Sex Work, and Consent." *Lateral* 5 (2), n.p.

Rende Taylor, Lisa, and Elena Shih. 2019. "Worker Feedback Technologies and Combatting Modern Slavery in Global Supply Chains: Examining the

Effectiveness of Remediation-Oriented and Due-Diligence-Oriented Technologies in Identifying and Addressing Forced Labour and Human Trafficking." *Journal of the British Academy* 7 (s1): 131–65.

Richey, Lisa Ann, and Stefano Ponte. 2008. "Better (Red)™ than Dead? Celebrities, Consumption and International Aid." *Third World Quarterly* 29 (4): 711–29.

Riley, Kaitlin. 2019. "Demi Moore Opens Up About Her Marriage To Ashton Kutcher." *Refinery29*, September 12. https://www.refinery29.com/en-us/2019/09/8396526/why-did-demi-moore-ashton-kutcher-break-up.

RMF. 2016. "The Ricky Martin Foundation Presents a New Educational Campaign." Puerto Rico. http://rickymartinfoundation.org/tag/education.

———. 2021. "RMF: About." Accessed August 11, 2022. http://rickymartinfoundation.org/about.

RMF and Inter American Development Bank. 2008. PSA: "Slaves of a New Era." September 9. https://www.youtube.com/watch?v=ySXTDlKVuRY.

Robinson, Cedric J. 2007. *Forgeries of Memory and Meaning: Blacks and the Regimes of Race in American Theater and Film before World War II*. Chapel Hill: University of North Carolina Press.

Rodriguez, Cheryl. 2016. "Mothering While Black: Feminist Thought on Maternal Loss, Mourning and Agency in the African Diaspora." *Journal of the Association of Black Anthropologists* 24 (1): 61–69.

Rodriguez, Peter, Donald Siegel, Amy Hillman, and Lorraine Eden. 2006. "Three Lenses on the Multinational Enterprise: Politics, Corruption, and Corporate Social Responsibility." *Journal of International Business Studies* 37 (6): 733–46.

Rodriguez-Coss, Noralis. 2020. "A Feminist Intersectional Analysis of Economic and Resource (in)Equality in Puerto Rico Before and After Hurricane Maria." *Gonzaga Journal of International Law* 23 (1): 97–113.

Rogers, Katie. 2020. "White House Holds Trafficking 'Summit,' but Critics Dismiss Lack of Dialogue." *The New York Times,* January 31. https://www.nytimes.com/2020/01/31/us/politics/trump-trafficking.html.

Rojek, Chris. 2001. *Celebrity*. London: Reaktion Books.

———. 2013. "'Big Citizen' Celanthropy and Its Discontents." *International Journal of Cultural Studies* 17 (2): 127–41.

Rose, Gillian. 2012. *Visual Methodologies: An Introduction to Researching with Visual Materials*. 3rd ed. Thousand Oaks, CA: SAGE.

Rotten Tomatoes. n.d. "Twisted: Reviews." Accessed August 11, 2021. https://www.rottentomatoes.com/m/twisted.

Rottenberg, Catherine. 2018. *The Rise of Neoliberal Feminism*. New York: Oxford University Press.

Rouse, Joseph. 2009. "Standpoint Theories Reconsidered." *Hypatia* 24 (4): 200–9.

Safer. 2021. "Safer: Get Started." Accessed August 11, 2021. https://safer.io.

Salazar Parreñas, Rhacel, Marie Cecilia Hwang, and Heather Ruth Lee. 2012. "What Is Human Trafficking? A Review Essay." *Signs* 37 (4): 1015–29.

Sanchez, Ray. 2019. "The Downfall of Puerto Rico's Once Powerful Rosselló Political Dynasty." *CNN,* August 3. https://www.cnn.com/2019/08/02/us/puerto-rico-rossello-father-son-legacy/index.html.

Sandberg, Sheryl. 2013. *Lean In: Women, Work, and the Will to Lead.* New York: Alfred A. Knopf.

Sarfaty, Galit. 2015. "Shining Light on Global Supply Chains." *Harvard International Law Journal* 56 (2): 419–63.

Savage, Mike, and Georgia Nichols. 2018. "New Directions in Elite Studies." In *Routledge Advances in Sociology,* edited by Olav Korsnes, 297–315. Abingdon, UK: Routledge.

Saward, Michael. 2006. "The Representative Claim." *Contemporary Political Theory* 5 (3): 297–318.

———. 2009. "Authorisation and Authenticity: Representation and the Unelected." *Journal of Political Philosophy* 17 (1): 1–22.

———. 2010. *The Representative Claim.* Oxford: Oxford University Press.

———. 2014a. "Afterword: Sovereign and Critical Grammars." In Rai and Reinelt, 217–25.

———. 2014b. "Shape-Shifting Representation." *American Political Science Review* 108 (4): 723–36.

———. 2020. *Making Representations: Claim, Counterclaim and the Politics of Acting for Others.* London: ECPR Press.

Schaeffer, Katherine. 2021. "The Changing Face of Congress in 7 Charts." Pew Research Center, March 10. https://www.pewresearch.org/fact-tank/2021/03/10/the-changing-face-of-congress/

Schaffer, Frederic Charles. 2016. *Elucidating Social Science Concepts: An Interpretivist Guide.* New York: Routledge.

Schlozman, Kay, Philip Edward Jones, Hye Young You, Traci Burch, Sidney Verba, and Henry Brady. 2015. "Organizations and the Democratic Representation of Interests: What Does it Mean When these Organizations Have No Members?" *Perspectives on Politics* 13 (4): 1017–29.

Schoen, John. 2017. "How an Obscure Tax Change Sank Puerto Rico's Economy." *CNBC,* September 26. https://www.cnbc.com/2017/09/26/heres-how-an-obscure-tax-change-sank-puerto-ricos-economy.html.

Schwartz-Shea, Peregrine, and Dvora Yanow. 2012. *Interpretive Research Design: Concepts and Processes.* New York: Routledge.

Schwiegershausen, Erica. 2015. "Lena Dunn Doubled Down on Her Stance Against Decriminalizing Sex Work." *The Cut,* August 7. https://www.thecut.com/2015/08/lena-dunham-still-against-legalizing-sex-work.html.

Severs, Eline, and Sara de Jong. 2018. "Preferable Minority Representatives: Brokerage and Betrayal." *PS: Political Science & Politics* 51 (2): 345–50.

Severs, Eline, and Suzanne Dovi. 2018. "Why We Need to Return to the Ethics of Political Representation." *PS: Political Science & Politics* 51 (2): 309–13.

Sharma, Nandita. 2003. "Travel Agency: A Critique of Anti-Trafficking Campaigns." *Refuge* 21 (3): 53–65.

Sherman, Rachel. 2019. *Uneasy Street: The Anxieties of Affluence.* Princeton, NJ: Princeton University Press.

Shih, Elena. 2016. "Not in My 'Backyard Abolitionism': Vigilante Rescue against American Sex Trafficking." *Sociological Perspectives* 59 (1): 66–90.

Showden, Carisa Renae, and Samantha Majic. 2018. *Youth Who Trade Sex in the U.S.: Intersectionality, Agency, and Vulnerability.* Philadelphia: Temple University Press.

Simich, Laura, Lucia Goyen, Andrew Powell, and Karen Mallozzi. 2014. "Improving Human Trafficking Victim Identification—Validation and Dissemination of a Screening Tool." Vera Institute of Justice, June. https://www.ojp.gov/pdffiles1/nij/grants/246712.pdf.

Simon, Yara. 2014. "Roy Rosello Alleges Former Menudo Manager Abused Him, Had Ricky Martin Dress As Woman." *Latin Post,* October 22. https://www.latinpost.com/articles/24208/20141022/roy-rosello-alleges-former-menudo-manager-abused-him-had-ricky-martin-dress-as-woman.htm.

Sitkin, Lea. 2017. "It's Up to You: Why Neoliberal Feminism Isn't Feminism at All." *Open Democracy,* July 18. https://www.opendemocracy.net/en/5050/neoliberal-feminism.

Skocpol, Theda. 2003. *Diminished Democracy: From Membership to Management in American Civic Life.* Norman: University of Oklahoma Press.

Smith, Michael D. 2011. *In the Company of Men: Inside the Lives of Male Prostitutes.* Santa Barbara, CA: Praeger.

Soderlund, Gretchen. 2005. "Running from the Rescuers: New US Crusades Against Sex Trafficking and the Rhetoric of Abolition." *NWSA Journal* 17 (3): 64–87.

Sorvino, Mira. 2009. Interview. UNTV, February 13. https://www.unmultimedia.org/avlibrary/asset/U090/U090213b.

———. 2011a. Speech in Support of Domestic Minor Sex Trafficking Deterrence and Victims Support Act (S. 596), US Senate, Washington, DC, March 16.

———. 2011b. Speech, "The Urgent Need for States' Legislative Reform on the Issue of Human Trafficking: Observations and Suggestions for Change." NCSL 2011 Legislative Summit, Washington, DC, August 11. https://www.ncsl.org/documents/statefed/mirasorvino.pdf.

———. 2012. Speech, "Progress and the Road Ahead: The Leading Role to be Played by State Legislators in Defeating Modern Day Slavery." NCSL Winter Meeting, Washington, DC. https://www.ncsl.org/documents/statefed/2012FallForum Speech.pdf.

———. 2013. Speech, "Beyond Awareness: Putting the Human Back in Human Trafficking." Georgetown University School of Foreign Service, Washington DC, January 30. https://www.c-span.org/video/?310697-5/mira-sorvino-anti-human-trafficking-symposium&start=$(start).

———. 2014. Speech, "Society's Role in Combating Human Trafficking." Catholic Bishops' Conference of England and Wales meeting on Combating Human Trafficking: Church and Law Enforcement in Partnership, Vatican City, April

9–10. https://dq5pwpg1q8ruo.cloudfront.net/2020/12/02/15/41/15/5abcbb2e-c2a2-4aec-bf75-2cf0234f0483/10_42_40_0_10_42_40_542_Society_s_Role_in_Combating_Human_Trafficking.pdf

———. 2016. Speech for H. Andrea Neves and Barton Evans Social Justice Lecture Series. Sonoma State University, Sonoma, CA, February 23. http://web.sonoma.edu/workplace/2016/02/16/mira.html.

———. 2017. Speech at the UN General Assembly on the appraisal of the United Nations Global Plan of Action to Combat Trafficking in Persons. September 27. https://www.youtube.com/watch?v=OYgxaSvlGSs.

Spivak, Gayatri. 1988. "Can the Subaltern Speak?" In *Marxism and the Interpretation of Culture,* edited by Cary Nelson and Nelson Grossberg, 271–313. Chicago: University of Illinois Press.

Spohrer, Erika. 2007. "Becoming Extra-Textual: Celebrity Discourse and Paul Robeson's Political Transformation." *Critical Studies in Media Communication* 24 (2): 151–68.

Steele, Sarah, and Tyler Shores. 2014. "More than Just a Famous Face: Exploring the Rise of the Celebrity Expert-Advocate through Anti-trafficking Action by the Demi and Ashton Foundation." *Crime Media Culture* 10 (3): 259–72.

Stever, Gayle, and Kevin Lawson. 2013. "Twitter as a Way for Celebrities to Communicate with Fans: Implications for the Study of Parasocial Interaction." *North American Journal of Psychology* 15 (2), 339-354.

Stolle, Dietlind, and Marc Hooghe. 2009. "Shifting Inequalities? Patterns of Exclusion and Inclusion in Emerging Forms of Political Participation." *European Studies* 13 (1): 119–42.

Stone, Deborah A. 2002. *Policy Paradox: The Art of Political Decision Making.* Rev. ed. New York: Norton.

Street, John. 2004. "Celebrity Politicians: Popular Culture and Political Representation." *British Journal of Politics and International Relations* 6: 435–52.

———. 2012. "Do Celebrity Politics and Celebrity Politicians Matter?" *The British Journal of Politics and International Relations* 14 (3): 346–56.

Strickland, T. S. 2017. "Oscars 2017: Purpose on the Red Carpet with Julia Ormond and PwC." *Triple Pundit: The Business of Doing Better,* October 26. https://www.triplepundit.com/story/2017/oscars-2017-purpose-red-carpet-julia-ormond-and-pwc/19351.

Strolovitch, Dara Z. 2007. *Affirmative Advocacy: Race, Class, and Gender in Interest Group Politics.* Chicago: University of Chicago Press.

Strolovitch, Dara Z., and Chaya Y. Crowder. 2018. "Respectability, Anti-Respectability, and Intersectionally Responsible Representation." *PS: Political Science & Politics* 51 (2): 340–44.

Stromback, Jesper, and Frank Esser. 2014. "Mediatization of Politics: Transforming Democracies and Reshaping Politics." In *Mediatization of Communication,* edited by Knut Lundby, 375–403. Berlin: De Gruyter Mouton.

Sullivan, Margaret. 2014. "Nicholas Kristof Should Give Readers a Full Explanation About Somaly Mam." *The New York Times,* June 2. https://publiceditor.blogs

.nytimes.com/2014/06/02/nicholas-kristof-should-give-readers-a-full-explanation-about-somaly-mam.

Superville, Darlene. 2020. "Trump Signs Order Creating White House Position Focused on Human Trafficking." *Fortune,* January 31. https://fortune .com/2020/01/31/trump-human-trafficking-bill-executive-order.

Sweetman, B. 2017. "The Judicial System and Sex Work in New Zealand." *Women's Studies Journal* 31 (2):61–68.

Szörényi, Anna. 2014. "Rethinking the Boundaries: Towards a Butlerian Ethics of Vulnerability in Sex Trafficking Debates." *Feminist Review* 107: 20–36.

Szörényi, Anna, and Penelope Eate. 2014. "Saving Virgins, Saving the USA: Heteronormative Masculinities and the Securitisation of Trafficking Discourse in Mainstream Narrative Film." *Social Semiotics* 24 (5): 608–22.

Taylor, Anthea. 2014. "'Blockbuster' Celebrity Feminism." *Celebrity Studies* 5 (1–2): 75–78.

———. 2016. *Celebrity and the Feminist Blockbuster*. London: Palgrave Macmillan.

Thakor, Mitali, and danah boyd. 2013. "Networked Trafficking: Reflections on Technology and the Anti-trafficking Movement." *Dialectical Anthropology* 37 (2): 277–90.

Thompson, Mark Andrew. 2019. "Now You're Making It Up, Brother: Paul Robeson, HUAC, and the Challenge of Institutional Narrative Authority." *Quarterly Journal of Speech* 105 (2): 156–81.

Thorn. 2014. "Thorn Hackathon to Fight Child Exploitation." Accessed August 11, 2021. https://www.thorn.org/blog/thorn-hackathon-fight-child-exploitation.

———. 2020a. "5 Things You Might Not Know about Child Sex Trafficking." Accessed August 11, 2021. https://www.thorn.org/blog/5-things-you-might-not-know-about-child-sex-trafficking.

———. 2020b. "How Vulnerabilities Increase Child Sex Trafficking Risk." Accessed August 11, 2021. https://www.thorn.org/blog/how-vulnerabilities-increase-child-sex-trafficking-risk.

———. 2021a. "5 Ways You Can Help to Defend Children from Sex Trafficking Right Now." Accessed August 16, 2021. https://www.thorn.org/blog/5-ways-you-can-help-to-defend-children-from-sex-trafficking-right-now.

———. 2021b. "Child Sex Trafficking Is a Cycle of Abuse." Accessed August 16, 2021. https://www.thorn.org/child-trafficking-statistics.

———. 2021c. "Spotlight." Accessed August 11, 2021. https://www.thorn.org /spotlight.

———. 2021d. "Technology Has Made It Easier to Harm Kids." Accessed August 16, 2021. https://www.thorn.org/child-sexual-exploitation-and-technology.

———. 2021e. "About." Accessed August 11, 2021. https://www.thorn.org /about-our-fight-against-sexual-exploitation-of-children.

———. 2021f. "Thorn: Partnerships." Accessed August 16, 2021. https://www.thorn .org/partnerships.

Thorn and Vanessa Bouché. 2018. "Survivor Insights: The Role of Technology in Domestic Minor Sex Trafficking." Thorn Digital Defenders and Texas Christian University. January. https://www.thorn.org/wp-content/uploads/2018/06/Thorn_Survivor_Insights_061118.pdf.

Ticktin, Miriam. 2016. "Thinking Beyond Humanitarian Borders." *Social Research* 83 (2): 255–71.

Tiku, Nitasha. 2013. "Who Is Getting Richer Off Twitter? Ashton Kutcher and a Saudi Prince." *Valleywag*, September 27. https://valleywag.gawker.com/who-is-getting-richer-off-twitter-ashton-kutcher-and-a-1411377807.

Tomich, Dale W. 2004. *Through the Prism of Slavery: Labor, Capital, and World Economy*. Lanham, MD: Rowman & Littlefield.

———. 2018. "The Second Slavery and World Capitalism: A Perspective for Historical Inquiry." *International Review of Social History* 63 (3): 477–501.

Tong, Rosemarie, and Tina Fernandes Botts. 2017. *Feminist Thought: A More Comprehensive Introduction*. 5th ed. New York: Westview Press.

Towler, Christopher C., Nyron N. Crawford, and Robert A. Bennett. 2019. "Shut Up and Play: Black Athletes, Protest Politics, and Black Political Action." *Perspectives on Politics* 18 (1): 111–27.

Tugend, Alina. 2019. "Exposing the Biases Embedded in Tech." *The New York Times*, June 17. https://www.nytimes.com/2019/06/17/business/artificial-intelligence-bias-tech.html.

Turner, Graeme. 2014. *Understanding Celebrity*. 2nd ed. Thousand Oaks, CA: SAGE.

UNICEF. 2011. Ricky Martin: Goodwill Ambassador since 2003. UNICEF People. *https://www.unicef.org/goodwill-ambassadors/ricky-martin*.

UNiFeed. 2005. Announcement: "Actress Julia Ormond appointed today, as a United Nations Office on Drugs and Crime (UNODC) Goodwill Ambassador to combat Human Trafficking and actress and human rights activist Bianca Jagger briefed journalists on Human Trafficking." December 2. https://www.unmultimedia.org/tv/unifeed/asset/U051/U051202d.

United Nations. 2014. United Nations Convention against Transnational Organized Crime and the Protocols Thereto. Vienna: UN Office of Drugs and Crime, September 29. https://www.unodc.org/unodc/en/organized-crime/intro/UNTOC.html

———. 2021. Guidelines for the Designation of Goodwill Ambassadors and Messengers of Peace. Accessed October 22, 2022. https://fliphtml5.com/kddq/dvke.

UNODC. 2016. Global Report on Trafficking in Persons. Vienna: United Nations. February. https://www.unodc.org/documents/Global_Report_on_TIP.pdf

———. 2021a. "Our Response." https://www.unodc.org/unodc/en/human-trafficking/our-response.html.

———. 2021b. "UNODC Strategy 2021–2025." https://www.unodc.org/lpo-brazil/en/unodc-strategy-2021---2025/index.html.

UPI Archives. 1991. "Report: Menudo Members Sexually Abused." May 22. https://www.upi.com/Archives/1991/05/22/Report-Menudo-members-sexually-abused/5282674884800.

Uranga, Rachel. 2020. "Ashton Kutcher's Sound Ventures Aims for New $150 Million Fund." November 20. *dot.LA*. https://dot.la/ashton-kutcher-2648998938.html.

Urbinati, Nadia, and Mark E. Warren. 2008. "The Concept of Representation in Contemporary Democratic Theory." *Annual Review of Political Science* 11 (1): 387–412.

US Department of State. 2005. "Trafficking in Persons Report." Office of the Under Secretary of Global Affairs, Washington, DC, June 1. https://2009-2017.state.gov/documents/organization/47255.pdf.

———. 2021. "Trafficking in Persons Report." Office to Combat and Monitor Trafficking in Persons, Washington, DC, June. https://www.state.gov/reports/2021-trafficking-in-persons-report/united-states.

Van Buren III, Harry J., Judith Schrempf-Stirling, and Michelle Westermann-Behaylo. 2019. "Business and Human Trafficking: A Social Connection and Political Responsibility Model." *Business and Society* 60 (2): 341–75.

Van den Bulck, Hilde. 2018. *Celebrity Philanthropy and Activism: Mediated Interventions in the Global Public Sphere.* London: Routledge.

van Elteren, Mel. 2013. "Celebrity Culture, Performative Politics, and the Spectacle of 'Democracy' in America." *Journal of American Culture* 36 (4): 263–83.

van Krieken, Robert. 2012. *Celebrity Society.* New York: Routledge.

Vance, Carole. 2011. "Twelve Ways to Do Nothing about Trafficking While Pretending To." *Social Research* 78 (3): 933–48.

Volcic, Zala, and Karmen Erjavec. 2014. "Transnational Celebrity Activism in Bosnia and Herzegovina: Local Responses to Angelina Jolie's Film *In the Land of Blood and Honey.*" *European Journal of Cultural Studies* 18 (3): 356–75.

Wajcman, Judy. 2009. "Feminist Theories of Technology." *Cambridge Journal of Economics* 34 (1): 143–52.

———. 2007. "From Women and Technology to Gendered Technoscience." *Information, Communication & Society* 10 (3): 287–98.

Walk Free Foundation. 2021a. "Country Studies: United States." Last modified April 13, 2021. https://www.globalslaveryindex.org/2018/findings/country-studies/united-states/.

———. 2021b. "Global Slavery Index." Last modified April 13, 2021. https://www.globalslaveryindex.org/2018/findings/highlights.

Wallace, Brandon, and David L. Andrews. 2021. "The Limits of Representation Activism: Analyzing Black Celebrity Politics in Lebron James' *The Shop.*" *Media, Culture & Society* 43 (5): 825–41.

Weitzer, Ronald. 2005. "Flawed Theory and Method in Studies of Prostitution." *Violence Against Women* 11 (X): 1–16.

———. 2007. "The Social Construction of Sex Trafficking: Ideology and Institutionalization of a Moral Crusade." *Politics and Society* 35 (3): 447–75.

———. 2013. "Review: Researching Sex Work in the Twenty-First Century." *Contemporary Sociology* 42 (5): 713–22.

Weldon, S. Laurel. 2006. "Inclusion, Solidarity, and Social Movements: The Global Movement against Gender Violence." *Perspectives on Politics* 4 (1): 55–74.

———. 2011. *When Protest Makes Policy: How Social Movements Represent Disadvantaged Groups.* Ann Arbor: University of Michigan Press.

———. 2019. "Power, Exclusion and Empowerment: Feminist Innovation in Political Science." *Women's Studies International Forum* 72: 127–136.

Wheaton, Hilary, and Samita Nandy. 2019. "The Value-Form of Persona: Celebrity, Scandal, Activism, and Commodities." In *The Political Economy of Celebrity Activism,* edited by Nathan Farrell, 51–65. Abingdon, UK: Routledge.

Wheeler, Mark. 2011. "Celebrity Diplomacy: United Nations' Goodwill Ambassadors and Messengers of Peace." *Celebrity Studies* 2 (1): 6–18.

Whittier, Nancy. 2017. "Identity Politics, Consciousness-Raising, and Visibility Politics." In *The Oxford Handbook of U.S. Women's Social Movement Activism,* edited by Holly J. McCammon, 376–97. New York, NY: Oxford University Press.

Wicke, Jennifer. 1994. "Celebrity Material: Materialist Feminism and the Culture of Celebrity." *South Atlantic Quarterly* 93 (4): 751–78.

Wijers, Marjan. 2015. "Purity, Victimhood and Agency: Fifteen Years of the UN Trafficking Protocol." *Anti-Trafficking Review* (4): n.p.

Wilson, Michael, and Erin O'Brien. 2016. "Constructing the Ideal Victim in the United States of America's Annual Trafficking in Persons Reports." *Crime, Law and Social Change* 65 (1–2): 29–45.

Willumsen, David M. 2018. "So Far Away From Me? The Effect of Geographical Distance on Representation." *West European Politics* 42 (3): 645–69.

WJSFF. 2021a. "About." Accessed August 11, 2022. https://www.wjsff.org/about-us/.

———. 2021b. "Our Work." Accessed August 11, 2022. https://www.wjsff.org/our-work/.

World Economic Forum. 2018. "Global Gender Gap Report." Geneva: World Economic Forum. https://www3.weforum.org/docs/WEF_GGGR_2018.pdf

Yang, Rachel. 2020. "The Biggest Celebrity Apologies on Social Media in 2020." *Entertainment Weekly,* December 10. https://ew.com/celebrity/celebrity-apologies-2020.

Yanow, Dvora, and Peregrine Schwartz-Shea. 2006. *Interpretation and Method: Empirical Research Methods and the Interpretive Turn.* Armonk, NY: M. E. Sharpe.

———. 2010. "Perestroika Ten Years After: Reflections on Methodological Diversity." *PS: Political Science & Politics* 43 (4): 741–45.

Young, Iris Marion. 2000. *Inclusion and Democracy.* Oxford: Oxford University Press.

Yrjölä, Riina. 2011a. "The Global Politics of Celebrity Humanitarianism." In *Transnational Celebrity Activism in Global Politics,* edited by Liza Tsaliki, Christos Frangonikolopoulos and Asteris Huliaras, 175–92. Chicago: University of Chicago Press.

———. 2011b. "From Street into the World: Towards a Politicised Reading of Celebrity Humanitarianism." *The British Journal of Politics and International Relations* 14 (3): 357–74.

Yuen, Nancy Wang. 2017. *Reel Inequality : Hollywood Actors and Racism.* New Brunswick, NJ: Rutgers University Press.

Zheng, Tiantian. 2010. "Introduction." In *Sex Trafficking, Human Rights and Social Justice,* edited by Tiantian Zheng, 1–22. London: Routledge.

Zilinsky, Jan, Cristian Vaccari, Jonathan Nagler, and Joshua A. Tucker. 2019. "Don't Republicans Tweet Too? Using Twitter to Assess the Consequences of Political Endorsements by Celebrities." *Perspectives on Politics* 18 (1): 144–60.

Zimmerman, Yvonne C. 2005. "Situating the Ninety-Nine: A Critique of the Trafficking Victims Protection Act." *Journal of Religion & Abuse* 7 (3): 37–56.

Zukin, Cliff. 2006. *A New Engagement?: Political Participation, Civic Life, and the Changing American Citizen.* Oxford: Oxford University Press.

INDEX

Note: *fig.* refers to figures.

Amnesty (Amnesty International): awareness, 62; CATW, 64–65, 75–77, 80,
88–89, 110, 209; celebrities and anti-
trafficking activism, 7, 62–65, 72, 73,
88–89; exploitation, 88–89; Judd,
Ashley, 110; Kristof, Nicholas, 88–89;
Ormond, Julia, 159; prostitution,
46*table*, 62–65, 75–76, 88–89, 110, 181;
sex trafficking, 64, 76; sex work, 64,
88–90; Sorvino, Mira, 159, 162, 170, 171;
women, 88–89
Andrees, Beate, 65
Andrews, David L., 38
Annan, Kofi, 164–65
anti-feminist consequences, 3, 17, 24
anti-trafficking activism: Black women,
17–18, 83; celebrity feminism, 5–6;
foreign policies, 6; gender, 17; immigration, 17; Judd, Ashley, 115–16, 118; labor,
175, 176–77; NGOs, 6, 111; Obama,
Barack, 70–71; Ormond, Julia, 160–61;
Pinkett Smith, Jada, 46*table*, 115–16,
118; race, 17; Rock Against Trafficking,
44; safe harbor laws, 182; US, 6, 146;
victims, 17. *See also* celebrities and
anti-trafficking activism
anti-trafficking movement: CATW, 209;
celebrities, 2, 4–5, 6, 17, 25, 60–62;
celebrities and anti-trafficking activism,
39–40; feminism, 19, 51; Global North,
51; Judd, Ashley, 62, 63*fig.*, 115; Kutcher,
Ashton, 62, 63*fig.*, 134; Martin, Ricky,
62, 63*fig.*, 126–27; Moore, Demi, 62,
63*fig.*; Ormond, Julia, 62, 63*fig.*, 195;
Pinkett Smith, Jada, 62, 63*fig.*, 98, 104,
115; religion, 173–74; sex work, 194;
slavery, 86, 88; Sorvino, Mira, 62, 63*fig.*,
195; US and globally, 6
anti-Vietnam war movement, 12
Archer, Alfred, 208, 210
Artemis Agency, 70
Asencio, Marysol, 144
ASSET (Alliance to Stop Slavery and End
Trafficking), 161, 168–70, 176, 190–91
Associated Press, 104
ATLAS.ti (software), 50
audiences, 54–55; accountability, 118;
authorizing and beneficiary audiences,

54; celebrities, 118, 214–15; celebrities
and anti-trafficking activism, 54–55,
59–61, 62, 89–90, 120; celebrity feminism, 118; the contextual, 54–55; human
trafficking, 59, 115; Judd, Ashley, 56, 115;
Ormond, Julia, 195–96; as performance
markers and performances, 26, 54–55;
Pinkett Smith, Jada, 115; political performances, 40–41; politics, 214–15;
"Real Men Don't Buy Girls" (campaign), 75; represented audiences, 54;
Sorvino, Mira, 191–96
awareness: Amnesty, 62; CAST-LA, 78, 85;
celebrities, 6, 13–14, 15, 16, 29, 44, 55, 65,
85, 158; celebrities and anti-trafficking
activism, 5, 6–7, 62, 65, 68, 72, 74, 98,
191, 198; celebrity feminism, 138; DHS,
71; end-demand initiatives, 194; feminist ideologies, 137; human trafficking,
6–7, 44, 114–15, 132, 138, 143, 180, 191,
198; Judd, Ashley, 99, 114–15; Kutcher,
Ashton, 122, 137, 138; labor, 176–77;
Martin, Ricky, 122, 126, 132, 137–38,
146, 156; MCF, 138; NGOs, 143;
Ormond, Julia, 158, 180; Pinkett Smith,
Jada, 114–15; RMF, 138, 143; sex trafficking, 99; solutions, 137–38; Sorvino,
Mira, 158, 163, 171; Thorn Digital
Defenders, 143; white women actors, 7.
See also PAC (Public awareness campaigns); PSAs (Public service
announcements)

Backpage.com, 46*table*, 69, 91
Bales, Kevin, 86
Baloch, Qandeel, 214
Barrientos, Stephanie, 169
Belafonte, Harry, 13
beneficiary audiences, 54–55
Berenson, Peter, 62
Bernstein, Elizabeth, 2, 66, 79, 175, 201–3
Beyoncé, 30, 31, 46*table*, 82
Biden, Joe, 203
Birkey, Rachel, 187–88
Black Entertainment Television, 38
Black feminism, 38, 47, 56
Black men, 17, 19, 24, 39, 61, 88, 111, 212
Black politics, 11–12, 14, 38–39, 215

Haynes, Dina, 44, 59

hegemonic masculinity: celebrities, 122–23; colonialism, 143; entertainment industry, 143; human trafficking, 143, 202; Kutcher, Ashton, 124, 143–44, 151, 153–57; Martin, Ricky, 124, 143–45, 149, 156–57; MCF, 27, 122–23; media, 143; politics, 22; "Real Men Don't Buy Girls" (campaign), 65, 74, 75; *Taken* (Morel, 2009), 143–44, 197; technologies and techno-masculinities, 153, 155; Trump, Donald J., 202; US, 143, 149

"Hero's Campaign," 162

Hesford, Wendy, 18, 49

Heynen, Robert, 112, 145

HIV/AIDS, 13, 14, 95–96, 118–19, 172, 198

Hobson, Janell, 32, 89

Hollywood studio system, 10–12. *See also* entertainment industry

homophobia, 112, 149–50, 151

hooks, bell, 50, 83

Hossein, Caroline, 83

House Un-American Activities Committee, 11

HRC (Human Rights Campaign), 149–50

Htun, Mala, 5

Huliaras, Asteris, 14

humanitarianism, 13–14. *See also* Amnesty (Amnesty International)

human rights, 50, 67, 149–50, 161, 165–66, 201. *See also* Amnesty (Amnesty International)

human trafficking, 22, 201–3; agriculture, 24, 25, 167; anti-feminist consequences, 3, 17; audiences, 59, 115; awareness, 6–7, 44, 114–15, 132, 138, 143, 180, 191, 198; Bernstein, Elizabeth, 2, 201–3; Black men, 17; Bureau of Justice Statistics, 24; Bush, George W., 22; Cambodia, 184–87; capitalism, 112, 175–76, 187, 188; carceral feminism, 51, 79–80; CAST-LA, 67, 77–78, 85; Catholic Bishops' Conference of England and Wales, 173–74; causes, 4, 50, 83, 101, 108, 109, 131–33, 135, 156; celebrities, 3, 5, 6, 7, 26, 29, 35, 43, 44, 45, 49–54, 59–60, 69, 78, 184, 197–98, 199, 211; celebrities and anti-trafficking activism, 26, 45, 48–49,

50–51, 69, 76–77, 85–88, 200, 208; "The Celebritization of Human Trafficking" (Haynes), 44; celebrity feminism, 6, 7, 60; children and youth, 3, 4, 131, 134–36, 139–40, 148, 156; choice, 40; coercion, 2, 3–4, 21, 25, 40, 71, 77, 135; colonialism, 17, 78–79, 156, 185; consumer activism, 189; crime, 130, 166, 168, 169; criminal justice solutions, 3, 23, 50, 51, 77–78, 79–80, 140, 146, 166, 179–83, 186–87, 201; critical trafficking scholarship, 20–21; CSR, 170; CTSCA, 187–88, 190; data, 4–5, 23–24, 132, 133, 136, 139–40; definitions of, 2, 3–4, 21, 77, 130, 166; deportation and dislocation, 4; DHS, 71–72; DOL, 23; domestic sector, 24, 25; DSB, 106, 112, 119–20; economics, 3, 4, 50, 84, 105, 130, 133, 155, 168, 174–75, 178; entertainment industry, 78; exploitation, 2, 3–4, 25; familial love, lack of, 108–9, 113–14, 120; feminism, 3, 17–25, 30, 45, 83–85, 198–208; feminist ideologies, 78; forced labor and labor, 2, 3–4, 7, 21, 71–72, 77, 85, 101, 105, 106, 130, 166; funds, 23, 181, 201, 217n3; garment industry, 25, 101; GEMS, 81; gender, 3, 4, 17, 22, 25, 78, 83, 85, 132, 133, 139, 155, 167–68, 172, 174–75, 199; globalization and internationalism, 3, 13, 22–23, 77, 168, 169, 186–87; Global North, 3; Global Slavery Index, 3; Global South, 104, 127, 138; GPG, 74; hegemonic masculinity, 143, 202; human rights, 201–2; ILO, 77–78, 105; immigration and migration, 4, 17, 25, 71, 77, 101, 146, 169, 199; imperialism, 78–79, 120–21, 184, 202; individualism, 80, 81, 84, 120; industries, 3; inequalities, 21, 51, 133, 168, 169, 211, 212; intersectionality, 47; involuntary servitude, 24; iPoint (consultants), 190; Judd, Ashley, 29, 35, 37, 93–94, 95, 98–100, 109, 112, 114–16, 118, 120–21; Kristof, Nicholas, 102; Kutcher, Ashton, 71–72, 74–75, 91–92, 122–23, 128, 129, 134–35, 143, 152, 154, 156–57; law enforcement, 22, 24–25, 54, 71–72, 120, 141–42, 159, 165–66, 181, 193; laws, 3, 22–23, 54, 132, 140, 146–47, 159, 166,

New Somaly Mam Foundation, The, 91

Newsweek, 90

New York Daily News, 219n1

New York Times: Abdul-Jabbar, Kareem, 215; celebrity feminism, 30–31; Faludi, Susan, 207–8; human trafficking, 2; Kelly, R., 207; Kristof, Nicholas, 66, 90–91, 94, 99, 102; nail salons, 3–4; Ormond, Julia, 160; Weinstein, Harvey, 203–5

NGOs (Non-governmental organizations): accountability, 119, 210–11; Ambassadors, 68; anti-trafficking activism, 6, 111; awareness, 143; beneficiary audiences, 54; celebrities, 14, 15–16, 56, 68, 210–11; celebrities and anti-trafficking activism, 48, 68, 72, 81, 85; children and youth, 167; DSB, 106; funds, 110, 139; global humanitarian concerns, 13; human trafficking, 71, 80, 84, 120, 139; Judd, Ashley, 110, 111, 112; Kutcher, Ashton, 74, 123–24, 134, 137; Martin, Ricky, 27, 123–24, 137; Moore, Demi, 74; Obama, Barack, 71; Ormond, Julia, 160, 176; Pinkett Smith, Jada, 94, 110, 111; political representation, 34, 35; Puerto Rico and RMF, 137; research and scholarship, 48; sex industry and sex trafficking, 20, 110; solutions, 136; US, 6; victims, 23–24. See also *individual NGOs*

Nichols, Georgia, 15

NIJ (National Institutes of Justice), 23

NOW (National Organization for Women), 79

Nyong'o, Lupita, 203–4, 205

Obama, Barack, 6, 22, 44, 70–71, 201, 202

Okyere, Samuel, 167

online sources, 44. *See also* social media; technologies

Open Democracy, 201

oppression: Black feminism, 56; CATW, 75; celebrities, 37, 55, 197–98, 216; celebrities and anti-trafficking activism, 6, 7–8, 27, 85, 185, 195, 197–98; celebrity feminism, 31; colonialism, 83; elites, 16; feminism, 50; gender, 67, 102, 175–76; intersectionality, 47; *A Path Appears*

(Chermayeff, 2015), 67; patriarchy, 79; racism, 83; radical feminism, 79; sex trafficking, 102; visibility, 198

organized crime: human trafficking, 3, 4, 71, 132, 166, 168; Kutcher, Ashton, 143; Martin, Ricky, 131–32, 143; neoconservatism, 22; Ormond, Julia, 168; women, 18, 22

organs, 2, 130

org-support (anti-trafficking organizations), 62, 64*fig.*

Ormond, Julia, 160–61, 166–70; accountability, 157, 158, 190–91; Ambassadors, 158–59, 160–61, 166–68; Amnesty, 159; anti-trafficking activism, 160–61; anti-trafficking movement, 62, 63*fig.*, 195; ASSET, 161, 168–70, 176, 190–91; audiences, 195–96; awareness, 158, 180; *Call + Response* (documentary), 66; capitalism, 158, 159, 174, 175–79, 187; carceral feminism, 174, 179–80; career, 158, 160; celebrities and anti-trafficking activism, 62, 63*fig.*; celebrity advocacy, 183; celebrity feminism, 159, 174, 195–96; children and youth, 167; the contextual, 27, 159, 166; criminal justice solutions, 175, 179–81; CTSCA, 176–77, 178–79, 187, 190–91; domestic sector, 166; economics, 84, 168, 175–79; exploitation, 168; fame capital, 183, 195; feminism and feminist ideologies, 157, 175, 195; forced labor and labor, 84, 158, 167; gender, 27, 158, 167–68; globalization, 84; Global Philanthropy Forum, 168–69; human rights, 161; human trafficking, 27, 84, 86, 157, 160–61, 166–70, 179–80, 195; ICE, 180; imperialism, 27, 159; industries, 158, 167; interviews, 46*table*; *Larry King Live*, 46*table*; law enforcement, 161, 180; laws and legislation, 176–79, 180–81, 190, 195; melodrama, 195; men, 168, 195; narratives, 27, 158–59, 166–70, 183, 195; neoliberalism, 174, 175; NGOs, 160, 176; organized crime, 168; patriarchy, 158–59, 174; performances, 159, 183, 195–96; the personal, 27, 157, 159, 160–61, 166; poverty, 168–69, 174–81; power, 27, 157, 159; prostitution, 166, 180–81; race, 27, 159, 191; representa-

prostitution: Amnesty *(continued)*
legislation, 183; Martin, Ricky, 130–31;
men, 20, 80, 109–10, 193; NOW, 79;
Ormond, Julia, 166, 180–81; public
policies, 21, 109–10, 180–81; Puerto Rico,
133; sex trafficking, 21, 75–76, 79, 220n3;
sexual violence, 132–33; sex work, 88–89,
100, 180–81, 220n3; Sorvino, Mira, 172,
182–83, 193–94; SVAW Campaign, 171;
technologies, 135; UN Protocol (2000),
21, 132–33; US, 22; victims, 25, 181; violence against women, 20; whiteness, 25;
women, 133, 180, 183. *See also* ECPAT
(End Child Prostitution and
Trafficking)
protests, 46*table*, 64*fig.*, 69, 150–51
PSAs (Public service announcements):
carceral feminism, 80; celebrities and
anti-trafficking activism, 48–49, 71–72;
CNN, 72, 218n7; DHS, 44–45, 71–72;
human trafficking, 71–72; ILO, 105;
Kutcher and Moore, 71–72, 218n7; law
enforcement, 71–72; Martin, Ricky and
RMF, 127, 131; narratives, 71; Pinkett
Smith, Jada, 98, 105; sex trafficking, 71
PSI (Population Services International), 29,
94, 95–97, 98–101, 112–13, 118–19
public policies: anti-trafficking, 24; anti-
trafficking activism, 6; carceral feminism, 80; CAST-LA, 67, 85; celebrities,
16, 41, 56, 199; celebrities and anti-
trafficking activism, 8, 46*table*, 52,
53–54, 56, 60, 70–71, 199; gender, 24;
HIV/AIDS, 172; human trafficking, 3,
17, 20, 24, 53–54, 139–40, 166, 175,
201–2; immigration, 24; inequalities,
212; labor, 71–72, 84, 176–77; narratives, 49–50; poverty, 71–72; prostitution, 21, 109–10, 180–81; race, 24; sex
trafficking, 109–10; slavery, 86; Sorvino,
Mira, 192; supply chains, 177–79;
Trump, Donald J., 202
Puerto Rico: awareness, 138; children and
youth, 27, 123, 127, 139–40; colonialism,
133, 146, 147–48, 185; domestic sector,
133; economics, 133, 146–48; exploitation, 133; forced labor and labor trafficking, 133, 147; gender, 132, 133; human

trafficking, 46*table*, 131–33, 137, 139–40,
146, 148; Human Trafficking Prevention and Awareness Month, 138; interviews, 132; laws, 140, 146–47; Martin,
Ricky, 123, 124–25, 132–33, 139–40,
145–46, 148–51, 156, 185; NGOs, 137;
politics, 148, 151; poverty, 133, 147–48;
prostitution, 133; research and scholarship, 132; RMF, 46*table*, 127, 131–33,
139–40; Rosselló, Ricardo, 149–51; the
state, 137; TVPA, 140; US, 133, 146–48,
151; US Congress, 146–47; victims, 132
Puerto Rico v. Sánchez Valle (2016), 147
Pugliese, Katheryne, 23, 217n3
purchased marriage, 132, 161

race: anti-trafficking activism, 17; capitalism, 38; carceral feminism, 111; celebrities, 44–45, 52–53; celebrities and
anti-trafficking activism, 26, 50, 72, 85,
94, 112, 159; celebrity feminism, 31;
Children for Sale (documentary), 107;
critical trafficking scholarship, 20–21;
entertainment industry, 117; human
trafficking, 3, 4, 17, 22, 25, 184, 199, 202;
inequalities, 116; Judd, Ashley, 109, 111,
112, 115–16, 120; law enforcement,
20–21, 24–25, 191; media, 19; migration,
18; *Nada Se Compara* (Nothing Compares) (music video), 119–20; neoliberal
feminism, 83, 111; Ormond, Julia, 27,
159, 191; Pinkett Smith, Jada, 109, 111,
114, 115–16, 117, 120; political performances, 38; political representation,
33–34; politics, 22, 33–34; positionality,
52–53; public policies, 24; representations, 57, 112; sex trafficking, 22, 145;
sexual predation, 19, 22; Sorvino, Mira,
27, 159, 162; technologies, 153; Trump,
Donald J., 202; US and US Congress,
42, 191; victims, 18, 19, 22, 25; violence
against women, 18–19; WJSFF, 97
racism: ASSET, 191; Black feminism, 38;
entertainment industry, 116; *Every Day
in Cambodia* (Cohen, 2013/2014), 173;
Global North and Global South, 83;
human trafficking, 21, 78–79, 114, 155;
individualism, 16; inequalities, 78–79,

slavery *(continued)*
 movement, 86, 88; Bales, Kevin, 86;
 Black men, 88; Black women, 18, 88,
 104–5; Britain, 86–87; *Call + Response*
 (documentary), 65–66; capitalism, 18,
 87, 187; CAST-LA, 67; celebrities and
 anti-trafficking activism, 85–88; children and youth, 167; colonialism, 169;
 consumer activism, 189; debt bondage,
 87; *Disposable People: New Slavery in
 the Global Economy* (Bales), 86; economics, 18, 87; exploitation, 87, 105;
 Free Produce Movement, 189; Global
 Slavery Index, 3, 23–24, 86; history of,
 87–88; human trafficking, 2, 4, 71,
 85–88, 104–7, 120–21; labor, 105, 169–
 70; market principles, 86; media, 4;
 migration, 87; Ormond, Julia, 86, 160,
 167–68; Pinkett Smith, Jada, 104–7,
 120–21; poverty, 168; public policies, 86;
 racism, 191; Sorvino, Mira, 86, 180, 182;
 supply chains, 169–70, 177, 220n2;
 technologies, 152; Tomich, Dale, 87;
 US, 71, 87–88. *See also* ASSET (Alliance to Stop Slavery and End Trafficking); "End Slavery Now!" (campaign)
slaveryfootprint.org, 189
Slavery to Freedom (gala), 67
"Slaves of A New Era" (PSA), 131, 138
SlutWalk, 32–33
Smith, Jada Pinkett. *See* Pinkett Smith,
 Jada
Smith, Will, 97, 103–4, 106, 113–14, 117
Smoot-Hawley Tariff Act, 176
Sobrino, Christian, 150–51
socialist feminism, 83–85
social media, 8–10, 59, 89, 136, 209–10, 214
social problems, 12–14, 211–12. *See also*
 inequalities; *individual social problems*
solutions, 136–41; ASSET, 191; awareness,
 137–38; CAST-LA, 77–78; CATW, 76;
 celebrities, 6–7, 25, 45, 60, 75, 115;
 celebrities and anti-trafficking activism,
 6–7, 26, 50, 60, 77, 78–79, 80, 83, 84;
 consumer activism, 189; feminist ideologies, 78–79, 109–14, 136–41, 174–83;
 gender, 142–43; human rights, 67;
 human trafficking, 6–7, 21, 45, 78, 81,

83, 109, 111–12, 119–20, 123–24, 136–41,
 142–43, 156, 187, 189; ILO, 77–78;
 individualism, 80, 111, 136; Judd, Ashley,
 98, 100, 109, 112, 115, 118; *Just Responsibility: A Human Rights Theory of Global
 Justice* (Ackerly), 50; Kutcher, Ashton,
 27, 123–24, 136–41, 142–44, 156; Martin, Ricky, 27, 123–24, 136–41, 142–43;
 men, 183; *Nada Se Compara* (Nothing
 Compares) (music video), 119–20;
 neoliberal feminism, 82–83; NGOs, 136;
 Ormond, Julia, 161, 174, 179–81, 195; *A
 Path Appears* (Chermayeff, 2015), 67;
 patriarchy, 80; philanthropy, 111;
 Pinkett Smith, Jada, 98, 109, 113–14, 115,
 118; radical feminism, 80; research and
 scholarship, 143; sex trafficking, 75, 161;
 social problems, 211; Sorvino, Mira, 174,
 179–83, 192, 195; the state, 136; structural factors, 78, 111; technologies, 136,
 156; victims, 143; visibility, 78–79. *See
 also* criminal justice solutions
Somaly Mam Foundation, 67–68, 90–91
Sonoma State University, 193–95
Sorvino, Mira, 161–63, 183–87; accountability, 157, 158, 190, 191–95; Agape International Missions, 175–76, 200; Ambassadors, 158–59, 162–63, 166, 170, 171–72,
 174–75, 180, 181, 186–87, 192, 200;
 Amnesty, 159, 162, 170, 171; anti-trafficking movement, 62, 63*fig.*, 195; audiences, 191–96; awareness, 158, 163, 171;
 Cambodia, 184–87; capitalism, 158, 159,
 174, 175–76; carceral feminism, 174,
 179–80, 182, 183; career, 158, 162; celebrities, 194; celebrities and anti-trafficking
 activism, 62, 63*fig.*, 69, 171; celebrity
 advocacy, 183, 193–95; celebrity-as-
 rescuer-of-victims, 69; celebrity feminism, 159, 174, 194, 195–96; children
 and youth, 172, 185, 192–94; child sex
 trafficking, 183, 193–94; CNN, 162, 172,
 183; commercial sex, 183, 193–94; the
 contextual, 27, 159, 166; criminal justice
 solutions, 175, 179–83; doc, 162; economics, 159, 175–76; end-demand
 initiatives, 182–83, 191, 193–94; Eng,
 Chou Bun, 184–85, 186–87; *Every Day*

supply chains: ASSET, 161, 176, 191; capitalism, 187; consumer activism, 189; CSR,
170; CTSCA, 176–79, 187–91; exploitation, 169; forced labor and labor, 169,
176–77; globalization, 169–70; human
trafficking, 169–70, 176–79, 187–88,
220n2; industries, 170; laws, 170, 176–
79; Ormond, Julia, 159, 161, 169–70,
176–79; public policies, 177–79;
research and scholarship, 187–88;
SB657 and SB1649, 177–78; slavery,
169–70, 177, 220n2; Sorvino, Mira,
192; the state, 170, 177; technologies,
170
SVAW Campaign (Stop Violence Against
Women Campaign), 162, 170–71
Szörényi, Anna, 143

Taken (Morel, 2009), 1–2, 3–4, 134, 143–
44, 197
Taylor, Anthea, 32, 51
Taylor, Lisa Rende, 176
TechCrunch Disrupt, 129*fig.*
techno-feminism, 153
technologies: causes, 156; celebrities, 48;
celebrities and anti-trafficking activism,
64*fig.*, 70, 208; children and youth, 92,
128–29, 134–36, 137, 139, 141–42; class,
153; consumer activism, 189; exploitation, 47*table*, 135–36, 155; gender, 142,
152–55; hegemonic masculinity, 153;
human trafficking, 47*table*, 135–36, 139,
140–41, 154–55; Kutcher, Ashton, 27, 71,
123, 124, 128–29, 134–36, 137, 140–42,
143, 144, 151, 152–55, 156; labor, 153; law
enforcement, 128–29, 140–41, 141–42,
152–53, 155; men, 154–55; Moore, Demi,
71; political representation, 34; power,
153; predation, 134, 137; race, 153; sex
trafficking, 135–36; sexual abuse, 128; sex
work, 135–36, 142, 152–53, 155; slavery,
152; solutions, 136, 156; supply chains,
170; techno-feminism, 153; techno-
masculinities, 155; US, 153–54; victims,
136, 137, 141–42, 155; visibility, 56–57;
whiteness, 154; women, 140, 153–54;
women of color, 154. *See also* Thorn
Digital Defenders

techno-masculinities, 155. *See also* hegemonic masculinity
Teen Revolt, 82
temporality: celebrities and anti-trafficking
activism, 7, 53–54, 62, 64*fig.*, 70, 94; the
contextual, 53–54; Judd, Ashley, 98,
114–15, 120; Kutcher, Ashton, 123, 129,
134; Martin, Ricky, 123, 129, 130;
Pinkett Smith, Jada, 98, 114–15, 120
Thailand, 29, 40, 112–13, 131
Thai persons, 40, 56, 67, 100, 112–13, 173
theater/art, 40, 47*table*, 64*fig.*
theater of pity, 100, 108. *See also* melodrama
Thistle Farms Bath and Body Care, 110,
111–12
Thompson, Emma, 46*table*, 47*table*, 62,
63*fig.*, 218nn1,13
Thorn Digital Defenders: accountability,
155; awareness, 143; children and youth,
136, 137, 153, 154, 155; child sex trafficking, 128–29, 141–42, 153; exploitation,
155; interviews, 219n2; Kutcher, Ashton,
123, 134–35, 137, 138; Moore, Demi, 134;
"Real Men Don't Buy Girls" (campaign), 75; sex trafficking, 134–36,
141–42; sex work, 153; the state, 155;
technologies, 140–42; victims, 134;
vigilante abolitionism, 154
Tillerson, Rex, 202
"Time's Up," 205, 207. *See also* #MeToo
movement
TIP (Trafficking In Persons Report),
22–23, 25, 132, 146, 202, 217n3
Together 1 Heart (organization), 91
Tomich, Dale, 87
Trafficking Victims Protection Act, 182
transgender persons, 4, 32, 74, 77, 112
Trump, Donald J., 77–78, 201–3
Trump, Ivanka, 201–2
Turner, Graeme, 9
T-Visas, 25, 202
TVPA (Trafficking Victims Protection
Act): carceral feminism, 22; celebrities
and anti-trafficking activism, 44; chil-
dren and youth, 24; human trafficking,
22, 77; law enforcement, 110; neocon-
servatism, 22; Obama, Barack, 70–71;
Pinkett Smith, Jada, 103–5, 110; Puerto

Founded in 1893,
UNIVERSITY OF CALIFORNIA PRESS
publishes bold, progressive books and journals
on topics in the arts, humanities, social sciences,
and natural sciences—with a focus on social
justice issues—that inspire thought and action
among readers worldwide.

The UC PRESS FOUNDATION
raises funds to uphold the press's vital role
as an independent, nonprofit publisher, and
receives philanthropic support from a wide
range of individuals and institutions—and from
committed readers like you. To learn more, visit
ucpress.edu/supportus.